Village
in the Vaucluse

Laurence Wylie

Third Edition

Harvard University Press, Cambridge, Massachusetts
and London, England

Library of Congress Catalog Card Number 74-77185

ISBN 0-674-93936-0 (paper)

Printed in the United States of America

To
A. Irving Hallowell

To Anja
Hopefully we'll get
to France again!
Hope you enjoy your reading!
Love B6
Christmas 2000

Preface to the Third Edition

In the twenty-five years since I became involved in studying French villages, France has become a primarily industrial country. The prediction of an American research foundation that France will lead European industry by the 1980's is proudly repeated by French officials and publicists. The basic shift in the French economy is reflected in the new symbol of national pride that government subsidies now support and encourage: the Concorde has replaced the Peasant as the emblem of French identity. With this change in the French economy, why, we may properly ask, should anyone be interested in French village life today?

Paradoxically, there is more popular interest in villages now than there was when I began this study. In 1950 most of our French friends could not imagine our voluntarily spending a year in France anyplace except Paris. And to choose a small, isolated community with neither modern comforts nor cultural facilities! Although the French were—and still are—proud of their non-urban roots, they traditionally spent only a few vacation weeks in a village or farm. In all but the richest agricultural areas many houses stood vacant most of the year. Now the rapidly increasing aggravations of city life have changed this pattern. City dwellers escape to the country as frequently and for as long as possible. Their dream is often to recreate what they assume the old communal life must have been. They reconstruct dilapidated houses and lay out new gardens, they play *boules* in the town square, and may even run for election to the city council.

There is a parallel between this movement and the overwhelming popularity during the last decade of the Astérix comic books. In this series, read by children and adults alike, the main theme is the miraculous survival of a lone village in Gaul; the naïve cunning and the "natural" strength of its citizens protect the village from the encroachment of "civilization." The same myth shapes the schemes of city planners as they adapt what they see as the secret of village happiness to modern needs. Although rural life has lost its place in the French economy, the public's commitment to the myth it nurtured is stronger today than ever before.

I had the good fortune to know Peyrane when it had a vigorous life and a rural personality. In 1950 it was still a viable community peopled mostly by artisans and shopkeepers catering to the farmers of the surrounding countryside. In 1957 my involvement in French villages was doubled, for in that year our family lived in Chanzeaux, a community in western France, some two-thirds of the way between Paris and the Atlantic. At that time Chanzeaux, too, was a viable rural entity. Although less spectacular than Peyrane, this Anjou village has the beguiling charm associated with "la douceur angevine." There is nothing soft and sweet about its ideological tradition, however. In 1792, Chanzeaux was in the van of the fierce Vendée Rebellion against the Parisian revolutionary government and, like other communities in the *Vendée angevine,* was not reconciled to the idea of a republic until the First World War. The Chanzeans still vote consistently to the right, and 85 per cent of the population (compared to 5 per cent in Peyrane) go to mass regularly. In 1966 my students and I published a book on Chanzeaux, a less personal but more solidly sociological study than this book on a village in the Vaucluse.* Peyrane and Chanzeaux represent the Red and the White, those traditional opposing forces that continue to shape French history.

Even though France has become predominantly urban, I have found that my almost annual visits to these two rural communities I know so well keep me informed of many current national trends. The presidential election of 1965 took place during the time I served briefly as Cultural Attaché at the United States Embassy in Paris. I was as impressed as other members of the Embassy staff to find that my forecasts of the election results were the most accurate of any in the informal Embassy poll. My predictions had been based mostly on what I saw in the crystal ball of Peyrane and Chanzeaux!

The first version of the new concluding chapter of this book was an article I wrote in response to a request from the editors of the *New York Times Magazine* (November 25, 1973) for an analysis of what had happened to Peyrane in the last twenty-five years. The few paragraphs retained from the article are reprinted by permission. Because I had just come back from a year in Paris and had had the opportunity to visit both Peyrane and Chanzeaux a number of times, the analysis seemed best set in the framework of a comparison of the changes in both villages.

---

* Laurence Wylie, ed., *Chanzeaux; A Village in Anjou* (Cambridge, Mass., Harvard University Press, 1966)

As this third edition of *Village in the Vaucluse* goes to press, I should like to bring to light a fact that should no longer go unstated. If you find that this book reads well, you will share my gratitude to Anne Stiles Wylie, whose critical acumen has influenced every word, every sentence, every paragraph of this account of a long experience we have shared.

L. W.

Cambridge, Massachusetts
February, 1974

Preface to the Second Edition

This book was written in the hope that it might give an accurate description of life in Peyrane, the French village where we lived in 1950–51. I also hoped, though with less evidence and less conviction, that it might more generally give an insight into life in France beyond the borders of the commune of Peyrane, and it has been pleasing to hear from other witnesses that through an acquaintance with the people of Peyrane one may understand the French people better. Now, thirteen years later, the description needs retouching. Because Peyrane, along with the rest of France, has changed, we must face the question of how much of the original picture is still valid. A partial answer is provided in my section of *In Search of France** but I have welcomed the opportunity to answer the question more directly in the chapter now added to the original text. I have tried to understand and describe the Peyrane of today, in some ways quite different from that of 1950 and yet in important ways very much the same.

This supplementary account is based on many sources, but primarily on our renewed experience in the community, for we returned there for visits in the spring of 1959 and again in the summers of 1959 and 1961. There have also been letters from Peyrane and reports from friends and readers who have visited the village. A French sociologist and an Italian psychiatrist have made studies of special aspects of life in Peyrane and have recounted some of their experiences to me. In November, 1962, I had an opportunity to meet the new mayor of Peyrane in Paris when he had just returned from the Vaucluse, where he took part in the national election. The censuses of 1954 and 1962 have, along with other data, furnished the basis for further studies I have made on population movement.

Of course, there is no longer a reason for hiding the real name of the commune — Roussillon — since any interested person could discover it rather easily and since the book is well known to the people of Peyrane. As soon as it was published in 1957 I sent a copy to Rivet, who had been

* "Social Change at the Grass Roots." (Harvard University Press, 1963), pp. 159–234.

particularly helpful in sending me information I had needed as I was writing. Other copies drifted into the community. American visitors brought theirs along. Mauron, the café owner, ordered copies through Unesco and a book dealer of Apt and sold several dozen to tourists and summer people. His own copy he keeps on the bar and uses as a guest book. Moïse and other principals have autographed their photographs. Moïse, in his enthusiasm, sends me a postcard now and then and signs it with his pseudonym, Moïse Jannel, instead of his real name.

Moïse's attitude toward the book is by no means shared by everyone in Peyrane, however. Even though I thought I had written sympathetically of this village of which I had been so extraordinarily fond, it was obviously unreasonable of me to hope that I might write an accurate account and still remain on good terms with everyone. As Monsieur Raynard reminded me later when we were discussing the subject: "You can't make an omelette without breaking the eggs!" Certainly any unfavorable statement I made about anyone was sheer flattery compared to the unpleasant things the Peyranais say about each other. Nevertheless, it was inevitable that I should have hurt a few people's feelings unintentionally. As the years have passed, however, the hurt seems to have healed. Our Peyranais friends are always extremely cordial when we visit them or when our American friends call to bring our greetings.

Most of our best friends in Peyrane — and these are the central figures in the book — seem less interested in the text than in other of its aspects. They love the photographs of each other, and they like having Peyrane better known. But most of them are not very "bookish" and are both less interested and less impressed by a text than people who have the habit of reading books. They have heard that the book contains intimate details, but so long as the facts are recorded in a language not understood by the neighbors, the Peyranais are not concerned. I sent several friends a copy of an abridged version translated into French and published in this country.* However, very few of the intimate "petites histoires" were included so there was not the risk of embarrassing people. Although the reaction to this French text was cordial, the people of Peyrane showed their greatest enjoyment in catching the professor in errors of fact, e.g., peas are *not* ripe as early as March; Roussillon is not a *monument classé* but a *site classé*. There was some feeling that I had given too good a character to some of the less popular individuals of the community. On the whole my relations

---

* *Village en Vaucluse.* Edition prepared by Armand Bégué. (Boston: Houghton Mifflin Company, 1961.)

with Peyrane have stood the test, and there is no greater pleasure for me than to return to Peyrane and have a glass of wine with my old friends — Bourdin, Carette, Rivet, Moïse, Favre, Jouvaud, Pascal, Mauron.

The only people who have expressed disapproval of the book seemingly as a matter of principle are a few of the city people who spend vacations in Peyrane or who have moved there since the book was written. They are interested in Peyrane as a resort and they see it and want the world to see it as an idyllic haven for artists and intellectuals. My picture of Peyrane does not reinforce this image. They criticize the book because it is a straightforward account rather than an artistically transformed reality. "Tout n'est pas bon à dire, n'est-ce pas?"

As a matter of fact, there is more I should have liked to add to the book than remove from it, for I am well aware how much is missing in my account of life in Peyrane. For the sake of anthropologists and sociologists I should like to have been able to give a more complete description of social structure, genealogy, land tenure. For the sake of historical completeness and general interest I should like to have known more of the facts I have learned since — like the fascinating detail I came across as I read Samuel Beckett's *Waiting for Godot*. My heart jumped when I read the passage in which one of his principal characters says to the other: "But we were in the Vaucluse together, I'd swear it. We worked in the harvest together on Bonnelly's farm, in Roussillon. . . . Everything is red down there." On the desk in front of me was the Roussillon election ballot of 1953 with Bonnelly's name on it!

Of course, I wrote to Rivet at once and found out that Beckett spent the war years in Peyrane. The next time I returned I went to see Bonnelly, who told me that he had sold wine and vegetables to Beckett, but he did not know him so well as our good friend Aude did. And I had spent hours with Aude without finding out about this wartime friendship!

When I think of the many facts I must have missed in studying Peyrane I am aware of the gaps in my account. "Mais c'est comme ça!" I hope, however, that with the new chapter bringing things up to date the book will still give a reasonably accurate idea of what life is like in Peyrane — both for the sake of the Americans for whom the book was written and for the sake of the people of Peyrane to whom I remain deeply grateful and warmly attached.

L. W.

Cambridge, Massachusetts
June, 1963

Preface to the First Edition

This is an account of life in a French village told in terms of the people living today in the commune of Peyrane. So it is human, actual, and specific. The details of life in Peyrane are often interesting in themselves. We are curious to know why the Gleizers threw money in the street when Michel was baptized, why Alphonse Peretti had his messy school work pinned to his back, why people approved when Olivier Borel went on a binge with other adolescents of the "Peyrane Jug," why Lucien Bourdin refuses to repair the slippery path leading down to his asparagus field, why Janine Imbert tried to shoot herself, why the Communist Chanon and the Catholic Jouve teamed up against the Socialist Radical slate in the election.

Yet this book is more than an anecdotal account. It is important to see how the everyday details and incidents fit together in a general way of life. Most accounts of rural France have made the people seem quaint and often like ridiculous puppets because their behavior is not seen in relation to a pattern. In this book an attempt has been made to depict living personalities in the framework of a systematic description of their culture.

Almost half of the people of France live in rural communes like Peyrane. This does not mean that half of the people of France are farmers, because the word "rural" means more than "agricultural." A rural commune is officially described as a commune in which the village has fewer than 2,000 inhabitants, so that the 46.8 per cent of the French population living in rural communes in 1946 included not only farmers but the artisans, tradesmen, industrial workers, and all who live in and around small towns. An accurate understanding of French culture must be based in part on a knowledge of the pattern of life of the 19,000,000 people living in the Peyranes of France.

This pattern becomes even more important when we learn that it has also shaped the lives of a large number of city people. It is well known that city populations in western countries tend not to reproduce themselves. Rural areas are the human nurseries that keep the cities populated and growing. Recent studies, however, show that the migration from farms and towns to cities is on an even greater scale than was suspected. In 1950, Charles Bettelheim and Suzanne Frère published a startling book on the city of Auxerre. They showed that this old city, which was thought to have a stable population, was in fact a center of demographic commotion. Very few families have lived there for more than two generations. Two-thirds of the present population was born elsewhere, and more than half came from rural communes. Studies of other cities indicate that this is a normal urban situation. Under these circumstances it is safe to say that a majority of the people of France — a substantial number of those living in the cities as well as those living in the country — were born and raised in rural communes.

It was to learn about this rural background that the author and his wife went with their two sons, then three and five years old, to live in Peyrane during the year 1950–51. The experience provided most of the information on which this book is based.

But why Peyrane? Out of the thousands of French villages where we might have lived, how did we happen to choose this particular place? Many villages would have been adequate. We assumed that the best village would be one which was not dominated by a set of unusual circumstances. It would not be too near Paris or any big city, nor would it be tucked away in too remote an area. It would not be dominated by the presence of a big army camp, factory, mine, school, hospital, or resort. It would not have suffered great damage in the war. The land should not be in the ownership of a small group of individuals, and its use should not be too specialized. The work techniques should be modern but not those of an industrialized agricultural area. There should be a normal flow of population moving to and away from the village. The dialect should not be too difficult for me to learn in a short time — that is, not Basque or Breton.

Preliminary consultation and investigation led us to the Vaucluse. One need only study the volumes of statistics published by the *Institut national de la statistique et des études économiques* to see that in many respects the Vaucluse is one of the least eccentric départements of France. In the general index of wealth it stands forty-fifth, exactly at the median for the eighty-nine départements. It ranks near the middle of most statistical tables — density of population, proportion of urban and rural population, the marriage and birth rate, the percentage of arable and fallow land, agricultural and industrial production, the number of 5,000-franc notes in circulation, the percentage of villages with running water and sewers, and the number of bars per capita. It ranks toward the middle in other ways that are less readily shown with statistics. In politics, for instance, it has been consistently middle-of-the-road. The elections are not one-sided, for there are substantial votes to the extreme left and to the right, but the characteristic contribution of the Vaucluse to French politics is Edouard Daladier.

In 1949–50, Lucien Bernot and René Blancard made a study of a village located on the old border between Picardy and Normandy. Through Monsieur Lévi-Strauss I met Lucien Bernot, and we discussed thoroughly the field work which he had just completed and which I was about to undertake. To increase the knowledge of French life as a whole it seemed sensible to place my project in southern France so that it might to a degree complement the Bernot-Blancard study in northern France. This consideration helped determine our choice of the Vaucluse département. There has been no formal relationship between our two projects, and although we have been in close touch with each other our reports were written quite independently. Our villages differed in many respects. Yet, in our conclusions concerning the basic motivation of the people there is essential agreement. In the case of these two villages the stereotyped differences between the northern and the southern Frenchmen, if they have any basis in reality, are more superficial than fundamental.

Investigation of the Vaucluse indicated that in choosing a village I should rule out certain areas within the département itself. Along the valley of the Rhône River the industrialized truck farms and vineyards give the communes more an urban than a rural atmosphere. In the mountains thirty miles to the northeast the communes are poor and isolated; they scarcely represent life in France today. But between these two extremes is an intermediate region that suited our purpose perfectly.

In August, 1950, our family settled in the little town of Pernes, in the center of the Vaucluse. During the next month we drove 2,500 miles in this small area, seeking our village and seeking a house in which we might live. We visited every commune, talking to all those who could give us pertinent information — mayors, teachers, town clerks, notaires, government officials, postmen, café owners, farmers. This procedure not only helped us find the location we sought; it was also valuable in orienting us to life in the area as a whole.

By the end of the month we had picked out three or four villages, any one of which might have been suitable. We chose Peyrane. It satisfied all our conditions, and besides we found there a house so strategically located that most of the people going in and out of the village had to pass by our front door. In retrospect our choice of Peyrane seems fortunate. The village has its peculiarities, which will be mentioned in the book, but on the whole they are unimportant. The only one that need be mentioned here concerns the school. The influence of the *Ecole nouvelle*, the indigenous progressive school movement developing in France today, has scarcely touched Peyrane. The school of Peyrane represents education in its more traditional form as it has trained most French adults; it is not what French educators believe education should be, and it undoubtedly does not represent French education of the future.

Some people who have read the manuscript of this book have assumed that Peyrane is peculiar because of the small part played by the Church, but this assumption is mistaken. In most French villages formal religion plays only a formal rôle. Catholic sociologists have shown that out of the 38,000,000 baptized French only about 8,000,000 are active in their religious practice. For most people observance does not extend beyond the rites of baptism, first communion, marriage, and burial. This is the situation in Peyrane. Before going to France I discussed my project with an official of the Philadelphia diocese, who gave me a letter of introduction to the priest of the village in which we might choose to live. When I called on the Abbé Malaval of Peyrane and handed him an envelope bearing the seal of the Philadelphia diocese, he was visibly upset. He was not accustomed to being treated with this consideration.

We had other letters of recommendation with us, but we did not need them. The fact that we came with our children was enough to open doors. The people of Peyrane love children, and they assumed we were not up to mischief since we brought ours with us. We told people exactly why we had come, "I am a teacher of French civilization," I said. "I have never lived in the south of France or in a village. We should like to live here a year to see what life is like." This reason was accepted. I was told that some of the Communists were skeptical at first. Their rumor was that we had come to prepare the next American landing, but before many weeks they, too, accepted our story. Indeed, the impression made by the American institutions of sabbatic leave and foundation fellowships was remarkable. In this village they increased respect for American Civilization more than any propaganda could have.

The first few weeks in Peyrane we spent orienting ourselves. I studied in books and in the field to learn what I could of local history, geography, and economy. I learned to understand the local dialect of Provençal. Since almost everyone in the community was bilingual, there was no real need to speak Provençal, but it was useful to understand it. During these weeks of orientation I gathered information on the basis of a questionnaire given to me by the dean of folklorists, Arnold Van Gennep. We copied the census reports of 1946 and a substantial part of the church records since 1900.

I had thought that a rôle I could fill in the village was that of supplementary schoolteacher. With the permission of the departmental school inspector in Avignon I taught English four afternoons a week to the "classe des grands," and I spent a great deal more time sitting in the school as an observer. Our older son was in the "classe des petits" and contributed to my fund of information. Mrs. Wylie was invited by the teachers to sit in the classes. We soon came to know the school intimately. By the end of the year I had found a way of securing information that might have been useful from the first: the teachers assigned a theme on a topic that interested me, and after the children's papers had served their purpose in school they were turned over to me. The teachers were coöperative in every possible way, and I wish I might use their real names so that I could thank them for their help.

It was not as a teacher that I came to participate in village life most naturally. After we had been in Peyrane a month I brought out my camera to take pictures of the firemen on their Sunday maneuvers. The following week I had a set of prints made for each fireman. From that moment my rôle was defined: I was the village photographer. Although my photographic record of life in the village could not be included in this book, my brief career as a photographer contributed substantially to it through the natural contacts it created for me with the people of Peyrane.

As we came to know people more intimately we found them eager to collaborate. I had no difficulty in obtaining information in either formal or informal interviews. The information gathered was recorded in diary form or organized according to the divisions of the *Outline of Cultural Materials* published by the Human Relations Area Files.

I had been warned by middle class urbanites that I should not try to use the Rorschach test. At worst, they said, peasants would be so suspicious of the ink blots that they would run us out of town; at best they would find the procedure so silly that they would not coöperate. I was too impressed by these warnings. I did not give the first Rorschach test until the last month of our stay in Peyrane when I knew I had nothing to lose in the attempt. The predictions were pessimistic, for the people of Peyrane loved the test. My only difficulty arose from the fact that some people's feelings were hurt because I did not have time to let them, too, tell me what they saw in the cards. I gave the test to ten per cent of the segment of the population in which I was most interested — the people in the village and those people living in the country who turned toward the village as a focal point in their life. Although the results of the Rorschach test are not formally included in this book, the months I spent studying at the Institute of the Pennsylvania Hospital and at the Klopfer Workshop and the time I spent giving the test in Peyrane were by no means lost. Through the test I established rapport with many individuals and gained insights that I could never have had without it. My only regret is that I lacked the time to get TAT protocols as well. The only other projective material I collected was a full set of drawings made by the children in the school.

Since the day we left Peyrane, the material in my files has continued to grow. Friends send us news, though at a diminishing rate. When I have needed further information, an inquiry sent to the teachers, to the grocer, to the postman, and to the town clerk has brought a prompt reply. Indeed, each time I look at my notes I am reminded that this book is not an individual project but a corporate undertaking. Collectively and individually the people of Peyrane did everything they could to make our year with them successful and enjoyable. It is frustrating not to be able to thank them by name for receiving us as they did, but perhaps the best way for me to show my gratitude is to conceal their identity. The name of the village, its exact location, and the names of all the persons used in this book have been changed. I am grateful to my friend, Paul Maucorps, for lending his name as a pseudonym for the most picturesque character in the book.

In placing my name alone after the title I feel presumptuous. It is literally true that the book, as well as the project on which it is based, has been a family enterprise. The four of us wish to express our gratitude to two institutions which made the enterprise possible: Haverford College, which gave me sabbatic leave, and the Social Science Research Council, which granted me an Area Research Training Fellowship.

From the day when I began to acquire the special knowledge and skills necessary to make this study to the day when the manuscript was sent to the publisher I have turned to many people for help. They have been unbelievably patient and kind. It is not possible to describe how each has helped, but I cannot resist mentioning their names. They and I know for what reasons I am grateful to them: Cletus J. Benjamin, Lucien Bernot, M. Carrère, André Casanova, Daniel Faucher, René Girard, François Goguel, Geoffrey Gorer, Martha Gordon, Georges Gurvitch, Maude Hallowell, Otto Klineberg, Bruno Klopfer, Martha and Paul Lawrence, E. Lee Porter, Louisa Kussin, Claude Lévi-Strauss, Marcel Maget, Paul Maucorps, Margaret Mead, Rhoda Métraux, Georges du Miffre, Henri Peyre, André Philip, Ira De A. Reid, Georges-Henri Rivière, Alphonse Roche, Eleanor Ross, Elbridge Sibley, Helen and Harry Stiles, Arnold Van Gennep, Evon Z. Vogt, Gilbert F. White and Anne Stiles Wylie. To this list should be appended a score of my colleagues of the faculty of Haverford College who have helped me at every turn of my interdisciplinary foray.

There is one man who must be mentioned separately. In both formal seminar and friendly conversation, A. Irving Hallowell introduced me to a world of ideas and techniques that underlie this book. He advised me in the practical problems of setting up my field work. He gave me counsel on the interpretation of my information, and he read the long draft of my manuscript. Out of gratitude, respect, and affection I have dedicated the book to him.

L. W.

Haverford College
May, 1956

Contents

Growing old in Peyrane

Epilogue

{All photographs were taken by the author.}

The Road to Peyrane

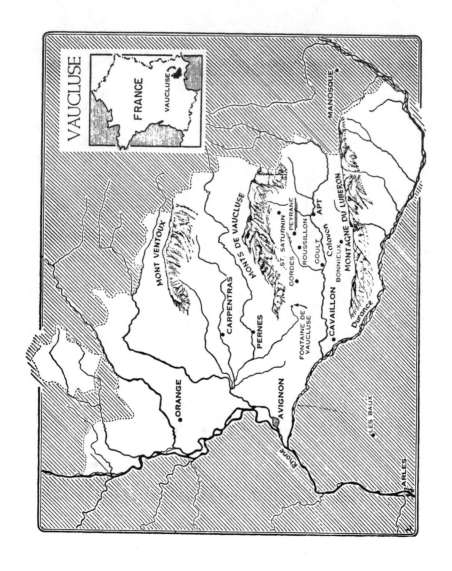

Chapter 1

In Space

Thirty-five miles east of Avignon on National Highway 100 is the turnoff to Peyrane. From there up to the village's nine-hundred-foot perch it is three miles on a gently rising black-top road. By car it takes only forty minutes to go from Avignon to Peyrane. It is even an easy bicycle ride if the wind is not blowing.

Without a car or bicycle the trip is complicated. Passenger service on the railroad that cuts across the tip of the commune has been discontinued. The only bus that goes directly leaves the bus station under the old Avignon ramparts every Thursday morning at eight o'clock. It does not follow the main road but meanders from village to village and reaches Peyrane only in midafternoon. Seven hours to go thirty-five miles!

It is more convenient to take a bus to Apt, a small town four miles from Peyrane, and wait for the bus that Monsieur Baume runs between Apt and Peyrane twice daily on Tuesday, Thursday, and Saturday. On other days of the week one must telephone the Peyrane exchange and leave a message for Monsieur Baume to make a special trip in the old car he uses as a taxi. But the message may not reach him, since he spends most of his time hunting. It avoids complications if the trip to Peyrane is made on Tuesday, Thursday, or Saturday.

The bus trip from Avignon across the Vaucluse to Apt is slow enough to give one a chance to see the curious pattern of windbreaks and canals that divide up the truck farms of the valley. This pattern was created by the men of the Vaucluse to adjust their way of living to the four elements that give the region its personality: the sun, the water, the wind, and the mountains.

The greatest natural resource of the Vaucluse Department is the sun. There are cold years and wet years, but in most the sun is so warm and so constant that a truck farmer can harvest eleven crops of lettuce a year. Carrots and cabbages can be grown all twelve months.

Cauliflower, celery, spinach, and artichokes are harvested from September to May. Peas, asparagus, green beans, new potatoes, and melons are ripe by the end of March. Tons of strawberries are picked in the early spring. All these are sent off by fast freight to the markets of the north in the cities of Germany, Belgium, Holland, Great Britain, and France. The sun makes the Vaucluse one of the best early vegetable gardens of France.

The sun also makes the Vaucluse one of the most prosperous departments of France. It ranks tenth among the eighty-nine departments for its standard of living. This does not mean that it is an especially wealthy region, for it ranks only forty-fifth in wealth. It does mean, however, that the wealth is widely distributed. On the whole, the Vaucluse is an area of small, prosperous farms worked by their owners.

In order to take advantage of the sun, the Vaucluse farmers must solve the problem of water. The total annual rainfall figures for this region are rather high, but the rain is not evenly distributed throughout the year. The winters are dry, and the summers even drier. Most of the rain comes in spring and fall, and it comes in storms so severe that they flatten the crops, erode the soil and sometimes bring hail, which means catastrophe to a truck farm.

Such storms do not produce the kind of rain that farmers pray for, and the Vaucluse farmers are not the type to pray for rain, anyway. Accepting the climate for what it is, they have elaborated an extensive system of irrigation canals utilizing the water of the Durance and Sorgue rivers. Now the fields of the low valleys get the gentle and regular watering they need.

Farther up in the hills around Peyrane, few farmers have the benefit of canals. Their fields get little more water than what the rains bring. Now and then a Peyrane farmer says longingly that when Peyrane gets its irrigation system his farm will be as rich as the farms down near Avignon, but he knows that this is wishful thinking, for no one is seriously considering the construction of such a canal. It is an attractive thought, however, for the soil of Peyrane is good, even if not so good as the soil of the valley. And Peyrane has even more sunshine than the valley, for often it is foggy in the valley when it is clear at Peyrane.

Because of its irrigation system, the valley landscape seems man made. Irrigation canals and ditches cut the fields into small, well-delineated geometrical shapes. The delineation is made even more striking by the heavy rows of cypress trees and thickets of cane that are planted along the northern edge of each field. Many of the fields are subdivided by high partitions of woven canes and reeds placed every ten feet or so apart.

These hedges and partitions are windbreakers designed to protect the crops from the mistral, a wind that hurtles out of the cold Alps, down the Rhone corridor to the warmer Mediterranean, at a rate of thirty to fifty miles an hour. In narrow passages and in gusts the mistral not infrequently reaches hurricane speed. According to an old saying, Provence suffers from three scourges — the Government, the flooding Durance, and the mistral. Popular tradition also has it that when the mistral starts to blow it will continue to blow in multiples of three: usually three days, often six days, and sometimes even nine days. Scientific observation does not bear this out, but it is true that when the mistral starts to blow it blows for hours and for days, especially in the months of December, February, and March.

This cold but dry, sunny wind has left its mark on every aspect of life in the whole region. One sees it not just in the cypress hedges that protect fields and houses (that Van Gogh found so picturesque). The olive trees all bend toward the south. The houses seem to bend southward, too, for they are customarily built so as to present a bleak wall and a long sloping roof to the north. Heavy stones are placed along the edge of the roof to keep the tiles from blowing away.

Regardless of precautions one cannot get away from the mistral. It comes in around the door. It comes in through cracks in the wall. It comes down the chimney and blows smoke through the house. As it continues to blow on and on, it gets on one's nerves. The teachers dread the mistral because when it blows the children are hard to manage. One cannot experience the mistral without being affected by it. Stendhal, in Avignon on June 14, 1837, wrote in *Mémoires d'un Touriste*:

A furious mistral started up this morning. That is the drawback of all the pleasures to be found in Provence.

Two weeks ago when we were going over the Beaucaire bridge the diligence had to be held down by eight men hanging on to ropes tied to the top. It looked as though the diligence might fall into the Rhone.

The north wind meets this river's long north-south valley which acts as a bellows to increase its velocity. When the mistral reigns in Provence you don't know where to take refuge. It is true that the sun is shining brightly, but a cold, unbearable wind penetrates the best closed rooms and grates on the nerves so that the most dauntless person is unwittingly upset.

It is appropriate that the six-thousand-foot outpost of the southwestern Alps dominating the landscape of the Vaucluse should be named Mont Ventoux — Windy Mountain. Since the fourteenth century when Petrarch wrote the first description of an ascent of Ventoux, writers and local patriots have adopted this windy mountain as a symbol of the windy Vaucluse. As you drive along in the bus from Avignon to Apt, the Mont Ventoux hovers on the horizon to the north, always visible when you pass a break in the cypress and cane hedges.

About fifteen miles from Avignon, the Mont Ventoux disappears behind a lower range of mountains that looms up ahead. A few moments later the road crosses the canal which brings irrigation water to the Rhone valley. This is the division line between the intensive truck farms of the valley and the more extensive farms, the vineyards, orchards, and grain fields of the foothills. Into the hills, the National Road No. 100 runs along the little Calavon River — of little use for irrigation since it does no more than drain the surface. In the summer its bed is dry; in the spring and fall after a storm it may flood its banks. The water from the mountains sinks into the limestone and flows away in subterranean channels.

Lined up parallel with the Calavon River for twenty-five miles and forming a basin of which the city of Apt is the center, are two mountain ranges — the Monts de Vaucluse to the north and the Montagne de Lubéron to the south. They are both lower than Mont Ventoux, but they are impressive because their fantastically eroded cliffs and sparse vegetation give them a wild appearance. Farms and half-deserted villages huddle in these mountains wherever water and a bit of fertile soil are found, but their poverty makes a shocking contrast with the prosperous farms of the valley below. More and more of this mountain land is being taken over for forests and hunting reserves.

The area lying between these two low mountain ranges is the Apt Basin. It is geologically complicated, but to the casual traveler it seems simple: mountains two or three miles to the north, mountains two or three miles to the south, and between them a valley studded with hills and divided in the center by a dry river bed. Economically, it is an intermediate region between the wealth of the Rhone valley and the extreme poverty of the high mountain farms.

The surprising thing, as you drive along vineyards in the center of the Apt Basin, is that you pass through so few villages — only two of them in a twenty-mile stretch, although the area is thickly populated. However, there are towns all the way. They are there, staring down at you as you pass, even though you may not see them. At almost any point along the road you can stop and, if you know where to look, you can see four or five villages, perched five hundred or a thousand feet up on the edge of the mountain, their limestone houses fading into the limestone of the background. Almost all the towns of the region are perched high on hills rimming and dotting the basin at the center of which lies their subprefecture and traditional market town, Apt.

When you first see these villages they all look alike, and they look rather like the "perched" villages characteristic of all of southern France. In most of them there is the old quarter of the town surrounding the ruins of a modest chateau at the peak of the hill. The older houses look as if they were massed in layers on the hillside, the red tile roofs emphasizing their horizontal lines. The newer quarter of the town straggles farther down the leeward slope of the hill and even ventures out into the valley. In some villages the old "perched" quarter has died completely and lies a mass of ruins above the new quarter. In other villages the process is almost completed. It seems to be the inevitable fate of these villages. It is as though they had tired of hanging on to their perch and slipped down to a more comfortable position.

When your bus drives into Apt you wonder what distinguishes it besides the yellow ochre sheds, the small winding streets, and the stagnant waters of the almost dry Calavon River. The guidebook does not add many details. It mentions the shrine of Saint Anne and the remains of the city wall, but it gives no hint of the real importance of Apt.

To understand the function and character of this city you must arrive on Saturday morning to see the market that has been held there — with the exception of a few years in the fourteenth century — every Saturday morning for the last eight hundred years. Vendors' stands fill the public squares. Streets and shops are so crowded that it seems as though all the people of the surrounding area have deserted their homes. This is far from true, of course, for it does not take a whole population to fill the narrow streets of Apt.

But there are many people, and they go to Apt for many purposes. Town officials go to discuss problems with the Sub-Prefect, who holds court then. Doctors' waiting rooms are crowded. Ear and eye specialists come from Avignon for their special Saturday morning clinic. Pharmacies do big business. To have a prescription filled you must stand in a line of fifteen or twenty people. Lawyers' offices are jammed. Notaires meet their colleagues and clients in Arène's café, the same café favored by mayors and town clerks. Each café is the headquarters for a special professional clientèle, so that if you are a politician, a coöp official, a labor union officer, a hunting enthusiast, a bicycle racer or a bowling enthusiast, you know to what café you can go to find people of similar problems and interests. Blacksmiths and garage mechanics have their busiest day of the week on Saturday. Welders, cobblers, watch repairmen, oculists, tailors — all accumulate a week's work. Young people come to Apt to court. Drinking companions come to drink. Some people come simply for the "promenade."

It is this Saturday morning market that gives real unity to the Apt Basin, a unity that is growing weaker as better transportation facilities permit people to turn toward the more modern railroad city of Cavaillon. The Saturday market gives Apt its personality. On other days it is as lifeless as a church on Monday morning.

It is natural that you, a foreigner, should be attracted to those features of the market that are not very important to the inhabitants of this region but which are exotic to you. You seek out the spots where farmers are selling hares, thrushes, essence of lavender, lavender honey, beeswax. If you get there early enough you can see Raymond Caizac, poet and truffle king, buy up a week's supply of truffles from the owners of the live-oak orchards and from the less civilized truffle hunters who live up in the mountains. The truffle crop is not what it used to be, so this transaction does not last long. Then it will take Caizac only a few moments more to carry his truffles home to his mother, who will combine them with minced thrush and can them for her son to sell to city dealers.

When Caizac has finished with his truffles he will be free to introduce you to the cafés of Apt and to the experience of drinking pastis and eating anchovies. He can send word to Monsieur Baume to hold the Peyrane bus for you, and after a few more rounds of pastis he will lead you to the bus — a few minutes after the scheduled time for departure. Of course, he knew that Monsieur Baume would not be ready to leave. Monsieur Baume has to do errands for the people of Peyrane who did not come down to the market. He still has to pick up several prescriptions at the pharmacy, get a spare part for Sautel's saw motor, buy some yard goods for Mademoiselle Pamard, and pick up some legal papers at a lawyer's office for Bourdin.

The people waiting in the bus try to appear indifferent to you, but they cannot help being curious. Their curiosity is legitimate. Peyrane lies on the road to nowhere. Except for the National Highway No. 100 which crosses only the tip of the commune, its roads lead only to and from the village. If you are going to Peyrane you are not simply passing through on your way elsewhere. You must have some reason for going there.

When Caizac introduces you to some of the people on the bus you have an opportunity to satisfy their curiosity. At the same time you have a chance to meet some of the leading personalities of Peyrane, for four of them are always on the Saturday noon bus.

There is Marcel Rivet, Secrétaire de la Mairie, an office which may be roughly translated by Town Clerk, although the Secrétaire has more responsibilities and is more influential in France than the Town Clerk in this country. Every Saturday morning Rivet brings official papers down to Mayor Ginoux, who meets him at Arène's café. Ginoux has his business in Peyrane but lives in the neighboring town of Gargas and comes to Peyrane only on Friday afternoons, unless there is an emergency. Since Rivet and he often have business at the Sub-Prefecture in Apt on Saturday morning they have gotten in the habit of meeting and transacting much of their business over a table at the café.

Rivet is from Marseille. During the war when it was hard to make a living and to find food for his wife and two little boys in the city, he brought his family to live with an aunt in her big house in Peyrane. After a short, unsuccessful period in the restaurant business in the Peyrane hotel he became Town Clerk. A warm, demonstrative person, he finds it difficult to live in a community where one must avoid becoming involved in quarrels and feuds. He protects himself by adopting the detached attitude of a city man looking down with amusement

on the "antics" of the villagers, but underneath he is hurt. He would
like to be one of the villagers, for he is fond of them.

Rivet's enemy is on the bus, Edouard Pascal, who considers himself
the Intellectual of the village. He was one of the bright boys in his class
at school, and since his family had money, he was sent off to the city
to continue his studies. Vaguely ailing, he came home two years later
and has remained in Peyrane ever since, though he makes much of
his connections and friendships with intellectuals elsewhere in the
department. He makes a scant living by running his moribund aunt's
moribund grocery. Since he has no car he has to go by bus to Apt on
Saturday for his supplies. Monsieur Baume brings them back in the
trailer he attaches to the little bus. Pascal has contempt for the people
in the village. He does not hide the fact that he considers them stupid
and uncouth. They resent his haughtiness and laugh at his peculiarities,
but — and it is this that makes Rivet furious — they still respect him,
partly because they are half taken in by his pose and partly because they
fear his sharp tongue.

Julien Vincent, the owner of the hotel-restaurant of Peyrane, also
goes to Apt every Saturday for supplies. He came to Peyrane to take
over the restaurant when Rivet had failed. Rivet's frankness with his
customers and his passion for the game of boules were the main causes
for his failure. Vincent has no such weaknesses. He says that he is
from Lyon and that he is in business for the sake of business. (He is
referring to the French stereotype of the people of Lyon who have the
reputation for being businesslike and lacking in humor.) More important, he is an excellent cook, the restaurant is beautifully located, and
his wife keeps the six rooms of the little hotel in neat order. Consequently Vincent has just "made" the *Guide Michelin* and has had the
façade of the restaurant remodeled. He adds distinction to his situation
by playing bridge every Thursday evening with three of the most conservative and influential men in the village. He is an outsider, like
Rivet, but he has been accepted by the people of Peyrane to the extent
of being elected to the Town Council.

Francis Favre always finds an excuse for going to Apt on Saturday,
but his real reason for going is simply that he enjoys the *promenade*.
He can justify the trip by finding an errand to do, for he is a man of
many errands. Not only is he the titular postman of Peyrane, but he is
at the same time the only plumber and the only electrician in the com-

mune. Any one of the three occupations could keep Francis busy and give his family a decent living, but Francis likes variety. He says that doing one thing all the time bores him, and besides three jobs are safer than one because one never knows. . . He likes being a postman best because it takes him around the commune every day and gives him a chance to talk to people. Consequently his roles as plumber and electrician suffer. Furthermore, Francis has a weakness for saying "yes" and a propensity for not finishing any job he begins. As a result he accepts many jobs, starts work on them, and leaves them unfinished for weeks and months. He goes off leaving his tools as an indication that he will return. He does return, but only to pick up a tool he needs on another job he has started. His tools are scattered all over the commune. People tear their hair, but they court Francis because he is the only plumber and electrician they can turn to, unless they want to pay to have one come all the way out from Apt. If a competitor moved in to take over the jobs that go begging, he might have trouble with Favre's relatives — and Favre is the most common name in the commune.

The second most common name in the commune is Jouvaud, so it is not surprising that there are two Jouvauds on the bus. There is Marguerite, the daughter of the prosperous mason and member of the Town Council. She goes to Apt every Saturday morning for a sewing lesson. Sitting at the back of the bus is her Uncle Simon, a shiftless individual who can hold down a job only with his brother. He has to go to Apt regularly to have his eye treated for a lime burn.

Caizac does not introduce you to Simon Jouvaud or Marguerite or to the three other women who are passengers on the bus. Rivet, Vincent, Pascal and Francis Favre will ask questions, answer your questions and keep you occupied until the bus leaves. When Monsieur Baume comes back he checks to make sure that all his expected fares are on the bus. Prayal is missing, but Baume knows where he is. A boy is sent to the Café des Sports, and in a few moments Prayal climbs unhurriedly on the bus. Sitting next to Rivet he explains that he has failed to persuade the owner of the Café des Sports, a champion boule player of the region, to team up with Rivet and him in the boules tournament at Peyrane's yearly fete.

With Prayal aboard, the bus pulls out, moving cautiously through the crowd of people, cars, buses, bicycles, and carts. Baume's horn and

his shout help clear the way, and finally the bus moves up the street
and out of town. For two miles it follows National Highway No. 100
over which you have come from Avignon. Then it turns off on a
smaller road that soon begins to climb the slope leading up to the hills
ahead. In the valley along a creek there are pastures and an attempt
at the kind of truck gardens you saw near Avignon. On the slope of
the hills are vineyards, wheat fields, and orchards. As you reach the
crest of the hills there are only woods, pine woods whose fresh green
stands out strikingly against the intensely blue sky of the Midi.

The road begins to wind, and as you twist around one particularly
sharp bend your breath is suddenly taken away by your first glimpse
of Peyrane's ochre cliffs. The soft red and yellow sandstone of the hills
has been carved away by ochre mines, gutted by storms, lashed by the
mistral so that it presents a confusion of steep cliffs shaped into weird,
colorful forms. On top of the hill, surrounded on three sides by two-
hundred-foot ochre cliffs, perches the red town of Peyrane.

Because of its color, Peyrane appears different from other villages.
It is gaudy against their dull limestone. Edouard Pascal has organized
a *syndicat d'initiative*, a sort of combined tourist agency and chamber
of commerce, to publicize the yellow and red cliffs of his village
"whence flow," he likes to say, "the gold and the blood." He even succeeded in having the Government classify Peyrane as a "national monument." This means that in order to preserve the beauty of Peyrane and
its surrounding hills, government approval must be sought before any
radical change — architectural or topographical — can be made in the
aspect of the houses or the woods or the cliffs. The beauty of Peyrane
is thus officially recognized, and on seeing Peyrane one must agree that
its beauty deserves to be officially recognized.

The people of Peyrane are conscious of the beauty of their village,
and they speak about it with admiration. The children draw pictures
that would curdle the blood of a psychologist if he were not told that
the red houses and red hills are in truth realistic. Now and then a
busload of tourists stops to buy postcards, gape along the precipices
and have lunch at Vincent's. Artists try to paint Peyrane without ending up with a hopelessly gaudy piece of canvas. The ochre town, the
green trees, the red cliffs combine with the blue sky and the brilliant
sun to make Peyrane a village apart.

It is surprising how little time it takes for the redness of a red village to seem natural. After a few weeks in Peyrane one almost forgets to be struck by the beauty of the cliffs and the color of the houses. As the flamboyance of Peyrane comes to be taken for granted, it becomes evident that this distinction is really superficial. Tourists and painters have little more effect on the people of Peyrane than a passenger liner has on life at the bottom of the sea. The real distinction of Peyrane is to be found not in its red cliffs but in the lives of the people who live in the town above the cliffs.

Chapter 2

In Time

Of the four men on the Peyrane bus only one is a native of Peyrane. Two were born in neighboring communes, and the other was born in Marseille. So far as their place of birth is concerned this group is a good sample of the population of Peyrane, for the majority of the people living in the commune were not born there. Most of them are from other towns around Apt, and many came from still farther away — from the poorer regions of the Alps, from Italy, and from Spain. There are Alsatian and Belgian refugees who did not return home after the war, the Breton wife of the farmer who once went to sea, and the Norman wife of the man who once worked in a Rouen cotton mill.

The diversified origin of this rural population surprises us because it does not fit into our American stereotype of the European peasant — the naive creature riveted to the same plot of soil which his ancestors have tilled since they stopped living in caves. It is easy to see how this stereotype develops. Nourished with Balzac's novels and Millet's paintings we arrive at a village that appears old to American eyes, so old that it seems that it has "always been there like that."

This impression is strengthened by what we learn of the village's past. Paleolithic remains have been found in a nearby cave. From the top of the village you look out over Perréal, the hill at the foot of which a famous battle was fought between Barbarians and Romans before the time of Caesar. At the southern tip of the commune is the Pont Julien, a Roman bridge which carried the Domitian Way across the Calavon River and which is still in use. In the museum at Avignon there are Roman coins and inscriptions that were found on farms in Peyrane. All this adds up to a feeling of antiquity, of continuity, and of stability.

As you go through the town archives (that is, the big pile of papers heaped in a closet in the Town Hall), it even seems as though the

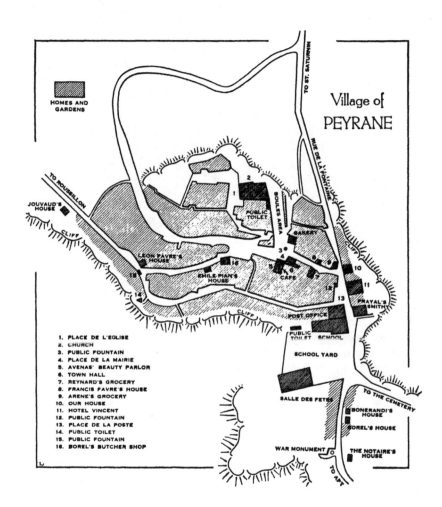

Village of
PEYRANE

1. PLACE DE L'EGLISE
2. CHURCH
3. PUBLIC FOUNTAIN
4. PLACE DE LA MAIRIE
5. AVENAS' BEAUTY PARLOR
6. TOWN HALL
7. REYNARD'S GROCERY
8. FRANCIS FAVRE'S HOUSE
9. ARENE'S GROCERY
10. OUR HOUSE
11. HOTEL VINCENT
12. PUBLIC FOUNTAIN
13. PLACE DE LA POSTE
14. PUBLIC TOILET
15. PUBLIC FOUNTAIN
16. BOREL'S BUTCHER SHOP

people of the village were permanent. An eighteenth-century list of town notables includes names that are also in the list of Municipal Councillors today. There is a legal document relating how in 1793 a man named Jouvaud led a group of young people dancing the farandole across the path of a group of boule players. One of the latter, named Favre, became so enraged that he killed Jouvaud. Today the Favres are Communists, and the Jouvauds are Radicals. It is difficult not to get the feeling that the Favres and the Jouvauds and their houses and their attitude toward each other are permanent fixtures of Peyrane like the ochre cliffs.

Of course, even the ochre cliffs change more rapidly than one might think. Monsieur Prayal points out a spot behind his shed where there used to be a road along the edge of the cliff. In the last fifty years the soft sandstone has eroded, and the road has fallen away into the valley. The cliff is sheer with the back wall of the shed, and before many years have passed the shed will fall into the valley.

Peyrane does change. The cliffs erode. The top of the hill is deserted, and the town spills down into the valley. The population changes. The impression of permanence is deceptive. Peyrane is old, but antiquity is not the same as permanence. Change may not be so spectacular as it is in some other places in the world, but over a period of time it is radical.

Just in the nineteenth century there were three distinct Peyranes. The Peyrane of today cannot be understood unless it is seen as one state of a kaleidoscopic process. Perhaps the best way to get a feeling for the constant transformation is to see how today's Peyrane grew out of the nineteenth-century Peyranes. To recreate this past we have only the census reports, sketchy historical accounts, and the evidence of the past that is still visible in the village. Pieced together, this factual information gives us in a few pages the past patterns from which today's pattern of life developed.

In 1801, the year of the first official census in France, there were 1195 people in Peyrane living as completely as possible to themselves. The village was the economic and cultural center of life, for roads were bad and communications with the outside were poor. Some silkworms were grown and the cocoons were sent off to Avignon, but most of the efforts of the peasants were devoted to producing what was needed by their own families and by their own community. The products were the traditional products of the Mediterranean area: wheat, dried vegetables, olives, wine, honey, figs, and almonds. A flock of sheep and goats produced milk, wool, a bit of meat, and — most important — it fertilized the fields. Ploughing was done with the *araire*, the wheelless plough which had been used in Mediterranean countries for at least two thousand years. Wheat was harvested with a sickle, but a new instrument, the scythe, was becoming popular in the Vaucluse.

Primitive methods of cultivation did not make for large harvests, and unfortunately, the soil, the terrain, the small size of the fields, and the climate of the Apt basin are not favorable for the production of the staple crops — wheat and olives. Even in good years the harvest was poor. The usual proportion of wheat harvested to the seed sown was five to one; in the best years it was seven to one. Under such circumstances the standard of living of the people was low. Not infrequently a sudden freeze, an epidemic among plants or animals, a hailstorm, or a flooding rainstorm wiped out a whole crop, and then there was famine. The five windmills on the hills around the town had no grain to grind, and the public oil mill had no olives to press. Travelers' descriptions and economic reports of this period often speak of the great misery among the peasants of the Vaucluse.

The Peyrane of 1851 was very different. Improvements in transportation had partly removed the necessity of self-sufficiency. The traditional crops were not abandoned, but they were more easily supplemented with wheat and oil shipped in from elsewhere. These shipments could be paid for because of the changed emphasis in the economy. Emphasis was no longer on self-sufficiency but on the production of goods to be sold outside the commune. A new crop had been introduced which substantially increased the income of the area — *garance*, the plant that produced red dye with which the French and British soldiers' uniforms were colored. The silk industry was also greatly extended in the first half of the nineteenth century. The peak of its production was reached in the year 1850, when the women and children of the Vaucluse (since raising silkworms is not a man's job) raised almost four and a half million pounds of silk cocoons.

The fear of famine was removed, and the silk industry made it profitable to raise large families. Between 1801 and 1851 the population of Peyrane increased from 1195 to 1484. During this same period, the

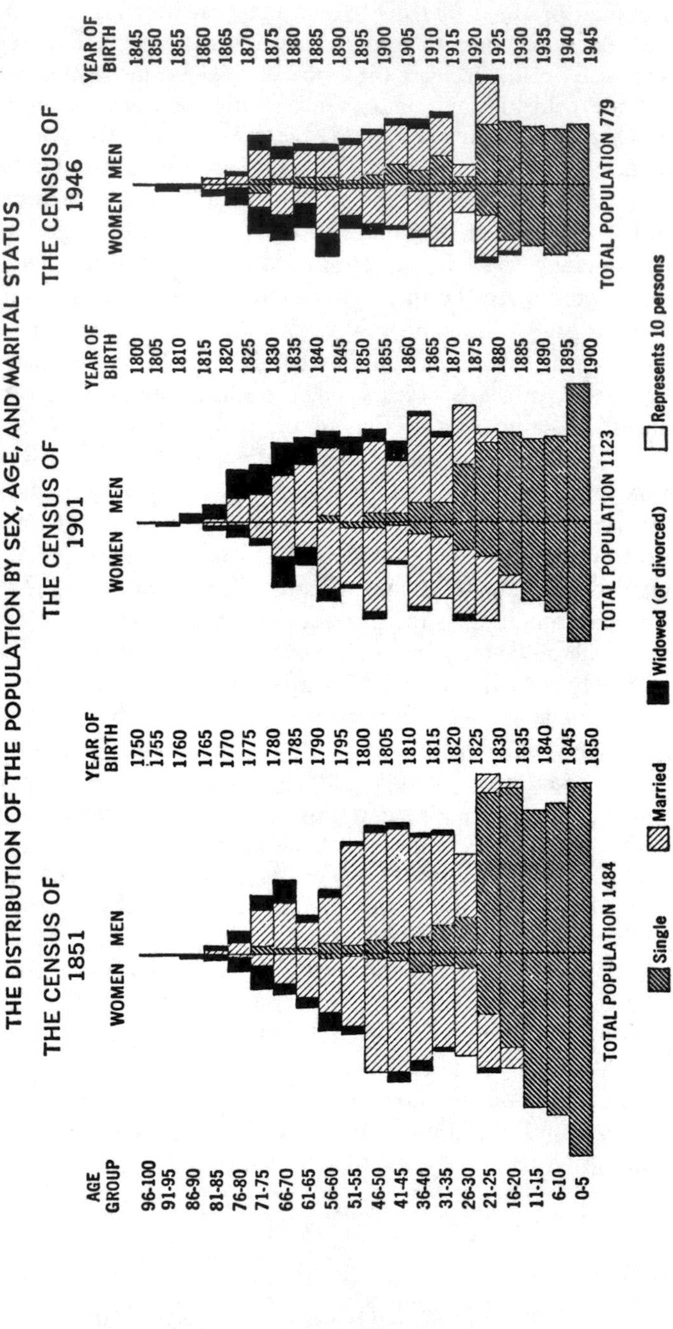

THE DISTRIBUTION OF THE POPULATION BY SEX, AGE, AND MARITAL STATUS
THE CENSUS OF 1851
THE CENSUS OF 1901
THE CENSUS OF 1946
WOMEN MEN
AGE GROUP
96-100
91-95
86-90
81-85
76-80
71-75
66-70
61-65
56-60
51-55
46-50
41-45
36-40
31-35
26-30
21-25
16-20
11-15
6-10
0-5
YEAR OF BIRTH
1750 1755 1760 1765 1770 1775 1780 1785 1790 1795 1800 1805 1810 1815 1820 1825 1830 1835 1840 1845 1850
1800 1805 1810 1815 1820 1825 1830 1835 1840 1845 1850 1855 1860 1865 1870 1875 1880 1885 1890 1895 1900
1845 1850 1855 1860 1865 1870 1875 1880 1885 1890 1895 1900 1905 1910 1915 1920 1925 1930 1935 1940 1945
TOTAL POPULATION 1484
TOTAL POPULATION 1123
TOTAL POPULATION 779
Single
Married
Widowed (or divorced)
Represents 10 persons

population of the Vaucluse and of France as a whole increased by thirty per cent. The twenty-five per cent increase in the rural commune of Peyrane was not far behind the increases in the larger industrial cities.

The population pyramid based on the census of 1851 shows that Peyrane was a growing community. This fairly symmetrical, broad-based pyramid shows a population composed of relatively few old people, a large proportion of younger children, and a substantial number in the middle age groups, economically the most productive group in the population. It is interesting to note that the irregularities in the pyramid were largely caused by the Napoleonic wars. The generation of men born between 1785 and 1795, the generation that was "bled white" by Napoleon, is reduced, and the generation to which their children would have belonged, the generation born between 1815 and 1825, is proportionately small. Except for these irregularities and except for the apparent excess of male over female births from 1825 to 1835, the population pyramid for 1851 is the kind one might expect of a thriving, productive community.

From 1851 to 1861 Peyrane continued to grow. The population increased from 1484 to 1568. Thirty-five new houses were built by the twenty-one masons and carpenters of the commune. Peyrane was a big *bourg* in 1861. It had two millers, seven bakers, three grocers and two butchers, two weavers, six tailors and five shoemakers. There were five blacksmiths in the commune. There were three cafés. There were two priests and three nuns.

But a peak had been reached in the growth of the commune. Within a few years Peyrane, like every village in the region, was hit hard by several catastrophes. First came the silkworm diseases. The silk industry had already been weakened by competition with other silk producing areas of the world. Perhaps the Vaucluse could not have continued to compete, so that production would have tapered off slowly, but the worm diseases gave it the *coup de grâce*. Abruptly the production of silk ceased to be an important factor in the economy.

In 1870 three other important sources of income were destroyed. First came the olives. The winter of 1870–71 was so severe that all the olive trees were frozen. In the same year an artificial dye was discovered that immediately replaced the dye extracted from the root of the *garance*, which had become a major crop in the Vaucluse. Finally, in 1870, the phylloxera, a vine-destroying insect which had been accidentally imported from America into a neighboring département and which was spreading throughout France, reached the Peyrane area. The vineyards of the commune were completely destroyed.

Thus, within a few years, four essential items in the economy were removed. At the same time the industrial revolution, which had hit France late, was attracting more and more people from the country to the city. In the four-year period, from 1876 to 1880, a primarily rural département like the Vaucluse lost 20,000 inhabitants who fled from the rural communes to the cities.

By 1886, seventy-nine of Peyrane's 349 houses stood empty, and 305 of its people had left. The population of the commune had dropped to 1213, almost exactly what it had been in 1801. The Peyrane of 1851 had disappeared, and the traditional wheat-and-sheep Peyrane reappeared, supporting about the same number of people it had supported a hundred years before.

The population pyramid based on the census of 1901 shows how Peyrane had changed. The proportion of old people is much higher than in 1851, and until 1895 the proportion of children born is much lower. A substantial section of economically productive adults, those born between 1855 and 1860, is lacking. These are the people who were in their twenties when the catastrophes hit Peyrane; they were naturally the first ones to leave the community and go off to the city.

The flight of the commune's population is even greater than the pyramid shows, but the loss is partially hidden by the fact that by 1901 a number of people had moved into the commune from the outside to take the places of some of the people who had left. This is shown in the fact that in 1861 the population of Peyrane had been fairly homogeneous. There were no foreigners living in the commune, and there were only ten people born outside the Vaucluse. By 1896 there were twenty-six foreigners and sixty-six people from outside the Vaucluse living in Peyrane. Almost ten per cent of the population was made up of *étrangers*, that is, people coming from other départements and from other countries.

The true loss in the population is also masked by the fact that the birth rate jumped after 1895. There were many more children born between 1895 and 1900 than in any of the preceding five-year periods. The influx of outsiders and the substantial increase in the birth rate are indications of a completely new development in the life of the village. A new Peyrane was forming, quite different from the Peyrane of 1801 and quite different from the Peyrane of 1851.

By 1901, the red and yellow cliffs of the commune, which are supposed to have furnished ochre for the Romans two thousand years before, were again being mined extensively. During the nineteenth century, the ochre extraction had been carried on in a very limited manner, but the expansion of the market and the development of modern machinery permitted rapid extension of the industry. By 1914, the Vaucluse was exporting 56,000 tons of ochre a year. Peyrane, one of the centers of the industry, had become a mining town.

The wide export market seemed to assure the industry of continued prosperity, but this turned out to be its weakest point. The war in 1914 immediately cut off the Russian market, and within three years all other foreign markets disappeared. Production dropped to next to nothing, and the population of Peyrane dropped to 900.

After the war production began again, and by 1929 it had finally reached the 1914 level. Then another catastrophe. The depression hit the building industry and consequently the ochre industry, for much of the ochre was used in making house paint. By 1938, the production in the Vaucluse had dropped to 18,000 tons. The next year war once more closed off the foreign markets, and this time some of the markets were closed for good. The end of the war brought little relief because in the United States a synthetic ochre had been developed that almost completely replaced the natural Vaucluse ochre. For political reasons the markets of eastern Europe were closed for an indefinite period of time. By 1951, the ochre mines of the Vaucluse were still producing ochre but on a much smaller scale. In Peyrane only fourteen regular inhabitants and a few transient Arabs are still employed in the ochre industry. The Peyrane of 1901 has disappeared as conclusively as the Peyrane of 1851 and the Peyrane of 1801.

The Peyrane of 1951 is different from those that have been described and yet it cannot be understood without reference to the past Peyranes. The size and distribution of the fields, for instance, have apparently changed little since 1801, and the general pattern has probably not changed much since 1501. Like other communes in this region of France, Peyrane is a community of small farms. Of the ninety-two farms in its territory about one-fourth are smaller than twenty-five acres, one-half are between twenty-five and fifty acres, and one-quarter are between fifty and one hundred acres. The division is even more extreme than it sounds, for the word *farm* is misleading. To an American, a farm usually means a relatively compact tract of land. A farm in Peyrane is rarely made up of one tract. It may have a central tract around a farmhouse, but the holdings of most farmers are split up into scattered fields widely separated from each other by fields belonging to other farmers.

Most of the farms, sixty per cent of them, are worked by the families owning them. Twenty-five per cent are worked by *fermiers* (cash-rent farmers), and fifteen per cent are worked by *métayers* (fifty-fifty crop-share farmers). This situation is also more complicated than it sounds. A man may own some fields, rent others, and work still others on shares. *Fermiers* and *métayers* may have special clauses in their contracts so that they do not fit exactly in the category in which they are placed for statistical purposes. The three categories of farmers do not necessarily imply social distinctions that one might be tempted to attach to them. For instance, the Rabouls are *fermiers* on the farm where they live in Peyrane, but they are landowners in the neighboring commune of Gordes and have rented the Gordes farm to a *fermier*. The Bonnels are *métayers*, but they have lived in Peyrane for many generations and have worked the same farm for four generations. They are more respected than the landowning Figeards. Each case, studied separately, seems to belie statistical generalizations.

A glimpse at the town platbook or at an aerial photograph of the commune shows strikingly how the arable land is divided into an elaborate network of small and irregular fields. The small size and irregularity of the fields may be attributed in part to the terrain, but the principal causes are buried in the archives dating back to medieval times. The intricate network of inheritance that has been elaborated over the centuries is, of course, a principal source of the complication, and the study of this network would be revealing, for its impact on family and personal relationships in the community is obviously great. For instance, Peretti owns most of his farm, but half of his house and some of the sheds belong to Reynard, the grocer, whose wife inherited them from her maternal grandmother. Reynard will not rent them to Peretti because he has reason to believe that Peretti would not be a good tenant.

The division of land also has a serious effect on the farmer's economic efficiency. In the eighteenth century when most of the farm work was done by hand this was less important. In 1950 small fields are incompatible with the use of farm machinery and with efficient farming methods. The traditional crops that were grown in the Peyrane of 1801 have never been completely abandoned. About one-third of the ploughed land is still devoted to the old staples — wheat and dried vegetables. For reasons that will be given later, this legacy of the past is disappearing slowly.

The legacy of the Peyrane of 1851 takes on the form of ruins of various sorts. In the countryside around the village only 472 people live today where there were 1075 people living a hundred years ago. In the village itself there were 493 people; now there are 307. The most striking evidence of this change is found in the ruined dwellings that dot the countryside. There were four hundred houses occupied in 1861; in 1946 there were fewer than two hundred fifty.

By poking around these ruins (and taking care not to fall into an abandoned well or knock down a weak wall) one can discover other remnants of the past. For instance, along the walls of what was the largest room in most houses are curious rows of holes about two inches across and an inch or so deep. These were the holes in which poles were inserted so that the silkworm trays might be placed in layers across the room. The growing of silkworms has almost completely disappeared in the commune. Only a few of the hardest working women still accept the frantic task of trying to keep up with the appetite of the worms.

The most picturesque monuments to the Peyrane of 1851 are the windmills perched on the tops of the hills around the town. Daudet's story, "Le Secret de Maître Cornille," describes how the windmills in this part of southern France, gradually lost out to the steam-and-water-powered mills of the cities. When the mills of Peyrane stopped grinding wheat altogether their wings were removed, the grinding mechanism was taken out, and the upper room was converted into a dovecote. Even the dovecotes have now been abandoned, and the old mills stand deserted. During the war, refugees were housed in two of them, and afterwards an artist lived in one of them until the mistral drove him out. Today anyone could buy the whole top of a hill in Peyrane complete with a windmill for ninety dollars.

A less obvious monument to the nineteenth-century Peyrane is the *Salle des Fêtes*. It was originally on open market building with only a roof supported by heavy pillars. When modern transportation destroyed Peyrane's function as economic center of the commune and made it in effect a suburb of Apt and Cavaillon, the old market building was abandoned. Then the mayor had the structure walled in. Now the old market building serves as a public dance hall, political hall, and ceremonial hall for the commune. It is hard to realize that this bleak building, deserted except on special occasions, should have once been the noisy, crowded center of Peyrane's life.

The Peyrane of 1851 also lives, or rather lurks, in the economic statistics which the Town Clerk records every year. These records state that about 3500 of Peyrane's 7000 acres are arable. It is further indicated that of the 3500 arable acres two-thirds are lying fallow. This is a remarkably high proportion of fallow land. The whole question depends on how the word "arable" is defined.

In 1851, when Peyrane's soil supported a much larger population than it does now, every available piece of land was put to use. Most of the work was done by hand, and labor was cheap. It was both imperative and profitable to cultivate plots of land that today would be considered unarable or at best marginal. However, since this land was once cultivated it is still listed as arable in the official statistics, even though it may never be ploughed again. It would be more accurate to record that of Peyrane's 7000 acres one-third are unproductive, one-third are marginal, and one-third are productive. The productive third would, of course, include not only the ploughed land but also the orchards, vineyards, and pastures.

The Peyrane of 1901 has left monuments still more spectacular than those of 1851. Some of the most colorful and grotesque cliffs have been formed by the erosion of ochre quarries opened fifty years ago. Halfway up Piedconil, the hill rising above the town, is a tremendous black hole in the middle of an orange cliff. This is the entry of an abandoned mine. The top of the hill above the entry is fenced in to protect *promeneurs* from a possible cave-in. Below the town a smaller hill, Roussens, has had one whole end slashed off. From the front of the school one can look off to the east and see similar cliffs and mine entries in the neighboring towns along the chain of ochre hills. Some of the mines and quarries are still actively worked, of course, but many of them are simply colorful monuments of a past economy.

Recently there have been attempts to grow mushrooms on a large scale in some of the abandoned mines, and in a few cases the experiment has been successful. The conditions in the mines are excellent for the cultivation of mushrooms, and if more manure were available for the mushroom beds the mines might once again offer the community an important source of income. At present, the number of mushrooms raised in Peyrane is directly proportionate to the number of horses in the stalls of the race tracks and cavalry barracks of Marseille, for these are the only large commercial sources of manure in the region.

As picturesque as the ochre cliffs, but less garish as a monument to the past, is the fountain at the bottom of the hill. Fifty years ago this was the only source of water for the village except for the rain water which was stored in cisterns. People had to carry their water a quarter of a mile up the hill from the fountain or buy it from watermen who brought it up in barrels mounted on wheels and pulled by donkeys. In 1912, the Mayor, Monsieur Prullière, aided by the député Georges Laguerre, maneuvered to get water piped into the village from a spring up in the Lubéron Mountain seven miles away. This was a difficult task because the water had to be piped beneath the bed of the Calavon River and then up to the reservoir at the top of Peyrane's nine-hundred-foot hill. Thanks to the initiative of Monsieur Prullière, Peyrane had running water decades before most of the surrounding towns, many of which still do not have it.

Monsieur Prullière owned an ochre quarry. One of the most expensive items in the mining operation was the carting of water to the quarry, for a great deal of water was needed to separate the sand from the ochre. The Mayor, that is Monsieur Prullière, had water piped to the top of the village hill. The quarry owner at the bottom of the hill, that is, Monsieur Prullière, contracted to take from the town all the excess water. As a result, since 1912 a gushing brook has been running from the reservoir at the peak of the village, through the open village gutter and down to the quarry at the bottom of the hill.

Although most of the monuments to the Peyrane of 1901 are related to ochre mining, there are others that recall the farming economy of that time. Looking out over the farms from the top of the Peyrane hill, one can easily distinguish the grain fields from the vineyards and the vineyards from the asparagus fields and the asparagus fields from the orchards. However, there is one kind of orchard dotting the countryside that is puzzling, for it is too dark to be olive or apricot or

cherry trees. These dark spots are live-oak orchards. When in the latter
part of the nineteenth century most of the money crops had failed, new
crops were sought to replace them. Until then truffle hunting had been
the occupation of the poorest members of the community who went
off into the mountains and wastelands with their truffle dogs. Since
truffles were most often found under live oak trees, it was deemed
worth the trouble to try growing live oaks and consequently, it was
hoped, truffles in orchards. The experiment was moderately successful.
At the end of six years or more, truffles did develop and were harvested
around the upper roots of some of the trees. The crop has always been
unpredictable and in recent years the orchards have produced fewer
and fewer truffles. Now the orchards are disappearing.

Wherever one turns in Peyrane there are ruins which evoke past
moments in the life of the village. When we take the census of 1946 *
and construct a population pyramid for the Peyrane of today, we find
that this modern population pyramid looks like a ruin, too. Compared
with the pyramid of 1851, the present-day pyramid is only a ragged
ghost. The proportion of old people is much higher, and the proportion of economically productive adults in the middle-age brackets
is much smaller. In reality there is an even smaller proportion of
Peyrane children than appears on the pyramid, for included in the
census of 1946 was a small colony of refugee children who had not yet
been repatriated after the war. The total population of the commune
has dropped from 1484 in 1851 (and from a peak of 1568 in 1861) to
779 in 1946 (to 713 in 1954).

Of course, all the vicissitudes in the commune's history in the last
hundred years are reflected in this transformation of the population,
but the most startling effects are those of the two world wars.

In the First World War thirty-eight men from Peyrane were killed.
One can see from the pyramid how the generation of men born in the
last two decades of the nineteenth century was decimated. The proportion of widows in the same generation is consequently high. The children who might have been born to these men are an element lacking

---

* Except in the war years 1871, 1916, and 1941, there had been a census taken in
France every five years from 1801 to the present. For reasons of economy the government
decided to omit the census of 1951. When the present study was made, therefore, the most
recent population information available had to be found in the census records of 1946.
Since that time, in 1954, another census has been taken in France, but we have been
unable to consult these records in detail.

in the population. Almost no children were born during the war; the births shown in the 1915–20 period took place for the most part in 1919 and 1920. Of course, when surviving men came home after the war and the ochre business picked up, the birth rate rose rapidly. Then came the depression and the Second World War. As has been noted, the pyramid shows a larger proportion of children born between 1930 and 1945 than it should because of the temporary residence of refugee children in Peyrane in 1946.

It seems almost ridiculous to speak of the effect of the war in terms of abstract numbers, for so far as the people of Peyrane are concerned, it is the psychological effect of the war that is important. Many times people said to us, "You come too late to study life in Peyrane. You should have been here before the war. Now it is different."

When one asks how life was different before the war, the answers are always the same: "We were better off then. Life wasn't so hard. We got along better. There was a dance every Saturday night, and we were always visiting back and forth with each other over a cup of coffee. Now everyone stays at home. The war changed life."

The effects of the war on Peyrane were relatively slight. No Germans or Americans came to the village, except for a patrol now and then which passed through without causing trouble. There was no fighting in the commune. There was no bombing. No French town could have been less molested physically than Peyrane. Yet from all the stories one hears, and from all the nasty incidents that people today allude to but prefer not to recount, the effect of the war situation on life in the village was devastating, especially insofar as the ability of people to live comfortably together is concerned.

Of the men of Peyrane who were mobilized at the beginning of the war, six were killed and fifteen were taken to Germany where they remained as prisoners for five years. The loss of this substantial number of able-bodied men not only broke up families and increased emotional tension; it removed an important group of productive workers. In spite of the loss, however, the population of the village actually increased because of the influx of refugees, broadly speaking a nonproductive group. At the same time, the ochre mines all but closed down, shutting off a source of income. So in a very short time the productive capacity of the community was seriously reduced, while the number of consumers was actually increased. At the same time, of course, goods of all kinds became scarce, both those produced in the commune and those brought in from outside. People had less and less money, and their money purchased less and less, and there was less and less to purchase. When an article was needed one had to get along without it, which was exasperating. If the article was found and if a way was found to pay for it, the price was so high that it was also exasperating.

Often, of course, people had to buy on the black market if they hoped to get what they needed, and that meant selling something on the black market in order to get enough money to pay black-market prices for the articles needed. This meant a double violation of the law. Even if one wanted to live by barter the transactions had to take place illegally. One could not trade a lamb for an inner tube because new restrictions forbade the free disposal of such items as lambs and inner tubes. There were more and more laws to violate and there were more laws one had to violate in order to live.

Normally, the people of Peyrane have relatively little compunction about violating minor restrictions laid down by the Government in Paris, but to live in constant violation is uncomfortable. It leaves one vulnerable to attacks by *les autres*, that is, by all the other people of the village. By a simple denunciation any one of *les autres* may threaten disaster to your family. In ordinary times *les autres* are a nuisance, but under these circumstances they are a menace. To protect oneself from them a family must isolate itself as completely as possible.

As individuals, families, and friendship clans tried to live more and more to themselves, and as they had more and more secrets to hide, the isolation and secrecy increased the suspicions of *les autres*. At the same time the issues over which people normally disagree became more acute, and the disagreement became more bitter. To a few people Pétain was a hero, or at least a *brave type* trying his best to help the French. To others Pétain was a villain or a stupid tool, and de Gaulle was the hero. To a few people it was patriotic to obey the Vichy laws; to others it was patriotic to disobey them.

The division between villagers and farmers also became more acute. The villagers, who had to depend on the country people for food, complained that the farmers charged them black-market prices, that often the farmers refused to sell them anything, preferring to sell their goods on the black market in the city. The farmers complained that the villagers tried to buy produce at legal prices and then take it to the city to sell it at black-market prices. Each incident increased suspicion and jealousy. Whenever anyone received a special gasoline or clothing or food ration there were always *les autres* who started a rumor that it was obtained illegally. It seemed that no one could do anything without arousing the antagonism of someone else.

Into this atmosphere of bitterness, deprivation, and distrust an even more violent element was introduced: the *maquis*. The *maquis* was the resistance movement of the commune, composed of young men, most of them from Peyrane but some of them *étrangers* to the region, who were fugitives from Vichy's brand of justice or who were avoiding forced labor in Germany. They roamed the country at night, armed with machine guns, seeking food, ration coupons, and other supplies which their group needed to carry on its activities. Most people gave supplies more or less freely. Those who did not were forced to contribute what was deemed their share.

The young men claimed to be motivated only by patriotic considerations, but after all most of them had grown up in the commune and were even living hidden at home or in houses of friends. As members of the *maquis* they had a patriot function, but as individual members of the community they had their own personal relationship with each other inhabitant of the commune. They were *in* with some and *out* with others. The motives of the members of the *maquis* were naturally interpreted by the rest of the people in the light of their own personal relationship with each of the young men. Consequently there is no agreement about the virtue of the Peyrane underground. To some people the men of the *maquis* were a pile of bandits; to others they were a group of patriots. The most reasonable judgement of them appears to be that of Lucien Bourdin, who was a prisoner in Germany during the war and knew about the *maquis* only what he had heard on his return: "I grew up with them, and I know what I'd have done if I'd been with them. The truth is that they were bandits part of the time and heroes part of the time. That depended."

Probably the most surprising thing about this tense situation is that it did not result in severe violence and tragedy as it did in other towns around Peyrane, all of which were in more or less the same predicament. At Gordes a series of denunciations and reprisals led to the partial destruction of the village. The Germans brought tanks up to the hill on which Gordes is perched and blasted away a whole quarter of

the village. At Saint-Saturnin a similar, and related, series of denunciations led to the capture of some of the men in the underground and
to their execution on the public square of the village.

At Peyrane nothing of the kind occurred. No serious denunciation
took place. No one was arrested. No one was killed by the *maquis* or
by the Germans or by the Vichy police. There was constant threat that
such violence might take place, but none did. According to rumors, the
Peyrane *maquis* played an important role in the incidents that took
place in Gordes and Saint-Saturnin. It is not unlikely that the young
men of Peyrane should have preferred to "faire leurs farces" in another
commune, for it is expected that a young man will "faire ses farces"
away from his own home, and as we shall see, the war situation in
Peyrane was considered a family situation. Within a family individuals
may quarrel, but their quarrel should stay within the family and should
never be allowed to harm the family group as a whole.

The quarrels within the Peyrane family brought no violence within
the commune but they were too bitter not to have had a lasting effect.
Undoubtedly people do not exaggerate when they say that they do not
get along as well together as they did before the war and that they
keep to themselves at home more than they used to. Just as the war
almost destroyed the ochre industry and transformed the economy of
Peyrane, it undoubtedly transformed the psychological atmosphere of
the community. It marks the end of one of the Peyranes of the past.

In the five years following the war there was a substantial increase
in the birth rate of Peyrane as there was in all of France. Because of
the increased birth rate a population pyramid based on the census of
1954 would show a high proportion of children under ten years old in
the village. This is the same sort of proportion that existed in the years
preceding 1851 and 1901 during which the economy of Peyrane was
expanding on a new basis. 1850 was a culminating year in the development of new money crops which changed the small, self-sufficient Peyrane into a large town closely dependent on outside markets and sources
of supply. In 1900, after the failure of important crops Peyrane was
entering another period of prosperity based on the ochre industry.

Since the war there appears to be another Peyrane emerging. It is
difficult to see because it is hidden by the vestiges of the past. The
ruins of old houses, the windmills, and the deserted ochre quarries flaunt
themselves so that the new apricot orchards and asparagus fields are

not noticed. The outmoded agricultural statistics, according to which 70 per cent of the arable soil lies fallow, conceal the fact that the land is used more efficiently than it used to be. The drop in the population from 1568 in 1861 to 713 in 1954 is so impressive that we miss an essential point: in 1954 a smaller population can produce more and enjoy a higher standard of living than the larger population of 1861.

The factors that contribute to the development of a new Peyrane today are the same that have transformed agriculture elsewhere in the world. In Peyrane, farming has become a more scientific undertaking. Most of the farmers of the commune have had no better than an eighth-grade education, and yet they speak in terms of soil chemistry and of the selection of seeds and fertilizers. The phase of the moon has become less important in determining the planting season than the advice of the seed companies, the agricultural agents, and the weather predictions heard over the radio. The radio also brings to the farmer the current market prices so that he knows the best price he can ask and get in selling his produce. He may not even have to bother about selling it; the coöperative may handle much of the marketing. He further improves his financial situation by buying material through the Apt coöperative, by having his wine pressed in one of the three nearby coöperative wineries, his brandy distilled by the coöperative distillery, his fields ploughed by the tractor coöperative.

The market of the Peyrane farmer has spread far beyond the limits of the Apt basin. Asparagus picked in Peyrane is sold in the markets of Paris the next day. Apricots, table grapes, and melons are also sent to the city markets. Tomatoes are carted to the tomato paste canneries in Apt, Pernes, and Carpentras. Wine is shipped from the coöperative wineries to the city in big tank trucks. During the cherry season, Louis Borel loads his truck with crates of cherries left for him by the farmers at the side of the road. If the market price is good he takes them directly to the canning and candied fruit factories in Apt. If the price is low he stores them in the big chemical vats which his son-in-law and he have built across the road from his house. In the vats he can hold the cherries until the price goes up. Of course, what little flavor these big, beautiful cherries have is lost in the vats, but the factories always supply the flavor anyway, so nothing is sacrificed and Borel's income is increased.

An American set down on a farm in Peyrane could not easily see that science has modernized Peyrane. Modernization is obscured not only by the ruins of the past, but also by the shabbiness of the present. There are none of the external signs of modernity — no chrome, no enamel, no electric iceboxes, no deep freezes, no television, no white kitchens, no glamorous bathrooms. Many of the operations done mechanically and electrically on a modern American farm are done by hand in Peyrane. Much of the shabby farm equipment might recall an American automobile graveyard rather than a modern farm. Instead of a shiny, new tractor one might see an old tractor that looks as though it were held together with bailing wire. The vine sprayer might be an improvised machine mounted on one truck wheel and one car wheel. The family might drive to market in a 1923 Renault with the back converted to serve as a pick-up truck. In this car it takes twenty-five minutes to go to Apt instead of the fifteen minutes it would take in a new car.

The contradiction between modernity and shabbiness is more apparent than real. The chrome, the enamel, the new paint are superficial signs by which we are inclined to judge but which have little to do with the essence of the problem. The contradiction arises from fundamental differences in attitudes between Americans and the people of Peyrane, differences which may be made clear in the following chapters.

Of course, it is only a moderate sort of prosperity that Peyrane can be expected to enjoy. Some of the limitations that handicap the indefinite expansion of Peyrane's economy are natural and insurmountable. It cannot be forgotten that only one-third of the land is really productive. Little can be done about the fact that there is scant rain in summer and winter and no likelihood of irrigation. There are the destructive spring and fall storms. There is the mistral which flattens crops and may bring sudden freezing spells. There is the division of land into small irregular plots, and it appears unlikely that this situation can be changed.

There is another hindrance which stands in the way of the development of a prosperous Peyrane, a modern and human hindrance rather than a natural or traditional one. Just as the past war almost wrecked what was already a rather feeble spirit of mutual confidence among the people, fear of a future war has destroyed confidence in the future. Without confidence in the future Peyrane cannot make the best of its natural resources.

According to agricultural experts the best crops for the terrain, soil, and climate of Peyrane are vegetables and fruits, and of these the best are grapes and apricots. The amount of grapes a farmer can grow is limited, however. Overproduction of wine in France has caused the government to forbid the planting of wine grapevines except to replace old stocks that are torn out. There are ways to get around the limitation, and if one wants to raise grapes legally there is no legal limitation on the production of table grapes and nursery stock. Unfortunately, the market for these is almost saturated. It would be dangerous to extend the production of grapes much further.

Better would be the cultivation of apricot orchards, but that means planting trees and waiting for them to bear fruit. Income would be postponed for several years. To plant fruit trees one must have confidence in the future. Most of the farmers with whom this problem was discussed had the same reaction: "We know we should plant trees, but what's the use? Who knows if we and our children would be here by the time they started to bear?"

In 1890 and 1900 the farmers of Peyrane planted live-oak orchards which could not bear truffles for six years — if indeed they were ever to bear anything. This sort of confidence has disappeared. Lucien Bourdin, whose father was killed in the First World War and who spent five years as a prisoner in Germany during the Second World War, spoke more bitterly than most people would, but he expressed a general point of view: "Plant an apricot orchard so the Russians and Americans can use it as a battlefield? Thanks. Not so dumb."

During the last war, the people who were best off in the commune were not those who had the most modern farms producing the best adapted crops. There was little use for quantities of asparagus and table grapes when the express trains were not running to Paris. The farmers who were best able to care for their families were those who had departed least from the old self-sustaining economy of the Peyrane of 1801. Wheat and sheep, even though they were produced inefficiently, gave bread and cheese and wool for the family or for barter. This was not an economy of prosperity but an economy of survival, and if a crisis threatens one must think first of surviving. In 1950 fourteen per cent of the best soil of the commune was still planted in wheat. Everyone knows that this soil could be exploited more efficiently than by growing wheat, but on the other hand a field of wheat is a kind of disaster insurance.

No one is foolish enough to think that he can fence off his family and his field of wheat and his flock of sheep and live isolated from the rest of the world. Two thousand years ago, if there were people living at Peyrane, they might have climbed to the peak of the town and watched with indifference while the Cimbrians and Romans fought it out at the foot of Perréal. Today the people of Peyrane have no illusion about the possibility of finding security in isolation. Relatively unscathed as they were in the last two wars, they nevertheless felt the effects so vividly that they have no illusions about security or about isolation in time of war.

They also believe that they can do nothing to prevent the threatened disaster because their fate is completely out of their hands. Before an election half of the people say it is the Russians who are bringing about disaster and half of the people say it is the Americans who are responsible. As we shall see, this official pre-electoral attitude is determined as much by the attitude of the people toward each other as toward the Russians and Americans. Less officially most of the people agree that both the Russians and Americans seem spoiling for a fight, and France is nothing but a pawn in the struggle between these two giants. They might be inclined to take sides if hope lay in one direction or the other, but in their experience there is no hope in war. They always have lost. A conservative newspaper of Marseille at the time of the Korean crisis carried the headline: "U. S. thinks in terms of victory; France thinks in terms of war." Since 1918 they know that the word victory is derisive.

In this situation the people of Peyrane do not act desperately. They simply plant no apricot trees. "C'est comme ça." One can only go on living from day to day, from year to year. Besides, the problems and pleasures involved in raising a family are so pressing that one need not think much about "all that." Wars come and bring disaster. Régimes change. Governments fall. But there is always the family.

Growing up in Peyrane

Chapter 3

Infancy

In Peyrane most babies are born in the homes of their parents. Only in unusual cases, when surgery is expected or when there is no one to care for the mother or the baby at home, are plans made to have the baby in the hospital. People say that hospital care is better than none, but it is necessarily inferior to home care because you cannot expect "strangers" to devote themselves to you as members of your family would. They know that in the cities some women prefer to have their babies in the hospital, and they know that in some small towns like Carpentras there are beautiful new maternity hospitals, but they also know that when a person needs care he needs to be with his family. When I asked Françoise Bonerandi whether she was going to have her baby at home or in the hospital, she seemed hurt that I should even have asked the question. Her house was big, her family had money, her family loved her and wanted to take care of her. Why should they have shipped her off to a hospital to be cared for by strangers? The birth of a baby is the most important event that can occur in a family. Both the mother and the baby deserve the best care the family can give them.

The person best qualified to deliver a baby is the doctor, and the most respected doctor in the area is Doctor Magny, so it is he who delivers most of the babies born in Peyrane. Midwives are not unknown in this part of France, but there is no midwife in the commune of Peyrane. The woman who most nearly qualifies is eighty-year-old Mélanie Favre, who is called in to assist whenever a family needs outside help. Since the State pays a large share of the obstetrical expenses, no money would be saved by asking someone other than Doctor Magny to deliver a baby.

Anyone may be present in the room in which the delivery takes place so long as he has business there. There is no taboo against the presence of a mother-in-law or a father, nor is the presence of a particular rela-

tive or personality required by tradition. The only important consideration is that those individuals are present who will give adequate attention to the mother and child. There is no need for an anesthetist.
Women say they have heard that in some places women are given an
anesthetic during delivery, but they think it is "more natural" for the
mother not to be put to sleep.

If the child is born normally and needs no emergency care he is
placed in the warm place prepared for him until the mother is well
taken care of. When she has been made comfortable the child is cared
for. He is washed, swaddled, and wrapped warmly. In the swaddling
his arms are left free but his legs are stretched out and held straight
by the bandage.

When I asked people why babies were swaddled I received a variety
of answers. Some said that it was because their bodies are so delicate;
if they were left free they might dislocate vertebrae. Others said that
babies move about so violently and unreasonably that they might kick
and harm themselves. Another reason was that legs should be kept
straight for several weeks; if a child were not swaddled he might become bowlegged. When I asked about the practice, people were on the
defensive because they know that in the cities babies are often not
swaddled. They also know that the schoolteacher in her lessons on child
care expresses disapproval on the grounds that swaddling prevents the
sun and air from reaching the body. The lack of sunlight means a lack
of vitamin D and causes rickets, she says. People respect the teacher's
point of view, but on the other hand they cannot see that swaddling
has done harm in the past, and the teacher has still not answered the
traditional arguments.

When I asked for details about the first feeding of the child, people
found my question rather silly. What difficulties could there be, they
asked. No one has to show a baby how to suckle. He is simply put at
his mother's breast, and the whole process takes place spontaneously.
Of course, they say, some mothers for some reason do not have milk
or do not have enough milk. In such cases it used to be that a wet
nurse was brought in, or the baby was taken to live with the wet nurse,
but wet nurses are a thing of the past. If a mother cannot feed her
baby, he is fed goat's milk or cow's milk or formula from a bottle,
but bottle feeding never replaces breast feeding if the mother can supply the milk. She expects to nurse the baby, and everyone else expects

her to. There is a general feeling, however, that mothers today have less milk than mothers of preceding generations. Fewer and fewer mothers are said to be capable of feeding their babies entirely at their breast.

Whether a child is fed at the breast or from a bottle, he is vaguely introduced to a schedule suggested by the doctor or by the instructions that come with cans of formula, but no attempt is made to adhere rigorously to the schedule. If he seems hungry, he is fed. If he is not hungry, no attempt is made to force him to feed, although some alarm may be felt since the lack of appetite may be a symptom of illness. Nor is there an attempt to establish a sleeping schedule. Generally speaking a baby eats and sleeps as he likes. If he cries he is cleaned and offered food. If he continues to cry for more than a few minutes, some one tries to pacify him by cuddling him. He may be picked up, held across the arms and walked to the accompaniment of singing. He is not rocked, since there are no rocking chairs in France, but he may be cradled in the arms of the person pacifying him. He is often kissed, and people talk constantly to him, either naturally or in baby talk.

If he has wet or soiled his diaper, the long bandage with which he is swaddled is unwrapped, and he is cleaned and swaddled again. It is a chore to keep a sufficient supply of clean diapers and bandages in Peyrane, for all laundry is done by hand, but in spite of the effort the baby is kept clean. One day when I was watching Françoise Bonerandi swaddle her baby, I remarked that it seemed to demand much time and effort. "It's not too bad in the summer," she said, "for then we swaddle a baby only for a month, but in the winter we do it for two or three months, and it's harder to do the laundry then, too. How long do they swaddle babies in America?" When I replied that babies were not swaddled in the United States, she seemed surprised. After a short silence she said, "Well, your children seem to have straight legs, so maybe there is something in what the teacher says." Then after another silence, "But this is the way we do it here."

At home the baby is left to himself as much as possible except when he is being shown off to guests. His mother is too busy to pay attention to him unless she thinks he is hungry or soiled or sick or has some such valid reason for demanding care. When he is taken out in his pram, the situation is different. Then he is on parade. No matter what may be the dimensions of the family purse, every effort is made to acquire an elegant pram which will do honor to the family when the baby is pushed through the village. The villagers greet the baby with a great show of cordiality and affection. He is taken from his pram, kissed and cuddled, passed from lap to lap. People poke him gently on the chin or in the stomach and make soft, hissing noises. They tell him in baby talk how beautiful and healthy he is. They jiggle him on their knees or in their arms. This show of affection and admiration is sincere. The people of Peyrane love babies.

As soon as a mother feels ready to receive callers, her friends come to see her and the baby. The tradition used to be that the first caller should bring a chicken from which broth might be made for the mother, but like most traditions which involve an economic sacrifice this one has been abandoned. However, the baby may still receive a few gifts, especially knitted clothing. The father is expected neither to receive nor to make special gifts, and although the other men may joke with him about the paternity of the child, there is no traditional joking ceremony he has to undergo.

A baby formally becomes a member of society within three days after he is born, when his birth is registered by the father or by the doctor at the town hall. His existence is inscribed on the *livret de famille* and he is given *civil status* which will be extremely important for him the rest of his life in any relationship he will have with the government or any of its agencies. Within a few weeks after he is born, usually from three to six weeks, he is made a part of the religious organization of the community; he is taken to the church to be baptized. Whatever their religious and ideological beliefs may be, all parents in Peyrane have their babies baptized. Some are eager to have their children baptized for religious reasons, but most insist on baptism for purely practical reasons. If, they say, the child should not be baptized and should grow up and want to marry someone who would insist on a religious ceremony, he would then have to be baptized, and it is both embarrassing and a nuisance for an adult to have to go through with the ceremony of baptism. It is better to have the ceremony carried out at the usual time. Besides baptism offers an opportunity for a family celebration.

Apparently there used to be a traditional way of handling every detail of the baptismal ceremony, but no one remembers exactly what the details were. Now the parents of the child talk with the priest informally and make arrangements for the baptism to take place at a convenient time, usually on some Sunday morning after mass. No narrow tradition governs the choice of godparents. The godparents of the first child are usually a close relative of the father and a close relative of the mother. For the successive children, an attempt may be made to choose godparents who may be of some practical help to the child in later life — a childless, well-to-do friend, for instance. In Peyrane, people say that such attempts are rarely successful. Godparents do not take a permanent interest in their godchildren. Their function is practically limited to being present at the baptismal ceremony, when possible, and to giving the child a name. Every child is given three names, one by his mother and one by each godparent, but only the name given by the mother is used except in official documents.

There is one onerous function which the godparents who attend the ceremony cannot avoid accepting. One Sunday noon our children came running into the house to ask if they could go up to the church with the other village children to get money which some people were throwing away. I thought they must have misunderstood what had been told them, but the possibility of seeing people throw away money in Peyrane was sufficiently fascinating for me to take my camera and run up to the church with the children. We arrived there just as the young Gleizer couple came out of the church with their baby, followed by its godparents and relatives. All the village children gathered around them, screaming, "Long live the godparents!" and the godfather reached in his pocket, pulled out a small handful of one-franc pieces and threw them to the children. While the children scrambled, the procession started down the street. In a moment the children were after them, screaming their refrain, and as he walked along the godfather occasionally threw out another handful of one-franc pieces. This continued as the procession made its way all the way down through the village. In front of Monsieur Vincent's hotel, the baptismal party got into cars and drove off with the children screaming after them. As he drove away the godfather threw out one more handful of francs. The children were organizing and counting their francs, and I stood and talked with old Monsieur Prayal, the blacksmith, "That," he said, "is one tradition that hasn't been lost, but there's a difference. We used to throw candy to the children, but now candy is too expensive. It's cheaper to throw away money."

As soon as the mother of a new-born child is able to return to her ordinary work, the question arises, who will care for the child? If her work consists of the usual domestic duties, the mother will care for her child herself, but if she must go to work in the fields, she has to find someone to care for the child while she is away. Usually a grandmother or an older sister of the child will assume this responsibility, but if neither is available, then almost anyone who is not engaged in economically productive work may be asked to help out — a brother, a grandfather, a relative, or a neighbor who is fortunate enough not to have to work or unfortunate enough to be unemployed.

Normally, the father is not expected to help much in the care of children, even when he is not working. He obviously loves his children and exhibits his tenderness for them openly, but it is not his responsibility to care for them. Only in unusual circumstances will he be asked to keep half an eye on them. There was one father in the village who apparently enjoyed caring for his baby, but it was recognized that his behavior was not normal and could be attributed to the fact that his wife and he came from Alsace. However, when a child is old enough to walk and to follow a normal diet, his father may be willing to take him to the café to show him off to his friends. In such circumstances the child is given a sip from his father's glass of pastis and is offered a glass of grenadine and water by the café owner's wife. Here the father is not sharing the responsibility of caring for his child; rather he is displaying feelings of pride for the child, and camaraderie with him.

No matter who cares for a child in Peyrane, the treatment he receives is sure to be tender and indulgent. Even brothers and sisters seem to enjoy carrying their baby brother or sister about, playing with it, kissing it, caressing it. Discipline of tiny babies is gentle. It usually consists of a scolding delivered with mock harshness in baby talk. Caring for a little baby is considered a pleasure rather than a chore by everyone except the mother, on whose shoulders rests the basic responsibility.

Weaning takes place gradually between the twelfth and twenty-fourth month, at about the same time as the child begins to walk. He is held at the table while the family is eating and is given a sip of soup or a bit of jam or pudding. Little by little he eats more and more with the family. Supplementary feeding is given according to the demands of the child, usually by bottle in the daytime and by breast at night, because bottle feeding is too much trouble at night. Between meals he may be given a pacifier.

When we moved to Peyrane, Dédou Favre was a year and a half old. Since he lived only a few doors from us, we saw him almost every day for a year, and we never saw him without his pacifier, which he wore on a string hung round his neck. Part of the time it dangled uselessly, but it was never forgotten; every now and then he would put it in his mouth and suck on it — not eagerly but in a rather friendly manner. A few doors down the street was a child a few months older, also named Dédou Favre. He did not have a pacifier. His mother thought pacifiers were dirty. She also disapproved of the way the other Dédou's mother let him play in the street and of the way she let him wander into Arène's or Reynard's store to beg for candy. If Arène or Reynard was not in a generous mood, the begging Dédou went to the café where he was sure he would find someone who would give him a few francs to buy candy. His mother did not encourage him to do this, but neither did she discourage him. The other Dédou's mother was horrified at the thought. Neither attitude seems prevalent. Some mothers are more like one Madame Favre; some are like the other Madame Favre. Both Dèdous seem to be happy children.

Whether a child in Peyrane is more like one Dédou or the other, he is sure to receive spontaneous offers of candy and cookies from the people he sees throughout a day. Many people carry candy in their pockets to give to children they meet, and most people keep a supply of candy and cookies at home for the express purpose of offering them to children who call on them. Candy is given to children only on the condition that they perform a social ritual.

By the time a child in Peyrane is old enough to walk and to lisp a few words, he has learned that "if you please, Monsieur," and "thank you, Madame" are potent expressions which will bring him what he wants. He knows that they must be said distinctly, directly, and that the "Monsieur" or "Madame" may not be left out of the expression. He has to stand up straight when he says them. And, of course, he has to shake hands with everyone when he greets him and again when he takes leave of him. He knows that if he omits any part of this social ritual anyone present, whether of his family or not, will remind him of the omission and will withhold favors until the omission is repaired.

Our children accepted with no difficulty the custom of eating candy and cookies any time of the day, but they considered it intolerable to be subjected to the social ritual before they were given the candy and cookies. The confusing linguistic situation, before they adjusted themselves to the French language, accounted partly for their shyness, but only partly. The main trouble was that there was little in their previous training to prepare them for a situation in which they had to conform rigorously and consistently to adult standards of politeness. They resented more than anything else the way everyone seemed to be trying to make them shake hands constantly. Their refusal to accept this French custom was embarrassing to us. Even though we thought that at home our children seemed normal in social situations, we saw that in Peyrane they were *mal élevés* (badly brought up) by the standards of any of the villagers, even the most humble villagers.

Marie Fratani, our "femme de ménage," undertook on her own initiative to improve the conduct of the children. Every morning when she arrived at our house and every noon when she left, she shook hands with Mrs. Wylie and me, and in spite of the obstinacy and hostility of the children, she insisted on their greeting her in the same way. Always smiling and always kind, she showed them she could be more obstinate than they. For five or ten minutes she would stay with them, greeting them over and over again with her hand outstretched, until they finally performed in a satisfactory manner. Other villagers showed almost as much concern for the politeness of our children. There was nothing personal about their attitude. They realized that we were accustomed to a more relaxed code of manners. They simply felt a collective responsibility for the manners of all children in the village including ours. Of course, our children eventually accepted the standards of politeness of the village as wholeheartedly as they accepted all the village standards. And besides, they learned that politeness often pays off in the form of candy.

When a child in Peyrane is old enough to sit at the table at mealtime, whether or not he has just been eating candy or cookies, he is strongly encouraged to eat all the food that is placed before him, for children must learn not to waste food. He is not actually forced to eat everything on his plate, but he must at least taste it. If a child refuses to eat at all, he is treated as though he were ill, since it is believed that only a sick child would ever refuse to eat. If he appears not to like a certain dish that has been prepared, he must show his good will in trying to learn to like it, but if it is obvious that he really can't eat it, his mother may prepare a substitute dish.

As a child learns to eat with the family he learns table manners, for everyone considers it important for a child to know how "se tenir comme il faut à la table." He must sit up straight and keep both wrists on the edge of the table when his hands are not being used for eating. An elbow must never be on the table, and a hand must never be below the table. If a hand slips down in his lap, his parents will say, "What's that hand doing, hiding down there? Put it on the table where it belongs!" He must say, "If you please, papa or maman," if he wants to be served, and he must say, "Thank you, papa or maman" after he is served. If he forgets to repeat the formula, his parents will pretend to be deaf and refuse to serve him until he remembers.

Traditionally, and even today theoretically, a child must not talk at the table, but the parents of Peyrane are not strict about this "mange et tais-toi" rule. They say that children are too much a center of the family interest not to share in the table conversation, and often the children have more interesting things to tell than the adults. However, children must learn not to interrupt their elders when they are talking.

Theoretically and traditionally, too, children may never with impunity contradict or show disrespect for their elders. In practice, however, many children speak disrespectfully to their parents, who retaliate only by threats which are usually not carried out. The attitude of parents toward disrespectful talk on the part of their children seems to vary considerably from family to family. Some parents, like Francis and Suzanne Favre, demand and obtain a respectful attitude from their children. Other parents, like Canazzi, the baker, and his wife receive insults from their children each time they try to discipline them. They are ashamed of the girls' behavior but they are unable to improve it. Janine and Suzanne continue to speak insultingly to their mother just as she speaks insultingly to them. Most children, however, are like Henri and Nicole Favre's children; they get away with a sly insult occasionally, especially if they can escape the attention of the parents until the insult is forgotten.

As soon as a baby is old enough to understand what is said to him, at the age of ten or twelve months usually, he is encouraged not to wet or soil his pants but to tell his mother so that she may help him perform in a more reasonable way. If he persists in his infant toilet habits, his parents and all those caring for him will shame him and ridicule him, trying to persuade him to be reasonable. If he still persists he may be threatened with and may even receive a few slaps on the buttocks. On the whole remarkable patience is shown on the part of the mother, even though it is not easy for her to launder the dirty clothes. If the child's clothes are dirty, they must be removed and laundered, for it is considered shameful for a mother to let her house be permeated with the odor of urine. Only people who "live like animals" allow themselves to live in such an atmosphere. There are some people like that in Peyrane but not many.

Usually toilet training takes about a year, although it is recognized that children differ considerably in the length of time it takes for them to be trained. It is also recognized that accidents may occur even after a child is trained. A mother may grumble about an accident, but she will punish the child only by shaming him. Parents do not customarily rouse their children during the night to urinate, although they may get a child up if he cries out in his sleep or if he seems unusually restless. Barring accidents, children have completed their toilet training by the age of four when they start to school.

Up to the age of four or five, children, especially boys, are allowed to urinate almost anywhere in the village, but when they are old enough to start school they are supposed to have enough control over their functions and enough *pudeur* (a sense of shame) to seek out a secluded spot. Seclusion, of course, is a relative matter, and considerable latitude is allowed in the interpretation of the word. At the very least it implies that a boy or a man should have his back turned to possible observers. At the most it implies complete solitude, but fewer men conform to this extreme than to the former.

The relative freedom with which children urinate enables them to learn at a very early age the difference between sexes. This observation is so natural that no undue curiosity is normally aroused. Of course, children are curious if the situation is not normal. One day when the Favres and the Wylies were picking cherries, their three boys and our two boys went to the side of the orchard to urinate. When we noticed that they lingered longer than usual I went over to where they stood in a group. Our older son was explaining to the Favre boys what circumcision was. No boys in the village are circumcized, and the Favre boys were fascinated by an unusual sight.

In Peyrane little boys who have pretty hair wear it long until they go to school. The small Favres had angelic faces, beautiful wavy hair which was bobbed, and of course they wore smocks which might look to an American like dresses. The first time I saw them I congratulated their father on his handsome daughters. He smiled and said that they were boys. Of course, I accepted his statement, but my sons did not. They continued to talk about the postman's little girls, until they began playing with them regularly.

Children are allowed to urinate rather openly, but rarely are they permitted to defecate in any but a most secluded spot. When I asked why the distinction was made between the two aspects of toilet training, people smiled and said that it was obviously a matter of privacy. Urination requires only a very rapid and very slight exposure, while with defecation the exposure must be long and rather complete. It is not, they said, that a person is ashamed of his body, the point is that one's private parts are one's own business.

One day when I passed the Fratani's house, I found Marie sitting out in front caring for Louis, her three-year-old grandson. At that moment Louis was squatting in the gutter having a movement. Marie was embarrassed and apologized for the spectacle. "But what can you expect?" she said. "We have no toilet in the house, and you can't expect a boy that age to wait until he goes to the public toilet. One shouldn't live like this, but that's the way it is." It did not seem to bother her that Louis had left a mess in the dry gutter. What disturbed her was the lack of privacy. In the whole toilet-training procedure emphasis is placed not on the filth or shame of excrement itself, but on the importance of the privacy of the individual and on the necessity of keeping clothing clean.

Children must learn to do their best to keep from getting their clothes dirty when they play. This is difficult in a village built on ochre cliffs, where the slightest contact with the yellow sand stains the clothing, but children do seem to learn to play without getting dirty.

One day I took our boys and eight-year-old Colette Favre out for a walk near some of the less precipitous cliffs. The boys immediately began to slide and roll down the slopes and jump from level to level. Soon their clothes and bodies were yellow; they looked like ochre miners returning from work. Colette had played naturally without complaining that she was not allowed to do what the boys were doing. As I watched them play, I did not even realize that she was playing in a different manner, but as we started back home I noticed that whereas the boys were yellow from head to foot, she had only two or three slight smudges on her sweater. As we got to her house, we saw her mother standing in front of it. Colette took off her sweater before her mother caught sight of her and tried to go in the house without being observed. Her mother noticed her and cried, "Colette! Why don't you have your sweater on? You'll catch cold. Here!" She took the sweater and started to help Colette put it on when she discovered the ochre smudges. "Oh!" she exploded, "so that's what you were up to! You got your clothes dirty and were trying to keep me from finding out! Vilaine, va! You'll go to bed without supper and without dessert. Get in the house."

Since I felt responsible, I tried to apologize. Madame Favre was not severe toward me, but she explained the situation. "You have Marie to wash your clothes, and I have to wash these myself. And besides the ochre is hard to get out and all the scrubbing ruins the clothes."

The next day when I told Colette I was sorry she had missed her supper, she said, "Oh, it didn't matter, Monsieur. They had forgotten all about it by supper time, and I ate as usual. But I should have known better than to go with you for a walk. I know how you let your children play."

The people were shocked not only at the way we let our children get dirty but by the way we let them expose themselves to danger. We were as strict as other parents in not allowing our children to go near the abrupt cliffs, but where the cliffs sloped down or were terraced we let the children jump from heights which seemed safe to them. I was scolded several times by the older people of the village for permitting the children to do such a dangerous thing.

One day when the boys and I were watching the Borels excavating beside their house, the boys got the idea of climbing to the top of the slope and jumping down into my arms. In spite of Madame Borel's warnings I enjoyed the play too. Finally she shrugged her shoulders and gave up. She simply stood and watched. In a few minutes she had been joined by ten other people. Everyone who passed stopped to witness the unusual sight.

The children of Peyrane must also learn to play carefully with their toys. In the first place, their toys are precious because they do not have many of them. We had taken a few of our children's toys with us, and at Christmas we bought others. Our house became a center for the children of the neighborhood who had never had so many toys and books to play with. They received no gifts at Christmas, and no child received more than one or two on New Year's Day, the usual time for giving presents to children. They might receive another present from a godparent on their feast day, but usually these were practical gifts of clothing. Toys were so scarce that children were naturally careful with them.

Moreover, French toys seem to be constructed so that they will last only if they are handled with great care. When we bought Christmas presents, we had difficulty in finding toys sturdy enough so that the boys would be able to "play naturally" with them. The big trucks looked appealing, but they were made of light wood and put together with brads. Little trucks were made of light metal and were of the wind-up variety with a spring that looked dangerous for fingers and so flimsy that it might break after a few runs. Most of the toys looked as though they were made for miniature adults rather than for children. From the point of view of an American parent on a Christmas shopping expedition, the toys we found most satisfactory were sturdy, little nonmechanical cars made in Great Britain, a large variety of very French lead soldiers, sailors, firemen, etc., and all sizes of extremely sturdy rubber soccer balls. There was also a type of colored building block that was more attractive than any American equivalent.

When a child of Peyrane received a toy, however, he was not given the kind of toy that we considered sturdy, hence satisfactory. He was given one of the flimsy wooden trucks or cars, or a toy made of very light plastic or celluloid. It was wonderful to see a child play with such a toy. He seemed completely satisfied to play with it in such a way that it would not break. He did not seem to need to bang it around or throw it. If eventually it did get broken, he accepted the catastrophe philosophically and continued to play with the broken toy. When children came to our house to play with the toys, we noticed that they would pick out one toy and concentrate on the pleasure it gave. Our boys were happier when they were making a long parade of toys.

Probably the toys of Peyrane last longer, too, because children are taught to get along together without fighting. If two children start to fight they are immediately separated by any adults who may happen to witness the scene. Only close relatives may punish a child, of course (because you may start a feud with a family if you assume the responsibility of punishing someone else's child), but if it is the relatives who separate fighting children, both children are punished. No inquiry is made into the question of which child started the fight or which was in the right. They are both fighting and consequently they are both guilty. Francis Favre told me that if he found two of his children starting to quarrel over the ownership or use of an object, he did not stop to inquire whose the object was. He simply took it away from the children and told them they could not have it again until they learned to play with it without fighting. Other parents shared Francis' point of view.

The fact that children are not allowed to fight does not mean that they are denied any means of aggression, for they are allowed to threaten and insult each other as much as they like. When the imprecations become too fierce, often an adult will try to shame the children or calm them down, but he will never punish a child for insulting another child.

When there was a large group of children playing at our house, it often sounded as though terrible carnage was about to occur, but actual fighting took place very rarely. I do not mean to imply that the situation in the courtyard was always hostile. To the contrary, it seemed to us that the children all got along together better than an equivalent group of children in this country, but when hostility did break out the threats of violence were fierce, and the violence rarely occurred. It was not uncommon to see Colette Favre and Janine Canazzi, who disliked one another, screaming insults and threatening each other with their fists as they backed farther and farther apart. The boys were a little less retiring than the girls. Paul Favre or Dédé Fraysse might occasionally land a blow with a fist, but fighting never went beyond the one-blow stage even with the boys. The attacking boy would run away after he struck, and the attacked boy would either cry and seek adult intervention or make a brief pretense of chasing the other boy without any apparent desire to catch him.

As our older boy began to speak French naturally, it seemed to me that his personality, or rather the expression of his personality, varied according to the language he was speaking. When he spoke English, he was usually shy, though given to occasional outbursts. When he spoke French, his expression was much more animated, and he seemed to disagree with other children more spontaneously and to insult them with more artistry. Of course, one explanation for this difference is obviously that he spoke English with his parents and his brother and

French with his friends, but I do not believe that this explanation is sufficient in itself to explain the difference. It would be interesting to know whether he actually felt less need for physical aggression when he had a better outlet for oral aggression.

Another lesson the children of Peyrane learn at an early age is that fatigue and physical discomforts are not excuses for failing to accomplish what is expected of them. As soon as a child is able to walk steadily, he is expected to walk at all times and never be carried. If a child capable of walking is seen being carried by a parent, people look at him with surprise and concern. They assume that the child must be hurt or sick. When we went for a walk and our three-year-old boy complained of being tired, I usually picked him up and carried him on my shoulders. If, upon inquiry, people learned that he was not physically disabled, they smiled indulgently and said, "So, the little fellow wants to be spoiled!" When I defensively explained that he was simply tired, because I did not like to admit that I spoiled my children, the response was a skeptical "Ah?" Then, so as not to hurt my feelings, "Well, he will soon get used to walking around these hills."

A child must learn to be stoical in face of heat and cold, too. As an infant he is not only wrapped in the swaddling band but is enveloped in layers of blankets even in warm weather. When he begins to walk he wears knitted wool garments, wool stockings, wool panties, wool sweaters, wool scarves, not only in the winter but on warmer spring days. His knees remain exposed, however. It is not unusual to see children as small as Dédou Favre playing outdoors in a cold winter wind, well bundled up, with a heavy muffler wrapped around their neck, but with their knees blue with cold. The neck seems to be considered the vital spot. It is always well protected from the cold, while the legs and knees are apparently thought not to need much protection.

Children learn to stay up late, to be sleepy without complaining and without becoming irritable. Some parents take their children to the movies, which never end before eleven or eleven-thirty. When they go calling in the evening their children always accompany them. The American institution of baby-sitting was a matter of amazement to them. When they learned that our children were usually put to bed at seven o'clock, a few people seemed to think that our practice might be a good thing for the children, but most were not convinced. The teachers, however, approved of our attitude, because children often fell asleep over their books after a night at the movies or at a family celebration. Their normal bedtime was nine o'clock, when the *marchand de sable* (sandman) was reputed to make his trip through the village.

If a child rebels against any aspect of his training, he may temporarily resist with success and he may retaliate occasionally by "talking back" to his parents, but in the end he must accept their will. If he resists discipline, they will at first try to reason with him, to explain why he has to do something, or at least explain that he is resisting something he cannot change, so he might as well accept it. If he still resists they will try to shame him into accepting by telling him that he is big enough to understand, so he shouldn't be baby-like. They ridicule him by comparing him with smaller children who, they say, are already conforming better to the accepted pattern.

If reason, shame, and ridicule do not secure the desired behavior, then parents may resort to fright. The traditional figures with which French parents are said to frighten their children are the *loup-garou* (the were-wolf) and *Lustucru* (the idiot), but these expressions are considered rather ridiculous to the people of Peyrane. They say their grand-parents might have used them, but no one uses them now. Some people may frighten their child with threats that some vague, dark, forbidding figure may come get them, perhaps *le barbu* (the bearded man) or *le ramoneur* (the chimney sweep), but even these figures are not sufficiently realistic to be accepted by most parents or children. There is no witch-like or ogre-like village character with which to frighten a child, for there are no frightening characters in the village. The dirtiest person is Monsieur Maucorps, but he is a sweet old man who frightens nobody.

More popular than bogeymen are animals that eat and gnaw. When we moved into the Martron house, Madame Martron warned our children to stay away from the well, for there were "nasty animals in the well that ate little children up." Parents said they kept their children away from the old town well — not in use, but not covered — by telling them there was a wolf in the well. When Louis Pian was naughty, his father told him he would put him in the basement and let the rats gnaw him. Francis Favre told his children that he would take them to the house of Monsieur Maucorps so the rats could gnaw them. Rats seem to be the most popular frightening agents, perhaps because the children know that there *are* rats in the basements and around the cliff and because they know that rats *do* gnaw.

Threats of physical mutilation are never used by parents, but along with threats of frightening experiences there are usually threats of deprivation and physical punishment. A child is constantly threatened with being deprived of something which his parents know he wants badly — dessert, supper, a chance to go outdoors, to go to the movies with his parents, to go to a celebration of some sort. However, these threats of deprivations are only mildly effective because children soon learn that they are never carried out.

Threats of physical punishment are taken more seriously because they are sometimes carried out. We found tucked away in the attic of our furnished house a *martinet*, a sort of miniature cat-o'-nine-tails, and we discovered that these instruments could be bought and were not rare in the houses of the region. However, people were unanimous in insisting that *martinets* were *never* used seriously. A child might be threatened with one, and very rarely his legs might actually be stung with the thongs, but never was serious physical punishment inflicted with such an instrument. The most common form of physical punishment was simply a spanking on the buttocks with the parent's hand.

Corporal punishment, however, is administered only as a last resort when a child has resisted all other means of persuasion. It is rarely necessary. Usually the mere threat of punishment is sufficient to secure obedience. Often one sees a father threatening by gesture to strike a child across the face with the back of his hand or arm, but this gesture is very rarely carried through to the act. It seems to represent the father's impatience rather than an intended punishment. The only time we saw a father strike his child was one day on the *Place de la Mairie* when Dédé Fraysse was extremely insolent to his father, André. André started to grab Dédé; Dédé ducked and ran away, but he had been too insolent for his father to forgive him, especially since the insolence had been witnessed by all the people on the *Place*. André chased Dédé, caught him and gave him an earnest boxing on the head and ears. Incidentally, Fraysse was the Alsatian, the only man in the village who apparently enjoyed caring for his baby, a younger son.

By the time a child in Peyrane is four years old, he is no longer an infant treated indulgently by everyone. His transformation has been gradual and apparently rather painless. Every step in his development seems to have depended on the development of what people call his *raison*, which to a large extent means his ability to understand what is said to him. As a tiny infant he is expected to have no control over himself. As soon as he seems able to understand what his parents are saying to him, he is expected to try to do what is asked of him. His parents are patient and tolerant. If he shows that he is trying to learn, trying to coöperate, he will be encouraged and not punished. Once a child has achieved control over one aspect of his behavior, however, he is no longer indulged in that aspect. Occasional accidents and relapses are forgiven, but the child is considered to have become *raisonnable* in that aspect and he is expected to remain *raisonnable*. Little by little the area of indulgence is narrowed and the area of the child's self-control is widened.

By the age of four, children have to a large extent accepted the discipline imposed on them. They are docile, stoical, usually courteous to their superiors, sometimes insulting — but at a distance. They play carefully without getting very dirty. Their toilet training is completed. They rarely fight among themselves, but they can express themselves orally with telling effect. They can get about the streets independently. They go on errands and begin to help out in the chores at home. If a new baby has come into the family, they have accepted him. They no longer insist on being the center of everyone's indulgent attention but join with others in the family in caring for and indulging their younger sister or brother. Their basic training at home has been accomplished. It will be continued and refined, but the children are now ready for training outside the home. They are ready to go to school.

Chapter 4

School

Madame Biron, the butcher's wife, lived in Apt before she moved to Peyrane. She likes living in Peyrane but she says that life in a city has one great advantage for a woman with a three-year-old boy like her Jeannot, for in the cities three-year-old children can be sent to school. In small schools like the one in Peyrane the teachers refuse to take children before their fourth birthday. Madame Biron talked to Madame Girard, the teacher of the *classes enfantines,* and tried to persuade her to take Jeannot a few months before his fourth birthday, but Madame Girard refused to make an exception, even though Jeannot was big for his age.

If Madame Girard had made an exception in this case she soon would have had all the three-year-old children in Peyrane. All the mothers are eager to send their children to school as soon as possible. A child in school is one less responsibility at home — at least for six hours of the day — and mothers welcome the opportunity to share their responsibilities with the teacher.

The fourth birthday is important in the life of a child, for he starts school that very day. The event does not come as a surprise to him, since there has been much talk about it in the family. He has new shoes, sturdy boots big enough so that heavy woolen socks may be worn with them. If the family purse is large enough he has a new cap or beret, new smocks, and a heavy muffler which his mother has knitted. He also has to have a brief case to carry his pencils and crayons and papers. The town furnishes school materials, but children usually prefer to have a set of their own, and Madame Girard will not allow them to be left at the school. If private materials disappeared she would be blamed for the loss, and she is unwilling to assume this needless responsibility. So even though children are given no homework until they are six or seven years old, they often begin to carry a brief case to and from school at the age of four.

The only children to undergo a special ceremony before starting to school are boys with pretty hair like Jeannot Biron and Bébert Favre. They have their long curls cut off and get a boy's regular haircut with a part on the side and a long lock held back with a bobby pin. Bébert's father cut his hair the day before he started to school, but Madame Biron, who was more accustomed to city ways and whose husband's business was prosperous, took Jeannot to Madame Avenas's beauty parlor because she said she wanted his first haircut to "look just right." One boy in the *classe enfantine* still had long curls and his mother felt it necessary to explain that she had a special reason for postponing his haircut. His aunt was to be married in a few months, and she wanted Loulou to look his best for the wedding.

On the day that the child is to start to school his mother accompanies him if she can arrange it. Otherwise an older sister or brother or a neighbor's child will take the responsibility of introducing him to the teacher and showing the required papers: birth certificate, diphtheria inoculation certificate, and vaccination certificate. Madame Girard greets a new child with a show of affection and interest. She shakes hands with him, hugs and kisses him, and tells him how happy he is going to be now that he is grown up and can go to school with the big children. When the child's mother leaves or when the older sister goes off to her class the child may cry and Madame Girard does her best to console him. She may hold him on her lap and mother him without interrupting her work with the older children in her room. If he is too demanding, she will call in Odette Peretti or one of the other big girls from the *classe des grands* to care for him until he adjusts to the new situation.

As soon as the child accepts the situation, and it rarely takes more than an hour or so, no more nonsense is expected of him. He must submit to the same rules and routine followed by all the other children. He must sit quietly at his desk for three hours in the morning and three hours in the afternoon. He must not fidget or talk to other children. He can move around freely only during the fifteen minute recess periods, one in the morning and one in the afternoon.

Officially, the *classes enfantines* are considered only a sort of *garderie*, a nursery where little children are kept for a few hours every day to free their mothers. Now and then Madame Girard may take the time to work with them formally, teaching them the alphabet, showing them how to copy letters and numbers, helping them learn songs or poems by heart, but most of the time she is kept busy with the older children on the other side of the room who have regular lessons to learn. The younger ones must learn to amuse themselves without making any disturbance. Paper, crayons, a few blocks, a few books are provided for them. A four-year-old may play with them or he may just sit still and listen to the older children recite. Now and then he may put his head on his desk and take a nap. Madame Girard lets the little ones sleep when they wish, for she knows that they may have been up until very late at a family dinner or at the movies the night before. And then she says, "There is nothing serious that they have to learn for a year or so."

The four-year-old and five-year-old children, however, *do* learn important lessons. They learn to sit still for long periods. They learn to accept the discipline of the school. They even learn about learning — that is, they are impressed with the fact that to learn means to copy or to repeat whatever the teacher tells them. They are not encouraged to "express their personality." On the contrary, they learn that their personality must be kept constantly under control. These attitudes are so thoroughly inculcated in the four- and five-year-old children that by the time they are six years old they are considered mature enough to begin their formal education.

When we moved to Peyrane our older son was almost five years old, and naturally he was expected to go to school. Madame Girard said we might do as we liked about sending him but she would be glad to have him. To us it seemed cruel to ask a five-year-old child to sit at a desk for six long hours a day listening to a language he did not understand, so we sent him at first only in the morning. After a few weeks, however, he asked if he might attend both the morning and afternoon sessions. He said he liked the Peyrane school much more than the kindergarten he had attended at home. "At home we always had to keep playing all the time. Here we can learn real letters and numbers and things."

One reason we hesitated to ask our son to spend six hours a day in the schoolroom was that the school and the room seemed unhealthy to us. Like most of the buildings in Peyrane the school seems ageless, but

it is only about two hundred and fifty years old. Built originally as a
Charitable Home for the Poor and Aged, it has served as a school since
1833 when public primary education was introduced in Peyrane.

It is a picturesque building, but everyone agrees that as a school it
is a disgrace to the community. The roof threatens to cave in at several
points. There are cracks in the walls that run from the roof to the
ground. The masons do their best to patch up the building so that it
will hold together, but they say that fundamentally it is beyond repair.
They have warned the Municipality, and the Municipality has warned
the Department of Education that the children in the upstairs classroom are constantly exposed to the danger of a cave-in.

The teachers complain that, apart from the question of danger, the
classrooms are inadequate. They may have seemed satisfactory fifty
years ago, but by modern standards they are too small, too dark, poorly
ventilated, and poorly equipped.

Each room is about twelve feet wide and twenty feet long, just large
enough to accommodate the ten double desks for the children assigned
to the room. In the center is a small wood stove surrounded by an iron
guard rail. Hanging from the center of the ceiling is a sixty-watt electric
bulb without a shade, the only artificial light in the room. Even on
sunny days there is not much light because there is only one window,
and the dark yellow walls reflect little light. In warm weather when the
window and door are open the air is sufficiently fresh, but in the winter
the room grows stuffy. Each teacher keeps a pan of water with strongly
scented herbs simmering on the stove.

There are few questions on which all the people of Peyrane agree,
but there is unanimous agreement that Peyrane should have a new
school building, a beautiful, modern *groupe scolaire* like the one in the
neighboring town of Goult. Just why Peyrane does not have a new
groupe scolaire, in spite of this extraordinary unanimity, is a complicated question which cannot be discussed at this point because it would
take us too far away from the actual problem of education. In 1950–51
it looked as though a new *groupe scolaire* might soon be built, but the
old school itself was a fact, the only fact that mattered to the child who
went to school and the only fact that concerns us here.

The teachers point to the old school building as evidence that the
parents are indifferent to the education of their children. "If they really
cared," said Madame Girard, "they'd work together in the *Conseil de*

Parents d'élèves and force through this business of a new school. But they won't even come to meetings of the *Conseil*."

Madame Girard was undoubtedly right in assuming that concerted action on the part of the parents would bring about the construction of a new school, but it was unreasonable of her to expect concerted action and unfair of her to blame the lack of action on the indifference of the parents. The adults of Peyrane do not unite to work together for any cause, as we shall see. They also avoid as the plague any involvement with the Government which they are not forced to accept. To expect them to organize spontaneously for the purpose of forcing the hand of the Government, even for a just and important cause like the erection of a new school building, is unreasonable.

Far from being indifferent to the education of their children, parents have a profound belief in it. This belief goes beyond the practical aspect of the question. It is obvious to them that all children should learn to read and write and do practical problems in arithmetic, that they should learn some history and some science and some geography. Such knowledge is recognized as essential for practical reasons. But quite apart from practical considerations they believe that education is a good thing in itself. "One can never know too much," was an aphorism that many parents used in talking to me about the school.

They are incapable of acting in an organized, official manner to support the school, but in the sphere of action where they feel secure and where their authority is supreme, that is within the family unit itself, they coöperate wholeheartedly with the teachers. In the first place, they see to it that their children attend school regularly. If a child is absent from school there is almost always a good excuse. There are legal sanctions to which the authorities can resort to enforce school attendance. The town can even cut off the government family allowances of a family which disobeys the school law, but it is never necessary to invoke these sanctions. People send their children to school voluntarily because they are eager for their children to be educated.

Naturally, there are exceptions. One of the least responsible inhabitants of the village, a Spanish ochre worker named Mariano, sent his older son off to work in the cherry harvest in another part of the department without securing the temporary work permit that can be obtained for children twelve years old. He told Madame Vernet, the boy's teacher, that he had gone to the city to visit a sick relative, but indirectly she learned the real cause of his absence from class. Even in the case of Mariano, however, it was not necessary to send the *garde-champêtre* (the constable) to remind him that he was disobeying the law. Madame Vernet simply told him that she knew the real reason for his son's absence. Two days later the boy was back in Peyrane, attending school regularly.

Most parents not only insist that their children attend school regularly, but they demand of their children the best possible performance in school. If the teacher tells a family that their child is not doing as well as he might in school, that he is not working hard enough, the child's life at home becomes uncomfortable. He is constantly reminded of his deficiency. He is told that he is disgracing the family. He is deprived of play opportunities and given extra work. Every possible pressure is brought to bear on him so that he may be forced to live up to the teacher's and the parents' expectations. The parents coöperate so wholeheartedly in this matter that the teacher sometimes has to intervene to prevent the child from being overworked at home. One of the problems of the teacher is to moderate the desires of parents who insist that their children be given supplementary lessons. Parents want their children to work hard, and they complain if they think the teacher is not sufficiently demanding.

The parents also coöperate with the teachers in enforcing the rules of social conduct. If a child is punished for misbehavior at school he can expect no sympathy from his parents when he gets home. In fact, he will try to hide from his parents the fact that he has been punished in school, for he knows that if they find out about it they will inflict another punishment on him. They will not even listen to his excuse, for they say there is no excuse for misbehavior. "One does what is expected! That's the way it is!" Only if the child can convince his parents that he has been discriminated against or punished unfairly can he turn their anger against the teacher.

A successful teacher must be very careful in all matters relating to the family. She must be scrupulously impartial in meting out punishments. She must never criticize parents in front of their children or in any other way weaken the parental authority. She must never take part in family arguments or clan feuds. In a general way she must never interfere with or imply criticism of a family as an institution.

The teachers are keenly aware of the importance of these unwritten rules, and far from wounding the pride of the families, they make a constant effort to flatter it. Two months of the school year are almost completely devoted to the preparation of programs in which the children perform as brilliantly as they can before their parents and the assembled community. Most of the month of December is devoted to rehearsing songs and skits for the Christmas party. Every child is given a role in which he may appear to the best advantage. Even Loulou Favre, who has a speech difficulty, is given a part, a silent part in which his difficulty will not be noticed. At the party every child is given a Christmas present chosen for him by the teacher.

From the middle of June until the middle of July the school building is almost deserted. The teachers and the children spend most of their time in the bleak *Salle des Fêtes*, practicing for the program of the Distribution des Prix, the Prize Awarding Ceremony which closes the school year. When the ceremony takes place every child in the school takes part in the program, and every child is awarded a prize for his work during the year. Obviously not every child deserves a prize, but it is important for every child to receive some recognition so that his family will feel that its dignity is respected.

If a teacher in a village school acquires the reputation of being a conscientious person capable of making the children work hard, if the parents think that the children both fear him and love him, if he is mindful of the honor of each family, if he has the tact to avoid becoming embroiled in village quarrels without being considered *fier* (aloof), if he is punctilious in making clear how every franc in the school budget is spent, if he gives gossips no cause to talk, then he will enjoy a favored position in the community. Obviously these conditions are not easily met; it would take a saint to fulfill them.

In spite of these conditions the life of a teacher is appealing. Socially the teacher is second to only the Notaire (the lawyer, broker, banker, and recorder of deeds). Culturally he is the incarnation of knowledge and civilization, which are highly respected in the community. Economically he is respected because he earns more money than any other salaried person in the village. He enjoys the prestige of being a representative of the government. People also respect him because of the security of his position and because of the pension he will receive when he retires. In some villages the teacher is more than a leading citizen; if he has the energy and tact he may become Town Clerk, and the

Town Clerk is frequently the real manager of the community, even though the Mayor remains the titular authority.

Economically and socially, then, a career as a village school teacher has an appeal. It is especially attractive to children of farm or lower middle class families who demonstrate unusual intellectual aptitude in school but whose ambition is modest. To qualify as a teacher in the primary school system is not easy, however. Before a candidate gets his permanent certificate he must have the equivalent of the baccalaureate degree; he must have studied in Normal School; he must have had two years' experience as a practice teacher; he must have passed a series of difficult oral and written examinations and practical demonstrations. There are few teaching positions open, and there are many candidates, so the competition is severe. There are no local school boards to exert pressure or to relax standards in behalf of a favored local candidate. The whole system is a part of the Department of National Education, which sees that standards are kept high.

Consequently, the three teachers in the school at Peyrane are professionally competent. Unfortunately they have no interest in the community of Peyrane itself. They were assigned by the Inspecteur d'Académie to their present positions and were forced to accept them because their seniority was insufficient for them to secure the positions they wanted in larger towns. All three have applied for positions elsewhere and will leave Peyrane as soon as more attractive positions open up. As a result, Peyrane is deprived of needed leadership, the kind of leadership teachers give communities in which they are interested.

Madame Girard, the teacher of the youngest children, spends most of her free time in the city of Apt where her little daughter lives with an elderly aunt and uncle. She is an attractive, rather stylish woman about twenty-eight years old. She became a teacher when she divorced her husband only a few months after their marriage in 1945, and she has been teaching in Peyrane ever since she completed her teaching certificate requirements. She has applied for a transfer to the schools in Apt so that she can be with her daughter.

Madame Druetta, who has charge of the intermediate grades, is the youngest of the three teachers and is still teaching on a practice teacher's license. She has been at Peyrane only one year and will not return next year if she can secure an appointment near the city of Pertuis, where her husband is an employee in a bank. She spends Saturday and Sunday nights at home. Monday morning her husband brings her to Peyrane on his motorcycle. Monday and Tuesday nights she sleeps in the lodgings supplied for her by the town of Peyrane. Wednesday evening her husband comes for her again and brings her back early Friday morning. On Saturday afternoon he comes to take her home for the weekend. When he is unable to make the trip she rides her bicycle seven miles to Apt and takes the bus to Pertuis. Madame Druetta obviously has little interest in remaining in Peyrane.

The head of the school and the teacher of the classes of oldest children is Madame Vernet. She is thirty years old, but she looks younger because her physical frailty gives her an air of immaturity. She came to teach in Peyrane during the war, and when she married Philippe Vernet, the son of the *garde-champêtre*, it looked as though she might spend her life in the village. However, Philippe was one of the most attractive, intelligent, and ambitious young men in the village, and he had no intention of spending the rest of his life driving a truck at the ochre mines. For the six years he has been married he has been taking correspondence courses, and with the help of his wife he has become a master mechanic. He hopes eventually to become a teacher in a technical school. Meanwhile Madame Vernet has applied for a transfer to a city school so that Philippe can work in a garage where he can get a better job than driving a truck.

Even though the teachers have little interest in the village as a whole, they are genuinely interested in the school and in the children in their classes. It is obvious that teaching is a true vocation for them. They are devoted to the children of Peyrane as they would be devoted to the children in any school, and they fulfill their duties conscientiously. Their superiors, their pupils, and the parents of the pupils all agree that Madame Girard, Madame Druetta, and Madame Vernet are good teachers.

It does not follow, of course, that they are not criticized by the villagers. No one can live in Peyrane and escape criticism. In spite of the respect in which they are held, the teachers are especially vulnerable to criticism. Their social prestige and privileges arouse resentment among the villagers who say that the teachers "have it easy," that they are well paid but do not have to work hard, that they have a long summer vacation and many shorter holidays throughout the year, that they have to work in the classrooms only thirty hours a week! Of course,

those who make these criticisms freely admit that they would be unwilling to trade places with the teachers and spend six hours a day,
nine months a year cooped up in the same room with twenty children.
People also know that the teachers spend many hours correcting papers
and working with pupils outside of class. Nevertheless, the basic resentment against teachers exists and is often expressed.

Probably the best testimony of the community's real approval of the
teachers lies in the fact that the sixty-nine children enrolled in the
school represent a large proportion of the children of school age of the
commune of Peyrane. Thirty-nine of the children live outside of the
village, and some of them living on the edge of the commune would
find it more convenient to go to other schools located nearer their
homes. The Marchal family, for instance, lives only two hundred yards
from the school in the hamlet of Les Pins; still the Marchal children
go to school in Peyrane despite the four-mile walk in the daily round
trip. Madame Marchal told me she disliked imposing this hardship on
her children, but the teachers in Peyrane were so much better than the
teacher in Les Pins that the sacrifice was worth while. The teacher at
Les Pins had been given his teacher's license during the war when the
scarcity of good teachers forced the Vichy régime to relax standards.

The schoolyard starts to fill up at eight o'clock in the morning. The
children who live the farthest away from school arrive first. Villagers
sleep later than country people. The village children drift down to
school only a few minutes before the eight-thirty deadline. Even five
or ten minutes after school has started one may hear a door bang up
the street, then the thumping of a child's heavy boots as Yves Biron or
Colette Favre runs down the street, late as usual but hoping to avoid
in some way the usual scolding.

At eight-thirty Madame Vernet blows her whistle, and lines form in
front of the three entries to the classrooms. There is some jostling in
the ranks of the four-, five-, and six-year-olds among those who want
to be first in line, but Madame Girard with a sharp word and clap of
her hands stops the confusion at once. The children seven to nine
years old in front of Madame Druetta's door, and those ten to fourteen
in front of Madame Vernet's door stand in a dignified manner and
look at the scuffling younger children with an air of amusement and
superiority. When order has been completely established the teachers
open the doors and the children file in, hang their wraps on the proper

pegs, sit down at their desks and start arranging materials from their brief cases.

The school day begins with a fifteen-minute *leçon de morale*. The teacher reads a short story or tells an incident from which she draws a moral lesson which may be summed up in a sentence, repeated in chorus and learned by heart by the children. Officially, the purpose of the *leçon de morale* is to teach the children to practice "the principal individual and social virtues (temperance, sincerity, modesty, kindness, courage, tolerance), to inspire in them the love for work, the taste for coöperation, the spirit of teamwork, the respect for one's word of honor, the understanding of other people, the love of one's native soil, the obligations toward one's family and toward France." *

Most of the teacher's moral tales are taken from ready-made texts like Souché's *New Moral Lessons* or *On the Straight Road* by Leterrier and Bonnet, and when she can she tries to relate them directly to the life of the children. This is an easy matter if, for instance, it concerns family obligations. It is harder if the moral lessons concern coöperation and teamwork, which are not characteristic virtues of the people of Peyrane. A few lessons are so completely in conflict with the customs of Peyrane that it seems futile to teach them.

One morning Mrs. Wylie was at school when Madame Girard was giving a moral lesson designed to increase the children's love and respect for Nature. The anecdote, from Souché's *New Moral Lessons*, concerned "Two Poor Little Birds," and the sentence which the children repeated and learned by heart was, "Let us be the friends and protectors of the little birds." In a region where a favorite dish is roasted little birds, where a husky man boasts of consuming fifty or sixty warblers at a sitting, there is little likelihood that this lesson will have much effect.

When the *leçon de morale* is finished, work is begun in earnest on the subjects in the curriculum. At ten o'clock the children file out to the school yard for a recess of fifteen minutes. Sometimes, especially at the beginning of the year, the teachers organize singing games for the girls and younger children, but usually the children are left to their own devices. They may run and yell and play at will so long as they do not attack each other physically, get wet or dirty or expose themselves to danger. The children break up into groups spontaneously,

* *Le Livre des Instituteurs*, 19ᵉ édition (Paris: Le Soudier, 1948), p. 161.

the younger children playing with friends of either sex and the older children playing only with friends of their own sex. The boys play tag or may organize a game of soccer if one of them has brought a ball to school. There is no play equipment of any kind in the school yard except for a climbing rope which children must learn to climb in order to get their *brevet sportif scolaire* (athletic certificate). The older girls sit in a sunny corner of the yard gossiping and petting one or two of the youngest children who turn instinctively to them when they need affection. The younger boys and girls run about madly in groups of two or three or four, often chasing and verbally tormenting a current scapegoat. The three teachers stroll about the yard, chatting and vaguely keeping an eye on the whole situation. Play is stopped only in case a child gets hurt or is punished. Then all the children crowd about the victim. If the child is hurt, faces of the other children are filled with sympathy, and there are murmurs that "he shouldn't have been doing that; he was sure to get hurt." If he is being punished, there is a mocking expression on their faces. Usually, of course, the play continues uneventfully until Madame Vernet blows her whistle and the children line up to march back into the school.

At a few minutes past eleven-thirty Madame Vernet sends a child out in the school yard to look at the town clock. When he runs back to report that the time is up, there is a scuffle to put away books. The two older classes are excused, and the children leave the classroom at will. The little ones in Madame Girard's class must line up outside the classroom and wait until all are ready to leave. They line up by twos, with boys and girls paired up and holding hands. When all is ready they march to the break in the wall between the school yard and the street where they stand poised for a moment. Madame Girard has them wait until they are all calm and until she makes sure no cars are coming down the street. Then she calls: "Avancez!" The children answer in one voice, " 'voir, Madame," and they start down the street, running and yelling, temporarily freed from the restrictive weight of discipline.

Most of the village children hurry straight home, for they have errands to do before lunch. Jacques Leporatti must carry a bucket and a pitcher of water home from the public fountain, for there is no running water in the Leporatti house. Georges Vincent has to bring bread from the bakery for his father's restaurant. Tatave Pouget has to run to the store to get a bottle of wine. Colette Favre has to take care of her little brother while her mother is finishing preparations for lunch, and when lunch is ready she has to go call her father at the café.

Back at school, lunch is being served to the children who live too far away from school to return home and to a few village children whose mothers are working and cannot prepare a proper lunch for them. Now and then children who could return home persuade their parents to let them eat at the cantine, for the children all enjoy eating there. They like eating together, and they say that the food which old Madame Bardin prepares is very good. It consists of three courses — two substantial dishes (stew, thick soup, spaghetti, or something of the kind) and dessert (usually jam or stewed fruit). Each child brings his own big piece of bread to school with him. This meal costs twenty-five francs, about eight cents.

Discipline at the cantine is strict. The children must sit up straight, keep their wrists on the edge of the table, and finish everything on their plates. There is a double purpose in requiring the children to clean up their plates. It teaches them not to waste food, and it also reduces the number of dishes which have to be washed. At the cantine as in most homes, when the main course is finished and each child's dish is wiped clean with a piece of bread, the dish is turned over so that dessert may be served on the back of it. The spoon is also inverted so that jam may be eaten from the handle.

During the meal absolute silence is maintained. A child may speak only if he receives permission from the teacher in charge. The teachers justify this rule of silence by saying that the acoustics in the cantine are such that the place would be a bedlam if the children were allowed to talk. They also say that lunch would last forever if the children were allowed to distract each other. As it is, lunch is so disciplined that it lasts no longer than fifteen or twenty minutes. Then the children are turned loose on the playground and play as they do during recess until class begins at one o'clock.

The afternoon session differs little from the morning session. It lasts three hours with a recess of fifteen minutes in the middle of the period. The children are dismissed at four o'clock in the same way as at eleven-thirty, with this difference, that at the end of the morning all the children leave the school. At four o'clock, five or six children are required to remain in their seats for any time from a few mintues to an hour in order to make up work that they have done improperly or as a punishment for misbehavior.

By five o'clock the school is cleared, and the cleaning woman comes to scrub and sweep. After she leaves the school is ready for the next day, and the shutters and doors are locked until morning.

When the village children leave school they run directly home for their *goûter*, or mid-afternoon snack. Since supper will not be served for three or four hours the *goûter* is important, and if a child does not return home directly after school his mother will send someone out to look for him. Some children sit down at the table for a fairly substantial meal, but most of them are impatient to get outdoors. They are given their large hunk of bread and a piece of chocolate or cheese and go out in the street to eat it in the company of other children.

After the *goûter* the younger children may play, but the older ones have work to do. Water must be carried from the public fountain. Armloads of wood must be carried from the basement room down the street where wood is stored. Trips must be made to the edge of the village to gather fresh grass for the chickens and rabbits or to pick mulberry leaves for the silkworms. When these chores are finished there is homework to be done. Finally at six or six-thirty the older children may go out in the streets to play, but even then the older girls have the responsibility of keeping an eye on their little sisters and brothers.

When the country children leave school they start their long walk toward home. Some of them live as far as two miles from the village. In winter when it gets dark early and the mistral is blowing, this walk is accomplished as fast as possible. In nice weather, however, groups of five or six children dawdle all the way home. This is the only time of the day when they are free from adult surveillance. They learn how to get along with other children without the pressure of adult authority but with the severe social pressure that can be exercised by other children of their group.

The groups grow smaller and smaller as children reach home and drop out. In the last few hundred meters there is usually a sudden rush to get home, for the children remember that they will be scolded if they have lingered too long. They may be late for the *goûter*, which is always a more formal, more substantial meal in the country than in the village. The men come in from the fields and the whole family sits down to a heavy snack of bread, cheese, sausage, jam, and wine.

After the *goûter*, all but the smallest children have their chores, more numerous and more important than the chores of the village children. They have the problem of carrying wood and water and getting grass for the rabbits and chickens, and when this work is finished they have to help work in the field or in the garden. They have to take their turn watching the sheep or goats, bringing them into the fold when it starts to get dark, and milking the ewes and nannies that are fresh. If there is time to spare between chores and supper it must be devoted to schoolwork. There is no time for homework after supper, for supper is not served until the men have stopped working, usually well after dark. By the time supper is finished it is time to go to bed. The next morning they must get up early to get to school on time, and in the cold early morning one has neither time nor inclination to dawdle or play. The walk home from school in the afternoon gives the country children their only playtime.

The four-year-old child who has just started to school soon falls into this routine. He has no homework. He has no chores. The routine is hard, however, and he must accept it without complaining. He knows that complaining would not relieve him of the pressure, for no one would listen to him. He has already learned that there are unpleasant aspects of life that must be faced. He is told that he is old enough to face the school routine, and he does so stoically. He is partially rewarded by his feeling of pride in being considered old enough, reasonable enough to accept the inevitable with resignation.

For ten years, until the child is fourteen, the school routine is the most important part of his life. His parents, his teachers, his friends constantly remind him of its importance. Confronted by this unbroken social pressure, he accepts the school routine as a serious responsibility to which he must measure up.

The educational program of the school of Peyrane is the same as that of every other public primary school in France. It is formulated by the Department of National Education which sends out precise and detailed instructions concerning educational goals, subjects to be taught, methods to be followed, distribution of class time, and all other aspects of the functioning of the school. As one reads page after page of these instructions, one gets the impression that the officials of the Department of National Education do not recognize the special needs of different communities and leave nothing to the imagination of the teachers. Even the games to be played in the nursery school are "determined by the decree of July 15, 1921."

In practice, of course, the program is far from being as rigid and impersonal as it seems. The teachers know that these official instructions are intended as a guide and should not be taken too literally. After all, the teachers are French and consequently recognize the gap that usually separates laws and regulations on the one hand from actual practice on the other. They know that they need not follow the daily program blindly so long as over a period of time they observe the relative proportions for the important subjects indicated in the program. They know that for everyone in Peyrane it is more important for a child to be able to read well than to take part effectively in choral singing. If they take the time allocated for singing and devote it to drill in reading no one will object.

Monsieur Valentini, the Primary Inspector from Avignon, who supervises the primary schools of the district, shares this flexible, reasonable attitude. The teachers speak as though they were in constant fear of his annual inspection visit and of the unexpected visits he pay now and then, but confidentially they admit that this anxiety is superficial, for Monsieur Valentini is a genial, tolerant person who expects teachers to carry out the spirit of the official program as best they can in their own specific, local situation. He calls the teachers of the district together for a meeting once or twice a year to discuss with them the program and their problems and to go over the new regulations sent out by the Department of Education. At one of the meetings I attended he explained at length a new ruling which some of the teachers had not understood. He concluded his remarks by saying, "That's what the regulation says, and I hope you all understand it now. Unofficially, of course, I might add that no one is going to object if you follow your own judgment in this matter."

Although the official curriculum prescribed by the Department of National Education is long and complicated * it may be described in simple terms as it is put in practice in the school in Peyrane. The children of the school are divided into five classes: *Classes enfantines* (Nursery Group) with children from four to six, *Section préparatoire* (Preparatory Section) with children from six to seven, *Cours élémentaire* (Elementary Course) with children from seven to nine, *Cours*

---

* *Le Livre des Instituteurs*, 19ᵉ édition (Paris: Le Soudier, 1948), pp. 150ff.

moyen (Intermediate Course) with children from nine to eleven, and the *Classe de Fin d'Etudes* (Concluding Course) with children from twelve to fourteen. Of course, the age division is by no means rigorous. A bright five-year-old may be placed with the six-year-old group, and a dull twelve-year-old may be kept with the seven-year-old group. Paul Jouvaud, who is mentally defective, remained in the room with the smallest children until he was thirteen years old and the biggest, strongest child in school. He was "graduated" from the Nursery Group and dropped from school, according to Madame Girard, when the stirrings of puberty made him too difficult for her to handle.

Madame Girard has charge of both the Nursery Group and the Preparatory Section. We have already seen how the Nursery Group spends its time. The Preparatory Section, to which Madame Girard devotes the major portion of her energy, concentrates on learning to read, write, and do simple problems in arithmetic. In an average six-hour school day about two hours are devoted to reading, a half-hour to writing, a half-hour to grammar, and an hour to arithmetic. The use of the remaining two hours depends on the mood of the teacher and of the children and on a variety of other human factors. Usually the time is split up into brief periods which are given over to singing, drawing, paper and scissor work, the *leçon morale*, short talks on such subjects as divisions of the year, points of the compass, parts of the body, hygiene, and so on. Recess, of course, takes up a half-hour.

There is no radical difference between this program and that of the children in the Elementary Course, which is Madame Druetta's sole concern. The same time is spent on reading and writing, but the emphasis is slightly shifted. Less time is devoted to reading and more to the formal study of grammar. Two new subjects are introduced, but in moderate amounts: history and geography take up about fifteen minutes of the school day.

In Madame Vernet's room are both the Intermediate Course and the Concluding Course, and it takes a teacher as skillful as Madame Vernet to handle these two quite different sections in the same schoolroom. The Intermediate Course is a continuation of the Elementary Course, and one sees in its program the same tendencies. Half the school time is still devoted to reading and writing, but the emphasis is shifted somewhat further: the study of formal grammar replaces reading as the primary concern of the class. No new subjects are introduced at this level, but the time devoted to arithmetic, geography, and history is doubled. Together these three subjects take up a third of the class time. Arithmetic alone takes up an hour a day. We noted that in the Preparatory Section, Madame Girard now and then gave brief talks on practical subjects such as divisions of time. By the time the children have reached the Intermediate Section these talks have become a formal subject to which a half-hour a day is devoted and which is called *leçons de choses*. This might be translated "lessons in things" or "exercises in observation," but it may be best understood as a kind of practical approach to the study of science.

The program of the Concluding Course is rather different from the programs of the other Courses. The study of French is still the primary consideration of the class, but the time devoted to it is reduced to an hour or so a day, the same time that is now given over to the study of arithmetic and science. History and geography take up about a half-hour, and what used to be called the *leçon morale* has now become civics, which the class studies for a half-hour daily. This makes for a more balanced program than that of the other courses, but of course the balance may not be evident from day to day. If the class is especially weak in one subject, most of the time may be spent on drill in that subject until the students perform adequately. This is especially true with the study of French, which is recognized by everyone as the most important subject taught in the school. Any other subject may be slighted or sacrificed in order to increase the time for drill in reading (silent or aloud) and writing (penmanship, spelling, grammar, composition).

The program is frequently interrupted. The visit of the Inspector or some other official, the illness of a teacher, preparations for the Primary Certificate Examination, a teachers' meeting which the teachers must attend in Apt, a visit to the ochre mine, the annual excursion to Marseille, and many other events frequently interrupt the routine. And then there is always the preparation for the two public performances — the Christmas Party and the Prize Awarding Ceremony — to which a substantial part of two months of the school year is devoted, as we have seen.

In spite of these interruptions and in spite of the rigidity, more illusory than real, of the official curriculum, when a child leaves school at the age of fourteen he has learned approximately what his parents expected him to learn in school. He can read with ease. He can write without making too many grammatical errors. He can solve most of the practical problems in arithmetic with which he is confronted in daily life. He knows enough of history, government, geography, and science to make him aware of his relationship to his environment; he is aware of the moral and ethical values professed by society.

To an observer who studies school life in Peyrane over a period of time it is apparent that the children learn much that is not explicitly stated in the curriculum. From the attitude of the teachers, from the way in which the school work is presented, from the textbooks, the children learn to make basic assumptions concerning the nature of reality and their relationship to it. These assumptions are not mentioned in the directives of the Department of Education. They are not prescribed by the Primary Inspector. If the teachers are conscious of them they never discuss them directly in class. Yet these assumptions are so important that they will determine to a large extent the frame of mind and the manner in which a child will approach the problems with which he is confronted throughout his life.

In teaching morals, grammar, arithmetic, and science the teacher always follows the same method. She first introduces a principle or rule that each pupil is supposed to memorize so thoroughly that it can be repeated on any occasion without the slightest faltering. Then a concrete illustration or problem is presented and studied or solved in the light of the principle. More problems or examples are given until the children can recognize the abstract principle implicit in the concrete circumstances and the set of circumstances implicit in the principle. When this relationship is sufficiently established in the minds of the children, the teacher moves on to another principle and set of related facts.

The principle itself is not questioned and is hardly discussed. Children are not encouraged to formulate principles independently on the basis of an examination of concrete cases. They are given the impression that principles exist autonomously. They are always there: immutable and constant. One can only learn to recognize them, and accept them. The same is true of concrete facts and circumstances. They exist, real and inalterable. Nothing can be done to change them. One has only to recognize them and accept them. The solution of any problem lies in one's ability to recognize abstract principles and concrete facts and to establish the relationship between them.

Another basic assumption is most clearly seen in the way history, civics, geography, and literature are studied, but it is important in all subjects. In learning history the children are first presented with a general framework which they are asked to memorize. Studying history consists partially in filling in this framework, that is, in learning how the facts of history fit into the framework. An isolated fact is unimportant in itself. It assumes importance only when one recognizes its relationship to other facts and above all its relationship to the whole framework. In learning geography a child first studies his own countryside, then the surrounding region, then France, then the world. Heavy stress is placed on the relationship of each geographical unit to a larger whole. In the study of morals and civics the children learn the proper relationship and reciprocal obligations of the individual to the family, to the community, to France, and to humanity.

This emphasis on the relationship of the part to the whole is also seen in the rather rudimentary study of literature that is carried out in the higher grades. No attempt is made to understand or to appreciate the text which is presented to the class until it has been thoroughly dissected and analyzed. It is broken down into its logical divisions, and the author's purpose in each division is explained. Difficult or obscure words and expressions are explained. Only when each of the component parts of a passage is understood and when the relationship of each part to the whole is made clear is the passage put back together and appraised as a unit.

Thus a child comes to believe that every fact, every phenomenon, every individual is an integral part of a larger unit. As in a jigsaw puzzle each part has its own clearly defined and proper position. They make sense only if their proper relationship is recognized.

Finally, it is assumed that knowledge is important only as it is related to human beings. There is no stress on learning simply for the sake of learning, no stress on the accumulation of facts without regard for their usefulness. This is most evident in the study of arithmetic and geometry. The principles studied and the problems solved are chosen exclusively on the basis of their usefulness in teaching the students to solve the problems which they will be confronted with after they leave school.

The purpose of the rudimentary instruction they receive in science is equally related to the children as human beings. No effort is made to have the children collect butterflies, learn to recognize different kinds of birds, study rocks simply for the purpose of being able to classify them. A bird offers no interest in itself. It is interesting because it is good to eat, or because it is harmful to the crops or eats harmful insects, or because it has beautiful plumage or a beautiful song. In the same way the study of geography does not consist in memorizing the capitals of all the departments of France; its purpose is rather to show the relationship of the people of Peyrane to their surroundings.

The learning of grammatical rules is so emphasized that at times it appears that the rules are considered important in themselves. This impression is false, however. The rules are considered important because it is believed that a person cannot express himself properly unless he knows them thoroughly. It is difficult for an Anglo-Saxon to comprehend how essential this language study is to the French. The French judge a person to a far greater degree than we do on the basis of his ability to speak and write correctly. Even in a rural community like Peyrane the way a person speaks and writes is considered an important indication of his social status. The study of grammar is thus strongly emphasized in school, not because of its intrinsic value but because it will be important to the children throughout their life.

The history course shows the same orientation. The framework of dates and facts must be memorized, it is true, but is important because it lends perspective to the two aspects of historical study which are emphasized in the course: the life of the French people at different periods of history and the study of the lives of great men.

In 1938, Monsieur Jean Zay, then Minister of Education, sent out a circular which Madame Vernet and Madame Girard told me they consider the most authoritative statement of purpose and method in primary education. Concerning the study of history the statement says:

In teaching history the teachers should emphasize the role played by those men who have helped bring about progress. Today we no longer believe that history can provide a means to foretell the future; we no longer believe that the study of history can provide us with solutions for present-day problems. It does teach us, however, to meet events in their unfolding with a more impassive attitude, and that is a valuable contribution. It teaches us the value of honest labor, the value of great example, the comfort to be derived from healthy admiration. Children should be told of the effective role played by those men and women whom we consider the benefactors of humanity. If they retain only a genuine feeling for such people we shall have accomplished much. For they will have learned that this material progress of which we are so proud was accomplished at the cost of great effort, that it is the ever-threatened result of an immense collaboration, that in enjoying it we are responsible to the great men who created it.*

Not dates or facts alone then, but human beings in relationship to dates and facts, should constitute the study of history.

So in their study of arithmetic, science, geography, grammar, and history, children learn that man is the measure of all things. Facts are important and must be recognized, accepted and learned, but they are important only as they may be related to human beings, and especially to the human beings living in the commune of Peyrane.

The most successful child in the school of Peyrane is the child who goes beyond the subject matter to grasp these basic assumptions. Without consciously realizing that he does so, he learns to recognize the relationship between abstract principle and concrete fact, the relationship between the part and the whole, and the relationship of knowledge and experience to himself as a human being.

Even the average child, who certainly has only a partial grasp of these relationships, is sufficiently imbued with their importance that they will help determine the manner in which he seeks a solution to any problem — in human relations, in politics, in mechanics. He will approach the problem as he was taught to approach all problems in school. In every problem he knows there is a principle involved, and it is important for him to recognize the principle. In every problem lurk practical, concrete difficulties which make the application of the principle difficult. There is no isolated problem; every problem is related to a larger problem. The only problems worth worrying about are those which affect people. To approach problems with these assumptions is to approach them sensibly, reasonably, logically, and therefore, it is assumed, correctly.

Of course, these assumptions are not new to the schoolchild, for they are also implicit in most of the home training he has received. One day

* Jean Zay, "Enseignement du Premier Degré. Instructions relatives à l'application des arrêtés du 23 mars 1938 et du 11 juillet 1938," *Journal officiel, Annexe,* 24 septembre 1938.

Madame Favre was sitting in front of her house sewing. Three-year-old Dédou, who was playing in the street, went too near the gutter and was about to get muddy. His mother looked up and called sharply to him:

"Dédou, you'll get yourself dirty. Get away from there!" Dédou was usually a docile child, but this time a naughty urge got the better of him. He looked up impudently and shouted:

"Why?"

His mother gave him a glance that he would remember and said through her teeth:

"Because I tell you to be good ("sage"). Because you're the child and I'm the mother. Because we're not animals. That's the way it is! So!"

Madame Favre was not merely exerting her authority. She was unwittingly explaining that there was a principle involved in this situation over which Dédou had no control. He could only recognize it and accept it. She was explaining that both she and he were part of a family and that each had a role that must be maintained. She was emphasizing the importance of human dignity. She was saying that those were the facts, pleasant or unpleasant, and that his only reasonable course of action was to conform.

There is no conflict between the principles of thought and action taught in the home and those taught in the school. The only difference is that in school they are taught formally. The basic assumptions are fundamentally the same.

Three afternoons a week a group of older children stayed at school from four to four-thirty to study English in the special course which the teachers and the Primary Inspector had authorized me to teach. One day, not long after I began to teach this course, I was talking to Henri Favre, the father of one of my pupils.

"How's Jacqueline doing in the English class?" he asked.

I was embarrassed because Jacqueline was the worst student in the class. Physically mature for her thirteen years, she was merely putting in time in school until her fourteenth birthday. She was attending the English class only because of its prestige value. However, I did not want to hurt her father's feelings, so I commented as favorably as I could:

"Oh, she's making progress."

Henri Favre looked pleased but surprised. "I'm glad," he said, "but, you know, it astonishes me because she's lazy and she's not very intelligent."

It took time for me to become accustomed to the honest, objective manner in which parents openly appraised the intelligence of their children. They recognize the fact that some people are more intelligent than others, and since it is a fact it must be recognized, faced and accepted like all other facts. They see no point in hiding it, or denying it, or even in minimizing it. One cannot hide what is perfectly evident to everyone, and little purpose would be served by minimizing it. It is better to accept such facts as they exist and to try to make the most of them. Consequently, parents, teachers and children discuss differences in intelligence with relative frankness. When a parent says, "My child is not so intelligent as yours," he is not fishing for a compliment; he is stating a fact.

The first day I attended Madame Girard's class I was shocked at the way in which she insisted on discussing her pupils with me in front of them. After each child in the Preparatory Course recited she stopped the recitation to give me an analysis of his capacity.

"There's an intelligent little one," she said after Jeanne Reynard had answered a question. "She works hard, too. It's a pleasure to teach a child like that."

Renée Chanon failed to answer her question. "There's Renée. Not stupid, but lazy. She sits there distracted with her mouth open all day. And untidy! You can't expect much of that kind of girl."

Marie Père tried painfully to give some kind of answer to her question but Madame Girard cut her off and gave me a look of despair. "Poor Marie. She tries, but — I think all is not right." She tapped her forehead significantly with her forefinger. Marie squirmed in her seat and looked as unhappy as I felt over the situation, but the recitation and the commentary moved on until all the children had had their turn.

Eventually I became accustomed to hearing teachers and parents discuss the children in front of them, although I was never able to force myself to speak with frankness in the presence of the children. I am sure that my lack of forthrightness was not considered an indication of tact, however. It was taken simply as an indication that I was no judge of intelligence.

Since children differ in the degree of their intelligence and since there is no point in hiding this no one expects them all to achieve the same standard of performance. Each one is expected simply to do his best, depending on his own individual capacity. This means that there is a different standard of intellectual performance for each child in the school. Of course, no formal recognition is given to the existence of different standards. The system is simpler than that. The teacher, as she gets to know a child, inevitably makes a judgment concerning his intellectual potentialities, and once this judgment is made she expects the child to live up to her conception of his potentialities. The goal she unconsciously sets for each child is high, probably too high for the child to reach, but she exerts constant pressure on him to make an effort to live up to it.

Only the child who makes an extraordinary effort to fulfill his individual potentialities escapes punishment. Georges Vincent, one of the brightest boys in the school, does far better in his lessons than most of the children, but he receives the most sarcastic criticism of which Madame Vernet is capable because she believes his performance could be even better than it is. On the other hand, Marie Père receives very little criticism because it is recognized that she does the best she can with her limited capacity for learning. After her class had been learning how to write the alphabet Madame Girard said to her mother one day:

"Marie is doing very well. She has learned how to make only three letters, but she makes them quite neatly."

The judgment a teacher makes concerning the potentialities of a child is based entirely on her common-sense observations. She knows about objective intelligence tests, for she has studied testing in Normal School, but she is sceptical of the usefulness and validity of objective tests. She is timid about expressing this scepticism — which, incidentally, is shared by her superior, the Primary Inspector — because she knows that "modern" education lays heavy stress on objective tests, and she does not like to be considered backward. However, she has confidence in her own judgment of a child's capacity, which almost always coincides with the judgment made by the child's parents and friends.

"Why," asked Monsieur Valentini, "should the teachers take the time and trouble to give these tests to their children only to find out what is already obvious?"

Differences in intelligence are recognized, and a multiple standard is set up for intellectual performance. Differences in personality and home training are also recognized, but there is a rigorous, single standard for social behavior. The teachers may understand the reasons for a child's misbehavior. They are not surprised that Joseph Mariano, the motherless child of a migrant laborer, is naughtier than Henri-Paul Favre, whose parents are benevolently strict in the matter of home training. To understand these differences is not to accept them, however. They refuse to tolerate misbehavior for any reason. Deviation from the standard set for all children brings immediate and stern punishment.

The code of social behavior which the teachers enforce is essentially the same that most parents have tried to maintain at home. The function of the teachers is to carry on this home discipline and to make up for omissions of lax parents. Since most parents are lax in some respect, this means that for most children the discipline is harsher at school than at home.

Whenever I went into Madame Vernet's classroom all the children would rise at once and say in chorus, "Bonjour, Monsieur." They would remain standing until Madame Vernet told them to sit down. In Madame Girard's room the six-year-olds would stand up, but the younger ones had to be prompted by Madame Girard who said to them harshly:

"Well! What does one do when a grownup enters the room? One stands up straight and says 'Bonjour, Monsieur.'" Then the little children would rise and the class would perform as directed.

It disturbed me that I should disrupt the class activities when I really wanted to slip in unobserved, so I asked Madame Vernet if this rite could be omitted when I came in. She refused.

"We're glad when you come in," she said. "It gives the children a chance to practice their lesson in politeness which they need so badly."

It is as important for the children to be polite in school as it is for them to learn their lessons. They must never speak to a teacher or to any adult without addressing her or him directly as "Mademoiselle" or "Madame" or "Monsieur." If an adult stops and greets them they must extend their right hand in a forthright manner. A boy must, of course, remove his hat when he is greeting someone; simply touching one's finger to a hat is insufficient. Children must never dispute the word of the teacher. Whatever she says must be accepted respectfully, absolutely and without other comment than "Oui, Madame" or "Non, Madame." If the teacher is in error, it is up to her to discover the fact. A child must never contradict.

In all circumstances a child must "parler comme il faut," that is, he must speak clearly and directly. He must not talk to another child in the classroom without the teacher's permission. If he wants to speak to the teacher he should hold up one finger and wait patiently for her to recognize him. He should not at the same time wave his finger and call out in a loud whisper, " 'dame, 'dame!"

Children must also be careful "se tenir comme il faut" at all times. This means that they must sit up straight and keep their hands no lower than the level of the desk top. They must not slouch or drape themselves over their desk. When they stand they must stand erect, squarely on both feet, without leaning on the desk in front of them.

Neatness is another virtue that is stressed. Children have already learned to play without getting dirty; now they must learn to work neatly. They must not get ink on their hands or clothing or books. The papers they write must be free of blots and smudges. An arithmetic paper with the correct answers is unacceptable if the problems are not written neatly. Finger prints and careless writing are an infraction almost as serious as a wrong answer.

The teachers try to maintain a high standard of personal cleanliness among the children, but home conditions beyond their control sometimes frustrate their efforts. If a child is always dirty they do what they can to teach him to keep himself clean, taking care not to criticize his parents. Only if the dirt is a menace to the health of the other children will they remonstrate with the parents. Of course, if a child is ill he is sent home at once. Running noses and coughs, however, are accepted as part of the normal winter condition.

The children are taught that needless daring is not a virtue. Physical danger must be faced only when it cannot be avoided. The teachers stress this lesson not only because it is part of the code but also because they feel the weight of responsibility for the safety of the children at school. They enforce the safety rules rigorously. Children must not climb on walls or jump from high banks. They must not bring knives to school. They must not expose other children to danger. Rough games are avoided. If two children start to fight they are separated, and both of them are punished, regardless of who started the fight and regardless of who was "in the right." Complete tolerance is shown to verbal attacks, but physical aggression is taboo.

If a child is hurt he tries to hide the pain. At recess one afternoon Jules Marchal jumped from a wall and hurt his arm. Everyone crowded around, but little pity was shown in spite of the fact that Jules was obviously in pain. He was used, rather, as an object lesson to remind the other children that they often get hurt when they disobey the rules. To minimize the criticism he was receiving from both teachers and children, Jules pretended he was not really hurt. He smiled and started to play, but his face was white and he was unsteady on his feet. He stayed at school the rest of the afternoon and discovered only that evening, when his parents took him to the doctor, that his arm was broken. A child in Jules' predicament learns to keep his feelings to himself. Expressing them only exposes him to criticism. I do not mean to imply that Madame Vernet felt no personal sympathy for Jules, in this case, incidentally. Her pity was simply overshadowed by her desire to prevent a recurrence of such an accident and the desire to clear herself of the responsibility for this mishap.

The worst sin of all — that is, the worst sin that could conceivably be committed by a schoolchild — is dishonesty, dishonesty in the form of either lying or stealing. For both these offenses a child is severely punished. If it is proven that a child has knowingly and maliciously taken an object which does not belong to him, he is even more severely punished.

I observed and heard of very few cases of dishonesty among the children, however. Two of the children were said to be habitual cheaters at school, and they were frequently punished. The only sensational case of dishonesty I knew of was that of one of the youngest girls, whose father came to school one day and told Madame Girard that she had taken forty francs from his purse. When she was questioned she denied having done it. The father then went to the store and asked Monsieur Reynard if she had been there. Monsieur Reynard said that she had come in that morning to buy forty francs' worth of chewing gum. This girl received the most severe punishment given at the school during the year. No doubt her punishment at home was even more severe.

This instance of collaboration between home and school in the enforcement of the social code is typical. The parents welcome the cooperation of the teachers and complain only if the teachers are insufficiently harsh. In general, they say that the teachers are more successful in disciplining the children than they, the parents, are. Times have changed, they say. When *they* were children they feared their parents and would not dare to offend them. Now, they say, children are impolite. They disobey their parents and insult them with impunity. Only the teachers can discipline them.

To an American, however, the children of Peyrane seem incredibly well behaved. They are courteous, docile, gentle, coöperative, respectful. They seem deficient in daring, but on the other hand there is no malicious destruction of property by gangs of children. They are cruel-tongued to their equals, but they are gentle and patient with children younger than they. Above all they have a sense of dignity and social poise. Regardless of what complaining parents say, the children of Peyrane appear to accept the social yoke that is placed on them. The teachers rarely have to punish a serious infraction. Their principal disciplinary efforts are directed toward insisting on courtesy and neatness, and toward repressing restlessness and talking out of turn.

The directives of the Department of National Education expressly forbid the infliction of physical pain as a punishment of children. There is no conflict between this injunction and the attitude of the teachers, or even of the parents, of Peyrane, for they seem to find physical punishment neither desirable nor effective. Madame Girard, when she is pushed to the limit of her patience, may give a spank on the buttocks or she may tug a child's hair or tweak his ear, but this is only incidental to the official punishment she is about to give.

Usually there is an attempt to make the punishment appropriate to the offense. If a child's fault lies in insufficient work, he is made to do extra work. If his work is careless he has to do it over again until it is done properly. This usually means that he has to make up work outside of regular school hours — during recess, after school, or on Thursday when the school is closed. A child may even be asked to go to the teacher's house to make up work on Sunday. This punishment means, of course, that the child is deprived of playtime or that he is unable to do chores expected of him at home. This, in turn, means that he will receive another punishment at home.

The punishment for restlessness in class might also be called appropriate. One afternoon when I went to school during recess I saw only

the four-year-olds and the older children in the playground. When I
asked Madame Girard where her five- and six-year-olds were, she said,
"They were naughty after lunch. They fidgeted so much that I kept
them in at recess." I looked in the classroom and saw the "little ones"
all sitting at their desks with their hands folded in front of them. They
were having no recess, and it was an hour and a half before school
would be dismissed. However, they grasped at a straw. When they saw
me they jumped to their feet and chorused, "Bonjour, Monsieur" so
politely that Madame Girard relented and let them go out on the playground for the remaining few minutes. Perhaps she, too, welcomed
this way out, for it is against the regulations to deprive children of
recess.

The most usual punishment and apparently the most effective one
lies in shaming a child by isolating him and pitting the rest of his
society against him. Every effort is made to make him feel ridiculous
or guilty in the eyes of others. Minor infractions bring forth a stream
of mocking criticism from the teacher as she calls on the rest of the
class to bear witness to the misbehavior. If a visitor is present the
teacher includes him in the jury.

Since I was at school so frequently I was pressed into jury service
more often than I wished. A scene that took place in Madame Vernet's
room one day after she had given a dictation was typical. I arrived just
as she was going over the children's papers.

"Ah, Monsieur, you arrive just at the right moment," she said. "Just
look at this dictation of Laure Voisin. Have you ever seen anything
so careless, so untidy? Six mistakes in three lines, and an ink smudge
to end it with!"

She was speaking to me, but her eyes were flashing at Laure who sat
staring at her desk.

"Just look, Monsieur," she went on. "She wrote *ses* instead of *c'est*,
so the sentence has no meaning at all. Stupid! It's only stupidity — and
I used to think she was fairly intelligent."

She paused for these remarks to sink in.

"And lazy. Maybe she could do good work if she wants to. But, no,
she prefers to sit there and dream! And to think that this girl insists
on presenting herself for the *certificat primaire*! I wouldn't shame the
school or her parents by letting her try. What candidate could pass who
writes *ses* instead of *c'est* on a dictation?"

The other children laughed mockingly. I would have preferred to be elsewhere. Laure winced and tears came.

"That's right. Now you cry. As though that would help you. It's not by crying that you'll learn to write a dictation. No, you will stay in after school and we shall do that dictation over until you do it right."

A child is also effectively ashamed if his performance, which should be good but is not, is compared with the performance of another child which is better than might be expected. Madame Druetta's class was practicing the multiplication tables one day. Marie Bourgues was one of the good pupils in the class, but she was weak on the multiplication tables.

"What is seven times nine, Marie?"

"I don't know, Madame."

"Ah! She doesn't know seven times nine. Everyone in this class knows that. Class, what is seven times nine?"

The class roared the answer.

"You see, Marie, everyone in the room knew but you. Do you know seven times eight?"

"........"

"No, of course, she doesn't. Aren't you ashamed? Even Alain Jouvaud knows seven times eight, and he's been out of school sick for a month. What is seven times eight, Alain?"

"Fifty-six, Madame."

"You see, Marie. Even Alain knew, and he's not as intelligent as you, either. You haven't worked on this or you'd know it. Have you?"

"Non, Madame."

"Well, you stay in here during recess and learn the table of sevens, and if you don't learn it then you can stay in after school. Do you understand?"

"Oui, Madame."

Since Johany Wylie knew no French when he entered Madame Girard's class she found him a convenient shaming instrument. When another child failed to learn something which Johany had learned she could always say: "You see, even Johany knows that, and only a few months ago he didn't even know French!" (The name "Johany" was Madame Girard's own version of Jonathan.)

A child's shame may be increased by exposing his guilt to a larger group. Madame Vernet may go to the door and call Madame Girard into her classroom to witness a particularly deplorable recitation. The situation may be extended even beyond the school. One day Alphonse Peretti turned in a *copie* which was full of errors, carelessly written, and covered with smudges. Later in the day he was sent with a group of children to Catechism at the church. The church is at the top of the hill; the school is at the bottom, so the children had to go through the whole village to reach the church. Before Alphonse left the school, Marame Vernet pinned the *copie* to his back so that his guilt would be exposed to the attention and mockery of everyone who saw him on the street. The villagers can be counted on to coöperate.

The little girl who took forty francs from her father's purse to buy chewing gum was punished by having pinned on her back a big sign saying VOLEUSE. During recess she was forced to walk in a circle around the playground while the other children were encouraged to run after her, taunting her and crying "Thief! Thief!" This was the most severe case of shaming which I observed.

For minor infractions a child is usually put *au piquet*, a punishment which combines mild social ridicule with immobilization in an awkward position. The child kneels a few inches away from the wall at the front of the room, places his forehead against the wall and remains there with his hands folded on top of his head until the punishment is ended. The children consider the *piquet* punishment more severe when, instead of kneeling, the child is asked to stand with his forehead against the wall and with his hands on his head. To increase the ridicule and shame of punishment the teacher may have the culprit spend the recess quarter-hour walking around a small circle on the schoolground with his hands folded on his head. It is not unusual during recess to see six or eight children being punished together, walking round and round in a circle with their hands atop their heads, stoically accepting the taunts that other children may shout at them from time to time.

Being put *au piquet* is a punishment primarily for the four-, five-, and six-year-old children. The prevalence of this punishment in Madame Girard's classroom may to a degree be attributed to the personality of Madame Girard, but it may also be attributed to the fact that the younger children are naturally more restless and less accustomed to discipline that the older children in Madame Vernet's and Madame Druetta's classrooms. By the time the children have been promoted to higher grades they have accepted the discipline imposed on them.

If, however, an older child forgets his dignity and reverts to misbehavior more typical of smaller children, he is shamed by being punished as though he were still a small child. One day in Madame Vernet's
class Odette and Alphonse Peretti seemed unable to keep from talking
to each other. Madame Vernet reprimanded them several times, but
they persisted. Finally she told them they were acting like babies, and
she sent them to Madame Girard's classroom where they were put
au piquet beside five-year-old Léon Pascal, who was being punished.

A child being punished can expect no pity from any quarter. Neither
tears nor a face twisted in distress arouse sympathy. To the contrary,
tears may release a new torrent of sarcastic remarks from the teacher
and mocking epithets from the children. The underdog arouses no pity
if he is being justly punished. Even his parents participate in the re-
crimination unless, as we have seen, the child can show that the teacher
has unjustly accused him or discriminated against him. If a punishment
is equitably inflicted, the child stands completely alone. What solace he
can find he must find within himself.

Outside of school and away from adult supervision the children as a
group appear to accept the responsibility of maintaining the social code.
Joseph Mariano has been mentioned several times because he seems to
reject almost every point in the code and is consequently the child most
punished in school. Outside of class when the children are playing in
the streets they continue to shame Joseph Mariano and to outlaw him
as the teacher does in school.

They obviously enjoy singling out an individual and shaming him
when his behavior is unacceptable, even in the slightest degree. A child
who forgets to wipe his running nose will find his playmates howling
at him: "Uuuuuuuuu, Uuuuuuuuu, Uuuuuuuuu, la chandelle, la chandelle!" and taunting him with their forefinger and middle finger
crooked to imitate the stream pouring from his nose. (*La chandelle*
means candle. The child's nose is dripping like a candle.)

When the teacher is forced to leave the schoolroom she often appoints
a child to police the room. On her return the observer faithfully makes
his report, and she punishes culprits without hesitating. The other children, even the culprits, accept this procedure and seem to harbor no
resentment against the informer. The child who informs spontaneously
on his fellows, however, without having had the responsibility placed
on him by the teacher, is subject to the disapproval of the other chil-

dren. One of the most infuriating insults a child can fling at another during a quarrel is *mouchard* (stoolpigeon). The teacher also discourages the telltale as a matter of principle and because sometimes the telltale forces her to punish misbehavior which she would prefer to ignore. The self-appointed informer who receives as thanks only the most barbed remarks of the teacher learns that it is better not to get involved with those in authority.

The child who is asked by the teacher to proctor the room during her absence is usually one of the teacher's pets. The teachers say they avoid favoring any child, but the children and the children's parents to whom I talked were surprised that I should even ask if the teachers had pets. Of course teachers have pets, they said! Teachers always have pets! Teachers have natural likes and dislikes as everyone else does. It would be silly to expect them to treat all the children exactly alike.

Because it seems inevitable that some children should be favored, little resentment is harbored against the teachers' pets. So long as a teacher distributes punishments justly and impartially, no one objects if she singles out a few pupils to whom she grants special favors. Favors are not necessarily a part of the official system of punishments and rewards. They may or may not be related to virtue and justice. They are often granted simply on the basis of indefinable and rather mysterious personal tastes. Instead of showing resentment toward a favored child, the other children may even join with the teacher in favoring him.

During the year that he was a pupil in the school of Peyrane, Johany Wylie was granted preferential treatment to an unusual degree. We pleaded with the teachers to treat him exactly as they treated all the children, but our pleas accomplished nothing. He was allowed to roam around the school at will. If he got bored sitting at his desk in Madame Girard's room, he went into Madame Vernet's room to sit next to Odette Peretti, the older girl he had adopted as his foster mother in the school. Madame Vernet allowed her to interrupt her lessons "to amuse Johany." Madame Girard usually chose him to check on the behavior of the other children while she was out of the room. The other children did what they could to increase his preferential treatment. They let him take their place at the head of the line. They brought him chewing gum and candy. The older boys let him join their games, and they played with him gently. The older girls mothered him and cuddled him as much as he would allow.

This case of favoritism was extreme, of course. No child of Peyrane could ever have hoped to receive this treatment. Johany was outside the system, and the rules did not apply to him. He was not expected to grow up in Peyrane so there was no need to force him into the pattern. The teachers felt no responsibility for the future of Johany as a citizen of the village. The children did not see in him a competitor. Their parents did not see in his freedom from discipline an insult to their family dignity. All felt that they could, without qualms and without criticism, follow their strong but usually frustrated inclination to spoil little children.

This feeling was intensified by the fact that Johany was considered a guest in Peyrane and must therefore be accorded privileges which the inhabitants deny themselves. As an American child, he was an exotic guest who aroused unusual interest. Finally, as a foreign child, he aroused the missionary zeal of the teachers. When I complained to Madame Vernet about his preferential treatment, she always said:

"Oh, Monsieur, he's with us only a few months. That's not long for us to teach him to speak French. If he doesn't have a good time in school he might not come. And we want him to love France and have good memories of it."

Johany was obviously a very special case. No amount of insistence on the part of his parents could make him fit into the regular framework of school discipline. To accomplish this we should have had to settle in Peyrane as permanent residents.

Children who are not teachers' pets may receive recognition and privileges by earning them through the official system of rewards, called the *système des bons points*. A *bon point* is usually a little colored print of some object — a flower, an animal, a provincial costume, etc. — of the type traditionally called *image d'Epinal*. Chocolate-candy manufacturers often package these prints as prizes, and they are printed in series so that children may be induced to collect complete series to paste in an album. The teachers may buy the prints in wholesale lots from an *imagerie*, a printing house specializing in these pictures.

According to this system of rewards, a child is presented a *bon point* for each meritorious act. He saves his *bons points*, and when he has received twenty of them he is entitled to receive a special prize. For the younger children the prize is usually a piece of candy, but by the time children are six years old they are considered big enough to be awarded "something more serious." Then they are allowed to go check the time by the town clock, to carry a message to one of the teachers, to distribute papers for the day. They may have their name written in a special notebook in which Madame Girard records unusual rewards of merit. In Madame Vernet's room the virtuous child's name is recorded on the weekly Honor List posted on the board.

The teachers say that the *système des bons points* effectively motivates children to do their best to surpass the comrades in both intellectual and social behavior. To the observer, however, it seems that there are two rewards which are still more effective in motivating the children to attain the high intellectual and social standards set for them.

The unusually intelligent and ambitious child is rewarded by his feeling of pride. A higher level of performance is expected of him, and the teacher devotes more time and effort to teaching him individually than to the other children. He receives no softer words and no more praise than they, because the level of the teacher's expectation is always fixed a little higher than the level of his actual performance. He receives no more extra favors than other children. He even has to spend more time studying than they, because more is expected of him. He is set apart from other children. The teachers, his parents, and the children tell him that he is more intelligent than they, and they place more responsibility on him. In family council it has been formally decided that if he lives up to expectations he will be sent away to learn a trade or prepare to enter a profession or government work. To accomplish this ambition the family must make financial sacrifices of which the child is made keenly aware. Responsibility has been placed on him in such a way that there is no escaping it, and he is constantly reminded of it by the teachers and his parents. This pressure supplies ample motivation for him to do his best to succeed in school.

This sort of motivation is completely lacking to the other children, of course. They have no lofty ambitions. The average child knows that he is not especially intelligent; he has been told so often enough by his teachers and by his parents. It would not occur to him to envy the brightest pupil, for it would not be *raisonnable* to entertain ambitions which obviously could not be realized. On the other hand, he knows he is not stupid and that he can get along in life.

Jacques Leporatti was considered an average student, just intelligent enough so that with great effort he passed the Primary Certificate exams. When I asked him why he worked so hard at his lessons his reply was prompt and forthright:

"Pour qu'on me laisse tranquille!" ("So people will leave me alone!")

For Jacques and for most of the children of the school the most sub-stantial reward for good behavior and hard work lies in *not* bringing shame to themselves and to their family, in *not* being punished, in *not* being saddled with avoidable responsibilities. They know that if their performance is satisfactory they will be left to themselves to enjoy the normal routine of life with a minimum of interference from Authority of any kind. This may seem a negative, uncreative kind of gratification, but to the average child it is sufficient.

The best pupils, like Georges Vincent, leave Peyrane when they are twelve years old to continue their studies in a more advanced school in the city. The poor pupils, like Jacqueline Favre, drop out of school without formalities on their fourteenth birthday. If a child is sufficiently intelligent, however, and if he is willing to work hard he is groomed to become a candidate for the *certificat d'études primaires*. This certificate, framed and hung in the *salle* (the kitchen-living-room), will bring honor to his family and will be a source of pride for him the rest of his life. Its possession brings practical advantages, too, for it is the minimum educational requirement for any kind of government position and for many other types of employment. A child of fourteen may not be interested in the kind of work requiring the Primary Certificate, but who knows? Perhaps some day for some rea-son he may want to qualify for the position of postman. If the Cer-tificate can be obtained with only extra hard work it is better to try for it as a hedge against the future.

For Madame Vernet, the Primary Certificate Examination is pro-fessionally the most important event of the year. The villagers and to a certain degree her colleagues and superiors judge her ability as a teacher on the performance of her candidates at the examination. It is given at Gordes, the *chef-lieu* of the canton seven miles from Peyrane. It is administered by Monsieur Valentini, the Primary Inspector, with the aid of primary school teachers called in from other cantons. Thus the candidates from Peyrane are placed in competition with candidates from all the other primary schools of the canton, and their work is evaluated by judges living outside the canton. The whole situation is beyond the control of the local teachers. Whether the candidates will bring shame or honor to Madame Vernet depends entirely on the candidates themselves.

Consequently Madame Vernet, like all the teachers of the Concluding Course of Primary Schools, is preoccupied with the question of which students to sponsor as candidates. Her sponsorship is not essential. A student may present himself as a candidate independently, but if Madame Vernet believes that he is likely to disgrace himself and her at the examination it is unlikely that he will persist in the face of her opposition.

In the spring of 1951 Madame Vernet chose as students likely to succeed Jules Marchal, Félix Raboul, and Jacques Leporatti. Laure Voisin also insisted on being a candidate, and although Madame Vernet told her she had no chance of passing the examination Laure could not be dissuaded. Madame Vernet grudgingly included her in the group, insisting that there was no hope but offering to help her as best she could.

The examination was to take place at the end of May, and during April and May, Madame Vernet devoted most of her time and effort to tutoring her three candidates and Laure Voisin. They were assigned extra lessons. Jules and Jacques stopped coming to my English class. The group stayed on at school after four o'clock almost every day for an hour or more. They went to Madame Vernet's apartment for tutoring sessions on Thursday and on Sunday. They were excused from chores at home so that they might spend all their free time studying.

The nature of the examination is specifically defined by the Department of National Education. It consists of a four-hour written examination in the morning followed by a two-hour oral examination in the afternoon. The subject matters and grading system are specified as follows:

WRITTEN EXAMINATION

Subject	*To pass, a candidate must get a grade of at least:*
I. Dictation, followed by questions on: 1. General understanding of the text 2. Grammar 3. Explanation of difficult words	10 out of a possible perfect grade of 20

II. Mathematics
   1. Geometry
   2. Arithmetic   } 10 out of 20
   3. Metric System

III. Composition
   1. A letter on a given subject   } 5 out of 10 on composition
   2. A free subject   } 2½ out of 5 on penmanship

ORAL EXAMINATION

Subject	To pass, a candidate must get a grade of at least:	
I. Geography	2½ out of 5	The candidate must
II. History	2½ out of 5	get a total of 10
III. Sciences	5 out of 10	points in this group
IV. Mental Calculation	No points given, but must be acceptable	
V. Drawing (for boys) Sewing (for girls)	No points given, but must be acceptable	
VI. Reading aloud, recitation, or singing	No points given, but must be acceptable	

To pass the examination the candidate must receive a total of at least forty points, so that he may get a low grade in one subject and catch up in another — provided, of course, that he receives at least the minimum grade in each subject. The examiners have the right to waive the rules and make a special decision in extraordinary cases, but such exceptions are rarely made. All the people I questioned about the examination — teachers, parents, and children — agree that the examiners and examination are severe but fair. There is no need to make special exceptions; a child who fails to pass does not deserve to pass.

Madame Vernet does not, of course, know the exact questions which are to be asked on the examination, but from her experience as teacher and examiner (since she is called to proctor exams in other cantons) she knows the kind of question which is usually asked. She knows the usual mistakes that are made. She knows which mistakes are passed over tolerantly and which ones are catastrophic to the chances of a candidate. She knows, for instance, that to write *ses* for *c'est* on a dictation may mean failure, whereas other mistakes may not even be counted. There are other peculiarities she is aware of. She knows that a student strong in arithmetic but weak in composition has a better

chance of passing than a student weak in arithmetic and strong in composition, because a perfect grade may be given in arithmetic, but a composition is never given a perfect grade. She knows that a child who
does well in French and Mathematics is almost never failed regardless
of his performance in the oral examination.

It is with all these points in mind that Madame Vernet drills her
candidates for the last few weeks before the examination. Each child
has weaknesses peculiar to him, some of which do not matter and some
of which are particularly vulnerable. If the weakness is too great to
overcome, then the child must be drilled in his strong subjects so that
he may pick up enough points in them to make up for his deficiencies.

On the morning of the examination two carloads of people left Peyrane at seven o'clock and went down the hill on the little road toward
Gordes. Jules Marchal was riding with his parents in their 1923 Renault.
In my car were Madame Vernet, Jacques Leporatti, Laure Voisin and
her mother. A few kilometers from Peyrane we stopped and picked
up the Raboul family who were accompanying Félix. I was surprised
that so many parents make the effort to go with their children to the
examination, for in most cases it is a serious economic sacrifice to give
up a day's work. Yet, of the parents of our four candidates only the
Leporattis, the poorest of all, stayed at home. When I asked Monsieur
Marchal why so many parents came he said:

"*Qu'est-ce que vous voulez?* Jules asked us to come. He said he'd
feel more sure of himself if we were there. And even if I had stayed
at home I'd have been too upset to work."

The ordeal of the child is the ordeal of the family. Each child knows
this. He bears the weight of the family dignity on his shoulders.

When we stopped to pick up the Rabouls we rearranged ourselves
in the cars so that all the parents were in Monsieur Marchal's car and
the four candidates were with Madame Vernet in my car. She wanted
to get them together with her for the last few minutes so that she could
go over the situation again with them. As we drove along she talked
with each child, warning him against the mistakes he usually made,
and drilling them all on points which were sure, she felt, to be included
in any examination.

When we arrived at Gordes, the *place* was full of cars, and the schoolyard was filled with parents, teachers, and children standing quietly in
little groups, too tense to carry on a normal conversation. Finally, at

eight o'clock Monsieur Valentini clapped his hands, and the candidates and examiners filed into the classrooms. The parents drifted out of the schoolyard. The mothers sat down in little groups on steps in the *place* and brought out their handwork. Some of the fathers took advantage of the trip to Gordes to carry out business; others gathered in the café. The teachers who were not serving as examiners remained in the schoolyard and sat talking in little groups.

A few minutes before ten o'clock the parents were all back in the schoolyard waiting for the children to emerge for their fifteen-minute recess. The bell rang, and they came out, blinking their eyes in the mid-morning sun. Their mothers gave them bread and chocolate, and Madame Vernet gathered the children around her to find out what questions they had been asked and how they had answered. She tried to evaluate the work of each child so that he might know if he had made enough points to give him a safe margin or if he had done so poorly that he would have to be particularly careful in the rest of the test. As the children left to go back to the examination she reminded them of pitfalls they should avoid the rest of the morning.

At twelve o'clock the parents were back again to take their children off for a picnic lunch and a rest until the oral examination began at two o'clock. I went with the teachers and examiners to the special lunch that had been prepared at the village inn. Monsieur Valentini did not come with us. When I asked one of the teachers why he was not included, she said:

"We like each other, but we don't feel comfortable together."

The situation at the lunch was already somewhat awkward because the examiners and the teachers of the candidates were thrown together. There was banter and professional gossip during the meal, but several of the teachers also talked quietly and earnestly with the examiners sitting next to them. Before lunch Madame Vernet had apologized for not sitting next to me, for she said that she wanted to take advantage of the opportunity to speak to a friend of hers. Later she explained that the friend was a teacher from a neighboring canton who was serving as examiner. The following week Madame Vernet was to serve as examiner in that canton. During the lunch she had tried to find out how the candidates from Peyrane were faring, but she did not try to probe too indiscreetly, for she knew that the next week the roles would be reversed.

At two o'clock everyone assembled in the schoolyard again, and the oral examination began. By four o'clock the written examinations had all been graded and the oral examinations had ended. The parents and children and teachers waited nervously outside while Monsieur Valentini met with the examiners. Finally he emerged, carrying under his arm the Certificates, each bearing his signature and the name of a successful candidate. He stood in the middle of the schoolyard and called off the names. One at a time the children came forward and were given their Certificates. There was no applause, no word of congratulation, no handshake. When Monsieur Valentini had finished I could recognize the successful candidates and their families only by the smiles on their faces.

There was a smile on the face of the children who had failed, too, but it was a frozen smile that did not conceal the tears in their eyes. Of the candidates from Peyrane only Laure Voisin had failed, just as Madame Vernet had predicted for several weeks. Madame Voisin was standing near Laure, but neither she nor anyone else made any effort to console the girl. When I moved over toward her, patted her on the shoulder, and tried to say a few consoling words, she looked at me in so bewildered a manner that I felt awkward and left her alone with her disappointment.

On the way back to Peyrane, Madame Vernet, Jacques Leporatti, Madame Voisin, and Laure were in my car. Madame Vernet and Jacques scarcely spoke a word. Madame Voisin talked most of the time. Her eyes were filled with tears as were Laure's. She was as disappointed as her daughter, but the emotions that she felt were turned against Laure. Laure had failed, said Madame Voisin, only because she had not worked hard enough. When her mother and father had tried to get her to study she had sat at a back table in her father's café dreaming with Jacqueline Favre and playing "Babyfoot" with the older boys. It was not the fault of her parents. And it was not the fault of Madame Vernet, who had certainly done her best to keep Laure from disgracing herself. It was Laure's fault and she was getting only what she deserved. It was only too bad that through her laziness she had disgraced her parents. Laure made no attempt to reply to her mother.

The month of June is one of the busiest months in the village and on the farm. The children who have taken the Primary Certificate Examination, now that they have in effect finished their schooling, could usefully be put to work at home. Nevertheless, they continue to go to school until the classes end on the Fourteenth of July. The hard work at school is finished, but the Prize Day Program is approaching. The three teachers spend most of the time in the *Salle des Fêtes* with the children of the school practicing songs, recitations and skits for the program. Laure Voisin did not come back to school after the examination, but Jules Marchal, Jacques Leporatti, and Félix Raboul were there every day. Their families were willing to sacrifice a worker needed at home in order to have their child — a child who had received his Primary Certificate — represent them in the Prize Day Program.

Chapter 5

Adolescence

The few weeks between the Primary Certificate Examination in June and the Prize Day Program in July were pleasant ones for Jules Marchal and Jacques Leporatti. No serious work was expected of them at school. At home they had only their chores. Their parents spoiled them, and people in the village complimented them. For the first time since they started to school they were under no pressure.

Félix Raboul shared in the honor, but he was unable to stop work and have a good time like Jules and Jacques. His school record was unusually good, and since Madame Vernet assured his parents that he was intelligent enough to go on with school, it had been decided that he was to become a skilled mechanic. So Félix spent the month of June preparing for the entrance examination given in July at the technical school at Sorgues.

Félix was not alone. Georges Vincent, the only child of the restaurant owner, was also preparing for the examination. He was thirteen years old and normally would have another year at the Peyrane school, but if he passed the entrance examination, he could transfer at once to the technical school without his Primary Certificate. His parents and Madame Vernet decided that he should try, for he ought not lose time in getting started on a career of civil engineering.

In July, when Félix and Georges took the entrance examination they both passed, and the following October they left Peyrane. If they were successful in their work at the Sorgues technical school, they would never come back to Peyrane except to visit. Every year their work would get harder as competition became more severe. Life would be lonely for them. However, if they succeeded in getting ahead, they would bring honor to their family and would also be able to contribute financial support which would more than equal the sacrifices the family had made for them.

Every year, two or three of the most intelligent and ambitious chil-

dren leave Peyrane to continue their studies. The only ones who return
to live in Peyrane are those who fail in their schooling. Then they return home in disgrace. Félix and Georges have before them the example of Edouard Pascal, the intellectual who failed and now can only
help his aunt run her little grocery.

For the children who are not sufficiently intelligent or ambitious to
go away to school, life suddenly becomes enjoyable and simple after
they have reached the age of fourteen. They are no longer children.
They are young people, and only two things are expected of the young
people of Peyrane: to support themselves and to have a good time.
They will have no other obligations until they become sufficiently
sérieux to settle down and establish a household of their own. The five
or ten years between school and marriage are relatively free, free of
the harsh discipline of school which the young people have left behind
them, free of the family responsibilities they will eventually have thrust
upon them. This is the period of life which the people of Peyrane call
"the happiest years of one's existence."

How to earn a living is no problem for the average child like Jules
Marchal. The day after the Prize Program, which ended his schooling,
he went to work on the farm of his father. There was no sudden break
between school and work, for Jules had always worked with his father
when he was not in school. Now he worked with him all the time, just
as he had expected to do when he finished school.

A few months before, Jules' class had been asked to write a theme
telling how their great-grandparents, their grandparents, and their parents earned their living, how their father chose his livelihood, how he
prepared for it, what the children themselves planned to do and how
they would prepare for it. This was Jules' theme:

My great-grandparents were farmers. My grandparents were farmers. My
parents are farmers. My father decided to be a farmer because he liked it
and because he didn't know how to do anything else. He learned to farm by
working in the fields with his father. I shall be a farmer, too, because I like
it. I am learning to be a farmer by helping my father in the fields. Whenever
he does some kind of work, I ask him to let me do it, too.

The attachment of Jules' family to farming has no basis in a romantic attachment to a single, specific plot of land, to a farm that has been
in the family for generations. The Marchals own no land. For three

generations at least they have been *fermiers*, working land that belongs
to other people in different parts of the Vaucluse. Their attachment is
to an occupation rather than to the land. In the themes they wrote on
this subject in school, the children of *fermiers* and *métayers* made the
same reply, generally speaking, as the children of landowning farmers.
They expected to be farmers like their fathers.

Most of the children of artisans, shopkeepers, and laborers also said
that they intended to continue in the occupation of their parents. Even
Jacques Leporatti, an intelligent boy with his Primary Certificate, expected to go to work in the ochre mine with his father, Aldo Leporatti,
one of the poorest men of the commune. This was Jacques' theme:

> My father works as an ochre miner. He chose this trade because at Peyrane
> there is not much work, and when he came to France he did not know any-
> one so he chose this trade. He learned this trade by meeting some men of
> Peyrane who worked in the ochre mine.
>
> My parents expect me to work in the ochre or else to work in the country
> with the farmers.

You could not say that it was Jacques' ambition to be an ochre miner;
it was rather his normal expectation. He was going to become a miner
because that seemed the natural thing for him to do. In spite of his
intelligence, in spite of his Primary Certificate, he would become a
laborer. If he had gone to the Departmental Orientation Center in
Avignon, he might have secured free, professional advice concerning
the way he might best earn a living, but his family — like the other
families — are unaware of this service. Whether they would avail themselves of it if they knew about it is questionable, of course.

The possibility of working on a farm, which Jacques mentions in
his theme, was a new idea to him. When I asked him about it, he reminded me of what had just happened to his older brother, Paul. Paul
had worked in the ochre mine since he was fifteen. (Families can continue to receive a government allowance for a child until he is fifteen
if he does not have a regular job, so no child takes a regular job "officially" until his fifteenth birthday.) A month before Jacques wrote his
theme a strike of ochre workers had been called. His father and brother,
Aldo and Paul, were thrown out of work. Aldo fell back on his supplementary livelihood — raising call birds to sell to hunters. Paul was able
to get temporary work on the Marnas farm since the asparagus season

was at its height. When the strike ended, Monsieur Marnas, who was old and ill, offered to keep Paul on indefinitely. So chance offered Paul the opportunity he would not have sought, and the younger brother, Jacques, got the idea that a future in the ochre mines was less inevitable than it had seemed.

Jacques might not be so lucky as Paul in finding a job outside the ochre mines, however, for few jobs are open in Peyrane to young people who cannot go to work with their parents. There are ninety-two farms in the commune. They are small, and family labor suffices to run them. There are only twelve hired hands on the farms of Peyrane.

There are other openings occasionally. Now and then the tractor coöperative takes an adolescent to drive a tractor, but the permanent employee is a young married man. The mushroom caves employ six men; two of them are adolescents. Simon Jouvaud, the mason and builder, employs six men, but only one of them is an adolescent. Even the ochre mines do not employ many men — only fourteen in the commune of Peyrane; but a young man can find a job in a mine in the adjoining commune and still live at home. The farms, the caves, the mines, and house construction are the only industries offering work to the young people of Peyrane.

The artisans and tradesmen have no jobs to offer. They barely support their families. Occasionally Biron, the butcher, needs someone to help him on his rounds in his truck, but he always calls on Mario Fratani. Mario lives in Biron's house and can be paid off in rent and meat instead of money. The tailor, Avenas, has an apprentice — Paul Rivet, the deaf-mute son of the Town Clerk — but this is not the regular sort of employment open to an adolescent in Peyrane.

Henri Rivet, Paul's older brother, is directly confronted by this difficulty which faces the young people whose parents have no farm or family business in which they can work. Henri is strong, healthy, pleasant, intelligent, in a word, highly employable, but he has had only odd jobs since he finished school five years ago. He has worked on farms at harvest time. He has worked for a few weeks at a time in the ochre mines. Whenever the Town of Peyrane has work, his father gives it to Henri. He worked on the town roads and on the census. He worked for several months as substitute postman, and now he is working on a cadastral survey. But Henri cannot continue working indefinitely at odd jobs. When he finishes his military service, the family

will have to reach a decision about his future, and it is assumed that
he will have to go to Marseille to find a job. He wants to stay in Peyrane, and his family would like him to stay, but, since he is not interested in farming or mining there is nothing to attract him. The Rivets,
like other families, constantly complain that they are losing their children because Peyrane has no work for them.

When one first arrives in Peyrane and meets the Jules Marchals and
Jacques Leporattis who are following the professional tradition of their
parents, one gets an exaggerated impression of stability. He does not
see the many adolescents who have left home. The only time they are
seen in Peyrane are on the two traditional homecoming holidays, All
Saints Day and Whitsuntide. Then they come home to visit — Gilberte
Reynard from Marseille, Paulette Biron from Apt, Louis Pascal from
Avignon, Renée Bonerandi from Sorgues, and all the others who have
left home to work or study in the city.

At Whitsuntide when Jeanne Favre came home from Apt, where
she works in the hospital kitchen, her father — Léon — had news for
her. Monsieur Vincent and his wife needed a girl to help them run
their inn which was to receive honorable mention in the Michelin
Guide. Vincent had asked Léon Favre if Jeanne would not like to return to Peyrane to work at the inn. Léon gave Jeanne the news eagerly
but assured her the decision was hers to make. She decided against it.
When she had gone to Apt she had been lonely, but now she had friends
and enjoyed living there. She was treated well in the hospital, and she
did not mind the work. The family agreed it was too bad the job had
not been available earlier, but now it was too late.

It is usual for adolescent girls in Peyrane to have a job, although
often it is only a temporary arrangement to support themselves until
they are married. Of course, they do not all seek a paying job. Their
first duty is to their mother. If she needs help at home, the daughter
will stay with her and share the household tasks and the woman's work
on the farm. This work is considered especially appropriate, since by
helping run the household, a girl is preparing for her future adult role.

Even if a family does not need the assistance of the income of an
adolescent daughter, she must at least give the appearance of working
seriously. Marguerite Jouvaud, the only child of the mason, goes to Apt
twice a week to take sewing lessons. On other days she spends several
hours sewing under the direction of her great-aunt who is a seamstress.

Jeanne Bonnel, a wealthy farmer's daughter, goes seven miles to Bon-nieux three days a week to take the free course in sewing given by a government teacher. Louise Paul, a mine owner's daughter, serves as apprentice to Madame Avenas, the village hairdresser.

Of course, the children who take lessons earn no money. Neither do the boys who work on the farms with their father or the girls who work at home with their mother. But their financial situation is no different from that of the children who work for wages, since wages for adolescents are given not to the children but to their parents. Although adolescents are considered mature enough to earn money, they are not sufficiently *sérieux* to be entrusted with the money they earn.

No matter whether they work for the parents or work for wages, all adolescents are faced with the same situation: they have no money of their own. If their earnings are more than enough for their support, the excess goes not to them but to the household.

On the other hand, a father is duty bound to give his adolescent children enough money so that they may have a good time. Not only do adolescents expect spending money, but society demands that a father be generous with them. The niggardly father is criticized. Three years ago Robert Cavaud, the sixteen-year-old son of Paul Cavaud, ran away from home. He went to Marseille, got a job and lived there for months before the family peace was made so that he could return. Madame Borel, who told me about it, said, "What else could you expect? Paul wouldn't give him enough money to have a good time like the other young people, so he left. He wasn't to blame, *pécaïre.*"

If the people of Peyrane unanimously took the side of the rebel against his father in this case, it is because they believe it to be the right of a young person to have a good time. More than that, they believe it is the *duty* of a young person to have a good time. And it is the duty of their parents not only to tolerate, but to abet their adolescent children in the quest for pleasure. An adult who has in some way been deprived of pleasure during his adolescent years is considered to a degree an incomplete person. He is looked upon with pity, or even with suspicion.

Roger Prayal is the son of a blacksmith. He is twenty-five years old, friendly, intelligent, reliable, hard-working, and yet people criticize him because as an adolescent he was more reliable and hard-working than a young man should be. He never let loose and had a good time like Olivier Borel, Louis Pascal, and other boys his age. Adult behavior on the part of an adolescent is neither normal nor desirable.

Lucien Bourdin did not have a normal adolescence, either, but people pity him. It was not his fault that he did not have a good time. His father was killed in the first war, and Lucien had to go to work as soon as he left school to support his mother and grandmother. By the time he was twenty-five his farm was prosperous, and he was well enough off to enjoy a brief period of belated adolescence. Then came the second war, and Lucien ended up in a prison camp in Germany where he stayed for five years. On his return home he found his farm run down and his savings destroyed through inflation; he had to start over again. He is now thirty-five, still unmarried, and considered peculiar. People attribute his peculiarity to the fact that he never had a good time like other young people.

Gaston Jouvaud is one of the most respected adults in Peyrane. Through hard work and intelligence he has become the principal mason in the commune and has six men working under him. He was not always so *sérieux*, however. Marie Fratani said that ten years ago no one thought he could settle down. He and his crony, Guy Vidal, were the terrors of the town. Then Jouvaud married Gina Pian, built his own house, and now he is one of the most serious men in Peyrane.

Gaston Jouvaud and Guy Vidal are normal adults. They went through their period of irresponsibility and have settled down. Their conduct has been normal, predictable, and therefore safe. Roger Prayal and Lucien Bourdin have never really had a good time. They might have within them passions still unexpressed which could burst out. They are not normal, predictable, and safe. The people of Peyrane do not say this, but the idea lies behind their insistence that young people *must* have a good time and that it is the duty of parents to provide means for their adolescent children to do so.

As soon as young people leave school they may take part in adult leisure activities. The boys and girls of fourteen are shy about participating, partly because they know that at first they will be teased. Sitting in the work-and-talk circles of the adult women and old men, adolescent girls have to learn not to be flustered by the sly remarks humorously associating them with likely or unlikely boys of the village. Boys, who until they finished school, have played card games only with other children at home or who have played boules only in the schoolyard may now take part in the belote tournament at the café on Saturday night or in the boule tournament on Sunday afternoon. They have played these games all through childhood and are as expert in them as most of the men, so they are at no technical disadvantage. If they lose, no one pays much attention, but if they win, the older men may kid them for days.

Philippe Aubenas and his partner, both fifteen years old, won the belote tournament one Saturday night and took home the prizes — enough thrushes for a family banquet. Philippe, who was the stronger member of his team, was at once nicknamed "Phili la Terreur" and was called "la Terreur" by all the men for several days. After a while the joking wore off and nothing was left but the admiration which all felt for him. If a boy proves to be good in a game, he is soon accepted as an equal by other men. They may even seek him out as a partner in preference to someone their own age.

Boys just out of school hesitate to go to the café by themselves, but by the time they are fifteen they feel as much at home there as the men. In the café the age groups mingle less than they do in games of boules and belote. Their interests and consequently their conversation tend to divide them into three groups: the old men, the mature men, and the adolescents. Conversation may spill over from one table to another, uniting groups in a general conversation temporarily, but when the conversation has ended, the groups turn back to their own interests. Boys fifteen or sixteen order their own drinks, but childhood patterns linger for they still prefer nonalcoholic fruit-syrup drinks. By the time they are seventeen or eighteen they will be following the adult pattern of drinking pastis or some other apéritif — except on days when they announce in an adult manner that their liver is upset, and that they are drinking only Vichy water.

Adults in Peyrane lament the fact that there is not more entertainment for young people. It is commonly recognized that the usual adult activities — work-and-talk circles, belote, boules, conversation in the café — offer amusement for serious adults but could not be expected to satisfy young people.

After the war a youth club, "Le Club des Jeunes," was organized. Officers were elected and it was decided that the group's main function would be to produce plays. The club soon disintegrated, for anyone who tried to take the initiative in a project was accused of trying to boss the others. The Communist members became angry and dropped out when they failed to elect their slate of officers. They claimed that the others dragged politics into the club by discriminating against Communist members. The non-Communists claimed that the Communists had tried to capture the organization so that they could make it serve the Communist Party. Everyone tired of bickering and the club died.

During the war Henri Viquier, a retired army sergeant who was acting as Town Clerk, had tried to organize a soccer team. Since many of the towns in the region have a soccer team, it seemed appropriate that Peyrane should have one. Besides, the Vichy government was encouraging local authorities to sponsor athletic activities in the hope that French youth might be strengthened physically and at the same time be diverted from political interests. Viquier persuaded the Town Council to pay for laying out a soccer field and constructing a dressing room with showers. Unfortunately, Viquier was at heart an army sergeant. He tried to discipline the boys as he would have disciplined a platoon of recruits. One day he slapped one of the younger married men who was late for practice. Everyone criticized him because "one does not treat the head of a family that way." The boys rejected Viquier, and the soccer team disintegrated. Viquier himself lost interest after the Allied landing in southern France. His own adolescent son ran off to join the Free French forces and was killed in battle a few days later.

The playing field and shower house remain as monuments to the soccer team. They have not been used since. Now and then someone decides that another attempt should be made to organize a team, but no one will take the responsibility for doing anything about it. Two years ago when a new grocery was opened by Monsieur Arène, a former semi-professional athlete, the mayor suggested to him that he might organize a team so that the facilities provided by the Town Council might be used. When Arène told me of the incident he said, "I didn't know the town very well then, but now I realize that I did well to refuse. No one will coöperate to get anything done around here. All I'd have gotten would have been criticism, and that wouldn't have been good for my business."

The only organized activity for adolescents that has a measure of success is dancing. There are two important dances in Peyrane every year. One is organized by the Volunteer Firemen, the other by the

Comité des Fêtes appointed by the mayor for the Michaelmas celebration. The Volunteer Firemen are not adolescents, but most of them are young bachelors who still enjoy dancing. At a dance they meet girls among whom they may find a sexual partner or even a wife. The firemen work hard to put on their dance and it is usually a success.

To manage the Michaelmas celebration, however, a new committee must be appointed every year. The mayor would prefer to see the same group function over a period of years, but he can never appoint a committee which will last. Anyone who shows initiative is accused by the others of trying to boss them, so by the time the celebration is over the Committee resigns, and the mayor must persuade a different group of people to take charge of the next year's celebration.

Arranging for the dances entails responsibility and hard work. First there must be a decision on the orchestra that will be asked to play. The Firemen usually try to hire a "big name" orchestra from Cavaillon; for the Michaelmas dance any orchestra will do since people will attend a free dance whether the orchestra is good or not. Once the date and the orchestra have been chosen the Committee must worry about publicity. An item is sent in to the Marseille newspapers so that it may be printed in the Vaucluse edition. Arrangements are made with a job printer in Apt for handbills and posters. When they are ready, the Committee delegates two or three members with cars or motorcycles to go around the countryside posting them on walls and in cafés. Bus companies serving the region must be told to send special buses through the surrounding communities the night of the dance to bring people who have no other means of transportation. An effort is made to make the *Salle des Fêtes* look less dreary and feel less damp. The orchestra platform is decorated with evergreen boughs and a few flowers. The fire chief drives the fire truck down to Sansom Favre's sawmill for sacks of sawdust to burn in the drum stove.

The dances are scheduled to begin at nine o'clock, but they never begin that early. Even the orchestra arrives after nine. The people coming by bus arrive earlier than the people of Peyrane because the bus driver has a schedule to keep, though the schedule is neither hard nor fast.

As the young people arrive at the *Salle des Fêtes*, the boys drift toward one corner and the girls toward another. Within each group they talk and joke and pretend to be unaware of the existence of the group on the other side of the hall. In fact, there is much eyeing between the two. Now and then, two or three boys, obviously discussing one of the girls, may even turn around and stare at her. She makes a desperate effort to ignore the attention she is receiving.

As the orchestra starts to play these two groups remain aloof, but the dancing begins because the young people are not the only ones in the hall. Some families in Peyrane — not many families, but a few of them — are always eager to participate in any form of amusement. They go to all the movies, traveling circuses, political meetings; they turn up immediately after any accident. So the Favres and the Bellets and Pougets always come to the dances. As the orchestra starts to play Henri Favre dances with his thirteen-year-old daughter Jacqueline, and seven-year-old Colette waltzes around the floor with her three-year-old brother Dédou. The older Bellet girls are dancing together. Léon Favre's little boys are not dancing but playing tag around the floor and teasing their cousins who are pretending to dance. The mothers of these children sit together at the side of the hall, talking and paying little attention to the rest of the family.

Soon a few young married couples join the dance: the schoolteacher and her husband, the baker's son and his wife, young Aubenas and his wife, who were married a few months ago and have come up from Apt. They are joined in a few minutes by some of the girls who have been standing in the girls' corner. Tired of waiting for the boys to make up their minds, these girls start dancing together. Some of them know that no boy will ever ask them to dance; others believe they can attract a partner better by dancing in front of him with another girl than by standing in a corner.

After one or two dances the boys prepare to act. The eyeing becomes more intense. Suddenly a boy breaks away from the security of his corner and walks across the hall. He stands before a girl and mutters something. She seems not to reply — often she does not even look at the boy — but they begin to dance. They do not look at each other; they do not smile. If they are poor dancers, they walk, rather than dance, round and round the hall. If they are good dancers, they execute intricate steps. Some of them even jitterbug. Both the good dancers and the poor dancers cling to each other but seem to dance only with their legs. The upper part of their body is rigid; their faces retain a blank expression. It is surprising how gracefully active their legs and feet can be when the rest of the body seems not to coöperate.

When the music stops the boy and girl, without a word or a glance, separate and go to their own groups. Once they have reached the security of their corner, they relax and smile and talk. Even engaged couples separate; only the married couples remain together and chat in a relaxed way between dances. However, when the music begins again there is the same wooden expression on the faces of the married couples as on the faces of the unmarried dancers.

From this one would not think that dancing is the favorite amusement for the young people in Peyrane, and yet their constant problem is to find means to attend every dance in the region. They never miss one if they can help it. Of course, there are only the two dances in Peyrane, but a dance can be found in some neighboring community every Saturday night. The boy who has a motorcycle is lucky; he can go to all the dances. If he has an adolescent sister, she is lucky, too, for she can ride on the back of his motorcycle. Every Saturday night Roger and Lucienne Prayal roar out of Peyrane on Roger's motorcycle. At about the same time the barber from Bonnieux comes into town on his motorcycle. He has come for his fiancée, Henri Favre's oldest daughter, to take her to a dance.

Some people criticize the Favres for letting their daughter go out unchaperoned with a man to whom she is not married, even though they are engaged. But it is admitted that times have changed and young people cannot be expected to conform to the pattern which older people had to accept in their youth. Restrictions were relaxed during the war, but still it is considered in better taste for a group of girls to go to a dance with the father or the older brother of one of them. Some fathers enjoy the task of escorting a group of girls to a dance, although they complain of having to stay up too late. After they tire of watching the dance, they go to a café and play cards until their wards can be persuaded to go home.

During the course of the evening the young people drift off to the café, too. The dance floor is almost deserted at times. A few of the older unmarried men "on the make" have located willing partners and have left. Most of the young people walk in groups to the café to relax as they never do at the dance. In the café they sit around tables laughing, joking, drinking. The drinking is moderate. Boys may become a bit stimulated, girls very rarely.

A group of young men on a spree is often the exception to this rule of moderation. They have little interest in dancing; they have little interest in girls beyond making remarks about them that are almost objectionable. If a boy has drunk more than he should and seems about to cross the line of decency, his comrades will keep him in check. They are interested in having a good time and have no desire to get into trouble.

Finally at two or three o'clock the orchestra stops playing, stows its instruments in a car and drives away. Buses go off with dancers returning to Bonnieux, Apt, and Cavaillon. Fathers and older brothers collect the girls for whose safe return they are responsible. The *Salle des Fêtes* is closed. The owner of the café finally succeeds in persuading people to leave. Soon the town is quiet except for the young men on a spree. For them the night is beginning. When they are evicted from the café, they pile into a car which roars out of town and heads for Apt or Cavaillon.

Although the two dances are the only organized activity for the adolescents, the adolescents themselves do not complain. Only the adults keep saying, "Somebody ought to organize something for the young people." When I talked to Philippe Aubenas and Robert Paul and Louise Imbert, they said they had plenty to do. Philippe said, "And besides we'd rather do what we want to do when we want to do it. Suppose we had a club and it was decided to have a party on such-and-such a date. Maybe when that day came we wouldn't feel like going to the party."

The amusement the young people are most enthusiastic about, after dancing, is taking a *promenade*. A *promenade* is so vague and formless that it can be defined only as "an occasion on which people go somewhere for recreational purposes only." It may be a short walk through the village, a picnic in the woods, or a long anticipated trip to the top of Mont Ventoux. It may be made by a family group to celebrate a first communion, by a group of girls to see the annual parade at Apt, or by a boy and girl in love. Even a single person walking in what seems to be an aimless manner may be said to be taking a *promenade*.

As I used to make my rounds through the village at different times during the day to see what was going on, the purpose of my walk seemed recreational to all those I met on the street. They would invariably greet me with "Well, out for a *promenade?*" It was difficult not to reply that it was my business to walk around and see what was going on. Their greeting did not imply reproach; if anything, it implied envy. The people of Peyrane think it is good to be able to take a walk any time of the day — especially when the sun is shining and the mistral is not blowing.

The dances, the *promenades,* and the usual forms of adult recreational activity are supposed to offer adolescent girls adequate opportunities to have a good time. A well-behaved girl will not seek others, and most of the girls seem content. Their work takes most of their time. They can go to the movie on Tuesday evening. They go to a dance on Saturday night. They go on a *promenade* on Sunday afternoons and holidays. They may go to the market in Apt on Saturday morning and remain in the city to spend the night with a friend. During the day and in the evening when they have spare time they may drop in at a friend's house for a cup of coffee. As they get older they can expect suitors to call in the evening.

Boys are expected to seek wilder forms of amusement. Three years ago there was a group of older boys called the "Bombonne peyranaise," perhaps best translated as the "Peyrane Jug," because the group seemed capable of holding an extraordinary quantity of wine. Louis Pascal had decided he wanted to become the village cobbler and had left his father's farm to set up his shop in one of the run-down houses of the village. After a year or so he gave up cobbling and went back to the farm, but during the year that he halfheartedly exercised his craft, his house was the center of activity for most of the young men of the village. Every evening and every holiday they congregated there and played cards and drank until late at night. Occasionally they went on a spree that lasted two or three days.

A spree usually began when the gang decided to go somewhere for a good meal. They would take the Borel car to Apt or to the Fontaine de Vaucluse for a dinner which would last two or three hours. The rounds of pastis before dinner, the bottles of wine consumed during the meal, the brandy or rum drunk after coffee kept them in good spirits until eleven o'clock when they would decide to go to a dance somewhere in the region. Even at the dance the group retained its unity. They would stand around and watch the dancers for a while, laughing and making remarks about the girls. As the effects of dinner wore off they would go to the café for a drink. There they played a pinball game or a few rounds of belote so wildly that the café keeper would threaten to kick them out. They kept distinct from the groups of dancers who now and then came from the dance. When the dance ended and the café closed, there was nothing more to do in the village, but with a car they could carry on elsewhere. In Apt and Cavaillon most of the cafés were closed, too, but there were always the brothels, now called "hotels" since brothels have been abolished, and these institutions remain open all night. The boys were not primarily interested in the prostitutes; they wanted a place where they could sit and drink and joke and play cards as long as they wanted. They enjoyed the girls who hovered around them because they could joke with them and dance if they felt like it. But on most of these occasions females were definitely of secondary importance.

By the time the sun came up the group was bored with the brothel and with sitting around drinking. Back in the car, they dashed up to Peyrane to get their guns and dogs, and in an hour they were off in the woods hunting hare or thrushes. The hunting lasted until they got tired and hungry and went back home to eat and drink. But then they were ready to start out again — this time perhaps for a fête in a neighboring town where they could "check up on things" and enter the boules tournament. Either success or failure in the tournament called for a few rounds of drinks, and eventually it would be time for dinner — a good dinner, since they had not eaten well for twenty-four hours. When someone suggested that there was a new restaurant in Gordes which was supposed to be good, they would set off and the night would begin again.

The "Bombonne peyranaise" took the idea of having a good time more seriously than most of the young people of Peyrane. They represented the extreme to which young people may go. Sometimes adults were inclined to feel that Pascal, Borel, Vidal, and others were going too far, but on the whole they approved. They respected them more than they did Roger Prayal who never did anything wild. The proof that their confidence was well placed lies in the fact that Pascal, Borel, and Vidal are now, three years later, serious, hard-working young men.

The "Bombonne peyranaise" did not spend every weekend on a spree. It costs more money than any of the boys had to carry on like that all the time, and a car was not always available to take them wherever they wished. Such a weekend was their ideal and they undertook to live up to the ideal as often as possible, but most weekends they spent quietly drinking and playing cards in Louis Pascal's old house.

Women played a subordinate role in these sprees, as we have seen. Even when the boys went to a brothel it was to drink and joke with the girls rather than to take advantage of an easy, though expensive, sexual outlet. On occasion, however, a boy might be induced to go upstairs with one of the girls. Emile Pian, a thirty-five-year-old, solid citizen, told me that one night he was on a spree. He was only fifteen, but he was big for his age and associated with older boys. In the course of the evening the group landed in a brothel in Apt where they drank and danced a good part of the night. The boys began kidding Emile because he had never had sexual intercourse, and naturally that led to their urging him to go upstairs with a girl. He resisted at first but finally gave in and had his first sexual experience in a brothel in Apt.

Emile said that afterwards he was almost ill from worry. It did not matter to him that he was no longer a virgin, but he was afraid he might have caught "one of those dirty sicknesses one catches in a brothel." He was worried only about his health — which was the reason he happened to recount the incident to me — and undisturbed by any moral implications. When I asked him about that he seemed surprised: "Why should that have worried me? It happened naturally. It was going to happen sooner or later, so it might as well have happened then. It's all just a part of growing up."

Emile Pian's attitude toward his first sexual experience is typical of the attitude most people of Peyrane display toward sex, as far as I was able to determine. They believe that since the sexual urge is a natural part of our existence, little may be gained by fighting against it. It is like all the inevitable aspects of life; since nothing can be done about them, they might as well be accepted. In this instance, acceptance happens also to afford one of life's greater pleasures. One would be stupid to deny oneself pleasures that come so naturally and that are so readily available. However, one must learn to control one's sexual urges because if they get out of control they may harm us.

Almost everyone, not just the men in the café, takes part in the banter about sex. The joking is usually centered about implausible situations, however, and the more implausible the situation, the more comic it is.

When one of the younger masons loudly makes an improper proposition to ninety-nine-year-old Madame Carbonnel, every one is convulsed with laughter. One of the wags at the bar may openly accuse the café owner's wife of illicit relations with Monsieur Maucorps, the dirtiest, most shiftless man in Peyrane; such an incredible accusation gets a big laugh.

Of course, one cannot joke this way with everyone. One would scarcely accuse the Notaire's wife face to face of sleeping with Monsieur Maucorps, because one does not joke with the Notaire's wife. One would not joke with Monsieur A —— about sleeping with Madame P——, since there are indications that Monsieur A —— does sleep with Madame P——.

A good deal of the gossip, and that means a good deal of the conversation, carried on at the café, at the grocery store, and in the knitting-and-sewing circles concerns the behavior of certain people of Peyrane who are rumored to have been indiscreet. Here the putative affair between Monsieur A —— and Madame P —— receives ample attention.

When men are playing games or arguing in the café a great deal of profanity is used, and most of it has sexual content: "con," "couillon," " 'fant de pute," "putain," "putain de sort," etc. No one is insulted by these words; in fact a person usually pretends not even to hear an insult unless it is placed in such witty context that it draws a laugh from all the other men present. In this case, a rejoinder is called for, a witty, devastating rejoinder highlighting — if possible — the irregular, or excessively active, or insufficiently active sexual behavior of the antagonist.

From the joking, gossip, and swearing one might think that sex is uppermost in the minds of most of the people of Peyrane. However, it is mentioned in so casual a manner that it is apparent that sex presents no serious problem to the majority of the people. Not that everyone in Peyrane is well adjusted sexually or that everyone in Peyrane has an adequate sexual outlet. Life in a "civilized" community necessarily frustrates everyone. However, the people of Peyrane by not denying the urge itself are relieved of one complicating factor which aggravates the sexual problem in certain other cultures.

In spite of the freedom with which the people of Peyrane talk and joke about sex, they are always discreet about their personal problems and experiences. The talk of sex remains on a superficial, impersonal level. Joking about sex is not funny if it becomes personal. One day when a group of men were joking about the sex life of Madame N——, I joined in the joking and recounted an episode which threw some light on the subject in question. One of the crudest jokers turned on me, and I realized as a foreigner I had failed to grasp the subtle difference between the jokes of the other men and my own. I had made too personal a reference.

It is considered bad taste for a person to discuss his own sex life with anyone else, just as it is in bad taste for anyone to inquire into another person's sexual experiences. As I came to know some of the people well, I found that I could ask direct questions because they understood the nature of my project. They realized that I had no interest in their personal experiences except as they helped me to form an idea of life in Peyrane. Even these people, however, firmly changed the subject whenever my questions took too intimate a turn.

People were willing to give me information on the sex life of others only insofar as others had been indiscreet enough to reveal themselves to the population as a whole. They delighted in telling me how Monsieur C—— had used the public hearse for rendezvous with his mistress. It was legitimate to talk about this because when Madame C—— had found out about her husband's infidelity, she made such a scene that the whole story became public property. However, no one was willing or able to give me information about the normal, discreet, sexual behavior of other people. They were unable because they actually did not know. Such things are not discussed.

The attitude toward sex is reflected in the education of children in sexual matters. Parents do not discuss sex with their children. It seems to them ludicrous and lacking in taste and *pudeur*, that any parent should feel the need of explaining the "facts of life" to his children. When I asked how children were expected to learn these facts, they replied, "Why just naturally. They learn those things as they grow up. Their instincts take care of that."

If young children ask questions about where a baby brother came from there is no embarrassment. They are told that the child was found under a cabbage or brought by the doctor. Such a lie usually does not fool the child, but it turns aside the question. Raoul Favre said that during the war a cousin of his and her two children — a boy and a baby girl — lived with him. The boy's task was to watch the cow and calf. One day when he asked where his baby sister had come from, his mother told him that the baby had come in a box. "That's silly," he said, "Babies come out of their mothers just as the calf came out of the cow's hind end." In a rural community like Peyrane it is inevitable that children learn about sex from observing the behavior of animals.

I was told that they also learn of "the facts of life" in school, but my informants could not tell me exactly what they thought the teachers told the children. The teachers themselves said that they had to be extremely discreet on the subject for fear of being criticized. The only information they gave was about personal hygiene and infant care.

In some cultures children learn about sex by observing their parents. In Peyrane even the poorest families try to make sure that no one but a small baby sleeps in the room with the parents. The worst housed family in the commune — the Pougets — complains bitterly because the whole family sleeps in three beds placed side by side in the one bedroom. Pouget says that only animals should live like that. The Francis Favres are badly housed, too, but they put the children in the bedroom and sleep in the kitchen themselves.

The most important source of information regarding sex is older children. Each generation of children enlightens the younger generation. I do not know at what age the information is revealed, and I do not know the precise nature of the information. My only piece of personal evidence is that Henri-Paul Favre, who was seven, told our five-year-old that "with girls it's different. It's round with a hole in the center." Apparently such random pieces of information accumulate and are refined so that a child is well-informed by the time he finishes school. People I talked to could not imagine that a child would not know all there is to be known by that time. "His instincts would take care of that."

When I talked to men in a confidential, relaxed situation they freely admitted that they practiced masturbation as children, although they said they did not remember at what age they began or how frequently they indulged. If a boy was caught by his parents, he would be scolded and threatened with a light punishment but the punishment was never carried out. Everyone denied that parents ever threatened a child with castration, although it was admitted that if a child were caught by someone other than his parents he might be so threatened.

When I inquired about men having intercourse with animals people were not shocked. There were said to be jokes about it, but I never heard one told. People knew only of an old man, held in contempt for other reasons also, who was found maltreating a goat. The reaction to this incident was that it was one of those instances of individual peculiarity which cannot be explained.

As children grow up they become aware that there is a discrepancy between the ideal and the real codes regulating sexual behavior. According to the ideal code no one should have intercourse out of wedlock. Probably a few adults in Peyrane really believe this injunction. No one, however, believes that the majority of the people of Peyrane adhere to it. It even conflicts with another rule of the social code which says it is good for a man to have intercourse before he is married. In the first place, it is believed that no man should attempt to settle down and accept the responsibilities of life until he has had an opportunity to release his passions. Furthermore, it is generally believed that marital sexual relations can be more successful if the man has had sufficient experience before marriage.

Most of the people of Peyrane would agree that the following statement, made by one of the men, is fair and realistic: "We're told that we shouldn't have intercourse except with our wife, but I don't believe that. I had my first experience when I was fourteen, and that wasn't the only experience I had before I was married. I was a healthy young man, so what can you expect? A young man has got to have a good time; there's nothing wrong with that if he's careful. Of course, with a girl it is different. I suppose it would be better for a girl not to have intercourse until she gets married; she might get into trouble. At least we say that a girl should be a virgin when she is married, and maybe there are a few girls who are still virgins when they get married . . . but I doubt it. There's no harm done, if they're careful. But once you get married you ought to be *sérieux* enough not to take chances. It's better for man and wife to sleep together and not get mixed up with other people. I can't say I've always been faithful to my wife. During the war when I was in the army and then a prisoner on a farm in Germany . . . well, it was different. I think my wife has been faithful to me, but I don't want to know about it if she hasn't. The important thing is not to get mixed up with other people."

This man had his first sexual experience with a girl when they stopped to play on their way home from school. It is not unusual for the children who live on farms at some distance from the school to have their first experience in this way. A few boys, as we have seen in the case of Emile Pian, may have their sexual initiation in a brothel, but this is unusual. Prostitutes are too expensive and there is "too much danger of catching a dirty disease." *Promenades* taken by young people sometimes offer opportunities for sexual experience. One boy said, "It's not that you go on the promenade with that in mind necessarily. Anyway, you're with a girl you're fond of or with a girl you've understood is willing. You get separated from the others in the group. One thing leads to another, you kiss — and there you are. You can't stop after that."

Whether a boy has intercourse with one of the more "willing" girls of his acquaintance or with "sa petite amie," a friend who has become a sexual partner, it is up to him to be careful. Since contraceptives are never used, someone has to be careful and a man is supposed to be able to control his passions more easily than a woman.

Raoul Favre told me that one day when he was ten years old he was engaged in sexual play with a girl nine years old. Their fathers happened to choose that inappropriate moment to walk through the corner of the field where the children were. His father sent him home and promised him he was going to "catch plenty" at supper time. When his father came home, however, he said nothing about it. In fact, the incident was never mentioned again. The girl was scolded and kept at home for a few days. Some parents would not be so tolerant as this boy's were. Undoubtedly both the boy's parents and the girl's parents would have been more severe if the children had been old enough for there to have been a possibility of pregnancy.

If a girl does become pregnant, it will necessarily become known. Such a dishonor is considered unfortunate, but gossip dies down, and there are examples in the village of "girl mothers" who found good husbands. Jeanne Imbert had a child when she was eighteen years old, and the child's father did not marry her. She was so upset by his refusal that she tried to commit suicide by shooting herself in the abdomen. (She recovered but people said, "The bullet must have almost killed the unborn child, for to this day she has a scar on her lip!") In spite of this incident Jeanne married well. She married Francis Favre, the postman, whose first wife had died a few years before.

Then there was Madeleine Fratani. When her father got sick and could not work, her mother took in a boarder. Madeleine was only sixteen years old, and the boarder made love to her. Madeleine became pregnant, and the man left town. There was gossip, but it soon died down. The only tragedy was that the child died when it was a year old. After that Emile Pian came back from Germany where he had been a prisoner. The Pian family is well-to-do, respectable, and hard-working. Emile fell in love with Madeleine and they were married a few months after his return. They are now one of the most *sérieux* couples in Peyrane.

Illegitimate birth is not a tragedy for the baby who is born out of wedlock, either. When I was talking to Madame Borel about cases of illegitimacy in Peyrane, I asked whether bastards were looked down upon. She flared up. "Why should anyone blame the child, *pécaïre*? He's not to blame. It's the fault of his parents who were not careful enough. In school no one would tease him, and when he's grown up people forget about it. Look at Robert Peretti. There's no difference between him and everyone else. His mother was a no good woman, so no one blamed Gaston Jouvaud when he refused to marry her."

If an unmarried girl becomes a mother, then, it is not a tragedy because of the moral issues involved or because the girl is permanently dishonored or because the child will bear the stigma of his birth. It is a tragedy because it places an unexpected economic burden on either or both of the families involved. It is tragic also because the birth of a child may prematurely end the adolescence of both the mother and the father. They may have to settle down and accept adult responsibilities before they are ready, before they have had their good time.

The idea of "having a good time" should not be exaggerated, of course. Except for occasional sprees the sources of entertainment for young people are card games, boules, *promenades*, visiting back and forth, and dances. In the telling, the good times which young people have are more emphasized than their daily work. However, since they are expected to contribute to the family purse an amount of money equivalent to the amount it takes to support them, they are kept busy working.

Nevertheless it must be recognized that having a good time is a serious affair in Peyrane. It is never expressed in that way. It is simply stated that "young people must have a good time," and all possible financial aid and tolerance are given to them. It is considered tragic when an individual's adolescence is cut short or when he is burdened with an adult's responsibilities before he can normally be expected to assume them. So even though the inhabitants of Peyrane are not explicit in recognizing that an adolescent's good time is a serious matter, it is obvious that they consider it to be so.

When a child leaves school at the age of fourteen he is in a sense fully indoctrinated from a social point of view. There is no aspect of the ideal social code of which he is unaware. Furthermore, his parents, his teacher, and society in general have brought about his submission to that code. The thirteen- and fourteen-year-olds give less expression to their individual personalities than any other group in the village. They are undoubtedly the best-behaved inhabitants of Peyrane.

Conformity has been achieved at the price of repression, however, and the people of Peyrane sense that this repression cannot be maintained. They know that adolescents have urges, and violent urges, that children do not have. Since adolescents cannot be forced to accept the social rules as completely as a child, behavior is tolerated that would not be tolerated in a child or in an adult. When adults see a sixteen-year-old boy making a fool of himself, they smile tolerantly and say, "Cette jeunesse, faut qu'elle passe," which is a way of saying, "Young people have to go through this stage." So long as a young man does not become too insulting, so long as he does not get in trouble with the law, so long as he does not make a mistake which will bring his adolescence to an end prematurely, his behavior is accepted.

Young people also have to learn for themselves that there are two social codes, the ideal code which their family and the school have forced on them, and the real code which governs the actions of adults. There is less difference between the real and ideal social codes in Peyrane than in some societies, but there is a difference. When, for example, the teacher has the class learn by heart, "We must be the friends and protectors of the little birds," the children repeat the phrase obligingly. They know, however, that as soon as they are old enough they will trap and shoot all the finches, titmice, and thrushes they can, just as their fathers do.

Children are taught that they must respect all elderly people. However, Monsieur Maucorps is one of the oldest men in the village, and they see their parents treat him disrespectfully. In school the children are taught that paying taxes is a civic responsibility, but as they grow up they learn that one pays only those taxes which one cannot avoid paying. Children are told that it is wrong to have sexual relations outside of wedlock. Before they are adults they will have learned that this rule is not always observed. Before they take their first communion the children must attend Catechism, and the priest indoctrinates them as fully as it is possible to indoctrinate this practical people. By the time they are adults very few of them will go near the church except for family ceremonies.

Before a child can grow up he must pass through this intermediate stage. The real social code has not been officially formulated like the ideal social code, and the difference between the two can be learned only through experience. A young man like Roger Prayal, who is too good, who is not wild enough for a young man, is not experimenting sufficiently. He will never have a full understanding of what one really can and really cannot do. "Il faut se faire une idée de la vie," people say. This implies more than learning the difference between the ideal and the real social code, but it does imply that. Roger will never learn to distinguish between the two because he has too little taste for testing the limits.

While testing the limits young people must also learn for themselves that some limits are desirable. People in Peyrane do not believe that man is naturally good, because it is obvious to them that children are not naturally good. They are more like little animals which must be domesticated, and they are thoroughly domesticated at home and in the school. They obey the rules imposed on them because they are forced to obey them, not because they want to. They must learn to hold themselves in check because they want to, not because there is a superior authority forcing them to.

It is assumed that in the long run, sins against social conventions do not appeal to people who have tasted the sins. If a person drinks to excess he discovers that there is more pleasure in drinking moderately. If a person stays up all night dashing from one town to another in search of pleasure, he will discover that there is a more satisfying pleasure in living a regulated life without walking farther than from home to the café. No one can become *sérieux* until he has tasted excess to the point of preferring moderation. A young man must fling aside as many of his responsibilities as he practically can; he must live as independently as circumstances permit. He must break away from family life as he knows it under the roof of his parents; eventually he will recognize how lonely he can be and will be prepared to sacrifice part of his independence for the sake of family life.

Olivier Borel told of friends of his who had left Peyrane and gone to work and live in Marseille at the age of sixteen or seventeen. Most returned after a few weeks or a few months. "At first they had a better time than they did in Peyrane, but they got tired of it and came home."

When, after the period of freedom and experimentation, a young person comes to accept the conditions and responsibilities of living in Peyrane, he is accepted as a full member of society. His adolescence is ended; he has become an adult. He has become *sérieux*. A person who is *sérieux* conforms to the rules of adulthood. He is predictable.

Of course, this process of becoming *sérieux* is never completed. No one in Peyrane is ever fashioned into the perfect citizen. Nor is the process of becoming an adult so clearly delineated as it may sound when analyzed. It is a gradual process differing from person to person. As a child grows up and shows himself to be *sérieux* in one phase of his behavior, he is considered adult in that phase and is granted appropriate responsibilities.

When a child shows that he can pour his own wine moderately he is given that responsibility. Most children pour their own wine by the time they are fourteen in Peyrane. Monsieur Maucorps, who is seventy-seven years old, has never learned moderation in the matter of pouring his own wine, and is considered childish in that respect. People tease him as they tease a child who through inexperience takes a few sips too many.

Boys are considered sufficiently responsible to go out alone at night by the time they are fifteen. At sixteen they may go out without telling their parents where they are going. Girls may go to dances in a group when they are fourteen or fifteen. When they are sixteen they may go to a dance alone with a boy unless their parents are conservative and insist on their having a chaperone.

The State, also, recognizes that individuals may be partially adult and may be given responsibility for certain types of behavior before they are ready to assume full responsibility for themselves as adult members of society. Young men may get hunting licenses at the age of sixteen. Men and women may obtain drivers' permits at the same age. With the permission of their parents young men may marry at the age of eighteen years, three months, and girls may marry at the age of fifteen years, three months. At the age of twenty, young men are considered old enough to serve a term in the army or navy. At the age of twenty-one men and women officially achieve adulthood; they are given full legal and political responsibility.

Among young people in the cities of France the age of twenty-one may correspond to the age at which they feel and act as adults and are treated as adults by other members of the community. In Peyrane, there is an unfortunate discrepancy. The men say that they are tired of having a good time and are ready to settle down, marry, and have a family by the time they are eighteen or nineteen — two or three years before they are considered adults by the State. Girls are usually considered *sérieuses* at seventeen or eighteen.

If the young people of Peyrane were left to themselves they would undoubtedly get married earlier than they do. They are not left to themselves. The State intervenes at this point and in effect prolongs the period of adolescence from three to eight years.

When a young man reaches the age of twenty he must leave Peyrane and spend several months (the actual length of time has varied considerably in the last fifty years) on active duty in the army or navy. Only those men who are physically disabled are excepted from this service. The young men grumble at having to serve in the army, but at the same time they look forward to this break in their life as a kind of adventure. It offers most of them the only opportunity they will have to see other parts of France. They do not mind the hardship of military life, they have been brought up to accept hardships. They dislike more than anything else the condition of anonymity which is forced on them. They dislike being thrown into intimate contact with people. They dislike having to obey without rational motivation. They dislike not being able to retaliate when a superior insults them. They dislike not being able to make their own decisions. They miss good food.

The most serious objection to military service on the part of both the boys and their parents, however, is that it makes a break in their lives at an awkward time. They do not lose just the year or two spent in the army or navy. They lose two or three years marking time until they go into the service. On their return home they must adjust to the life of the village again and make decisions about their livelihood which they could have made when they were eighteen. Then it takes time to find a suitable spouse and to earn enough money to establish a household. Finally they marry, about five years later than they would have if they had not had to cope with military service. The State loses far more in economic productivity and a lower birth rate than it gains from their services.

The effect of military service can be seen in the case of Rivet's two sons. Paul is a deaf-mute. Since it has always been obvious that he would be exempt from military service, he began to learn a trade when he was fifteen years old. Now he is eighteen and ready to qualify as a journeyman tailor. He will be able to make his own living while learning to "cut," and by the time he is twenty-one he will be a full-fledged tailor.

Henri, as we have seen, has had only odd jobs although he is nineteen years old. When I asked him what he was going to do when he settled down he said, "I don't know. No use thinking about it until after military service." By the time he decides how he is going to make his living and whether he will go to Marseille or try to live in Peyrane, his younger brother will already be professionally established. Meanwhile Henri continues to work at odd jobs and at having a good time without finding pleasure in either.

One of Henri's worries is that his family will not let him think of marriage until after his military service. He is in love with a girl from Apt but both his family and hers agree that it would not be wise for them to become engaged or to marry before he went away.

Olivier Borel, one of the leaders of the Peyrane Jug, came home on sick leave from the army, and since he had more spare time than most people in Peyrane we talked a great deal together. His main worry concerned his engagement. Before his departure for the army he had asked Lataud's sister-in-law to marry him. They had always had a good time together and it seemed logical for them to consider themselves engaged. Now he had become more serious, and he was afraid she was not serious enough for him. "Things look different when you are away from home," he said. "Then when you come back they look even more different." He did not feel comfortable with her any more. It would have been better if they had not become engaged. Never, he said, would he let a son of his make plans for the future before he got his military service out of the way.

By the time young people are ready to marry they are acquainted with other young people from the whole area of the Apt Basin and even from more distant parts of the département. Family connections, visits, *promenades*, and above all the dances which they have attended have enlarged their circle of acquaintances beyond the limits of Peyrane.

Choosing a husband or wife from among these acquaintances is limited by both legal and popular restrictions. It is forbidden by law to marry a lineal relative, whether the relationship is legitimate or illegitimate, whether the relationship is by blood, marriage, or legal adoption. Marriage is also forbidden between brother and sister, uncle and niece, aunt and nephew, brother-in-law and sister-in-law (if divorced). These are laws which the people of Peyrane would follow even if the State did not enforce them. At this point the articles of the Civil Code and popular interdictions coincide. Popular and canonical restrictions go even one step further, to forbid marriage between first cousins. To prove the wisdom of this rule people point to Simon and Marcelle Jouvaud, whose eldest child is feeble-minded, they say, because his parents are first cousins.

It may be that a common but less recognized prejudice still further limits the field of choice; young people apparently prefer to find a spouse living beyond the boundaries of the commune rather than to marry someone from the village whom they have always known. Unfortunately, the census records are incomplete on this point, so that we cannot know exactly to what extent people go outside of Peyrane to find a spouse. Of the eighty-two married couples for whom we have information, only seven were endogamous and seventy-five were exogamous! Guy Vidal and Yvon Fraysse, who took the census in the commune, failed to record the information concerning the eighty-three other married couples of Peyrane.

When a young man decides he would like to marry a certain girl, his behavior makes his intentions obvious. At dances she is his only partner and he tries to keep other men from dancing with her. He tries to be with the girl on *promenades*. He drops into her home frequently, sometimes bringing a bottle of his sparkling wine. After a while the visits become so much a part of the family routine that he is almost accepted as a member of the family. In most families he is allowed to take the girl to a dance without a chaperone. He may take her on his motorcycle to visit relatives in a neighboring hamlet. The girl's family makes a point of retiring a little earlier than usual so that the young people may be alone.

After a few months the young man surprises no one when he asks the girl to marry him. If she consents, it is traditional for him to ask her father officially for his consent. This is legally necessary if the young people are minors. Family approval is not hard to obtain if it is evident that two conditions are fulfilled.

The first condition is that the couple should be in love. All the people of Peyrane whom I questioned on this point agreed that the most important condition for marriage is love. When they were asked what they meant by love they found the question silly, but if they were pressed for a definition they agreed that two necessary elements in love are passion and compatibility. If these two are missing, they said it is unlikely that a marriage will be successful.

The other important condition is that both the young man and the young woman should be *sérieux*. *Sérieux* means several things in this context. A serious husband or a serious wife is first of all faithful. A man who might "run after other women" or a woman who might be capable of "making horns grow on her husband's brow" is not serious. The most disgraceful thing that can happen to a person is for one's spouse to be so flagrantly unfaithful that the infidelity becomes generally known in the village.

Seriousness implies more than fidelity, however. A serious husband will try to earn as much money as the family needs to live "decently." He will not drink immoderately or spend too much time playing cards or boules. He will supplement his income by cultivating a garden. He will live so that he will be loved and respected by his wife and children.

A serious wife will be a hardworking, reasonable, and moderate woman. She will keep her house neat. She will feed and clothe the family economically and well. She will be on good terms with her neighbors but will not spend too much time gossiping. She will know how to stretch a hundred-franc note without having the reputation for being stingy. She will supplement her husband's income by making clothes, raising chickens and rabbits. If the need for money is desperate she will even take over the arduous task of raising silkworms or working in the grape harvest, without neglecting her regular household duties. She will not object if her husband goes to the café so long as he does not spend too much money or drink too much or come home too late for meals. She will not even object if he is moderately immoderate — that is, if now and then he goes on a bit of a binge. She will keep the children from running the streets when they are young and she will keep them clean. She will teach them good manners and will encourage them to love and fear their father. She may expect her husband to coöperate in disciplining the children, but except on rare occasions she may not ask him to spend his free time taking care of the children.

There are other qualities besides "seriousness" that one welcomes in a prospective son- or daughter-in-law. Since marriage brings the families of both spouses into close contact it would be preferable that the two families be compatible with each other, so that neither will be ashamed of the other or awed by it. Then there is the matter of money. Everyone says that it is stupid to marry for money, but when conversation falls on a particular ménage it becomes obvious that people do associate the question of money with the question of marriage. They say, for instance, that Madeleine Fratani was lucky to marry Emile Pian; her family was poor, and he was the favorite nephew of a well-to-do uncle. Philippe Vernet married well; he drove a truck at the mines and married a schoolteacher who earned more money than he.

Money is not beside the point, therefore, but it is still commonly said that wealth is not an essential quality to look for in a prospective wife or husband. It is better to have a serious wife or husband whom you love than a rich one who would make your life miserable. Hélène Monier is the unmarried thirty-year-old daughter of one of the wealthy farmers in the commune. Although she is attractive, people say that in spite of her money she will never marry because she is too devout and has too sharp a tongue.

If a girl's parents refuse to give their consent to a marriage, the young couple often elopes. Rather than face a public scandal, the family soon expresses its approval of the marriage and tries to convince other people in the village that they had never had any real objections. Probably no one is fooled by this talk, but face is saved and the family maintains its dignity by accepting the inevitable. The Sol family objected violently to Louis Martron when he was courting Mireille, for he was only an apprentice chef, and she was the daughter of a mine owner. Although the young people eloped, Louis was not only accepted as a son-in-law, but became the virtual head of the family because of Monsieur Sol's poor health.

Shortly after a girl's parents give their consent to a marriage, the families of the boy and girl have a dinner together to celebrate. In Peyrane marriage contracts are extremely rare. So little wealth is involved in most alliances that it would be ridiculous to go to the expense of hiring the Notaire to draw up a legal document to preserve it. Such contracts used to be more common, but since the last two wars no one has much money, it is said, and the formality has been discarded.

After the betrothal the boy and girl are at once accepted into each other's family. The boy spends every evening at the home of the girl. The girl spends part of the day in the household of her fiancé, visiting with her future mother-in-law, sewing with her, even helping in her household tasks. They are allowed to kiss each other on both cheeks in public when they meet or say goodbye. An observer might note that kissing is not limited to the cheeks or to farewells, but this kissing is not intended for the public.

Long engagements are avoided. Two months to a year is the usual time between betrothal and marriage. During this time the engagement may be broken without any formality and with little gossip. People assume there must be good reason for the break, and no one would deny that it is better to discover the reason before the marriage than after. Sometimes a wedding is postponed until a brother returns from his military service, or until an ailing grandmother gets well or dies. So long as the couple does not have to wait too long it is better to start married life under the most favorable conditions.

Marriages may take place at any time during the year, except during the month of May, "le mois de Marie." Since there is less need to work in the fields and gardens toward the end of June and beginning of July, most of the marriages in Peyrane take place within two weeks of the first of July.

One preoccupation of the young couple is to comply with legal formalities. The establishment of a family is the most important event that can occur in France. Codes have been elaborated to define completely and precisely the rights and duties of husband and wife toward each other, toward their children, toward their relatives and toward society. The State has done what it can to make sure that these relationships are understood and observed. If exceptions must be made the Prosecuting Attorney has the power to make them so that the law may be adjusted to individual cases. Even an incestuous marriage may be authorized — but only by the President of the Republic!

First the bans must be published. This means that for ten days an announcement of the marriage intentions must be posted on the doors of the Town Halls of several communes — the commune where the marriage will take place, the communes in which the bride and groom have been living for at least six months or the commune in which each was born, and the commune of the parents or guardians if the bride or groom is a minor. The announcement must include the full names of the bride and groom, their residence and domicile, and the name of the Town Hall in which the marriage will take place. To secure the publication of the bans, the bride and groom must present an official certificate showing that they have had a physical examination within two months.

Any person may state his opposition to the marriage by protesting to the mayor, and the mayor may use his judgment in heeding such unofficial protests. However, certain persons — a close relative, a guardian, or the District Attorney — are legally qualified to oppose a marriage, and if they formally notify the mayor through the intermediary of the bailiff that they oppose the marriage, then it must be postponed. The opposition must be serious, for if it is eventually overruled by legal authorities, the person who has registered opposition is liable for damages.

At least four days before the wedding the bride and groom go together to the Town Hall where the ceremony is to take place. There they must present their medical certificates, the certificates showing that the bans have been properly published, the certificates showing that there has been no opposition raised, certificates of domicile if they are requested, their birth certificates unless they were born in the commune. Other papers may be required — a marriage contract if one exists, a death or divorce certificate if one of the spouses has been married before, a military certificate if the groom is in active service.

At least a month before the marriage the couple must also see the priest to arrange for the religious ceremony. The bans must be published on the door of the church for at least three weeks. It is not unusual for the young man to object to a religious ceremony, since the law does not require it. His objections are invariably overruled by the women in the families, and he gives in, he says, "to keep peace in the family." No one, probably not even the young man himself, takes his grumbling seriously. In Peyrane everyone is married in the church, regardless of belief and political affiliation. Charles Pouget, the hot-headed secretary of the Communist Party, was married in the church just as the devout Joseph Gleizer was.

If the bride insists that "things be done well," the groom must go to Apt to rent formal clothes for the ceremony. Especially since the war, however, it is felt that this degree of elegance is unnecessary. A black suit in good condition will do very well for the wedding. The groom is sure to have one, for it is an essential part of the wardrobe of every man in Peyrane. Some of the black suits seen at ceremonies have become shabby over the years, for they are always worn to both funerals and weddings.

It is true that I never saw Monsieur Maucorps wearing a black suit, but I dare say that he does have a moth-riddled one somewhere in the old house where he lives. Perhaps he dare not wear it for fear it will fall apart, and he must save it to be buried in. Perhaps the suit he wears day and night *is* his black suit. It would be difficult to know for sure just what color this suit used to be.

Apart from making sure his black suit is in good condition, the fiancé has few worries concerning preparations for his marriage. Years ago there were traditional ceremonies to be observed, but these have been lost. Formerly the fiancé was expected to "ferrer l'épouse" by giv-ing her an earring. "Ferrer" means to apply iron to something: to shoe a horse, to put an iron tip on a tool, to put hinges and lock on a door. By giving his fiancée an earring a young man "put the iron to his wife." He demonstrated his domination over her. Many people have never heard of this custom, although the oldest remember hearing about it when they were children.

The only traditional prenuptial ceremony that the young man need think of today is "the burial of his bachelor life." Formerly in some parts of France this was an elaborate ceremony at which a mock funeral was actually carried out. A coffin was made and the groom's bachelor life was symbolically buried. Today the expression remains, but the ceremony is lost. The "burial" consists only of a dinner which the groom has with his male friends — the last of the feasts they have together as bachelors.

The bride and her mother are busy with preparations for the wedding banquet and with the important task of making the wedding gown. It may no longer be essential for the groom to wear formal dress to the wedding, but every effort is made for the bride to have a long, white dress with a veil. Its elegance depends on the purse of the family, but every family is willing to make a sacrifice so that their daughter may be as beautiful as possible on the day of her marriage.

On the wedding day the party meets at the home of the bride's family and the procession starts for the Town Hall. The bride's father leads the way with his daughter on his arm, and the guests fall in behind, walking in couples. The groom is the last in the procession with his mother on his arm. At the Town Hall they find the mayor waiting for them in the *Salle des Mariés*, the official ceremonial hall of the commune.

The marriage ceremony is legally open to anyone who wishes to attend, but there must be at least two witnesses present. The mayor inscribes on the *Registre de l'état civil* the Marriage Act, which contains the essential information given on the various certificates which the bride and groom have been required to present. The bride and groom, the witnesses, and the consenting parents then sign the Marriage Act. The mayor reminds the couple of their new rights and duties. These are listed, along with all the sanctions and penalties and exceptions, in several pages of the Civil Code. In essence the Code states that husband and wife owe each other fidelity and assistance. The husband is the Head of the Family. His wife must live with him, and he must receive her. (Of course, the Code defines possible exceptions for this as for every rule: for example, if the husband keeps a mistress at home, his wife is not obligated to remain there: if a husband or wife contracts a venereal disease in an adulterous relationship, the spouse is not required to care for him or her.) The couple is reminded that they must bring up their children as well as they can and that they are legally responsible for the actions of their children.

The mayor pronounces the couple man and wife. Their marriage is noted marginally in their birth certificates. They are given a Marriage Certificate if they ask for one. They are presented with their *livret de famille*, the family record on which all the official events of the family will be recorded at the Town Hall throughout the life of the family.

The couple are legally married and the wedding party starts for the church. The bride and groom now lead the procession; the bride's father takes the place of his son-in-law at the end of the procession with the latter's mother. The priest, l'abbé Autrand, and Georges Vincent, the acolyte, are waiting at the church. Monsieur Autrand witnesses the exchange of vows, blesses the wedding ring, reads the religious ceremony, and says Mass. The Mass may be more or less elaborate, depending on the money which the families are willing to spend for it. However, there are few devout families wealthy enough and few wealthy families devout enough in the commune of Peyrane to provide for an elaborate ceremony. The important thing is to have had both ceremonies, to be considered in order by both the civil and religious authorities.

When the procession leaves the church and starts down the narrow streets it may find its way barred by a crowd of townsfolk who have set across the street a long pole decorated with flowers and ribbons. The tradition is that the newly wedded couple must "pay for its passage" through the village by placing candy and money on a tray held before the barrier. Formerly, candy was given in preference to money, but today the wedding party usually offers money only. Once this barrier is passed the party meets new demands. The children of the village run after them shouting, "Vivent les novi," and the party is supposed to throw money to pacify the children.

Back at the bride's home the party prepares for the wedding banquet which is given at home or at the hotel if the girl's family can afford this luxury. The meal is elaborate with many courses and the best wines available in the village. There are always a professionally decorated wedding cake and a sparkling wine.

Toward the end of the meal one of the men dives under the table. Everyone giggles and the bride squeals. He reaches up and removes from her leg a special garter which she has put on for the occasion. This is one of the few old customs preserved in Peyrane. It is a widespread custom in France, and there has been discussion among scholars concerning its symbolic significance. The people of Peyrane think of it as only a trick to be played on the bride to embarrass her.

An older unmarried sister of the bride must be prepared to face the embarrassment of having her spinsterhood brought to the attention of everyone, for during the dinner she is formally presented with an onion. Unsuccessful suitors of the bride are also publicly reminded of their failure. During the night following the wedding bouquets of sage are tied to the doors of their house.

The wedding dinner is followed by a dance, however simple the arrangements may be. During the dance the married couple try to slip away to the house of the parents of one of them. At two or three o'clock in the morning they are aroused by loud knocks on the door. The noise grows louder until the groom goes to the door to receive a boisterous crowd of friends. The couple, presumably in need of nourishment, are presented with two bowls of onion soup.

There are charivaris in Peyrane, but they are reserved for remarrying widowers. Three years ago the foreman of one of the ochre mines, Monsieur Artigues, was married. He was sixty years old and had lived alone for many years. When he met a young widow in Avignon, married her, and brought her to live in Peyrane, Monsieur Maucorps and several of his cronies organized a charivari that awoke the whole village. It did not last long. Monsieur Artigues came running to the door with a bottle and glasses, the sight of which immediately brought an end to Maucorps' dishpan ceremony.

The ideal of all young married couples of Peyrane is to have enough time and money to take a wedding trip to Nice for two or three weeks, but very few are able to realize this dream. If they can afford to go anywhere it is usually only to Digne or to Marseille to visit relatives for a few days. Some people must be content with a *promenade* of a few hours to the Fontaine de Vaucluse, but most manage to leave Peyrane for a few days.

When the couple returns to Peyrane to settle down in the quarters which have been prepared for them, they find that their status in the community has changed. Their adolescence has ended. They are man and woman, adults who must face problems seriously for the rest of their lives.

Adult Problems and Worries

Chapter 6

Setting Up a Ménage

The House

When Louis Bonerandi and Françoise Borel decided to be married they thought their engagement would be short, but it dragged on for months as they tried to find a house where they could live. Finally they had to accept a temporary solution: they would be married and stay with Françoise' family until they found a place of their own. No one in Peyrane thinks it is good for a young couple to settle down with the parents of either the boy or the girl, but marriage cannot be postponed indefinitely. To Louis and Françoise it seemed better to be married and live with the Borels for a while in spite of the lack of privacy and the possibility of parental interference.

A year later, when a baby was born and still no house had been found, the temporary solution was accepted as permanent. Borel and Bonerandi built two rooms onto the rear of the Borel house, and the two families settled down together. Now they have become used to the arrangement, and it even seems reasonable. Madame Borel takes care of the baby. Françoise works with her uncle, the tailor, who lives next door, and Louis works with his father-in-law. The combined households function smoothly, but no one would say that the arrangement is ideal.

The housing shortage that prevents young couples from setting up independent households is paradoxical. One third of the houses of Payrane are vacant, and yet they are not available to villagers. The owners say governmental rent controls discourage them from renting their vacant property. Rent ceilings are too low; few houses in Peyrane could be rented legally for more than fifteen dollars a month. Furthermore, it is said to be almost impossible to evict a tenant without going to law, so the owners would rather keep the houses vacant, with the hope of selling them, than let them be occupied by tenants whom they cannot evict and who will not pay enough rent.

The house in which we lived illustrates the situation. It had stood vacant for seven years. Monsieur Martron was willing to rent it to us because he was sure we would move out at the end of a year, and the high rent he was able to charge Americans for a furnished house — thirty dollars a month — made it worth while. With the rent we paid, Monsieur Martron made necessary repairs to the house, and a few months after we left he sold it to a Belgian who had retired to the sun of southern France.

This points to another reason for the housing shortage. Inland Provence has become a modest resort region for northern city people who cannot afford to go to the Riviera or who prefer the simple life of a small town. They can pay more for a house than villagers can, so the owner holds it in the hope of selling to city people. He will not rent to villagers and the villagers cannot afford to buy.

The biggest house in the center of Peyrane was bought by an architect from the city of Moulins. In the summer his family vacations in Brittany, but during the Easter vacation they get away from the rainy north to camp out in the Peyrane house for a few days. The rest of the year the house stands vacant and gloomy.

One must know the personality and history of each house and each owner to understand why other empty houses are not available. Monsieur Prayal will not rent his extra house because he has adolescent children; he wants it for one of them to use sometime. Monsieur Reynard owns a vacant house but he uses it to store supplies for his grocery. Madame Baume lives in the country, but she will not rent her house in the village because she uses the front room for her newspaper and magazine business. Lucien Bourdin lives with his mother, but he will not rent another house which he owns because he uses it as a refuge where he can be by himself now and then. Madame Magne has moved to Apt to live with her daughter, but she will not rent her house; she hopes to move back when her health improves. The house north of ours has been vacant since Madame Favre died, but it is not habitable. The house to our south looks vacant, but it belongs to a blind broom salesman who roams over southern France and occasionally comes back to Peyrane for a week or two.

The older children in Madame Vernet's room were asked to write a theme on these questions: What is the most beautiful house you know? Why is it beautiful? What is the ugliest house you know? Why is it ugly? What kind of house would you like to live in when you grow up? The themes they wrote emphasized the difference between the sort of house people live in now and the ideal house they would like to live in. Jules Marchal, like most of the children, saw his ideal in the Notaire's house:

The most beautiful house is the Notaire's. It is beautiful because on the outside it is well stuccoed and painted a beautiful red brown. There are flowers around it everywhere, and beautiful roses in summer. Inside the walls are painted and shining and the tiles are polished.

The ugliest house is the Charrins' because the kitchen is next to the cow and you have to go up a ladder to get to the bedroom. The house where the Arabs live is ugly, too, because there are cracks in the walls and the floors are falling in and everything is dirty.

When I'm big I'll have a well stuccoed house exposed to the south with beautiful windows and a beautiful door and flowers all around it. Inside I'll have a dining room with a colored electric light and a divan. In the kitchen there will be hot water. There will be a W.C.

The Notaire's house is a new "villa" that would not be out of place in a middle-class suburb of any French city. The only house comparable to it is the more modest one which Jouvaud, the mason, built for his own family. These are the only houses constructed in Peyrane in the last few decades, and they are the only two surrounded by the flower gardens which all the children admire.

Compared to these two houses all the others are very old, and they would look bleak if the stucco covering the native stones were not painted one of the various shades of ochre. There are no flowers except for an occasional pot of geraniums. Most of the houses are two stories high and about twenty feet wide. The roofs are made of rounded tiles; big stones must be placed along the edge of the roof to keep the mistral from blowing the tiles away. If the house stands by itself in the country it faces south and presents a bare, windowless wall to the windy north. If it is in the village it is cramped between the adjoining houses. The façade is flush with the narrow street. If there is a garden or court it is in the rear of the house. The value of the property depends partly on whether the garden gets the winter sun and is protected from the wind.

There have been so many alterations, additions, demolitions, partitions, patches, and repairs that it is a philosophical question whether the houses as they now stand are the same as those from which they evolved. Many of the original houses were built one hundred or two hundred years ago, and some are much older. They were built to last, and barring catastrophes, they do last.

In 1936 part of the upper hill fell away and crushed a dozen houses in which Algerian ochre workers were living, so there are occasional catastrophes. When he was plastering the wall of our back room one day, Simon Jouvaud looked out the window over the cliff. "The way the cliff's eroding your shed will go soon. Then your house will follow," he remarked. Anxiously I asked how soon he expected this to happen. "I wouldn't give this house more than a hundred years," he answered.

Because of their age — or rather their agelessness — and because of their common ochre color the houses look much alike to a foreigner walking through the streets for the first time. He cannot distinguish between the Leporatti house and the Charrin house, which stand side by side, but any child in the village could tell him that the houses are totally different. In his theme Jules Marchal pointed to the Charrin house as the ugliest in town. The Leporatti house, which resembles it, has a stairway, is clean, and in repair. The Allibert house and the Martron house look alike from the outside, but the Alliberts have neither running water nor electricity while Martron has all the "modern comforts." On the other hand the Alliberts have a courtyard bathed in sun all winter while Martron's courtyard, shadowed by the house next door, is cold and damp. Francis Favre's house and Fraysse's house seem indistinguishable, but Francis has built a toilet behind his house while the Fraysses have to use the public toilet a hundred yards away.

Francis' mother died a year ago and her house is vacant. To the outsider it looks like most other houses, but it has a half-inch crack running down the back wall from the roof to the foundations. Francis could repair it by pulling the walls together and securing them with long steel rods; many of the houses are held together in this manner. But because of its location the house is not worth it. The sewer empties nearby, and the Charrins with their cow live across the street. The house is directly exposed to the mistral and it never receives the direct rays of the sun. It is hard to imagine a more undesirable house. Instead of repairing this house Francis will remove its roof so that he will have to pay taxes on the land only. This is the fate of houses that are not worth repairing.

The principal room in every house is the *salle*, which serves as living room, dining room, and kitchen. In the center is a dining-room table covered with oil cloth. Hanging directly over the table is the electric light, a small bulb within a shade that is often decorated with fringe or beads. There are several straight chairs. Along one wall there is a sideboard. The furniture appears neither antique nor new. At the windows are simple curtains, never draperies of any sort. The walls give a feeling of bareness, although there may be one or two pictures or photographs of a mountain or forest scene tacked up. Sometimes there is a framed *certificat primaire* or a military certificate on the wall, too. There is always a little radio placed in the window, on the mantel, or on the covered sewing machine in the corner. The mantel is crowded with various objects: spice jars, a calendar, a formal wedding photograph, a snapshort of one of the men in military uniform, perhaps a jar with artificial flowers. In the spring there are sometimes real flowers, but they are put into a glass or vase with no thought to their arrangement. Very often the fireplace is closed up and a woodstove placed in front of it.

On the whole the room gives an impression of bareness, but also an impression of cleanliness and neatness. It would not occur to people to praise any but the Notaire's and mason's houses for their beauty, comfort, or modern conveniences. These are criteria that may be important for the rich, but any woman, regardless of her wealth, can keep her home clean, and it is for this that houses and housewives are judged.

This respect for cleanliness does not imply an interest in hygiene, although the houses of Peyrane are very hygienic. There is no upholstered furniture, not even in the house of the Notaire. There are no rugs on the floors. The floors are made of tile rather than of wood. But hygiene is a simple coincidence here. People are not interested in upholstered furniture because they are not interested in what they contemptuously call the "comfort of the buttocks." The houses have tile floors because tile is cheaper than wood in that part of France. Of course, tile has other advantages: it is cool in summer; it is durable; it can be cleaned and polished easily. But the fact that tile is hygienic as well as cheap, durable, and easily cleaned is a coincidence that interests no one.

The indifference to hygiene is illustrated by the toilets. Most of the

farm houses have an outhouse, a simple shelter built of cane. Inside
the shelter the only convenience is a beam placed across the center
of the pit at knee height. This outhouse is invariably located next to
the manure pile, and when the manure is taken to fertilize the gardens,
the night soil is taken, too.

In the village some houses have no toilet at all, but there are three
public toilets strategically located around the town. These consist of
a neat concrete shelter, although inside they are anything but neat. The
convenience in these shelters is a hole in the concrete floor. When the
odor of these toilets becomes a matter of public concern the firemen
bring their hose and wash the accumulation down the hill.

Other village houses have as a toilet a little shelter surrounding a
shallow pit. When the pit is full its contents is removed and carried
out to the family garden for fertilizer.

About ten per cent of the houses have a toilet with a flushing mechanism but without a water closet, so that a bucket of water must be
used to flush the toilet. Some of the flushing toilets are connected with
a sewer which empties almost at the edge of town. Houses like ours
which back up to the edge of the cliff do not need to be connected
with the sewer. Our toilet was at the back of the court. A long gutter-
pipe extended over the cliff and sent a cascade to the valley below.
The other houses along the cliff used the same convenient system.

The whole sanitation system of the village depends on this elevation
above the valley. Surplus water from the reservoir at the top of the
hill runs down the hill day and night, carrying with it the debris from
all the houses. It would be more convenient if the water were distributed through several gutters, but it runs through one main gutter to
an ochre mine in the valley. The mining company uses the water for
washing ore and pays the village for canalizing the water in its direction.

When we asked our landlord how to dispose of our trash, we were
told we might put it in front of our house where the street sweeper,
Monsieur Anglade, would cart it away. "But it's farther from your
kitchen to the front door than to your back window so you might as
well dump it over the cliff. That's what Monsieur Anglade will do
with it anyway." Everything over the cliff! The area at the bottom
of the cliff is left to dogs, cats, rats, and chickens.

Francis, the plumber, was amused and perhaps shocked that I should

1. Peyrane

2. Baptism procession

3. French and American boys

4. Dédou Favre and his pacifier

5. The school

6. Monsieur Arène and his store

7. Raoul Favre delivers branches

8. Jacques Roussel ploughs

be interested in plumbing. He was not surprised because he had noticed in American movies "all the porcelain bathrooms with bathtubs and hot running water and water closets." "We don't make so much fuss," he said. "For us when you have to go one corner is as good as another." Since Francis had gone to the trouble of building a W. C. behind his own house, his quip cannot be taken literally. He does not disapprove of hygiene but he is not obsessed by it.

Francis' lack of enthusiasm for modern comforts and conveniences is shared by most of the people of Peyrane. They admire them in the Notaire's house, and they say they would install them in their own houses if they had enough money. It is true that most of the people are too poor to install modern bathrooms and kitchens, but the absence of conveniences in the houses of some of the wealthiest people indicates that money is not the only factor involved. The two richest farmers in the commune do not have running water in their houses. One of them does not have electricity; the other installed it because he found it would be profitable in the farm work. One of the wealthiest mine owners lives in the family house in Peyrane, and the house has neither running water nor electricity.

The teachers and the Doctor, who are the principal propaganda agents for modern hygiene, complain that whenever a family gets enough money to improve its sanitary facilities the money is invested in some other way that will increase the family's capital without drawing attention to its prosperity. If prosperity is publicized, it means a rise in taxes. Only the middle class Notaire and social climbing Martron are willing to invest in conveniences. For most families investments must increase income.

The Martron house, in which we lived, had electricity, running water — even *hot* running water — a bathroom with a bathtub, a flushing toilet with water closet, a central heating system. Such houses are not so rare as one might expect in villages of the Vaucluse. Almost every village has its big house which has been modernized by a son who went off to the city, made money, and acquired city tastes for comfort and display. So we were not surprised to find a house with modern conveniences in Peyrane. We were surprised to learn how the conveniences functioned.

The central heating system consisted of a small stove connected to four little radiators in the four rooms on the second floor. When cold weather arrived early in November we decided to light the furnace. Monsieur Martron had asked us to let him know when we wanted to use the central heating system so that he could show us how it worked. When I telephoned him, he first tried to persuade me that we did not really need to use it. The cold snap would pass, he said, and warm weather would return. In some winters the Martrons never lighted the furnace at all, and Monsieur Martron felt sure we would not need to light it either. When I insisted, he said that it might even be dangerous to start the central heating plant. We would first have to fill the pipes with water, and then there might come a day when the weather would get very cold; we might forget to light a fire in the furnace, and the radiators would freeze and burst. I assured him that if it got that cold we would certainly not forget to make a fire in the furnace, and I continued to insist that we wanted a fire. Monsieur Martron then came up to Peyrane from Apt to discuss the matter. Finally he gave in and began to instruct me in the art of running the central heating system. As we examined the details of the system we discovered at once that a few repairs would have to be made. The water tank had rusted through and the pipes were filled with rust. Obviously the central heating system had not been used for years.

I cannot go into all the detail of explaining how much effort and time it took to put the system back into order. But by Christmas it was ready to be used. Monsieur Martron and I carried gallon after gallon of water to the third floor, climbed a ladder, and emptied the water into a storage tank, for the system was not connected with the regular water pipes of the house. When water gurgled down through all the pipes and radiators we started a fire in the furnace, and after a while the radiators lost their chill and began to heat up. Monsieur Martron left, and I continued to urge the fire along. I soon discovered that in spite of all the trouble the heating system was scarcely adequate to its task. The temperature of the rooms upstairs could not be raised above 52° — even when I fired up so that the wallpaper near the stovepipe caught fire.

Our hot running water system and the bathing arrangements worked even less efficiently than our central heating system. Basically the problem lay in the fact that the hot water was heated in a coil which ran through our cookstove and was then stored in a tank in the bathroom above. There was no radiator in the bathroom, for as Monsieur Martron had said, "It wouldn't be logical to put a radiator there when there's already a big tank of hot water." But since the bathroom was huge, most of the heat from the water in the uninsulated tank was dissipated without really warming the room. Through a crack in the wall the mistral flapped the wallpaper back and forth. When the hot-water faucet in the bathtub was turned on — filling the tub with tepid water — the coils in the kitchen stove filled with cold water, so that the stove could not be used for at least an hour.

On the whole, the modern conveniences and comforts in our house were not very convenient and comfortable. The Martron family, it was clear, had scarcely used them. Martron had installed them less to increase his family's comfort than to raise its prestige.

Accustomed to our American house where a movement of the finger regulates the heat of the whole house, we had taken the radiators of our Peyrane house seriously. When we found that they would not heat the whole house we looked for other means. There were fireplaces in every room; there was the kitchen stove; there was a salamander — a kind of closed Franklin stove — in my study. I was determined to keep the house warm, since with all this apparatus it was theoretically possible. For a few days I went from stove to fireplace to salamander to furnace, nourishing the various fires with wood and coal briquets. It did not take me long to discover that it was a full-time job to keep all these fires burning. Worse than that, the coal and wood bills were alarming in this land where coal and wood are scarce. Even by spending time and money to heat the house, I was not accomplishing my purpose. When the mistral blew, no fire could keep my study warm. I gave up heating it and brought my typewriter and books and papers into the *salle*. Then it seemed foolish to have fires going in the fireplaces in the bedrooms when the only times they were useful were when we were dressing and undressing. It was more sensible to dress and undress in the *salle*. The bathroom was no longer a comfortable refuge as it was at home. Taking a bath meant undressing in a cold room, stepping into lukewarm water, and at the same time upsetting the kitchen routine. We found that we needed fewer baths than before.

Little by little our family life, which at home was distributed throughout the entire house and which we had tried to distribute throughout the Peyrane house, withdrew from all other rooms and was concentrated in the *salle*. This change solved some problems: I spent less time keeping the family warm, and the fuel bill dropped gratifyingly. Other problems were raised. I had to learn to work while the children were playing. The children had to learn to play more quietly. I had to learn to pick up my papers from the table so that it might be used as a dining-room table. Most of our meat was cooked over the coals in the fireplace. When one of the children had an earache at night we could not sit in his room and rock him; we brought him down and held him on our lap in front of the fire. The fire of oak logs which burned day and night for six months became the focal point of our family life.

Without realizing it we had adapted ourselves to a necessary condition of life in Peyrane where families learn to live together in one room. The only warmth of the house is found in the *salle* around the fireplace, or more usually nowadays around the stove. Around this fire, food is prepared and eaten, the family councils make decisions, friends and neighbors are entertained, the doctor even examines a patient whose bed has been moved into the heated room.

In the summer this center of life is less important. The fire is lighted only to cook the food. The family lives outdoors in the sun as much as possible. But in the long, winter months the family is drawn together about the fire in the *salle*, the core of the family's existence. It is inevitable that the English word *home* cannot be translated directly into French. The nearest equivalent in French is the word *foyer*, the hearth.

The Family

There are few childless households in Peyrane. The Notaire and his wife have no children, but that is scarcely surprising since they were in their late forties when they were married. Among the couples who might be expected to have children only two are childless, the Peyrouxes and the Arènes.

The Arènes had the grocery store across the street from our house, so we saw them every day. And every day we heard from them the same complaint: they loved children, they wanted children, but for some reason they had never had any. Both Monsieur and Madame Arène assumed that it was Madame Arène's fault. Arène never blamed his wife, but she complained constantly of being barren.

Years ago, to assure her fertility, Madame Arène might have gone to Apt to rock Saint Anne's cradle in the shrine of the church, or she might have gone to pray nearby at Notre Dame de la Lumière. Today most women of Peyrane would not resort to these means. The thing to do, Madame Arène knew, was to see Doctor Magny, but she dreaded the tests she had heard about and worried about the possible expense. She preferred to consider her childlessness inevitable.

Although the Arènes have given up hope of having children they are not resigned to their fate. They are bitter that a normal happiness has been denied them. They relieve their feeling of bitterness by criticizing the children of the village, who are so badly brought up, Madame Arène says, that they come into the store and beg for candy. When she gives them a piece, off they go without even thanking her. Or they tell their parents who bring the younger children to the store so that Madame Arène will give them candy, too. Or a parent will come in and complain because a neighbor's child has been given candy and his has not. Madame Arène says that although she loves children, she has given up being nice to them because neither they nor their parents appreciate it. If *she* had children they would not be brought up in that manner!

To add to their bitterness, the government penalizes the Arènes for their childlessness. Since they have no children their taxes are higher than those of other people in their income group. They are struggling to make a living out of this little store, and they say they would almost break even if the government did not take so much in taxes. It seems unfair to them that the government should take their money and pay it to families with children as *allocations familiales*. The more children you have the more the government gives you. The government deliberately encourages people to live like animals, says Madame Arène.

"Take the Malitournes," she says. "They have five children and he doesn't work. All he does is go to the government office to get his family allowance checks. They squander that money and come here to get groceries. We're softhearted enough to give them credit because the children have to eat, and it's not their fault, poor dears, if their parents are like that. So here we are, barely able to support ourselves, and yet we have to support this family of do-nothings who live better than we do."

Although society as represented by the government in Paris seems to look with favor on the Malitournes, the society of Peyrane generally agrees with the Arènes in their contempt of families like the Malitournes. There are only four or five such families in Peyrane, and the consensus is that most of them are shiftless, improvident, lacking in the rational control that distinguishes human beings. They live like animals.

Only two big families are respected, and they are referred to as "beautiful families." The Jouves are a young couple from the city, devout Catholics who have "returned to the soil" because of idealism. They hope to help bring religion back to the religiously indifferent rural areas of France. Few people of Peyrane share the ideals of the Jouves, but they respect them because of their social rank and admire their family of four little children.

The family of Charles Mitan, the president of the Tractor Coöperative, is also respected. They have nine children, eight girls and the last a boy. After the birth of their son the Mitans stopped having children. Everyone in Peyrane understood and appreciated the Mitans' determination.

The Malitournes, the Pougets, the Pellegrinas, the Doucets are different. These families have no money. The husbands have the reputation of working as little as possible; the wives are not good housekeepers; the children are dirty and badly brought up. Nor do these parents seem to want big families. They complain more bitterly than other people about the trouble their children give them. The people of Peyrane accuse them of raising big families just so the government will support them through family allowances.

The accusation is probably false. To say that most of these parents produce big families by design is to attribute to them more forethought than they have. They live much better than they would without the family allowances, but from conversations with the parents I infer that they have big families not through forethought but through lack of forethought. While the government system of family allowances has improved the standard of living of big families in Peyrane, it has had little influence on the birth rate. Couples who would have had big families without the family allowances have them more comfortably. Couples who would not have had big families without the family allowances still do not have them.

It also seems that religion has little effect on the birth rate of Peyrane. Most of the parents of big families are ardent Communists. Most of the devout Catholics have only two or three children; they are among the most respectable people of the village and are quick to accuse parents of big families of living like animals. It would almost seem that, except in the case of the bourgeois Jouves, people reproduce in inverse ratio to the intensity of their religious zeal.

The Arènes and the Malitournes represent two extremes that most newly married couples hope to avoid. They do not want to remain childless like the Arènes, even though they are not able to explain just why. As Madame Bonerandi said, "No one knows why we want babies. We . . . love those little beings." Newly married couples are explicit about why they want to avoid the example of the Malitournes. Having so many children wears out the mother. If there are too many children in a family they're too much of a worry and they can't be brought up decently. When the children get older their parents can't help establish them as they should. And besides, human beings are human beings, not animals.

In Peyrane a family of two or three children is the ideal. Marie Fratani summed up this point of view when she said to my wife, "You have two children. That's enough. Now you should put in the cork."

What most people in Peyrane use for a "cork" I am not sure. One thing is certain: no one uses any devices secured at the drugstore or from the doctor. One can buy them at Apt, but they are expensive. Some people have heard about the rhythm method, but no one trusts it. I gather that *coitus interruptus* is frequently practiced. The ubiquitous *bidet* with soap and water is a trusted method. Among some married couples there may more frequently be cessation of sexual relations than one might expect.

A newly married couple need not worry about methods of contraception for some time, however, for they expect to have their children as soon as possible. The parents of the three babies born in the village during our stay had been married a year when the babies were born.

Pregnancy brings no great change in the life of a young woman. She is expected to continue living as normally as possible. When Madame Vidal, the wife of a poor ochre worker became pregnant, she did not give up her job of cleaning the town hall every morning. Madame Bonerandi continued to help her mother around the house and to work for her uncle, the tailor, in her spare time. If either of these women had become ill everyone would have come to her aid, but so long as they were well they were expected to live as usual.

Both women went to see the doctor at the end of the third, sixth, and eighth months of pregnancy, and both had urinalyses at the pharmacy at Apt at regular intervals between medical examinations. Since the government pays for prenatal examinations every pregnant woman in Peyrane sees a doctor regularly.

In spite of the reassuring words of the doctor after each examination, Madame Bonerandi and her mother were anxious about the pregnancy. Rationally they gave no credence to the superstitions they had always heard; they scoffed at the idea that a pregnant woman's fear can give her offspring a birthmark. Yet it was not without concern that Madame Borel told me of Charles Pian. "They say when his mother was pregnant she was scared by a pig. Her husband was butchering it, and it got away and ran toward her all covered with blood. Two months later Charles was born with half his face covered by a red birthmark."

When Madame Vidal was six months pregnant her younger sister, who had been living with her, died of the rheumatic fever which had crippled her since childhood. Madame Vidal went to stay with relatives and did not attend the funeral. Madame Bonerandi, a close friend of the deceased girl, was not present at the funeral, although all the other friends of the girl were there, six of them serving as pallbearers. Pregnant women avoid unhappy spectacles like funerals.

Toward the end of the period of pregnancy the Vidal and the Bonerandi households were on the alert. Baby clothes and linen had been gathered. Arrangements had been made with relatives to help at the time of delivery and to keep the household running. They kept in touch with Doctor Magny in St. Saturnin.

Twice within two weeks the gendarmes had to rouse Doctor Magny to tell him that he was needed in Peyrane. First it was Madame Bonerandi who in the early hours of the morning gave birth to a boy. A few nights later it was Madame Vidal's turn. She gave birth to twins, a boy and a girl. Both women had been in labor five or six hours, an average time in the opinion of most people.

Everyone was aware of these events early in the morning after they had taken place, and everyone seemed especially happy about them. Relatives, neighbors, friends, even villagers who were more or less "on the outs" with these families, all agreed that the Bonerandis and the Vidals had started "beautiful little families" now.

Within a few days both women began to return to normal life. Madame Bonerandi was lucky, people said. She lived with her mother who helped take care of the baby. Madame Vidal, although she received government assistance, felt obliged to return to work as rapidly as possible, and in a few days she was again washing the floors of the town hall every morning. She made arrangements with a sister to take care of the babies while she was working. Since she was well, she was expected to assume her usual burden, to return to normal.

But "return to normal" is a phrase that has little meaning for a young couple with their first child, for this is nothing they have known before. After the glamor of being the parents of a first child has worn off, after they have become accustomed to thinking of themselves as a household of three instead of two, they realize with a shock what normality means for the adults of Peyrane.

All their life they have heard their parents and other adults of Peyrane complain about how hard life is, this "bitch of life," as the men say. You can't help wanting peace and happiness, yet these hopes are never realized. Children are the worst disappointment of all. You want them; you love them; you work for them. Yet from one point of view they are just a nuisance or a worry. Madame Canazzi, the baker's wife, says, "When they're well they make your life miserable and when they're sick you worry yourself sick over them." And when they grow up there's no gratitude. They go away and leave you. The only happy time in life is when you're young and having a good time before you're married.

As young people settle down to raise a family they find their freedom is gone, and their work, their responsibilities, and their worries have increased many times. They accept the situation, since nothing can be done about it; but they join in the general chorus of adults complaining about it. Of course, much of this talk is superficial. One complains about life the way one complains about the weather. It is a way of relieving oneself of pent-up feelings and of being friendly with other people. One does not mean to be taken too seriously, for certainly no parents of Peyrane would change places with the childless Arènes. And one may long for the days of adolescence without really wanting to trade for them the present life with all its hardships and worries. To complain of one's children is to relieve oneself of the aggression one cannot help feeling toward the little beings that you have to feed and wash and discipline constantly. You can't beat them when you feel like it, so you talk about them. There must be some relief from the constant struggle all parents have in raising their families as they think they should.

Chapter 7

Making a Living

Making Ends Meet

The main worry of every family in Peyrane is the main worry of most families everywhere: how to make ends meet. Prices in Peyrane are high, and income is low, so every family is preoccupied with the question of increasing family resources to cover the cost of living.

The problem seems to be rather well solved. People complain of their poverty, but there is no misery. Everyone is sheltered; everyone is clothed; everyone is fed. On Sunday afternoon a tourist walking through the streets and seeing the villagers out for a walk or sitting in front of their houses would have the impression that Peyrane is even prosperous. The father of the family in his black suit and black hat, the mother in her simple, neat dress, the children — especially the little boys — even stylishly dressed: the Peyrane family out for its Sunday walk would be indistinguishable from any family of solid, though modest, circumstances in Apt or Avignon. Compared with villagers in poorer regions of France, like inland Brittany, the people of Peyrane live comfortably and securely. However, their comfort and security are relative, and they are achieved only by hard work, constant worry, vigilance, and ingenuity.

Food is expensive. In Peyrane, as elsewhere in France, the largest single item in the family budget is the cost of food. Using the convenient rule of 1000 francs for $3.00, we can get an idea of the cost of a few foods that are really important in a family budget: bread costs 15 cents a loaf; sugar costs 15 cents a pound; peanut oil, 70 cents a quart; olive oil, $1.50 a quart; the local cheese 45 cents a pound. For three essential items alone — bread, oil, and wine — a family of four must spend about $15.00 a month.

With the aid of grocers and other informants we found that the cost of the average monthly market basket for a family of four is about sixty dollars. In our own family of four we spent four dollars a day for food, but we were far more extravagant than other people in Peyrane and we ate far better than we do at home. The normal experience is that of the postman's family. Madame Favre says that it costs her three dollars a day to feed her family of six, consisting of two adults, an adolescent daughter and three little boys. She did not include in this estimate the eggs, chickens, rabbits, and cheese that the Favres produce themselves or get from her father's farm.

Rent is the least expensive item in a family's budget. For our furnished house we paid thirty dollars a month, the highest rent in Peyrane. Everyone except our landlord said we were being exploited. The lowest rent was the three dollars a month Pouget paid for a wretchedly furnished house in poor repair. No one in Peyrane seriously complains of high rents. The difficulty, as we have seen, lies not in paying the rent but in finding a house to rent.

Clothes, on the other hand, are expensive even by American standards. The best clothes cost more than those of the same quality in the United States, but of course no one in Peyrane wears clothing of high quality except the Notaire's family. Most people wear the kind that would be bought in an Army and Navy Store or from a big mail-order house in this country, and it is more expensive in France than it is here.

Fuel is expensive in this part of France where there are no coal mines and no heavy forests. Wood costs $9.00 a ton. Coal briquets cost $1.50 for a hundred-pound sack. Bottled gas costs $3.00 a bottle, and a family uses at least one bottle a month for cooking in the summer. Electricity costs 6 cents a kilowatt hour.

Some people confine their expenditures to the necessities of life, but most people spend some money for amusements. If a person goes to the movies in Peyrane, it costs him 15 cents. It costs 25 cents to enter a boules or belote tournament. The usual drink at the café costs 10 cents, and it is difficult to go to the café without being caught in a round of drinks and having to pay for two or three. *Babyfoot*, a pinball game in the café, costs 3 cents a game, and the loser must buy drinks as well as pay for the game. He must also pay for drinks if he loses at boules or belote. One cannot decently entertain at home without offering guests coffee, and coffee costs $1.25 a pound. Cigarettes cost 20 cents a package for the most ordinary and popular, *gauloises bleues*. If you roll your own cigarettes, you pay 25 cents for a package of the cheapest tobacco. It costs 15 cents to take the bus to Apt. If you have a car, gasoline costs 75 cents a gallon.

Compared to the cost of living, the average income in Peyrane is low, although no one knows exactly what the average income is. A family's income and the sexual behavior of normal individuals are the two most closely guarded secrets in the village. The tax commission itself, faced by the impossibility of discovering all the facts concerning income, sensibly contents itself with apportioning taxes according to its estimate based on "exterior signs" of the wealth of each family.

The calculation of income is further complicated by the elaborate family aid program of the French government. In determining the income of each family, one must take into account not only the family's earnings but also the amount of money it receives from the government in the form of family allowances, single-income allowance, lodging allowance, health allowances, etc. The allowances have become a very important part of the village economy. Several families receive more financial aid from the government every month than they receive in wages for their work. Henri Favre, for example, has a pregnant wife, three small children, and an older apprenticed child. He earns less as an ochre worker than he receives in the form of family allowances and single-salary allowance from the government.

It is possible to speak of Henri Favre's wages precisely because he belongs to the one group of people in the commune who speak of their income readily — the salaried people and wage earners whose incomes are a matter of public knowledge. They have nothing to gain by hiding the facts of their incomes. Indeed, they believe they may gain by publicizing them, since they say they are too low. Their standard of living is not noticeably different from that of other people, so their salaries and wages may offer some indication of the normal income in the village.

The highest-paid salaried workers are the teachers; the best-paid teacher receives about ninety dollars a month and a free apartment above the school. The lowest regular wage is that of Pouget, the poorest of the ochre workers. He showed me pay stubs which averaged about twenty-five dollars a month. Between these two extremes is Rivet, the town clerk, whose salary is forty dollars a month. Henri Favre, one of the better-paid ochre workers, receives a wage of about thirty-two dollars a month. His government family allowances and single-salary allowance bring his monthly income up to about seventy dollars per month. Pouget's total income is sixty dollars: twenty-five dollars in wages and thirty-five dollars in government allowances. Other men who talked to me about their financial status seemed to use the round sum of 20,000 francs — sixty dollars — to describe their monthly income. On the basis of what evidence we have, we can suggest that the average income of the families of salaried workers and wage earners might be between sixty and seventy dollars a month.

In short, the family income is about the same as the cost of the monthly family market basket, sixty dollars. And in addition to food one must pay for clothing, fuel, rent, doctor's bills, medicine, utilities, transportation, insurance, savings, and amusements. It is not surprising that the people of Peyrane talk and worry constantly about their economic problems! How can they make ends meet?

The question is serious, but the situation is not so desperate as it sounds. The economy of Peyrane is not simple. It is infinitely complicated. The pay check and the government allowance check are far from representing the total income of the families. There are many ways of supplementing income. The number of transactions involving exchange of goods and services, rather than money, is so great, and the nature of these transactions is often so subtle and complicated that a full accounting of the economy of Peyrane is impossible. Many of the transactions pass completely unnoticed, and some are kept secret. Many seem so natural and insignificant that people scarcely realize that they are related to income. The complexity of the economic system may best be understood if we analyze the sources of income of a few families.

In Francis Favre's family there are two adults, an adolescent child and three small children. Francis is the postman and receives his regular check from the government for his services. Since he travels over the whole commune every day it is only natural that people should ask him to perform all sorts of special services. Rigaud asks him to tell Joly to send his boy over to help get in the hay. Monsieur Reynard asks him to deliver a package of rice to Madame Chanon who is sick and has sent word she needs it. The town clerk asks him to spread the word that a meeting of the schoolchildren's parents will be held on Sunday afternoon. He is asked to announce the funeral of Thérèse Roget. Figeard asks him to tell the hunting guards to come gas out a den of foxes near his farm. These services are freely performed on a friendly basis, but that does not preclude the offering of a gift which Francis usually accepts, depending on the importance of the favor — a chicken or a bottle of wine or some eggs or a cheese. Then there are the innumerable trifles that Francis is offered — the glasses of wine and liqueur and brandied cherries.

When Francis returns from his round as postman other work awaits him. He is the only electrician and plumber in the commune and people literally squabble over him. If he had the energy and determination to do all the jobs he is constantly begged to undertake he would be one of the wealthiest men in the village, but Francis has little ambition. He prefers a life of peace and leisure. To secure peace he never says *no* when he is asked to do a job; to secure leisure he never does the job he has accepted if he can avoid it. One morning during his vacation after he had promised to come to our house at nine o'clock and did not arrive, I learned from Monsieur Reynard and Monsieur Vincent that he had also promised to be at their houses at nine o'clock. None of the three of us saw him all morning; he had gone to the market in Apt.

But when Francis cannot avoid undertaking a plumbing or electrical job, when he actually finishes a job, when he gets around to submitting a bill, when the bill is actually paid, then Francis makes a substantial, extra contribution to the family income, more usually in money but sometimes in goods.

Another source of income is the government. For their three little boys the Favres receive a monthly check equal to fifty per cent of the basic salary of the zone in which Peyrane is located. Moreover, Francis' wife is pregnant, and he has filled out the necessary forms declaring that they will have a fourth child in seven months. As soon as the formalities are arranged the Favres will receive a family allowance for the unborn child dating from the beginning of pregnancy. The allowance for four children will be eighty per cent of the basic salary — an important sum for this family.

Suzanne Favre, Francis' wife, is one of the best mothers and housekeepers in Peyrane. Her house is always neat. Her children are well-dressed and well-trained. She has contempt for mothers who let their children run the street. She keeps hers at home and devotes much time to them. In addition to caring for the house and for the children, she raises chickens and rabbits and has to go out each day to get grass for them. These are normal duties for a wife and Suzanne does them well.

Since Francis' salary is sufficient only to buy food for the family, Suzanne has assumed the responsibility of clothing them. This involves not only knitting and sewing all the clothes, but earning the money to buy the materials. For articles like shoes that she can not make, she also earns the money.

During the grape and asparagus harvest Suzanne takes a full-time job working eight hours a day at the Marnas farm. The two older boys stay at school all day, eating their lunch at the canteen. Since the farm is not far from the village she takes three-year-old Dédou along with her. Thus she manages to carry on her normal domestic activities and her job as harvester at the same time. If at the peak of the harvest she has to work longer hours, she sends her children to her father's farm, but she prefers to keep them with her.

Of course, Suzanne must be careful not to earn too much money. If she earns more than half the amount of the basic salary of the zone in which Peyrane is located she must forfeit still another source of income — the government "single-salary allowance." So long as Francis is the only full wage earner in the family, the Favres receive every month from the government fifty per cent of the basic salary in addition to the usual family allowance. These amounts are further increased because of Francis' position as a government employee.

In the late winter and spring Suzanne raises silkworms. This involves very little work at first, but as the worms hatch out and begin to grow the work increases unbelievably. One would never suspect that a few little worms could consume so large a quantity of mulberry leaves. To get the leaves Suzanne walks a mile from the village, strips trees (she has obtained permission from the owners), and carries huge sacks of leaves to the village on her back.

Francis and Suzanne own a small cherry orchard which they inherited a few years ago. It is only a half-mile or so from the village, and in June when the cherries are ripe Suzanne walks there with her children after school. They carry pails and baskets with them and pick cherries until almost dark. Then Francis comes down from the village with a hand cart. They load the cart with crates of cherries and push it back up the steep hill to the home of Monsieur Borel who buys them to resell on the Cavaillon market the next day.

Whenever Suzanne finds time she goes on beyond the orchard two miles or so to her father's farm, or rather to the farm which he works, for he is a tenant farmer. When she has visited with her parents for a few moments, she and her little boys walk back to the village taking eggs, cheese, and vegetables. When her father or sisters or brothers come to the village they never fail to bring some farm produce as a present. Her father owes his relative prosperity to Suzanne. During the early days of the war before she married, she lived on the farm. Her father was sick. Her brothers were prisoners in Germany, and her sisters were too young to work, so Suzanne ran the farm, ploughing and cultivating and harvesting and caring for the horses and goats and sheep.

No work seems to be too hard for Suzanne. When Francis had an accident and was unable to go on his mail route for several days, the Mayor could find no one to take his place. Suzanne got on her bicycle and rode the twenty-five mile route, delivering the mail more promptly than her husband usually did.

With his talent and training as electrician and plumber Francis could make an excellent living for his family, and Suzanne would not have to work so hard. But, as people say, Francis has no taste for work, so Suzanne must make up for his deficiency. Together they succeed in making ends meet and in raising their children decently. It takes work, but Suzanne does not complain because life is like that — especially for women.

Compared with Francis, Emile Pian is a model husband. As a mason he has a good job working for Gaston Jouvaud who pays him three dollars a day. It is hard work, sometimes dangerous work when he is on top of an old house trying to pull back into place a wall that is ready to fall. He is a regular worker and never misses a day when he can help it. Last winter when he had lumbago he went back to work after two days in bed, even though every effort made him groan.

No one is more *sérieux* than Emile. He almost never goes to the café. He never plays boules or belote. On Sundays and in the evening after he has finished work he walks out a half-mile from the village where he has his garden on a plot of land that is partly owned by him and partly rented from a neighbor. On the rented land he grows enough vegetables to feed the family all season, and since cold weather does not last long he often manages to supply the family with salad greens for nine months of the year.

On his own land he has a vineyard. In a good year the vineyard produces enough grapes to supply his family and his wife's family with wine for the entire year. They all harvest the grapes, and Emile borrows Moïse Jannel's wine press and presses the grapes himself. When the wine is good, and when there is more than enough for ordinary needs, he fabricates a few special drinks. With herbs that his wife gathers he makes some bottles of vermouth according to his Uncle Pierre's recipe. He also decants several bottles of juice while it is still fairly sweet, before it is completely fermented, and pours a few ounces of alcohol in each bottle before he corks it; this makes *angélique*, a dessert wine which may be served to friends spending the evening with the Pians. In other, heavier bottles of not completely fermented wine he puts a little sugar; he then corks them with extreme care and covers the cork with a heavy coating of sealing wax; this makes sparkling wine to be served at special celebrations.

When Emile has pressed the wine from the grapes he does not throw away the residue, even though it looks dry and useless. He takes it to Monsieur Hugon, the man from Rustrel who makes the rounds of the villages every fall with his portable still. For a small sum of money (openly paid) and for a slight share in the product (surreptitiously donated — since the government maintains strict control), M. Hugon distills from the residue enough alcohol to last the Pians and Fratanis all year. Some of this is used for medicinal and household purposes, and some of it is either drunk straight by the men after their supper coffee or else made into *pastis* to be drunk as an apéritif.

Pastis is a sweet, anis-flavored drink that is drunk so diluted with water that one can consume several glasses without experiencing much effect from the alcohol. The men of Peyrane insist that it gives them an enormous appetite. Since he has his own supply of pastis, Emile does not have to go to the café in the evening. When he feels the need of companionship he invites his friends to his house to drink his pastis. The café owner complains that since the war and inflation many men have their apéritif at home.

Even though Emile has a good job and uses his leisure time to provide the family with vegetables and beverages, his income is not sufficient. Since Madaleine and he have only one child they receive no government family allowance to supplement the family income. They would like another child or two, but Madeleine has had several miscarriages. However, since Emile's wages are the only official family income, the Pians do receive the government single-salary allowance, which amounts to twenty per cent of the basic salary every month. The twenty per cent will be reduced to ten per cent on the child's sixth birthday.

Like Suzanne Favre, Madeleine Pian takes full-time jobs during the grape and asparagus harvest, and she raises as many silkworms as she can care for in their small house. The rest of the year, when she has no regular work, she goes with her mother and Madame Biron out into the woods and fields around the town every afternoon to bring back whatever they can find that will be useful. In the fall they pick baskets of mushrooms, some of which they eat fresh and some they preserve. In the winter they go out with a hand cart and bring back loads of twigs and branches for fuel. In the cherry season they bring back cherries from Monsieur Rastello's orchard where they buy them at a big reduction because they pick them themselves. Every day during the year they must go out to cut grass for their chickens and rabbits.

A year ago Emile's brother, a petty officer in the air force, returned from three year's service in Indo-China and was stationed at an air field not far from Peyrane. He brought back with him his daughter, a two-year-old girl whose mother, he said jokingly, he "bought" when he got out there and "sold" when he left. He brought the little half-Chinese girl back to France, and she lived with Emile and Madeleine in Peyrane for several months. They enjoyed keeping their niece, partly because they had always wanted a daughter and partly because Emile's brother made a financial arrangement with them. The arrangement was kept secret, and officially Emile assumed the financial responsibility of raising the child. Consequently the Pians were credited by the government with the support of two children, and they received a family allowance equivalent to twenty per cent of the basic salary until Emile's brother was transferred and took the little girl away.

Emile and Madeleine have not only their immediate family to support; they also contribute to the support of her parents, Marie and Mario Fratani. Mario is an ochre worker. He is industrious, but his health has gotten worse and worse in spite of a serious operation he underwent many months ago which the doctor said would help him. Whenever he tries to work regularly he has a bad attack that keeps him in bed for several days. Doctor Magny, Mario's family, and everyone in the village think it obvious that Mario should be allowed to retire on a government disability pension, but whenever Mario makes the trip to Apt to be examined by the social-security medical examiner he is told that he is not ill enough to draw more than partial disability benefits. He cannot receive even these benefits unless he tries to work regularly. So Mario goes back to work — and has another attack. The social-security complication seems as mysterious to Mario and the people of Peyrane as it does to me. There must be an explanation, but I know only the story that Mario and the villagers tell.

When he is recovering from his attacks — and he never stays in bed as long as Doctor Magny says he should — he does what work he can around home and around town. He works in Emile's garden. He cleaned our gutters. He helps Moïse Jannel press wine.

Marie and Mario live in the back of the house of Biron, the butcher. They used to have the whole house to themselves, but their landlord sold it to Biron. The Fratanis refused to move because they could find no other place to live. Biron could probably have had them evicted if he had gone to law over it, but it seemed to everyone's advantage to seek a friendly solution. Now the Birons and the Fratanis live together on an amicable and coöperative basis. The Fratanis have two rooms to themselves, and Mario works off their rent by helping Biron. He helps him butcher and prepare the meat; he helps him make sausages; when he is recovering from his attacks he goes with Biron in the big red truck with pink plastic pig heads on the front to make the daily rounds through the countryside, bringing meat to hamlets and villages which have no butcher.

Marie is not in good health either. She has an occasional heart attack which she ignores whenever she can for fear the doctor will tell her she cannot work. She has no full-time employment but takes whatever work she can find around the village. She goes to the Notaire's house one afternoon a week to help Madame Barbier. She would prefer a full-time job if she could find one, but there are only three regular openings for cleaning women in Peyrane — at the school, at the town hall and at the hotel — and these three jobs are filled.

During the year that we lived in Peyrane, Marie cleaned our house every morning. This was her first regular job since the Martrons moved away seven years before. We paid her the wages she asked — fifteen cents an hour for several months until she raised her demand to seventeen cents. For this sum she swept and dusted the entire house, washed all the tile floors on her hands and knees, cleaned the courtyard and toilet, and did the washing and ironing. All this was done without the benefit of warm water or mechanical aids, except Madeleine's thirty-year-old electric iron. When the weather got cold Marie insisted on continuing to do the washing in the cold water in the stone tubs in the courtyard. When she could endure the cold no longer she would put a bucket of embers between her feet so that the heat would rise within her skirt. After pleading with her and insisting that her family bring pressure to bear we succeeded in persuading her to do the washing in the kitchen with warm water.

Marie asked for no pity and no help. She knows that human beings — especially women — are born to work and suffer. She accepts her lot and makes the best of it. She takes any kind of work she can find. When we wanted her to come back in the afternoon she was often not able to. She had gotten word that she was asked to help butcher a pig at a farm two miles or so from the village or to help prepare a banquet at another hamlet. After working at our house all morning she walked to the farm where she was hired, did her work, and walked back to the village. The last we heard she has had no more heart attacks than usual.

The Fratanis and Pians live in separate houses, but they find it economical to have their meals together at the Pians. I do not know how the cost of the food is divided between them, but there is undoubtedly some definite arrangement, for the people of Peyrane prefer to have everything clearly arranged so there will be no misunderstanding.

The Favres, the Pians, and the Fratanis are average families in Peyrane. Some people are better off; some are worse off; most are in a similar situation. All people have in common the inevitable problem of supplementing income in order to make ends meet, and everyone with work and ingenuity finds his own particular solution.

Henri Favre was an apprentice butcher as a boy; now he is an ochre worker, but he takes time off to butcher most of the pigs raised by villagers for their own use. Leporatti, another ochre worker, raises *appelants*, decoy thrushes, finches, warblers, etc., which he sells to hunters. His wife is the cleaning woman at the hotel. Lataud, the owner of a café which finally "went on the rocks" a few months before we left, worked part time in the ochre mines. Madame Grandgeon takes in sewing. The Rivets have a summer boarding house. Arène works on the commune roads for three weeks every year to pay his taxes. The mechanic, Ricci, finds that the income from his garage is too small to support even a bachelor; he helps Borel collect cherries and asparagus from the farms and drive them to the market in Cavaillon. Many of his jobs are paid for in merchandise rather than in money. Biron gives him meat; Marchal gives him vegetables; the café owner gives him drinks. On his way to the café in the evening Pascal often stopped at our house with a melon or some peas for which we gave him enough money to pay for drinks.

Pascal is a farmer, and the farmer's economy is more complicated than that of the artisan or tradesman or worker in the village. Most of the farmers have to keep records in order to furnish the commune with statistics and to compute their taxes, but the records — especially those which a tax collector might examine — are somewhat removed from reality. One could never establish from a farmer's records exactly what his real income is. Pascal did not make a record of the fact that he had dropped by our house to sell us two pounds of peas on his way to the café. He certainly never recorded giving Ricci three melons to pay for welding a hole in his gas tank. It did not even occur to him that such items represented income for him. When I asked him how much he had made the previous year he said his income had been about two-hundred and seventy dollars. But this sum represented only the amount of cash he received for selling his crops to Monsieur Borel and at the Saturday morning market at Apt. To discover his real income Pascal would have to be shadowed for three hundred sixty-five days of the year so that each of his many little transactions could be recorded and the value of items produced by him and consumed by his family could be estimated.

These theoretical questions concerning the definition of income are matters of which the people of Peyrane are unaware, but even if they were aware of them they would not be interested. The problem that preoccupies them is the practical problem of feeding and clothing and housing their family. This problem does not confront them in abstract terms of income and expenditure; it is composed of an infinite number of concrete situations. To resolve these situations one resorts to whatever means lie at one's disposal: payment of money, exchange of goods, exchange of services, gifts, psychological devices, social pressure. Any one of these is as good as another, but no one means is sufficient to solve all problems.

Cutting Corners

The financial problem of a family is only half solved when each member contributes as much as he can to the family income. To make ends meet everyone must also coöperate in reducing expenses to a minimum. This endless need to cut corners has left a deep impression on every part of the daily routine.

Food is the largest item in the budget of any Peyrane family. Unfortunately, this is a most difficult item to reduce because of the importance attached to food. The subject of food is one of the principal topics of conversation. Like the weather and like the hardships of life, it can be discussed freely and with pleasure by people who appear ready to fly at each other's throats when politics are mentioned. Good recipes are discussed not only by women in the work-and-talk circles; men standing at the bar enjoy telling how to roast thrushes properly just as they enjoy going out to shoot thrushes. The people of Peyrane do not eat simply to satisfy their hunger; for them eating is one of the things that make life worth living.

This attitude toward food makes the task of the mother especially difficult. She must satisfy her family's and her own high standards of taste, and at the same time she must economize. It is no coincidence that traditional dishes are made of inexpensive ingredients. One of the most popular is *daube*, which is made of a cheap cut of beef. To prepare *daube* the Peyrane housewife first soaks the meat in wine to soften the tough fibers and to bring out the flavor. The wine has been carefully seasoned with herbs and condiments. After the meat has been marinated for several hours it is drained and browned in oil. Finally it is put in a casserole with the original wine concoction and simmered for three or four hours. This dish is inexpensive, but it is a family treat that can be served on special occasions.

The housewife's situation is complicated by the fact that it takes so long to prepare good but inexpensive dishes like *daube*. Time is valuable to her since she must contribute at least as much as her husband to the family resources. Even if she does not have a job picking grapes or asparagus, she still has the house, the children, the chickens and rabbits, the sewing, the cleaning, and the washing to occupy her. So the woman's position is difficult. She must spend as little money as possible on food. She must take care and time in preparing it, and she has little time to spare.

Breakfast is the easiest meal. Most members of the family have a bowl of warm milk flavored with hot coffee. With this goes bread that is dunked in the bowl or eaten with honey or jam. If anyone is going to spend the morning at hard physical labor, he is not satisfied with a "bowl breakfast" of *café au lait* and bread. He wants a "fork breakfast" of cheese, sausage, and hot soup. This soup may still be called a "fork" dish because there is as much solid as liquid in it. Wine, rather than coffee, is the drink that goes with a "fork breakfast."

Dinner is served at noon. There is sometimes a meat dish, but more usually a meat substitute is served, a heavy dish with a macaroni, noodle, rice, potato, or egg base. A fresh vegetable is often served as a first course with oil and vinegar. For dessert there is fruit and cheese or jam or pudding. For supper a hearty soup is most likely served, and there is a green salad if there was none at noon. Cheese and fruit are served for dessert again.

A large quantity of bread is eaten at all three meals and at mid-morning and mid-afternoon snacks. Everyone agrees that the smallest loaves are best because they have the highest proportion of crust, but the largest loaves are most economical and therefore most popular.

Wine is drunk by almost everyone. The town water is excellent, since it is piped from mountain springs, but it is considered tasteless. Even people who do not drink wine will put a few drops in their glass and in the glasses of the children to flavor the water.

The Peyrane diet is healthy, although it may be somewhat high in starch and low in protein. The lack of protein from meat is partially made up by the protein in cheese and eggs. Butter is too expensive for most people to use, but the large quantity of oil in the cooking makes the fat content of the diet high. Sugar is expensive and is used sparingly; it is safe to say that no one gets too much sugar. Fresh vegetables, tossed salads, and fruit furnish plenty of vitamins.

People would laugh to hear their meals analyzed like this. From their point of view, a person who is not starving eats not for health but for pleasure. However, they are not so discriminating in their enjoyment of this pleasure as they used to be. Technological change and the high cost of living have taken their toll on the palates of the people of Peyrane. Through need and eventually through habit they have been led to prefer the mediocre to the good in certain items.

Peyrane lies within the olive-producing region of France, and formerly olive oil was a staple in the community. Modern transportation has made it cheaper to buy African peanut oil at the store than to grow and to make one's own olive oil. For reasons of economy, peanut oil has been used instead of olive oil for so many years that people have actually come to prefer its flavor. The local olive harvest is now so small that the public olive press stored in Francis Favre's shed is hardly used.

The taste for good wine has also deteriorated. The larger producers take all their grapes to the Wine Coöperative where good and indifferent grapes are all put into one chute. This encourages the growers to raise varieties of grapes that give the largest amount of juice and sugar regardless of their flavor. This coöperative wine is produced impersonally and on so large a scale that the final product is necessarily mediocre. Most of it is sold to large distributing companies, but each grower reserves enough for his family. So the wine that most of the grape producers of Peyrane drink is precisely the same wine that is sold in the cities as "ordinary wine." They have grown so accustomed to drinking mediocre wine that they find it acceptable.

Small growers like Emile Prayal who press their own grapes produce a wine that is usually better than coöp wine, but they are also obliged to sacrifice quality for quantity. They press their grapes until they have extracted every possible drop, and this procedure does not make for a wine of high quality. Only a few vintners, like old Monsieur Sanape, care enough about good wine to sacrifice quantity and to spend the time it takes to produce wine of quality. Sanape does not drink much wine, but when he does, it must be good.

When you buy *vin ordinaire*, Monsieur Reynard or Monsieur Arène fills your bottle from his wine cask. If you do not have a bottle, you must buy one. Since we occasionally bought good wines in Apt and Avignon and since the bottle is included in the price of expensive wines, we usually had a supply of bottles which, we were surprised to learn, was a real treasure, not something to be thrown away. The men need all the bottles they can get for their homemade wine, marc, angélique, and pastis. The women must take bottles to the store every time they buy wine, oil, ammonia, disinfectant, fuel alcohol, and vinegar. When people brought us bottles of their wine as a present, they had no qualms about asking us to be sure to return the bottles, or to give them others in exchange.

The junkman of Apt, lou Bey, finds only broken bottles on the dump at the foot of the cliff in Peyrane. In fact, he rarely finds anything worth picking up there because no one throws away a rag or tin can or piece of paper that has any possible use. There is little paper in the village to throw away. The grocer never wraps up an article if he can avoid it. The customer brings her own net or oil cloth shopping bag into which potatoes, onions, tomatoes, and cabbage are placed without wrapping. When the grocer is obliged to wrap something — an order of rice, for instance — he turns to the pile of neatly cut-up newspaper, chooses a piece of appropriate size, folds it, holds it by corners, and gives it a twirl so that the corners become twisted. This will hold until it reaches the customer's kitchen. The grocer has string but only in balls on the shelf — for sale. For olives or a piece of soft cheese news-paper cannot be used. For such articles he regretfully tears off a piece of waxed paper he has had to buy for that purpose. When the customer arrives home after a shopping expedition she has only a few little squares of newspaper or oily wrapping paper to dispose of. These are saved to help light the fire.

There are no heavy cardboard boxes available — even at a price. When Monsieur Reynard and Monsieur Arène buy their goods at the wholesale grocery they are responsible for supplying the containers to carry them home. The wine merchant in Apt occasionally let me use a heavy cardboard box in which to carry home my purchase if I would be sure to return it on my next trip.

Since we subscribed to the *New York Times* and since I bought a copy of all the newspapers distributed in Peyrane, we had another treasure almost equal in value to our treasure of bottles. To please Monsieur Arène or any tradesman in Peyrane we needed only to present him with a pile of old newspapers. Each grocer bought his own newspaper each day, but a six-page Marseille newspaper cannot serve many customers. Monsieur Arène could not ask other people to give him newspapers because he knew they needed them. He knew that ours were available because we were among the very few customers who bought toilet paper.

Just as every scrap of paper has some value, so every piece of cloth is put to use. Best clothing is carefully preserved for special occasions;

everyday clothing does not soil or tear easily. In cold weather the children wear wool clothing, but it is protected by a cotton smock which is cheaper and easier to clean. Since washing requires soap, takes a mother's time and energy, and wears out the cloth, children must learn to play so as to soil their clothes as little as possible. Garments are patched and repatched. People do not think that patches are attractive, but they are indifferent to them on work clothes. The clothing worn by the ochre workers often consists of more patching than original material.

Outgrown garments are passed from one child to another, from one family to another, from one generation to another. Outgrown knitted articles are unraveled and reknit. A pair of shoes is worn by one person or another until it falls apart, and then the cobbler usually finds a way to put it back together. Many people save their shoes for special occasions; for daily use they wear carpet slippers which are cheap and comfortable. In the summer most people wear *espadrilles*, inexpensive shoes with rope soles and canvas tops. The poorer children of the village often wear canvas shoes even in the winter. The country children need heavier shoes, but these are made as durable as possible with hobnails, steel tips, and steel coverings around the sole of the shoe.

When a family wishes to dress up for a special occasion it has the means to do so. For ordinary days, however, clothing is designed for protection and warmth; its style and attractiveness are appreciated, but they are secondary considerations that parents cannot afford to worry about.

The warmth of clothing is especially important because the houses are cold in winter. The Provençal fireplaces are big enough for a roaring fire, but we saw no roaring fire in any fireplace except in our own. We tried to heat the *salle* to 65°. We let the fire burn all night so that the room would be warm when we came down to dress in the morning. We put more wood on the fire when we left the house so that the *salle* would be warm when we came home. People found our behavior shockingly wasteful and our *salle* stiflingly warm.

It is considered dangerous for anyone to get too cool in summer and too hot in winter, so by heating our *salle* to 65° we were exposing ourselves to illness as well as wasting fuel. The accepted way to keep warm in winter is to dress warmly so that either outdoors or indoors one can be comfortable. The only rooms in the village warmer than ours were those of the postmistress, the town clerk's secretary, and one of the teachers, and these three women were always a bit ill. People were not sure whether they insisted on heat because they were already ill or whether they were ill because they lived in overheated rooms.

For most people the *salle* is comfortable if the extreme cold and dampness are removed, and a small fire is sufficient for that purpose. The accepted way of building a fire is to get a small flame started in the center of the fireplace. Then two logs are placed at right angles with each other, with two ends sticking out the corners of the fireplace and the other two ends barely meeting at the flame. As the logs burn away at this point of contact, they are pushed slightly closer together so that a small, constant flame is maintained and a minimum of fuel is consumed. When the family leaves the house, or when everyone goes to bed, the fire is extinguished. In temperate weather a fire may be lit, but for cooking only. A temporary fire of this kind is usually made of twigs or grape-stock trimmings which are allowed to burn themselves out. If a log is used, it is taken out in front of the house and extinguished as soon as the fire is no longer needed.

In many houses the fireplace has been replaced by a cookstove which stands directly in front of it so that the smoke pipe of the stove may be run up the chimney of the fireplace. The best fuel is anthracite briquets, but they are too expensive for most people. The usual fuel burned in stoves is *petits bois*, that is, branches of live oak, one-half to two inches in diameter, that have been sawed into pieces three to six inches in length. If they are too dry, they are mixed with greener wood so that they will not burn too fast.

Most of the stoves have a small boiler to supply the household with a little warm water, but this water is used sparingly. Dishes are usually washed in cold water with washing soda which is considered more effective and is less expensive than soap. When the clothes are ·too dirty to clean with cold water, they are placed in an immense percolator and allowed to cook on the stove. Water for sponge baths, which the ochre workers take every night after work and which other people take about once a week, is heated on the stove and poured into a large tin tub placed in the *salle*. In the summer warm water is scarcer than in winter because the cookstove is not used. It is cleaned and polished, and on it is placed a two-burner gas plate supplied with bottled gas which is used sparingly. Gas is too expensive to heat water for normal purposes.

To bathe, families go down the hill to the washing basins of the ochre mines.

The Notaire and his family have none of these household worries, for their new house is run with electricity. It has not only electric lights but an electric furnace, an electric stove and an electric water heater. Everyone else in the village uses as little electricity as possible. In most houses its use is confined to the small bulb hanging in the center of the *salle* and to a radio.

We put a seventy-five-watt bulb in the fixture over the table in the middle of our *salle*, for we were unable to read comfortably with the twenty-five-watt bulb we found in it on our arrival. As the other bulbs burned out around the house we replaced them with sixty-watt bulbs. When the meter reader for the *Electricité de France* came, he told us that we used far more electricity than any other householder; we ranked with the hotel and the café. Even the Notaire's bill was lower than ours because all his appliances were run not by the normal current but by *force*, a high-voltage current for which the consumer is charged lower industrial rates.

There are not many electrically powered tools in the village. Some people have an electric iron, some an electric sewing machine, and a few have motor powered buzz saws to cut the *petits bois*. The list of artisans and merchants using electric equipment is short. The garageman has a battery charger. The blacksmith has electric bellows. The butcher has a big new refrigerating room, the only electric refrigeration system in Peyrane. Neither the plumber-electrician nor the masons have any electric tools.

The taxes one pays, like all expenditures, must be cut to a minimum. Because there is a tax on radios, the official statistics for the number of radios in the commune are unreliable. Because of the dog tax, there are on the official records many fewer dogs in Peyrane than exist in reality. According to official statistics there are no donkeys and no mules in the whole commune, but it is a fact that there are two donkeys and one mule in the village itself, and there are others on the farms.

The run-down appearance of property can be explained partly by the desire to keep the property tax down. Houses, fields, cars, clothes sometimes look shabbier than they need to because evidence of poverty means lower taxes. One day when Lucien Bourdin was taking me to see his asparagus field, he led me down the hill back of his shed along a path that was so slippery and treacherous that he felt called upon to explain. "I could easily repair it," he said, "but if I made it safer, I would make it look better. Then someone on the tax commission might think me wealthier than he does now. In the next meeting of the commission he would be sure to get my assessment raised."

There are a few situations when appearances are more important, when the family dignity depends on the family's ability to present an attractive front. The baby must have attractive clothes and it must ride in a shiny perambulator. The whole family must appear well clothed on Sunday afternoon. When guests are invited to dinner, the dinner must be extraordinarily good. But only on very special occasions can a family afford to endanger its economy by making wasteful expenditures. Even when a family acquires enough wealth so that the economic struggle is in reality not desperate, it is not tempted to display its wealth publicly. Useless display might endanger it. In Peyrane the problem is not "how to keep up with the Joneses" but "how to stay behind the Joneses."

The shabbiness in the village is especially striking to an American because of the value he attaches to newness. For the people of Peyrane an object need not be shiny and new; the question is whether it functions adequately and economically. They experience no special satisfaction in using an article that has been used by no one else before them. The latest models and newest gadgets may arouse curiosity, but people are fundamentally indifferent to them unless they fulfill an essential need at less cost.

Given this attitude it is easy to understand the general indifference toward modern plumbing. The doctor's and teachers' campaign for more sanitary toilet facilities can hope for little success. It cannot be proved that water closets function more effectively and more cheaply than the traditional facilities. It cannot even be proved that sanitary water closets are necessary for reasons of sanitation and health, since the health of Peyrane is good. On the other hand, the Ploughing and Tractor Coöperative cannot fail to arouse genuine interest, for men have found that by working together in the coöperative they can get their fields ploughed not only efficiently but also more cheaply.

Because people do not insist on newness, their ingenuity in "making do" with an old thing is everywhere in evidence. When Monsieur Viquier needed a chicken coop, he constructed one in the cheapest and simplest way possible. In the soft sandstone cliff beside his house he hollowed out a shallow cave of appropriate dimensions. To enclose the opening at the front he built a wall from stones found at the foot of the cliff. Of course he needed a small doorway, and to make a doorway in a stone wall one needs a lintel. In an abandoned ochre mine near his house he found half a mine-cart wheel which serves as a strong and not unattractive arch for the chicken coop door.

The stone laundry basin in our courtyard was divided into two sections, one for soapy water and one for rinse water, but there was only one faucet. The problem was to get water into the basin lacking a faucet. It would have cost money to install two faucets or a double faucet or an extra pipe. Such an expenditure was easily avoided because Madame Teste (who lived in the house until her death in about 1900) found an old gun barrel which she tied under the faucet with a cord. The barrel still channels the water where it is wanted. It is not the primary function of a gun barrel to channel water. It is rusty. It looks old. It is inefficient because some of the water is lost. It is inconvenient to replace the cord each time it rots away. However, the gun barrel serves its purpose adequately and at no cost.

The farmers around Peyrane use pitchforks that are, so to speak, grown rather than manufactured. A certain type of tree is planted, and as it grows all the branches are trimmed away except for three which are trained to grow in position for the tines. When the trees grow to the proper size, they are cut down, the bark is stripped off, the three branches are cut to a suitable length, and their ends are whittled to a point. The result is a pitchfork which is light, sturdy, safe (since the tines are not as dangerous as steel ones), and cheap. They cost only about sixty cents apiece. They are not heavy enough to be used with manure, but they are adequate for light work with hay and straw.

The ingenuity, the thrift, the stress on adequate function rather than on appearance may best be illustrated by the automobiles in Peyrane. The département of Vaucluse has the highest number of light automobiles per capita of all the départements of France, not excepting those of the Parisian region. The National Statistical Institute uses this fact — along with several other key data, such as savings accounts, taxes paid, etc. — to help prove that the Vaucluse is economically one of the most progressive départements of France. There is no doubt that many départements are poorer than the Vaucluse, but before one draws exag-

gerated conclusions about the wealth of the Vaucluse, it might be well
to take a look at the cars of Peyrane, for they are typical of the cars
of the whole département.

There are two cars in Peyrane less than five years old, the big Citroën
of the Notaire and the butcher's red truck with pink plastic pig heads.
If we exclude these two, the cars of the commune of Peyrane average
about twenty-five years in age.

One day Madame Borel came to our house to ask if I would be willing to photograph their new car so that they could send a picture of it to
their son in Morocco. I hurried to the Borels, for the acquisition of a
car was an unusual event in Peyrane. The "new" car proved to be one
that I had seen the garageman working on for weeks in his spare time.
It was a 1929 Fiat which had been towed to Peyrane because it could
not run on its own power. The lighting system was completely out
of order. Three tires were gone. There was a hole in the gas tank, and
there were probably other ailments I did not know about. Ricci had
rewired the car, rebuilt the engine, welded the gas tank, found three
usable tires. Now the car ran. The paint and the upholstery were in
poor condition, but the engine functioned adequately. The Borels said
that they might paint the car some day.

The difficulty in repairing such cars is that spare parts are often not
available, but even the lack of an essential part is not too discouraging.
It is always possible with ingenuity to adapt some object. Pascal has a
Renault which he bought second hand in 1923. He keeps the motor in
good condition so that it runs smoothly, provided he does not make unreasonable demands on it. The car looks a bit peculiar because of its
wheels. The two front wheels are from a truck. One of the back wheels
was taken from a *sulphateuse*, a vine-spraying machine. The other back
wheel is one of the original wheels of the car. Pascal could not afford
a new car and does not even feel the need for a new car. All he needs
is a vehicle adequate for carrying produce to the market and for bringing home supplies. His Renault is not an object of beauty and it cannot go fast, but it does its job.

The Borels' car and Pascal's car are typical of most of the cars in
the Vaucluse. Originally they were passenger cars, but the present
owners have adapted them for work. To transform his old Citroën
into a truck Monsieur Arène simply sheared away the back of the body
and fastened it on again with hinges. Gaston Jouvard stripped his old

Francis Favre at his plumber's bench

10. *Madame Prayal washes lettuce*

11. Rivet at the noon apéritif

12. *Rivet ready to "fire" a boule*

13. *Rivet "points" a boule*

14. *The big tournament*

Panhard down to the chassis and built a wooden bin on it so that he could haul sand and gravel. None of these cars is comfortable or beautiful, but they all fill a need adequately and inexpensively. Their owners are satisfied with them.

The question of buying a car on the installment plan rather than "making do" with what one has does not occur to the people in Peyrane. They do not like to be in debt. To be in debt is to be obligated to someone, giving someone rights over you, giving someone the possibility of prying into your affairs and criticizing the way you run your life. Being in debt is a threat to your independence.

People do not even like to receive gifts if they are not in a position to make some kind of gift in return to acquit themselves of obligation. When I took Pierre Pian to Apt, he brought us a bottle of his best wine the next day. When I took Monsieur Graziani's picture so that he could put it on his application for an old-age pension, he was embarrassed that I would not accept payment. Our relationship was uncomfortable until he brought us a dozen eggs one day, thus cancelling the obligation and reëstablishing his independence. When I helped Paul Rivet get a hearing aid, his parents invited us to a dinner that was obviously beyond the family's means. In addition Rivet gave me a highly prized possession, three stainless steel boules that he had won in a contest. We had to learn that to refuse such gifts, which represented serious sacrifice, was more unkind than to accept them. Only by accepting could we permit a person to regain his feeling of independence. This meant that we had also to learn not to make gifts and not to render services unless we were sure they were really wanted by other people. They felt as obligated to return an unwanted favor as a wanted favor, and to make a person pay for something he does not want is to render him a disservice.

Economic Success and Failure

It may seem surprising that people ever succeed in saving money, but they do. In the constant and bitter struggle to make ends meet, most people seem able to produce enough more than they consume to have a little left over. The National Statistical Institute lists the Vaucluse high in the number and size of savings accounts, and according to gossip in Peyrane a substantial percentage of the savings in the commune is not deposited in savings accounts but hoarded at home. This hearsay flatters the traditional belief held by city dwellers that all peasants have a hoard of gold coins sealed up in a wall, but only a few men in the commune are wealthy enough to have accumulated a substantial hoard.

Louis Borel was born in a little village in the mountains north of Peyrane, the poorest region in the Vaucluse. His parents died when he was a little boy, and he left the mountains to wander around the Vaucluse working at whatever job he could find. When he was in his early twenties he came to Peyrane to work for a master mason. He had learned several trades, but he preferred building houses. His great handicap was that his education was limited. He had been to school only a few months and had learned no more than to read figures and sign his name.

In Peyrane he met and married Françoise Béchade, who had her primary certificate and could do accounts. Together they have prospered. Louis does the work, and Françoise keeps the books. For a while he continued his mason's work. His big job was building the finest house in Peyrane, the Notaire's. During the war there was little work for a mason, but Louis had a truck and found it profitable to buy produce from the farmers and sell it in the city. When the war ended he acquired a big truck which had been confiscated from the Germans, and with it he expanded his business. Now he is the most active middleman in the commune, buying vegetables and fruit from the farmers and selling them either at the market in Cavaillon or to the candied fruit factories in Apt. In the winter he cuts wood in the mountains, brings it back to Peyrane, saws it up, and sells it to villagers. The only place to buy coal in Peyrane is at Borel's. He trucks it in from Cavaillon and sells it in fifty pound lots. He also has the only filling station.

The standard of living of the Borels is no different from that of most families. They dress the same, eat the same, live in the same manner as most people. Louis obviously makes a substantial profit from his business, but the only external sign of wealth is that he is constantly increasing his matériel. Across the road from his house he is building vat after vat in which to preserve cherries. Without the vats he has to sell at the low prices of harvest season. When he finishes his vats he can preserve the cherries for weeks or even months and sell them when the market is high.

Monsieur Anselme is said to be the wealthiest farmer in the commune. Like Borel he came from the mountains north of Peyrane and from a family so poor that he had to start making his own living when he was still a boy. For years he walked five miles down from the mountains every morning to work as a hired helper on a farm in the plain, and at night he walked five miles home. He had a little house and a plot of land which he cultivated carefully, working on it before he left for the valley in the morning and after he returned at night. Working his own land or working on the valley farm would either one have been a full-time job for most men, but Anselme carried on both for years. Finally, when he was in his late forties, he had saved enough money to buy a farm of his own in the valley. He did not change his habits, however. He continued to work with the same tenacity until he was able to round out his holdings in one of the most fertile and best exposed areas of the commune. His main crop is table grapes. During the peak of the harvest season he never goes to bed. He hires a few pickers whom he pays well and from whom he expects the kind of work he himself would do. He helps as he can in the harvest, but his main job is to move the crop to market at Cavaillon, fifteen miles away. To keep up with his pickers he makes two round trips a day, driving a big wagon pulled by a team of horses — a total of sixty miles. When he gets home from one trip he loads his wagon again and changes teams, for horses need rest even though he does not. Of course, the horses know the way well enough that Anselme can doze as he rides along the dark roads.

Anselme is seventy-three years old now and shows no indication of slackening his pace. He lives isolated from the rest of the community. No one calls on him, and he never appears in the village except when he has to come on official business to the town hall. When I stopped at his house one day to ask for directions, he received me with dignity but without cordiality. He did not ask me to sit down, and he offered me nothing to drink — an almost unheard of lack of hospitality in this region.

Anselme has never married. He lives with his sister-in-law, the wife of his brother who died a few years ago. His brother had no children. His only heir is the daughter of his sister, and he has scarcely even seen this niece. The people of Peyrane like to tell the story of Anselme because it exemplifies two ideals. They admire Anselme's ability to work tirelessly, to live frugally, to accomplish his own business without getting entangled in relations with other people. On the other hand, they are unable to understand why he works so hard to amass a fortune which will be inherited by someone in whom he is not interested. If he had children it would be different. Borel has a son and daughter to work for, but Anselme has only a niece with whom he is vaguely acquainted. Furthermore, although they admire his ability to avoid human entanglements they think he carries it too far. It is hard to understand how a person can live without enjoying contacts with other people, whether it be cordial contact with friends or bitter feuds with enemies. The people of Peyrane approve of work, but they do not approve of work simply for the sake of work. They approve of minding one's own business, but they do not approve of cutting oneself off from society.

Borel and Anselme are examples of the few men in the community who have started with nothing and have amassed what most people consider a substantial fortune. To generalize on the basis of these examples would be to create a false picture. There are just as many men in Peyrane who started life with ample resources and who have wasted them. Raoul Chanon's father was a prosperous farmer and for many years a Town Councillor. Chanon père died just before the war, and Raoul inherited one of the best farms in the commune. It soon deteriorated. Raoul was not to blame at first. He was called up for service in Germany and to avoid it he joined the *maquis*. He was popular among men in the underground and became the leader of the Peyrane *maquis*. He could scarcely be expected to run his farm efficiently under those circumstances. But even after the war Chanon did not settle down. He became involved in politics, and just after the Liberation he was elected Peyrane's first Communist mayor. He spent too much of his money in the election and in furthering his party's interests. To recoup his losses he did not go back to the farm but started a butcher shop with two friends. Perhaps one of the three men could have made a living out of it, but all three could not — especially since all three shared a passion for pastis and boules and politics. In the election of 1948, the Communist party was defeated, the butcher shop failed, and Chanon was finally obliged to withdraw to his farm. He is working it now, but he is so poor that he never comes to the village to play boules or to have an apéritif at the café.

Chanon's sister inherited land and money from her father, too. She is one of the hardest-working women in Peyrane and her children are two of the "best raised" children in the school. Unfortunately, she married Lucien Peretti who has become a chronic alcoholic, the only one in the commune. Work as she will, she cannot make up for her husband's conduct. Her money is gone. They still have the farm, but people wonder how long they will be able to keep it.

Monsieur Maucorps' family was fairly well-to-do, but in his hands the family's savings have dribbled away. Monsieur Maucorps never married and has never worked except in his little garden plot. All he wanted was enough money to buy bread and wine. Now at seventy-five he is the dirtiest man in the commune. His house is a shambles. He never washes and never changes clothes. He does no work except to walk down the hill to tend his garden, and that, he says, is difficult because by the time he gets there he has to come home to rest. He is followed everywhere by his mongrel pup which, he says, he is training to hunt truffles — a pastime that would be equivalent to fishing in a community where there is a river.

Chanon, Peretti, and Maucorps form a counterpart to Borel and Anselme. No one of them represents the normal situation in Peyrane. We cannot generalize on the basis of either Maucorps' extreme insouciance or Anselme's psychopathic will to work. Very few peasants have gold secreted in their walls, and very few live in squalor. Most work hard, make ends meet, and save a little besides.

Paul Roussel probably presents a fair example of the usual Peyranais. He is sixty-five years old, and until two years ago he was a tenant farmer. Finally, after forty years of working hard, living austerely, and saving his money he was able to buy his own farm. He has one child, a son forty years old, who works the farm with him and who hopes to get married and raise a family now that his parents and he have achieved their goal. They have had to struggle, but they have not isolated themselves like Anselme. Paul and Jacques both come to the village to play in the boules and belote contests, and the family is cordial to anyone who drops in to see them. They feel the necessity of working constantly, but their feeling is not a compulsion.

Among the artisans and workers of the village there is evidence of the same ability in normal circumstances to put aside a little money. One afternoon a big truck rolled into the village and after some difficulty managed to squeeze its way up the main street to the public square. Two men got out, set up stands, and piled up a supply of dry goods which they hoped to auction off. In a few minutes a crowd of thirty people had gathered around the display. The number of sales was not great, but I was surprised at the size of some of the purchases. Most of the people spent from three to six dollars on yard goods and towels and scarfs, but some people spent more. Roger Prayal, the son of the blacksmith, bid twenty-five thousand francs, seventy-five dollars, for a pile of sheets and blankets. This won the lot, and Roger went home and brought back five five-thousand franc notes with which to pay for it. (He has since married one of the teachers; his purchase at this auction was obviously part of his trousseau.)

The normal impulse of most of the people of Peyrane is not to buy luxury items but to save whatever surplus they have when all their expenses are met. They save to buy land to increase the productive resources of the family. They save to help the young people get established. They save in order to splurge when a splurge is called for — a first communion dinner or a wedding or a pink angora sweater to adorn the three-year-old son on Sunday afternoons. They save to provide security against the unknown menace that probably lies lurking in the future, for they have no confidence in the future. They live in a land where unforeseen disaster is traditional, all kinds of disaster — from the invasion of the Cimbri to the silkworm disease, from the great freeze which destroyed the olive orchards to the invention in the United States of synthetic ochre coloring, from the modern wars that have killed so many of their sons to the ensuing inflations that have made life even harder. These are public disasters. There are also private disasters, like serious illness, that can be faced more calmly if the family has money saved up.

Credit

When catastrophe hits, what can a family do? Its savings are soon gone. Aid from relatives and friends is soon exhausted. Payments from the government in the form of family allowances, sickness insurance benefits, invalid's benefits, and so on, may prevent complete disaster, but these payments are never great enough to permit the family to live normally. The only way out of the dilemma is for the family to reduce its cost of living. The rent is not paid. No clothing is bought. There can be no social life.

Since food is the largest item in the family budget, it is the item on which the greatest saving can be made. Instead of eating meat two or three times a week, the family is fortunate if it sees meat once in ten days. The protein in the diet is reduced to practically nothing, and the family fills up on carbohydrates — potatoes, spaghetti, bread. Even the cheapest food costs money, but if the family has no money there is still a way out of the dilemma. The cost of the food must be charged. However disgraceful the idea of being in debt may be to many people, a family faced with catastrophe soon finds itself living on credit.

"Ah, Monsieur, credit is a festering sore on the body of commerce!" says Monsieur Reynard. This is a favorite phrase of all the merchants of Peyrane. Even in the case of solvent citizens who are sure to pay for what they charge, the merchants do not extend credit willingly. A request for credit makes the merchant uneasy, though he may smile and say, "Why, of course. Pay whenever you like." An unpaid account is an account that despite the best intentions may, through some unforeseen accident, never be paid.

If a merchant feels anxious when he is obliged to extend credit to someone who is certain to pay his bill, his anxiety is intensified when he sees Madame Malitourne come into his shop. Malitourne has gone off to Marseille to look for a job; the family is living off government allowances; two of the several children are sick. Madame Malitourne gives her order which the grocer fills silently with a furious frown on his face. He knows what is going to happen. She is going to say, "Charge this. I'll pay when my husband sends me some money from Marseille." He'll grumble about the big bill she already has, but he knows that eventually he will write the sum down on a slip of paper and add it to her bill. He knows that the whole transaction is fiction, that she does not intend to pay.

The merchants are not equally vulnerable to the credit attacks of Madame Malitourne. Reynard has a solid, well established business. He can afford not to extend credit to her. He can and does refuse to let her and anyone like her charge a single item. Fortunately for Madame Malitourne, there are four other groceries in Peyrane, too many groceries for so small a town, but each of them continues to struggle along, hoping that the others will fail first. Of these four groceries Arène's is the least secure, so it is there that the poorest families shop. When Arène fails, as he inevitably will, they will turn to the next most insecure grocer. In effect, the credit system amounts to a poor tax on the merchant who is least able to afford it.

Of course, legal recourse is open to the merchant. He could try to get the courts to force the customers to pay their bill. He could get the bailiff to seize the property of Madame Malitourne. He could do this but he wouldn't for several reasons. Such a procedure might destroy the good will of regular customers. It would get the grocer involved in legal complications and legal personalities; the people of Peyrane have the utmost distrust of Law and anyone connected with it. ("Homme de loi, homme de merde," the men say.) Finally, legal recourse is not a realistic solution, since "you can't get something from nothing." The shabby bits of property belonging to the Malitournes would not bring enough money to pay for the cost of the seizure. There's nothing to do but accept the situation, and to hope against one's better judgment that the Malitournes will win the lottery and have the decency to pay their bills.

As a matter of fact, it happened that Malitourne did win in the lottery before he moved away from Peyrane. It was kept a secret so that Malitourne could make a special trip to Marseille, cash in on the ticket secretly, and thus avoid being troubled by his creditors. I was told that this was a common practice of those who won in the lottery.

Only rarely does the town government intervene in cases of credit. One day when I was at the town hall the Mayor and the Town Clerk were discussing Monsieur Maucorps' debt to Bonerandi, the baker. Maucorps bought bread from Bonerandi every day, and he had not paid for a loaf in two years. He now owed $120.00! Bonerandi had come to ask if the municipality would pay the bill.

The Town Council had budgeted a small amount for aid to the poor, and the Mayor thought the town should pay the bill and then send Maucorps off to Apt to the Old People's Home. Rivet was against sending Maucorps to the Home. "It would kill him," he said. "He couldn't live away from Peyrane." He thought Bonerandi should receive only what it had cost him to make the bread and in the future the town would continue to pay the actual cost of Maucorps' bread. Rivet's proposal finally prevailed. Maucorps was the town mascot!

The Malitournes were a different case. The Malitournes were not even natives of Peyrane. They had moved there two years before. Malitourne had opened a shoestore but it had failed after a few months.

According to village gossip Malitourne had never paid the shoe factory for the stock which he sold; he spent the money he took in, and when all the stock was sold he merely declared himself bankrupt. He had lived off the shoe factory for a few months, and now he was living off Arène's grocery store. Arène himself was a newcomer to Peyrane. The municipality felt no moral responsibility for either Malitourne or Arène. People felt sorry for Arène, for he was "a nice person." They felt sorry for Madame Malitourne because she had an irresponsible husband, but nevertheless the sooner the Malitournes used up their credit and were forced to leave town the better it would be for everyone.

The Malitournes moved away from Peyrane a few months after our arrival there. But at almost the same time another family came to Peyrane. The father got a job at the ochre mine, but he was laid off after a few weeks. He went to Marseille to look for work, and his wife did her marketing at Arène's. When I mentioned to the Notaire the similarity between this family and the Malitournes, he smiled and said, "Whether it's the Malitournes or some other family, it doesn't matter. There's always at least one like that living here. They stay as long as they can. Then I suppose they go to another village where they're not known and repeat their performance."

Reynard was eager to talk to me about the Malitournes. "When I was first in business," he said, "my heart was tender, and I tried to help people like that. But it's no use. They have no sense of responsibility. Now I can spot a family like that ten meters away, and I get myself ready so that I can tell them at once that I won't give them credit. You know that credit, Monsieur, *c'est la plaie du commerce.*"

"But what about your regular customers?" I asked. "Don't some of them get into trouble sometimes and have to ask for credit?"

"Then," he replied, "the situation is delicate. Very delicate. Sometimes I am obliged to extend credit to certain persons, so as not to offend their relatives and friends who are good customers. But I avoid giving credit when I can. People must not be encouraged to fall to the level at which the Malitournes live. No self-respecting person will ask for credit."

Monsieur Prayal, the blacksmith, cleared up the matter of credit for me when I asked him about it. "No one will ask for credit if he can avoid it. No one wants to be obligated to anyone. All we want is to be left alone, each of us."

"But," I said, "I've seen one woman whose family has always lived here go into Arène's store and buy things on credit."

"That is a different situation," he replied. "Arène is not from Peyrane. He is sure to go bankrupt and move away from town. People who owe him money will not have to live with him forever, so some people feel that Arène is fair game. But you know who these people are, and you know that you mustn't judge us all by them, Monsieur. They've no sense of dignity."

Chapter 8

Health

It might be expected that Peyrane, with its open sewers, its open privies, and the use of night soil as fertilizer, the quantity of animal excreta in the streets, the custom of disposing of trash and garbage by simply throwing it over the cliff, and with the absence of screens in the windows, would be an unhealthy community in which to live. We found it healthy, however, even though we took no special precautions. We ate raw carrots and green peppers and lettuce from the gardens. We accepted all that was offered to us to eat and drink. Yet we suffered no gastrointestinal attacks. After we had learned to live in a cold, tile-floored house, we had even fewer colds and attacks of tonsilitis than usual. Contrary to our expectations, we found Peyrane an unusually healthy place in which to live.

Our experience was consistent with the information I had received from the Director of Public Health for the Vaucluse département. While I was still investigating possible sites where we might spend the year, I had called on him. He assured me that the Vaucluse was generally a healthy département. His only real problems, he said, were in the slum sections of Avignon, so that any village in the département in which we chose to live would be good so far as public health records are concerned. There was no typhoid, no smallpox, no dysentery, no polio to speak of, nothing unusual to worry about. Most of the few tubercular cases in the rural area were city people who had moved to the country for their health.

The several people we met who had moved to Peyrane from the cities for reasons of health, however, were disappointed. None of them had been seriously ill, and they had come with an exaggerated idea of the health of a rural atmosphere. They underestimated the hardships that faced them: the lack of city facilities, the lack of social contacts to which they were accustomed, the difficulty of earning a living. Peyrane does have a healthy atmosphere, but it is no sanitarium.

The winter we stayed in Peyrane was one of the worst winters in years. In this part of France which is supposed to be dry and sunny, the sun did not shine, and a cold, penetrating rain fell for days. The weather was an even more constant topic of conversation than usual. An epidemic of grippe spread over France and took its toll on Peyrane. People kept saying, "If the mistral would only blow!"

The mistral is no pleasure in itself. When it sweeps over the town at forty or fifty miles an hour, it drives its chill through the heaviest garments, raises the dust in the street, makes you catch your breath. The people of Peyrane dread the mistral, but at the same time they are grateful because, they say, "It sweeps illness away." There is probably truth in this belief. The mistral is cold and unpleasant, but it is a dry wind. When it blows, the sky is its bluest and the sun shines brightly. Undoubtedly the combination of low humidity and sunshine is beneficial to the health of the community.

In the spring when the rainy season has passed and the sun shines without the accompaniment of the mistral, the direct rays of the sun are considered unhealthy, however. Then people walk with their heads well covered and they avoid sitting in the direct sunshine. After weeks of cold, rainy weather we were eager to soak up the heat of the spring sun, but when people saw us, they clucked their tongues, "You'd better get out of the sun," they warned. "It's dangerous this time of year." When, after a few days of enjoying the sunshine, I developed acute sinusitis, Marie Fratani could not refrain from saying, "I warned you not to stay in the spring sun. Now see what's happened to you!" Her explanation of the situation sounded logical: "This time of year the sun is hot, but the air is still cool. The sun heats you, and the air cools you. You get a chill and you catch cold."

Marie felt called upon to justify her fear of the spring sun by offering an explanation that would sound logical. Like most people of Peyrane she has a rational attitude toward illness and medicine. They seem a bit mysterious to her, but she believes they are mysterious only because of her ignorance. She thinks that the more education and training one has the less mysterious they are, and that the doctor is therefore the best qualified adviser in matters of health.

A few of the older people in the village, while they share this confidence in the knowledge of the doctor, still believe that there are some cures that may be more effective than the doctor's prescriptions. They say, for instance, that Madame Calas can make signs on burns that take the pain away, that Madame Bourdin can utter words and say prayers that will cure a toothache. They believe that if you take a live toad or rabbit or pigeon, split it open and put it on the head of a person suffering from meningitis, it will cure him. There is an old man at Les Pins who has a secret recipe, passed down in the family for generations, which will cure many diseases. It is so bitter that it is hard to swallow, but sometimes it works when the doctor's prescription won't. Some people believe that a snake skin placed on the stomach will cure an ache. If the ache persists, the best cure is to go up in the mountains to the sanctuary of St. Gen and lie down in the hollow of a big stone called "St. Gen's bed."

The few people who believe in these cures do not like to talk about them because they fear being laughed at; they know that most of the villagers consider these "old wives' cures" ridiculous. However, certain of the less dramatic traditional panaceas are accepted by everyone, and the necessary herbs are gathered from the fields. Sage, thyme, rosemary, and serpolet teas are good for a stomach-ache. A lily petal dipped in lime water beaten up in olive oil is good for burns. Saint-John's wort is good for cuts and fever. Borage in brandy is good for chills. A gargle of mallow tea is good for a sore throat. An inhalation of vapor from a brew of thyme, *romarin*, and eucalyptus and pine oils is good for sinusitis. (I offer my personal endorsement of this remedy.) Most of these herbs are packaged and sold by drug stores and some are even prescribed by the doctor. Many of the traditional remedies have been forgotten. Even the oldest people, when questioned about a traditional cure for a certain ailment, will say, "Yes, there used to be one in the old days, but I can't remember what it was. Nowadays if we get sick, we call the doctor."

The word "sick" is not frequently used in Peyrane. It has been largely replaced by the word *fatigué*. A person may be *un peu fatigué*, which means that he is not well but not seriously ill. Madame Chobaut and Monsieur Avenas were *un peu fatigués* when they moved to Peyrane. A person drinking Vichy water instead of his usual apéritif says that he is "a little tired in the liver." A person who is *un peu fatigué* is expected to carry on his normal life as well as possible. He may rest more than usual. He may be given special foods and home remedies, but no one would think of calling the doctor.

When he feels that he can no longer function normally, he gives up and goes to bed. Then he is *fatigué*, and some alarm is expressed. If his temperature is not high or if the illness is one with which the family is familiar and which it knows how to treat, the doctor still will not be called. The patient will stay in bed, take the remedies offered him, and wait to get better. If he is suffering, he is given aspirin, but the doctor would not be called simply to alleviate suffering. The patient usually gets well without professional treatment, but if disturbing symptoms develop, then everyone is alarmed and the doctor is called. The patient is *bien fatigué*.

Calling the doctor is not a simple matter, because there is no doctor living in Peyrane. However, within a radius of seven miles there are a dozen doctors. Most families would not hesitate in their choice because one, Doctor Magny, has won their confidence. Only people who owe him too much money would call another doctor. Magny is a pleasant-mannered, energetic man of about forty-five who has no intention of letting himself go to seed in this rural district. Every year he goes to Paris for two weeks for a concentrated course at the medical school, a course organized to acquaint men like himself with the important developments in medicine. His office is equipped with an X-ray machine and other aids. It seemed to us that through Doctor Magny the people of Peyrane had access to good medical service.

Doctor Magny makes two regular trips to Peyrane every week. On Monday and Friday at noon he drives into town in his little Citroën and stops at Prayal's blacksmith shop. He talks to Prayal a moment and then goes to see Vincent, the owner of the hotel. Prayal and Vincent are Doctor Magny's agents in the village. If anyone wants the doctor to call on his regular visit, a message is sent to one of them. If he calls on his regular visit to Peyrane his fee is $1.50, but if he has to make a special trip he charges $4.50, so that a family will make every effort to postpone calling the doctor until the day of his regular visit.

In a really critical case, however, the Doctor will be asked to make a special trip. Between nine in the morning and five in the afternoon he may be reached without difficulty. One has only to place a call from the Post Office in Peyrane to the village in which Doctor Magny lives. At five o'clock the switchboards in both villages are closed, but the hotel in Peyrane has a special line that remains open until eleven o'clock, and the police station in the other village has a line open all night. If the Doctor is urgently needed, one may ask the police in his village to go to his residence and call him to their phone. After eleven o'clock Peyrane has no easy means of communicating with the outside world. If you want the Doctor, you have to go get him.

Doctor Magny rarely sees a patient in Peyrane who is not seriously ill. Many people may be *fatigués* and the whole village may be coughing and sneezing, but officially he will not know it. One Friday noon when we met at the hotel for an apéritif, he said he had no calls to make that day. I knew from Madame Vernet that over half the children were out of school with mumps or grippe, but for none of these cases had Doctor Magny been called.

Illness and taxable property are alike in a sense: official records concerning them are not to be trusted. When the Director of Public Health of the département had told me of the good health situation in the region, he was perfectly honest. He was basing his judgement on the official information at his disposal; there was no way he had of knowing about the many cases of illness that never come to the attention of the authorities. He had a rather accurate idea of critical illness, and of course a perfectly accurate idea of illness resulting in death, but the teachers of the département undoubtedly have better information concerning the general state of health of an area than the public health authorities.

Continuing to act as we would have at home, we asked Doctor Magny to come see us when we were just *fatigués*, hoping thereby to prevent any of us from becoming *bien fatigués*. Under these circumstances he was a bit embarrassed for he said he was not used to treating patients who had no serious symptoms. When David had an earache, Doctor Magny examined him and prescribed aspirin and ear drops. I asked about the possibility of using penicillin. Doctor Magny was amazed. "The child may be suffering but it's nothing serious. You don't use *les grands moyens* (that is, antibiotics) for little things; you save them for serious cases. And by the way," he added, "some time when you're at a pharmacy buy a rectal thermometer. How do you expect to get an accurate reading orally, especially when you have to go through all the mathematics to change Fahrenheit to centigrade?"

If Doctor Magny avoided using *les grands moyens* except in critical cases, he did not fail to prescribe a long list of *petits moyens* at the slightest opportunity. Every time I went to the pharmacy in Apt to get a prescription filled for us or for some other family in Peyrane, I found that the prescription listed at least three of four medications. For a bad sore throat: a box of mallow petals, a bottle of peroxide, sulpha pills, sulpha in liquid form for swabbing the throat. For grippe: *cryogénine, phénergan, privine, rectocalcium*. It is not surprising that all of the pharmacies in Apt are busy; it is impossible to get a prescription filled without standing in a line.

Doctor Magny carries with him as large a supply of medicine as he can, for many of his patients find it practically impossible to get to the pharmacy in Apt or to send someone in their place. There is nothing unusual about the list of ailments endured by the people of Peyrane: diseases of childhood and old age, farm and mine accidents, grippe, earache, sore throat, pneumonia. Doctor Magny's work consists in treating extreme cases of these diseases, accident cases and, of course, he also has most of the obstetrical cases of the commune.

Since there is no unusual amount of sickness in Peyrane, and since the people have so spartan an attitude toward pain, one might expect not to hear much talk about health. Yet it is a main theme of conversation. A surprising number of people are preoccupied with the question of their health or the health of some member of their family. In some cases the worry is specific and serious. It is not surprising that the Fratanis should worry about Mario who has ulcers and Marie who has heart trouble, or that the Favres should worry about Louise who has a rheumatic heart.

Most of the worries are less specific, however. The Imberts worry about Monsieur Imbert who has always been *un peu fatigué*. The Reynards worry about Monsieur Reynard who has had a headache for twenty years. Madame Baume often does not come to the village to open her newspaper stand because she is *un peu fatiguée*. When the usually dapper Edouard Pascal appears unshaven, you may be sure that he is disturbed by the malaise that has plagued him periodically for years. The term *un peu fatigué* is used to describe these ailments. It is so conveniently vague that it indicates both a general depression in the rhythm of life or a more specific ailment.

The liver frequently gets the blame for vague cases of *fatigue*. At the apéritif hour in the cafe there is almost always some habitué who orders Vichy water instead of his usual drink. When his friends express surprise, he explains that his "liver is tired," and he is giving it a rest. They sympathize with him because most of them are periodically troubled by their liver, too. The next day it will be one of them who is drinking Vichy water. This preoccupation with the liver is so general that I asked Dr. Magny whether the incidence of liver trouble was unusually high in Peyrane. He assured me that he treated very few cases of liver trouble and that he did not think there were any more cases in Peyrane than elsewhere in France.

When I put the same question to Doctor Jouve, the director of a clinic in Avignon, he replied half jokingly. He said that the people of southern France consume so much oil that their livers become unusually large and healthy. People are aware of their livers not because they are diseased but because they are healthy! He added, more seriously, that the constant consumption of alcohol may have something to do with the question, but that he did not think the incidence of liver trouble was so high as one might gather from the complaints one hears. "Perhaps," he said, "liver trouble in France is equivalent to ulcers in the United States."

One reason for the preoccupation with illness is the concern with its economic consequences. Many people live on so close a margin that if their income is cut off, their resources will soon be exhausted. Pouget, an ochre worker, said, "Last year I had sixty dollars saved up. Then I got sick, and before I was able to go back to work the sixty dollars were gone, and we were in debt." As we sat in his house talking, the baby and the two-year-old boy were playing on the floor. When Pouget saw that I noticed them coughing, he added, "Now both children have whooping cough. The baby was coughing up blood so badly yesterday that we had to ask the doctor to look at her, and he said he was coming back Friday. I can't afford to pay him. We haven't paid our rent for six months. If I get sick now and can't work, we won't have any savings to go on this time. *Ce sera la catastrophe.*"

Léon Favre was out of work for weeks after a serious collision he had with Francis Favre (no relation), Léon on his motorcycle and Francis on his bicycle. Francis was hurt in the accident but not seriously. As postman injured while on duty, he received full pay for three weeks. By the end of two weeks he had recovered and had a week left in which to enjoy his leisure. Léon, however, was critically injured. For two weeks he was in the hospital, but even after several weeks convalescence at home it appeared doubtful that he would be able to work normally.

"We can keep going for a little while," he said, "but I can't know for how long. I had a little saved up. Marie and Marcel (his adolescent children) are working, and we get a government family allowance for the two younger children and the baby that's not yet born. But unless I can get back to work before long, we'll be *foutus* (done for)."

"What about your social security?" I asked.

"Oh, the government! I'll probably get what's coming to me, but it's all so tied up in red tape that you can't be sure of it."

Two notorious cases had helped undermine confidence in social security. The first case was that of Mario Fratani which I have already described. So far as the villagers could see Mario unquestionably deserved to be pensioned indefinitely for his disability; for some reason that no one clearly understood he was denied all aid. The other case was that of Elie S—, a mason, who had been temporarily blinded by lime. An eye specialist in the city had given him prompt and effective treatment so that Elie could see as well as he could before his accident. However, he continued to receive a monthly check from the government for his "partial disability." Elie, who told me the story himself, said that the doctor had been willing to make this arrangement in return for a share in the check.

Undoubtedly, most of the people who qualify for social-security payments receive them regularly, but because of the lack of confidence in the government people feel that ultimately their security depends on themselves. They trust their capacity to withstand minor sieges of illness, but they fear the utter catastrophe that serious illness may bring.

The Arènes were managing to survive in their precarious grocery business in spite of the fact that Madame Arène was *un peu fatiguée*. She could keep the store while Arène tried to increase their resources by other means. It was while he was working on the commune roads to work out his taxes that she took a turn for the worse. She became *bien fatiguée* and had to stay in bed. Arène gave up the road work and kept the store going while he nursed her. The doctor was unable to diagnose her illness, and she continued to get worse. Finally she was sent to the hospital in Aix.

While she was in the hospital, Madame Arène pined for her husband, and the doctor told him that to keep up her morale it was necessary that he visit her twice a week. This meant closing the store two afternoons a week, losing the business he might have had at that time, perhaps losing for good some of his few regular customers whom Reynard would woo during his absence. Madame Arène could not eat the hospital food; she wanted home cooking. Arène spent two mornings a week cooking appetizing dishes to take to her. Their 1925 Renault had been adequate for a weekly trip to the market in Apt; it could not take the high hills and 50 kilometers between Peyrane and Aix four times a week.

As Madame Arène's illness dragged on, Arène became more and more depressed. The emotional and economic stress was becoming intolerable. "We've taken it before," he said, "but this time it's the end. *C'est la catastrophe!*"

Chapter 9

Getting Along With Others

When we arrived in Peyrane, it seemed as though everyone were trying to warn us against the danger of getting involved with everyone else. Our first and most natural contacts were with our landlord Martron, with the Provins family next door, and with the Arènes across the narrow street. Martron warned us to stay away from both families. "I'm not saying why, you understand, but it's a friendly warning. Take it as you will." He added with a suggestive wink, "And I am sure you will enjoy trading more with Reynard than with Arène who is . . . well, you'll see for yourself."

The Provins family was less discreet in talking about Martron. They detailed their griefs against him and warned us never to trust him under any circumstances. When we talked to the Arènes, we found that they agreed with Martron that the Provins were shady characters and agreed with the Provins that Martron was not to be trusted.

As we came to know other families, we found that their relationships were frequently no better. It seemed to us, with the exaggeration which comes with first impressions, that all the families were suspicious of each other. "Of course, you can trust me and my family and a few other people I'll point out to you, *mais les autres, ils . . .*" *Les autres, ils . . .* was the inevitable opening of a diatribe against the other villagers. "*The others*, they criticize you, insult you, meddle in your business, try to tell you how to bring up your children and your dog and how to treat your grandmother. *They* try to turn other people against you by casting doubts on your honesty and morality. *They* talk behind your back and then when you catch them at it they try to lie their way out of it. *They* don't respect your rights and your property. *They* are unreasonable and dishonest."

So far as respect for private property is concerned, we found that there was no justification for distrust. Martron told us, for instance, that we should never leave the house when the masons were working in it or when Francis Favre was patching up the plumbing for fear that these individuals might be tempted to steal. Despite this warning we frequently left the house when men were working there, and no article ever disappeared. Everyone told us that we should never leave the house without locking the door. Nevertheless we frequently left the house with the door not only unlocked but standing open. Henri Favre's dog — who is definitely *not* trustworthy — soon found her way to our kitchen, and we learned to keep the door closed. But it was a dog and not people who forced us to close the door. No human beings stole anything from us while we lived in Peyrane.

Only once during the year did the gendarmes have to ride their bicycles up the hill from headquarters to investigate a theft. Madame Fraysse had left a bathrobe hanging on the line at the public laundry, and it disappeared. She told the constable who telephoned the *gendarmerie*, and two men were dispatched to the scene of the crime. When they arrived, they asked no questions of anyone. Instead they went directly to search the house where the Algerian ochre workers lived. They took it for granted that a theft would have been committed by someone outside the social structure of the village, as the Algerians are. The search of the Algerians' house revealed nothing, but the people of Peyrane agreed that the gendarmes had acted logically in investigating the Algerians rather than the normal inhabitants of the village. Even though people constantly accused each other of being dishonest, when it came to an overt case of dishonesty they at once suspected outsiders rather than any of themselves.

There was one other case of overt theft that took place during the year. Gaston Gayol, a farmer living in a remote corner of the commune, went to the market at Cavaillon one spring morning to sell some tomato plants. The market was glutted with tomato plants that day, and he sold very few. Nevertheless, when he loaded his unsold plants back into his car he stowed away not only the plants belonging to him but many of those belonging to the farmer parked next to him. His action was observed. He was arrested, brought to trial, and sentenced to prison, though the sentence was suspended because of his good record and because he had two young children who depended on him for their support.

Naturally this case received considerable attention in Peyrane; everyone talked about it. The consensus of the men at the café was expressed by Henri Favre: "One mustn't hold it against Gayol. No one in his right mind would have done what he did." When I pressed Henri on why he thought Gayol was out of his head, he said that no sane person would give way to his "natural impulse" to take what didn't belong to him.

One day when Lucien Bourdin and I were walking down to his asparagus field he pointed to a sickle stuck in a post along the path. It was sheltered from the rain by a projecting board, but it was well exposed to the view of anyone passing along the path.

"I've been watching that sickle for three years," Bourdin said, "Someone left it here and forgot it and hasn't passed this way since. Everyone going by sees it. Still no one has touched it."

"But," I asked, "what about all the dishonesty people talk about? Everyone keeps warning me to be cautious with 'the others' because they say 'the others' aren't honest."

"Have you missed anything that you think might have been stolen?"

"No."

"Well, there you are. If you listen to all that 'the others' say you'll never know the truth. The fact is that people here are honest, as you see for yourself. You have to learn to ignore 'the others' if you live here; they can't be trusted."

Lucien was not contradicting himself. He meant that people were honest insofar as private property was concerned, but they would gleefully destroy the reputation of other people by dishonest means. Martron could be trusted not to steal the material possessions of the Arènes and Provins, but he could not be trusted to give an honest judgment of their character. On the other hand, we found that anything he had to say about his friends the Pians or Fratanis could be accepted as true. The reason for this difference was that he was *brouillé* with the Arènes and with the Provins, but he was *bien* with the Pians and Fratanis.

If you are *brouillé* with someone, it means literally that you have been *mixed up* with him; your mutual relationship has become *confused*. You have quarreled and are now "on the outs." You have broken off relations. You avoid passing each other in the street, and when you cannot avoid passing you turn your head to avoid having to speak. You try not to be caught in a social situation in which you would normally be expected to shake hands. Through your behavior you try to create the impression that the person with whom you are *brouillé* has ceased to exist.

If by chance you cannot avoid meeting, you appear to lose your temper. You threaten physical or legal sanctions against each other. Friends plead with you to be calm. You give the impression that only their restraining influence keeps you from carrying out your threats of physical violence or legal action. In reality you know that your loss of rational control is not so complete as it seems. You have tried to frighten your opponent and to dramatize the situation, not to endanger your security by committing an irrational and irreparable act. The intervention of your friends has merely enabled you to play a violent role more convincingly.

Even though you do not injure your opponent through physical or legal action, you may still harm him by attacking him orally. Oral aggression is socially acceptable, it rarely endangers the aggressor, and it may sometimes be even more effective than other types of aggression. The purpose of oral aggression is to arouse suspicion and resentment of your opponent so that he will be destroyed socially.

Suspicion is aroused by creating the impression that your opponent is a danger to society in general and a threat to the security of each individual. You recall incidents which put him in an unfavorable light. You may even invent incidents, but it is dangerous to lie about someone. If your opponent proves that you are a liar, then he has won a round against you. You suggest that he is deceitful, malicious, dishonest, and disrespectful without actually saying that he is, hoping your listeners will assume that there is a factual basis for your insinuations.

Thus Martron had tried to arouse our suspicions against the Provins by saying, "I advise you to stay clear of the Provins family. I'm not saying why, you understand, and we'll pretend I have said nothing. It's a friendly warning. Take it as you will." His significant wink was intended to imply that he could give us plenty of proof if he weren't so discreet and kindly disposed. He used the same technique against the Borels: "If you want to buy wood, it would be better for you to order from a man I know in Apt. I'm not saying the Borel would cheat you, but it's my duty to warn you that you *might* find it preferable to deal with my friend in Apt." Martron was *brouillé* with both the Provins and the Borels.

Indeed, Martron seemed to be *brouillé* with almost everyone in the village, except the Pians and Fratanis. The people with whom he was *brouillé* circulated stories that slandered him as viciously as he slandered others. It was said that when Martron, a poor fifth-rate *chef de cuisine*, married into the well-to-do Sol family and became head of the business and the family, he was cruel and disrespectful to his wife's parents and relatives. One old uncle, who had lived with the family for years and had become dirty and careless, was relegated to the attic. He was forced to live in a cold, drafty room in which the sun never shone. When he came downstairs he was not allowed to be in any room but the kitchen. This treatment broke his heart and he died, a victim of cruelty, say Martron's enemies.

There was also a tale that years ago Martron wanted to buy an ochre mine from old man Jaumard who was as eager to sell it as Martron was to buy it. Martron, however, did not want to disburse capital to pay for it, so he persuaded poor innocent, illiterate old Jaumard to co-operate in a most unusual deal. Jaumard was to sign the mine over to Martron, and at the same time he would give Martron a false promissory note for 20,000 francs which Martron would take to the bank to offer as collateral for a loan with which to finance the purchase of the mine. He would pay off the loan little by little with earnings from the mine. When the loan was paid off the promissory note would be destroyed. Jaumard would have sold the mine at a fair price, and Martron would have purchased it without dipping into capital. Jaumard accepted the plan, too innocent to suspect the treachery of Martron. He deeded the mine over the Martron and gave him an IOU for 20,000 francs. Then Martron, the villain, as soon as he had the deed for the mine, went to his lawyer instead of to the bank. He sued Jaumard for "recovery" of 20,000 francs which Jaumard legally owed him, and the court decided the case in favor of Martron. Thus Martron got the mine for nothing and extracted 20,000 francs from Jaumard whose family was ruined by the transaction.

Jaumard himself and the Notaire both told me this story, but I have no idea what the basis for it is. Jaumard and the Notaire were both so badly *brouillés* with Martron that it would be unfair to judge him by what they said about him.

The teacher of the older children assigned a theme on *brouilles*. They were asked: "What makes me angry; what I feel like doing when

I'm angry; what I actually do when I am angry, how long *brouilles* last; how they end." Here are some of the themes.

The things that other children do that make me angry are: funny faces, teasing, cheating. What makes me most angry is for them to call me bad names, when they take my cap or when they pull my hair. When I am angry at someone I want to kick him and throw at him anything I can lay my hands on. What we really do when we're angry is to go away from each other and not speak anymore.

There is no time when one should fight except for wars. Angry spells last a few hours or a few weeks, so they're different from *brouilles* among grownups which usually last years and years and sometimes cause fits of jealousy when for instance someone kills a chicken in a neighbor's field.

The things other children do that make me angry are: when they cheat or tease me or decide in the middle of a game that they won't play anymore. The names that make me maddest are: "imbecile," "shut up, silly," "you talk too much," and "liar, it's not true."

It makes me want to run after him and show him what's what, but what I really do is to go off in a corner and yell at him, "You wait and see after school. You'll see what happens. You won't get home with your nose in the right place."

It's all right to get angry when someone teases you, but there is no excuse for fighting. *Brouilles* last a week at the longest. Some last a day, an hour, a half-hour or a quarter of an hour. They end when we shake hands.

The things other children do which make me angriest are cheating just so they can win. The thing they say that makes me maddest is to tell me I'm a cheater when I haven't cheated. It makes me not want to play anymore and not speak to him for forty days. Usually when I get angry with someone I don't speak to him for two or three days even though I had promised myself not to speak to him for forty days. There is no excuse for fighting. *Brouilles* last a week at the most. Then they're settled by a handshake. Children's *brouilles* last no more than a week but grownups may stay mad at each other forever.

The things children do which make us mad are: they cheat in games, kick our marbles when we're playing, nudge our pen when we're writing so we'll make blots on the paper.

The worst insults are: "imbecile," "idiot," and other nasty words.

The teasing which makes us angriest is when you're working a problem and are absorbed in the work and they pinch us or pull our ear. It makes us want to fight him when we get out of school. Usually when we do get out we don't think about any of this any more, and we talk about something else.

It's all right to get angry when, for instance, a friend slams shut a book we're reading or when I tell him to move down the bench a little because he's spreading out and taking all the space and he won't move.

There are times when fighting is all right when we are playing and someone cheats and his side says he didn't cheat even though our side saw him cheating. Then we get angry and take sides.

Our *brouilles* last scarcely a day. Sometimes we ignore a "bad comrade" for three days. When grownups get angry they stay *brouillés* for a year and sometimes for their whole life.

Children's *brouilles* seem to differ from those of adults only in their duration. The causes are the same: lack of respect for an individual's dignity and property, unwillingness to adhere to the social code, interference in an individual's serious and legitimate occupation. The reactions are the same: tempers flare, but there is no violence; physical aggression is threatened, but not executed; oral aggression brings some release, and the individual tries to withdraw into himself or to isolate his opponent from contact with other members of society. The *brouille* is brought to an end and contact is re-established by handshake.

The opposite of being *brouillé* with someone is being *bien* with him. Being *bien ensemble* means being "in" with each other, being on friendly terms. You play games together. You have your apéritif together. Your families often spend the evening together. You support each other in your *brouilles*, and you may even participate in them. When you need someone to do a favor you can count on the friend with whom you're *bien*.

If you are neither *brouillé* nor *bien* with a person you have little to do with him. You say of each other, "There is nothing between us," meaning that you have no griefs against each other on the one hand and no reason to establish a more cordial relationship on the other hand. You recognize and respect each other's existence, and neither one of you seeks to change this relationship. It is my impression that many people of the village are either *brouillés* or *bien* with each other. People about whom you say, "There is nothing between us," are those who live in another part of the commune or others with whom you naturally have little contact. The Notaire would not be *brouillé* or *bien* with Monsieur Maucorps, and Monsieur Prayal would not be *brouillé* or *bien* with the Curé because the Notaire and Monsieur Maucorps, Monsieur Prayal and the Curé have almost no social contact with each other. There can be "nothing between them." Monsieur Joly and Monsieur Gayol live in opposite corners of the commune and rarely see each other, and it is natural that there should be "nothing between them."

It is impossible to predict these relationships. Monsieur Joly lives at some distance from Monsieur Jouve, but they are *bien* with each other because of their similar views in politics and religion. On the other hand, Joly lives close to the Malens who agree with him on political and religious questions, and yet they are *brouillés* with him because the Malens are *bien* with Joly's divorced wife's family.

The relationships are constantly changing. Sometimes the shift from a *bien* relationship to a *brouillé* relationship is abrupt. At one time four of the leading men of the village — Baume, Viquier, Prayal the tailor, and Martron — were extremely *bien* with each other. They played cards together, drank together, hunted together, played boules together, and their families often spent the evenings with each other. One day they went off on one of their usual hunting expeditions. In the middle of the morning, they returned to the village separately. Each one went directly home instead of going to the café for the usual drink together. Something had happened, and each of the four men was *brouillé* with the other three. No one knew, or at least no one would tell me, the reason for the *brouille*. The only explanation I was given was that there had been a quarrel over which one of them had shot a bird. The situation has lasted for years. The men have done their best to avoid recognizing the existence of each other, although it is difficult for four such prominent men to ignore each other in so small a community. A friend has written recently that two of them have finally shaken hands and ended their part of the *brouille*. My informant was malicious enough to add that they had come to an understanding because together they could do more damage to the other two men.

The causes for *brouilles* are not always what they seem to be. When the news reached the village that Gayol had been convicted of stealing tomato plants but that the judge had suspended sentence, a violent argument broke out in the café between R—— and A——. A—— approved of the judge's action in suspending sentence, and R—— felt strongly that Gayol should have been sent to prison. The argument reached so violent a pitch that A—— and R—— became publicly *brouillés*.

The true cause for the high feeling between them became apparent and it had nothing to do with Gayol's tomatoes. A friend of A—— discovered R—— writing something on the wall of the public toilet. When R—— realized he had been seen he tried to erase what he had written and to substitute the innocuous insult, "A—— is a Communist." It was too late. He could not erase completely what he had written: "A—— sleeps with Madame P——." A——'s friend called A—— and two friends to witness what was written on the wall. The next day A—— brought suit against R——. On the advice of his lawyer and his friends he dropped it after a few days because there was no chance of winning it.

Gayol's theft had little real relation to this *brouille*. It was only the apparent cause for the quarrel. The real cause was jealousy. R——, who was over eighty years old, is said to have received Madame P——'s favors for years, but now she was bestowing her favors on the younger and handsome A——.

Such *brouilles* as those between A—— and R——, between Martron and Jaumard are serious. Of course, there are minor quarrels that provoke high feeling but which sometimes do not last much longer than those among children. Rivet, who had lived only a few years in Peyrane, found it dangerous to listen to gossip. "You're friendly with Monsieur X and Monsieur Y," he said. "One day they quarrel and you meet Y at the café where he pours out a long tale of grief against X. The next day X doesn't speak to you, and you can't understand why. Finally you find out that X and Y have been reconciled, and Y has told X you criticized him when all you did was listen to Y criticize him. It doesn't matter. X is *brouillé* with you, and the worst is that Y takes X's side in the quarrel!"

The perfect Peyranais does not exist, but there is an unexpressed ideal to which people are expected to conform. Everyone deviates from the ideal in some way. It is this deviation that interests other people especially and becomes a subject of conversation. Since this conversation is usually unkind, people prefer not to be talked about. But everyone is aberrant in some respects; no one can avoid being the target of gossip. One could list all the inhabitants of Peyrane with the reason for which each person is criticized. Nicole Favre lets her children run the streets; Suzanne keeps hers in too much. Pouget is too hotheaded; Baume is too calculating. Reynard is too unsociable; Francis Favre wastes too much time talking to people. Martron is too shrewd in his dealings; Monsieur Pascal lets himself be duped too easily.

Bourdin said, "If Christ himself came to live in Peyrane, *the others* would find something wrong with Him. You can't win here. If you're not too much this way, you're too much that way. You get criticized if you do something, and you get criticized if you don't do it. So you have to decide that *the others* don't matter. Don't tell anyone what you think, what your plans are, how much money you make. Don't tell them anything that matters. Just live to yourself as much as you can."

Raymond Caizac, the truffle dealer from Apt who is more interested in poetry than in truffles, has written a novel about a village in the mountains not far from Peyrane. The following passage from this unpublished novel conveys something of the feeling that the people of Peyrane seem to have for each other.

The few families that lived in the village were *brouillées* with each other. The only time they spoke to each other was when someone was born or was sick or died. Then they all came running together to see if there was anything they could do to help. As soon as the crisis was past they stopped speaking again — unless it was to quarrel over a disputed boundary line or right-of-way. Then someone might run and get a rifle to threaten his neighbor — but, of course, no shot was fired. The worst that ever happened was for someone to let fly with his fist. Then they ran to get the constable, and the justice of the peace smilingly mediated the case at point — a couple of chickens that had been caught pecking at the seed in a neighbor's field.

In this village they lived this way — conscientiously *brouillés* with each other. They didn't even like to read the same newspaper. Everyone had a car, but each family had a different kind of car. Rouget had a Peugeot, Paul had a Fiat, Féli had a Citroën, and Jacques had a Ford. That way there was no possibility of lending each other spare parts. They did lend their horses to each other to get the ploughing done, and after the work was finished they had a big dinner, a great feast, for each family wanted to show off. But these dinners always ended in a quarrel. They lived mad at each other, because when you're *brouillés* you don't speak, and so you imagine no one can stick his nose in your business. As if that were possible up there on the mountain!

Caizac's village was much smaller, poorer, and more ingrown than Peyrane. The relations of the people of Peyrane were not hostile to such a degree, but allowing for the important difference in degree — and for the novelist's exaggeration — the spirit is the same in the two communities. The people of Peyrane would agree with the people of Caizac's village that the essence of wisdom lies in the injunction: Don't get involved with people!

Only a handful of people in Peyrane fully succeed in following this injunction. Old Anselme has never thought of anything but work, it seems, and he has worked by himself except during the harvest season. He has never become involved with anyone, not even with a wife. Old Marnas has always avoided involvement, too, He never discusses anything with anyone except the weather and the state of the crops. Old Allibert never appears in public. Reynard is absolutely the same with everyone; he is neither *bien* nor *brouillé*. No one likes him, but no one has anything against him. He says it is better that way for his business. It is undoubtedly not a coincidence that these four men are among the most prosperous men in the commune. They have not been diverted from their business by the difficulties with other people that plague so many of the inhabitants of Peyrane.

These men are admired for their ability not to get themselves involved. Yet the admiration for them is not unqualified. People look on them with something of the same feeling they might have for a saint. They admire them, but they would not trade places with them. There is something unhuman, unsociable, and cold about these men. They may avoid the worries that arise from close contact with other people, but they miss the pleasure, the stimulation, the excitement that stem from the same source. Their lives are drab. A *brouille* may cause the blood pressure to go up. It may cause unhappiness. It may add to a person's many worries. At the same time, it is exciting. It gives a person an opportunity to dramatize himself and a situation. The struggle to make a living, the frustration of desires, the worries about health, about the family, about the future, would at times be almost unbearable if one were not able to find release in the excitement and drama of a *brouille*.

Furthermore, a person who avoids *brouilles* at all costs also avoids the kind of contact with people that leads him to be *bien* with other people. He denies himself the pleasure of having an apéritif with other men in the café, of joining in a boule contest, of spending an evening in the company of other people. He even denies himself the pleasure of conversation.

Most people believe that it is wise to keep important things to oneself, to avoid involvement with "the others" insofar as it is possible. At the same time, contact with other people is important for them. Most of them are temperamentally unsuited to cut themselves off from society as Anselme, Marnas, Allibert, and Reynard have done. Faced with the conflict between the desire to live apart from other people and the need to be with other people they have found a practical solution that works adequately most of the time. When they are with other people they are cordial, friendly, hospitable, even jovial, but this behavior is superficial. As Bourdin said, "Don't tell anyone what you think, what your plans are, how much money you make. Don't tell them anything that matters." By presenting a sociable front to other people while at the same time concealing what one feels to be one's true self, the people of Peyrane try to live with each other and yet remain apart from each other.

Most of them have not read Montaigne, but they would appreciate his advice: We may receive people cordially in the front room of our shop; still we must reserve a little back room where no one but ourselves can penetrate.

Chapter 10

Peyrane and the Outside World

When Madame Arène says, "They (*ils*) have raised the price of coffee on us again," she is not referring to the *ils* of the village, but to a more dangerous set of *ils*. She means the *ils* that threaten from beyond the limits of the commune. Of course, the *ils* within Peyrane are a nuisance, but since they are specific individuals whom one knows and sees every day, one can guard against them. The *ils* outside Peyrane are dangerous because they are anonymous, intangible, and overpowering. Against the outside *ils* an individual has little defense, and yet from them come the greatest evils that beset the people of Peyrane: inflation, taxation, war, legal restrictions, administrative red tape. It is the outside *ils* who are blamed for raising the price of fertilizer, for forcing young men to spend eighteen months in the army, for preventing a farmer from planting as many wine grapes as he wishes, for taking a substantial portion of the family income in the form of taxes, for complicating existence with waiting-room queues and forms to be filled out.

The identity of the outside *ils* varies. The term may refer to Big Corporations or to Newspapers or to the *Syndicat d'Initiative d'Avignon*. It may refer to the French People or to the Americans or to the Russians or to People in general. Usually, however, it refers to the French Government in all its manifestations, for it is the Government which collects taxes, makes war, controls the wine production, and employs impersonal civil servants.

This attitude is in direct conflict with what the children are taught in school. In their civics books they read that the Government is simply the concrete manifestation of the State, which is the political personality of *La patrie*. They learn by heart such sentences as:

The French nation has a body formed by the soil and the men who live on it; a soul formed by the history, language, tradition, and symbols.
When men feel love for their nation it becomes a *patrie*.

The State is the nation organized and administered.

The Government is the directing organism of the State.

A good citizen always seeks to become educated. He respects the law, pays his taxes loyally, accepts the military obligation, and defends his *patrie* when it is threatened.

A good citizen possesses the spirit of coöperation and mutual aid.

Politics too often arouses distrust, disdain, and even disgust.

Politics should not be an excuse for furthering private interests and above all it should not unleash our passions.

Politics should be a great public service, the art of bringing about more justice and happiness among men." *

The children have no difficulty in accepting the concept of *la patrie*, for at home and throughout the village they hear *la patrie* spoken of only with love and respect. One of the most hallowed spots in the village is the *Monument to Those of Peyrane who Died in Defense of the Patrie*. Several times a year they see the men of the village temporarily forget their personal differences and march together to lay a wreath at the foot of the monument. The children know that France is a country favored above all others — "Sweet France" of the marvelous hexagonal shape. They know that the French language is the language of Civilization and that Civilized People everywhere consider France as their second *patrie*. Culturally, emotionally, geographically, aesthetically, the people of Peyrane feel they are an integral part of *la patrie*. They recognize also that officially, legally, statistically, they are a part of the State, which they respect but do not love.

Unfortunately, *la patrie* and the State must be translated into human terms, and it is at this point that the people of Peyrane refuse to accept the "beautiful sentences" of the civics textbook. Theoretically, Government may be an alter ego of *la patrie*, but in point of fact it is made up of men — weak, stupid, selfish, ambitious men. It is the duty of the citizen *not* to coöperate with these men, as the civics books would have people do, but rather to hinder them, to prevent them in every possible way from increasing their power over individuals and over families.

This is a point on which everyone in Peyrane would agree: a man

* These sentences are taken from the sections entitled "Retenons par coeur" of chapters 26, 36, and 37 of Ballot and Aveille, *Education morale et civique. Classe de fin d'études* (Paris: Charles-Lavauzelle, 1952).

with power over you is essentially evil. They readily admit that a man may be virtuous when he goes into politics, but they would deny that he can remain virtuous if he attains power. Except for a few supporters of the MRP, the voters of Peyrane say that the heads of their parties, and of all other political parties, are "a pile of bandits." Even people who are not in politics but in government administration are tainted by the corrupting force of power. They become insensitive to the feelings of others.

In preaching civic virtue to the school children, the authors of the civics book recognize that their precepts describe an ideal rather than an actual state of things. They warn:

Many honest and intelligent people, who could be the best guides in public life, avoid politics, and condemn it harshly.

1° Indeed, politics arouses much *distrust*. People avoid talking about it in family gatherings, in friendly professional or social groups. It is excluded from the army, which must remain impartial (*la grande muette*), and from the judiciary branch of the government. It must be kept out of school. This phrase is almost always found in the constitutions of clubs and societies: "All political and religious discussions are formally forbidden." Thus, distrust seems general.

2° The *disdain* in which politics is held is no less great. "Politics is a specialty which I am willing to leave to the specialists," says the writer Georges Duhamel. Thus he expresses the *disdain* which many intellectuals feel for what one of them calls "the housework of the nation."

3° Hence the *distaste* for politics and for politicians who are often portrayed as men of little morality, of slight merit, incapable of making their way honestly and serving usefully.

The authors of the civics text then go on to preach a different and democratic ideal to the students, but in these paragraphs they have described the reality that the children have witnessed. They constantly hear adults referring to Government as a source of evil and to the men who run it as instruments of evil. There is nothing personal in this belief. It does not concern one particular Government composed of one particular group of men. It concerns Government everywhere and at all times — French Governments, American Governments, Russian Governments, all Governments. Some are less bad than others, but all are essentially bad.

Of course, much of the talk against Government and politicians must not be taken too seriously. People do not mean all they say. They recognize the necessity of government, and on a rational level they recognize the necessity of a certain amount of civic spirit. However, when they are confronted by the frustrations caused by these outside *ils*, they fulminate against them. The outside *ils* are like the weather: they are necessities which one must accept, because "that's the way it is." It makes a person feel better to curse the weather and to curse the outside *ils*. We should be naïve to take much of the cursing seriously, but still we should be equally naïve to ignore the cursing. The hostility toward government is real and it is deep.

It might seem that this hostility to the State should be tempered by the extension of the welfare function of Government, that is, of the social-security system. The Government as a welfare agency is a relatively new concept, however, dating mainly from 1928, and as yet the distrust of Government has not been tempered by the fact that people receive extensive family allowances, sickness, unemployment, old age, and many other benefits. In a sense the system of social security has even reinforced the antipathy toward the Government. People accept the benefits, but they complain that they are not large enough to make up for what the Government takes away in taxes, or for what is lost through inflation, which is blamed on Government. People complain also because the benefit payments are tied up in governmental red tape. They complain because payments sometimes seem capriciously allowed or disallowed by arbitrary administrators who have the claimants at their mercy. People complain because some (for example, the childless Arènes) are forced to help support others (for example, the large Malitourne family).

They see that Mario Fratani is refused disability payments; yet everyone agrees that Mario is too sick to work. On the other hand, they know that Elie S—— has "arranged" to continue receiving disability payments for a damaged eye that is now cured. They know about the case of Paul Rivet, who has been deaf from birth. The doctor says that an operation would permit Paul to hear with the help of a hearing aid. The Government would pay for the operation, but would pay only $6.00 toward the hearing aid, which costs $95.00. Since the family cannot afford the hearing aid, the Government assistance is cruelly tantalizing.

Undoubtedly there is another side to all these stories, and there are many examples that could be cited to illustrate the beneficial aspects of social security as it is applied in Peyrane, but it is the unfavorable rather than the beneficial aspects that people talk about and that seem important to them.

In 1945, when Peyrane was liberated along with the rest of France, the chief of the local *maquis*, Raoul Chanon, took over the government of the commune. A few hours afterward he received a telegram from the departmental *Comité d'épuration* saying: "Arrest the following collaborators — Barbier (Notaire and Vichy Mayor), Viquier (Town Clerk and Légionnaire), Allibert (owner of ochre mines), Reynard (the principal grocer), Baume (owner of the bus and taxi), Bonerandi (the baker), Marnas, Anselme, Sanape, Laplace, Massot, and Arnoux (the last six among the wealthiest farmers).

When Chanon read the telegram he did not hesitate. He tore it into pieces and said, "Nous réglons nos affaires en famille!"

No act and no phrase could have more completely captivated the people of Peyrane. I heard this story from many sources, from Communists on the Left and from the intended victims, Barbier and Reynard, on the Right. Regardless of what people thought of Chanon's role in the resistance, and regardless of what people thought of him as a farmer, as a businessman, as a husband, he became the village hero. By his action he had defied what then seemed to be the Government, and he had gotten away with it. He had thumbed his nose at the worst of the *ils*. He had asserted the right of the people of Peyrane to manage their own affairs. He had given expression to their feeling that in spite of all the squabbles (or because of them?) Peyrane is one big family, composed of individuals who disagree among themselves, but who unite when faced by a common enemy threatening from outside.

This feeling of unanimity is in reality only a vague emotion which disappears if an attempt is made to translate it into action. People agree that war, inflation, taxation, restrictions, and red tape are evil, and they agree that Governments are largely responsible for them. They agree that Government and the men who run Government are essentially evil because they have power over individuals and over families. They agree that individuals and families should be protected against Government, but at this point action rather than feeling is required, and when action is required, unanimity disappears. Just how to make Government, the necessary evil, function so as not to crush the individual and his family, so as to help them if possible, is a question on which disagreement within the community is extreme and bitter.

Thus political bitterness is more than an effect of people's disagreement. It is also a cause for their not getting along together. The existence of party labels gives them the opportunity of blaming on each other not just the evils that arise from living together but also the evils that threaten from without.

When the price of coffee goes up, Pouget can blame it on "Reynard and people like him who vote for men who help Big Business rob us little men." Reynard, on the other hand, blames the high taxes on "people like the Pougets who live like animals, have lots of children, then vote for politicians who pay them to have still more children — paying them out of the pockets of 'decent' people (like Reynard, that is) who have only two children."

It would be an exaggeration to say that all the people who are enemies for personal reasons are also political enemies, as it would be false to say that all people who vote for the same candidates get along well together. Raymond Laurens and Henri Jouve are close friends, although Laurens is a Communist and Jouve is a devout Catholic. Raoul Favre and Chanon are personal enemies although both of them are Communists. These cases are exceptions, however. It is more usual for people who dislike each other for personal reasons to disagree politically. Of course, if personal grievances are too intimate to mention in public, then political differences become particularly violent, for politics carries the whole burden of hostility.

Even when political differences are not complicated by personal hostility, political discussion may become violent. If you blame the woes of high prices, taxation, and war on men who are favored by your neighbor, it is hard not to react violently against the neighbor. Jouve and Laurens can remain friendly only because they do not discuss politics. For the same reason, political discussion is avoided in family gatherings. As the authors of the civics book say, political discussion may be banned from social organizations because politics may threaten their existence. It may be recalled that Paulette Bonerandi explained the disintegration of the Youth Club by saying, "Politics showed its head, and naturally that was the end of the club." The only proper place for political argument is a neutral area like the café, but even there the men are careful not to unleash their political feelings. They are especially careful with outsiders whose motives and reactions are unknown.

For the first six weeks we lived in Peyrane I heard almost no mention of politics, even though every day I attended both apéritif sessions at the café. One day I told Henri Favre I was surprised the men did not seem more interested in politics. He almost choked on his drink.

"But that's a passion with us!"

"Why don't you ever talk about it then?"

"We talk about it all the time, but naturally not when you are there. . . After all, you know what they (*ils*) say."

He was referring to the rumor that I had come to help plan the next American invasion. However, after a few more weeks, when the men realized that I was probably not a spy they began to talk freely about politics in front of me. Of course, Henri's remark that they discussed politics all the time was an exaggeration. Hunting and boules and food were spoken of just as frequently, though never with the same emotion.

In view of the passion which politics arouses in Peyrane, one might expect the political parties to be well organized and active. This is not the case. Even the Communist Party is loosely held together and constantly threatened with disintegration. In the winter of 1950–51, it was split with such dissention that some people thought it would not be in a position to support its candidates in the next elections. The trouble was that some members of the party like to hunt rabbits with ferrets, and others like to hunt them with a gun. Since the ferret is more effective than the gun in exterminating rabbits, the gun men accused the ferret men of ruining the sport by ferreting all the rabbits in the commune. The political parties of Peyrane rest on the same fragile basis of human relations as the other organizations in the village.

Sometimes the activity of a few men, abetted by outside influences, gives the impression of strength and unity to political parties. To a tourist walking through the village it might appear that the Communist Party was more active than it is because the Communist posters are prominently displayed on the village walls. In truth they are a false indication of the strength of the party. They are sent in from outside and putting them up is the work of only two men. Moïse Jannel and Charles Pouget do all the work of the party. They put up the posters. They pass around petitions. They sell almanacs. They peddle *la Terre*, the Communist weekly newspaper for farmers. They take up collections for the defense of Communist martyrs like Henri Martin. The other members of the party take advantage of Moïse and Pouget — and hold them in contempt for letting themselves be used.

So the display of posters is deceptive. It indicates no party strength, and furthermore it exercises very little influence on village opinion. Its main effect is aesthetic. People rarely stop to read the posters, and they rarely talk about them. There was only one poster which became a topic of conversation. It was a Communist poster showing French children being blown to bits by an American atomic bomb, a poster so horrible one could not avoid being struck by it. But instead of being converted to Communism, people resented having to look at the picture, and they criticized Moïse for putting it up. Usually posters arouse so little interest that they are not even defaced!

Personally, I found the posters fascinating. One day I noticed Jouvaud, the blacksmith, looking at a Communist election poster and started to take his picture. He saw what I was doing and obligingly held his pose until I had finished, but then he turned to me and asked, half amused and half suspicious, "Why did you take that picture?"

"I've wanted a shot of someone looking at a poster."

"Why?"

"To show how interested you are in politics."

"All that," he waved his hands at all the posters on the wall, "is propaganda, and propaganda does not interest me."

"Ah?"

"All sides have thrown it at us since '39 — we don't pay attention to any of it any more."

People look with the same skepticism on radio broadcasts and newspapers, but at least the radio and the newspapers are not ignored. Most families have a radio, and most adults listen to some news broadcasts regularly. Most people have an opportunity to see a daily newspaper, too, though it is impossible to say how much of the newspaper and what sorts of articles are read. Madame Baume's news agency distributes about fifty newspapers every day — twenty copies of the *Marseillaise* (Communist), twenty copies of the *Provençal* (Socialist), ten copies of the *Méridional* (vaguely conservative), and two or three copies of the *Dauphiné libéré* (Socialist). According to the postman, about the same number of newspapers is distributed every

day by mail and in about the same proportions. The Voisin café sub-
scribes to the *Marseillaise*, and several men who do not buy their own
paper read the café copy. Other newspapers are passed around informally from family to family during the day, so that it is difficult to
know how many people read a newspaper every day, but with one hundred newspapers circulating in a population of 779, it seems right to
assume that a large proportion of the population regularly have an
opportunity to see one.

In conversations, a regularly occurring phrase is "I was reading in
the newspaper. . ." Usually what was read was a human interest story,
but when the speaker is referring to a political item he often adds,
"That's what the paper said, and, of course, you can't trust newspapers."
If the speaker does not add this phrase, one of his listeners will.
Skepticism is widespread. Even the hard-bitten Communist Moïse said
to me when he sold me a copy of *la Terre*: "It's interesting, but don't
think I believe it all."

It would be unwise to infer from this skeptical attitude that the
people of Peyrane are able to sift the true from the false in the broadcasts and newspapers. They are no better able to do this than most
other listeners and readers in the world. They lack both the knowledge
and the objectivity to make an intelligent analysis of the news that
reaches them. However, after years of being pulled one way by the
Third Republic and another by the Vichy Government, one way by
the radio of Occupied France and another by the BBC, one way by the
pro-German posters and another way by pro-American posters, they
have become extremely sensitive to the fact that the outside *ils* are trying to manipulate them. Consequently they resist attempts to change
their point of view. They tend to accept only that part of radio and
newspaper information which substantiates the point of view they have
already adopted.

Above all, they are suspicious of political party platforms. Even if
they take the trouble to read such statements on posters or in newspapers, they have no faith in them. Most people know very little of
the specific programs of the political parties, although there are some
exceptions. Rivet, the Town Clerk, knows in a general way what the
different parties say they stand for. Edouard Pascal buys three newspapers daily and reads them; he can and does speak with authority
about party programs. Charles Pouget, the Secretary of the Communist

Party, worked in a factory in Lyon and learned enough of Marxist theory to introduce the basic terms into his arguments. Most people, however, retain only a few of their party slogans, especially those slogans that aptly express their own bias.

What determines this bias? On the one hand, family tradition, economic and social standing, individual personality, relations with other individuals; on the other hand, the conception each person has of his political party. This conception has little to do with official party platforms or with the way the party actually functions in Paris. The essential determinant is the nature of the party as it is conceived in Peyrane.

The RGR (Le Rassemblement des Gauches Républicaines), as heir of the Radical and Socialist Radical parties, is the oldest political party functioning in Peyrane. Except for the years 1945–47, Peyrane has had a Radical mayor since 1895. For forty-five years of this period the Mayor was Monsieur Prullière, who is still spoken of with affection by people of all parties. No one has really filled his place in Peyrane since his death in 1940. He owned an ochre mine, but he was "not proud" and people went to him for discreet advice on any subject. He knew how to get things done and to keep peace in the village without a show of authority. It was his party that nationally supported the Separation of Church and State, but in Peyrane this separation caused no bitterness. Le pauvre Monsieur Prullière disregarded the edicts of the Government and made his own arrangements with l'abbé Olivier. It was also le pauvre Monsieur Prullière who had water piped into Peyrane from the Lubéron mountain seven miles awey, so that Peyrane had running water long before other villages in the neighborhood.

The present mayor, Monsieur Ginoux, is supposed to have made a considerable amount of money by selling farm supplies to the farmers and by buying their produce from them. He is not considered a proper heir of the Prullière tradition, for he has the reputation of being "hard" with people. They do not come to him for personal advice. He receives a smaller number of votes than other candidates of his party on the ballot. Nevertheless the Municipal Council always elects him mayor because he is supposed to be "in" with Daladier and thus in a position to get favorable treatment for the village.

Edouard Daladier, until 1954 the national president of the RGR, has represented the Vaucluse in the Chamber of Deputies since 1919, except for the years 1940 to 1946. Because the electoral system has been changed periodically, he has not always been the representative of the district of which Peyrane is a part, but today he is a representative of the whole département and hence of Peyrane. Daladier has been the faithful representative of his voters of the Vaucluse. He has tried to protect the individual against both the menace of the Left and the menace of the Right. When the Left has been too strong, he has joined hands with the Right. When the threat is stronger from the Right he has joined hands with the Left. In 1936 he participated in the Popular Front. When war threatened in 1938, he signed the Munich Pact. In 1939 he outlawed the Communist Party. When in 1940 the honor of the *patrie* and the freedom of the individual were threatened, he voted to carry on the war to the bitter end. In 1954 he joined with the Communists to fight EDC and to stop the war in Indo-China.

Political observers have been surprised by Daladier's ability to retrieve his position again and again when he has been on the losing side. They are surprised only because they do not know the people who vote for him and who feel that they too, have been on the losing side often — buffeted by the Left and by the Right, by Germany, by Russia, and by the United States. As the threat to the individual has shifted, Daladier has shifted, but he has never ceased to try to protect the individual from the overwhelming *ils*, whoever they were at the time.

Most of the RGR strength in Peyrane comes from the older people, especially from the more prosperous traditionalists who have seen candidates with the Socialist Radical label win all but two national elections in Peyrane since they were children. In voting for the Socialist Radical candidate, they are voting as their father did, or rather, as their father appeared to vote, for if the party label has remained the same, the program of the candidates has not. Before the first World War, Peyrane voters preferred a Socialist Radical candidate farther to the right than the Socialist Radical elected by the surrounding region. In 1924 and 1936, the Socialist Radical was to the Left. Today he is a Moderate. But they have all been Socialist Radicals.

As the older generation dies out in Peyrane, it appears that the RGR will die out, too. It can no longer win an election alone but must count on the support of other moderate parties like the MRP and SFIO.

Traditionally and theoretically, the SFIO (the Socialist Party) lies to the left of the Socialist Radical Party. The Socialist Party proposes to protect the individual not only against Government and Church and

Foreign Powers, as does the RGR, but also against Wealth. The differences in the platforms of the RGR and the Socialist parties have little to do, however, in determining the vote of most of the people of Peyrane. In reality there is *no* difference between the political ideas of the RGR and the Socialist voters, except for a few people like the schoolteachers, who cast a positive vote for the socialist tendencies expressed in the Socialist Party platform. Most of the people who vote Socialist do so to distinguish themselves from the people who vote Socialist-Radical. Some of the Socialist voters are middle-aged, that is younger than the Socialist Radicals, and they resent the domination of the older group. Other Socialists are somewhat less well established economically and socially than many Socialist Radicals; their vote indicates a feeling of resentment. Other Socialists are *brouillés* with Socialist Radical neighbors and refuse to support the same political party.

The essential difference between the Socialist Radical and Socialist voters is best illustrated in the two assistant mayors. The second assistant, Monsieur Roche, is a Socialist Radical. He was born in 1871, has lived in the village all his life, and is supported by the income from two farms he owns. The first assistant, Monsieur Aubenas, was born in 1896. He lived in the country until recently, and still works his fields on the edge of the village. When there is no work on the farm, his sons work in the ochre mines. The economic and social differences between Roche and Aubenas are exacerbated by a personal feud over a property boundary. One could not expect Aubenas to support the party of which Roche is a leader, and yet he could not vote for the MRP or RPF or Communist Parties, for they represent tendencies with which he wishes even less to be associated. The Socialist Party offers Aubenas the outlet he needs. This poses a problem for Aubenas's son, who has to vote Communist in order to differentiate himself both from his father and from Roche.

In the election of 1951, the MRP (Popular Republican Movement) received thirty-seven votes in Peyrane. This is about the number of adult practicing Catholics in the village. Most of the MRP voters are women who believe that their vote is a vote for the Church. For the two or three men who support the MRP candidate, however, their vote is more than a vote for the Church. They are openly enthusiastic in their support of this new party which, they say, is the only really liberal party and the only party with honest leaders. They say that their vote

is a vote for social reform and a vote against corruption of the RGR
and Socialist politicians.

When General de Gaulle's rightest Rassemblement du Peuple Fran-
çais was still in existence, it had supporters in Peyrane, but they did
not make their support public. They did not campaign openly and
would admit their preference only in confidence. Most of the RPF
voters are lower middle class people who moved to Peyrane from the
city and are forced by circumstances to remain there. By voting RPF
they were showing their contempt for the village louts who either supported the "corrupt" moderate parties or "stupidly" voted Communist,
that is, for a "foreign power." They wanted a strong man to clean up
France and get rid of all the politics and politicians. These people seem
to have a craving for discipline — or at least a desire to see *les autres*
disciplined — which the villagers do not share.

It is difficult to generalize concerning the people who form the
largest political group in the community, the Communist Party. Whatever generalization one is tempted to make must be immediately at-
tenuated to account for important exceptions. Thus one can say that
on the whole the Communist are made up of the youngest generation
of voters, but it must be added at once that some of the most fervent
members are Moïse Jannel, Raoul Pascal, the Charrins, the Mazons,
who all were born before 1900. On the whole, the Communists are economically less favored than the Socialist Radicals or the Socialists, but
among their leaders are Chanon and Laurens, who own their own
farms, Biron, the most prosperous butcher in the region, Léon Favre, a
foreman in the ochre mines. On the whole, the Communists are less
established socially, but the entire Favre clan votes Communist, and
the Favres are probably the oldest family in the commune. Most of the
former prisoners of war and most of the men who lived and fought
in the *maquis* are Communists, but Emile Pian, who spent five years
as a prisoner in Germany, and Gaston Jouvaud, who was one of the
most ardent *maquisards* in the commune, are Socialists.

The one point on which all the Communists are in firm agreement
with each other and with the party program is that they believe most
of their problems may be attributed to the outside *ils* — to the Government, to Wealth, to Foreign Powers, to Selfish Interests which threaten
the helpless individual. Of course, in this belief they are also in agreement with their neighbors who vote Socialist Radical and Socialist.

The essential difference is that the Communists are more dissatisfied, more outraged by the State of Things, and consequently their protest vote is even more violent. They vote as far to the left as they can. If there were a party to the Left of the Communist Party, they would vote for it. Furthermore, by voting Communist they are voting against their neighbors who vote Socialist and Socialist Radical. A Communist vote permits them to express their contempt of the inside *ils* and the outside *ils* at the same time.

Since the Communist Party has not participated in a French Government for several years, it enjoys an advantage over both the Socialist Radical and Socialist Parties. It can blame these parties and the Governments which they have supported for all their present problems: high prices, high taxes, war in Indo-China and North Africa, the economic and military invasion by the Americans, the strengthening of Germany, the eighteen months' military service, the lack of housing, the inadequate social security benefits, the competition brought about by lowered customs barriers, the prohibition against increased wine-grape acreage. All this the Communists blame on the Government, on the parties which participate in the Government, and on the people of Peyrane who vote for these parties.

However, it is only on this negative aspect of the Communist program that the members of the party find themselves in agreement. The only Communist who seems interested in the more positive aspect of the Communist program is Charles Pouget, whose mother was a Favre and who was therefore born into the Communist clan. Pouget left Peyrane as soon as he finished school and went to Lyon to work in a factory. There he received indoctrination in Communism which he now preaches. He was made Secretary of the local party because of his zeal and because of his willingness to do the party work which others wish to avoid, but for some time there has been talk of removing him from his office. The leaders of the party say that Pouget goes too far. He is hard to get along with. He frightens people by his talk of revolution. They would like to replace him but it is difficult to find another secretary. Moïse is willing to work but he is too stupid. Maurice Favre is willing but his education is insufficient. Peretti is only too willing; he is a hothead who quarrels with everyone. If Pouget goes off to the city to work in a factory again, as he says he is going to, the party will be left without a secretary, or else the leaders will have to name someone like Raoul Pascal, loved and respected by everyone, but indifferent to party doctrine.

What if the Communists should win an election and take over the government? Would the Church not be suppressed? This question brings from the Communists only a reaction of amused tolerance. Communism and religion have nothing to do with each other, says Léon Favre who is considered the brains of the Communist party. He points out that Chanon has just had his child baptized, that Raymond Laurens' son has just taken first communion, that there is no difference between the religious practice of the Communists and the non-Communists in Peyrane. This is an obvious fact.

What about the collectivization of farms? Wouldn't Laurens and Chanon and Mitifiot lose the land they own? No, says Chanon. The soil and terrain of Peyrane would make collective farming inefficient there. Collectivization would take place only on the plains of Beauce and of the North, in other parts of France.

What difference would a Communist victory have on Peyrane? None, directly. Indirectly, when the people took over the Government in Paris, prices would be controlled, taxes would go down, military expenditures and service would be reduced, war would end in North Africa. . . Unless, says Léon Favre, you Americans think you have to come over and save us again. That would be *la Catastrophe*.

But what about the controls on prices and everything else? Wouldn't it mean that Peyrane would feel more than ever the restraints of Government? If, says Chanon, our rotten leaders betray us and try to dictate to us what we think and what we do, then there is always the *maquis*. Laval and Hitler couldn't make us give in. Just let any other *salauds* try it. We know how to resist. . . Thus many of the Communists would be among the first to resist a Communist government. As Chanon said, the people of Peyrane prefer to handle their *own* affairs.

The Communists usually get about one-third of the votes of the registered voters. The moderate parties — RGR, SFIO, and MRP — get another third. In national elections there is normally about a third of the voters who do not bother to come to the polls. Among these there are, of course, some who are physically unable to do so. There are also a few people who seem indifferent to, almost unaware of, any election. Most of the nonvoters, however, refrain from voting as a matter of principle, for they believe it is a waste of time to take part in a meaningless ceremony. They agree with the voters in deploring the Government and other Impinging Forces, but they think it is stupid to believe that a vote can weaken the strength of these forces.

The attitude of most of the nonvoters I talked to was that of Figeard: "Why should I take time off from work to go all the way up to the Town Hall to vote? And for a politician? They're all a pile of bandits." When Figeard spat he added an exclamation point to what he said.

Of course, the people who vote would not disagree with nonvoters like Figeard in their contempt of political leaders. The MRP supporters are an exception in believing that their leaders have "clean hands"; the supporters of all other parties agree that their leaders cannot be trusted. Even the Communists express contempt for their leaders. In their eyes, leaders are good not because they are more trustworthy than others, but because they are more violent in their opposition to the government.

Basically there is little difference in the attitude of the people who vote Socialist Radical, Socialist, Communist, and those who do not vote at all. In every case their behavior simply indicates a condemnation of the hardships of life which may be attributed to governmental authority. They are acting against the outside *ils* who oppress them and against the inside *ils* who are the local incarnation of the outside *ils*. The difference in their behavior is a difference in degree, not in essence. What determines the intensity of their reaction has more to do with family traditions, personality, health, personal experience, and with their relations with other people in the village than with political credos. Since the personal differences are so keenly felt, the elections are keenly contested.

The elections are all the more tense because of the even division of the adult population into thirds — the Moderates, the Communists, and the nonvoters. A slight shift in the population can change the course of an election. A few people who change their vote, or a few abstainers who are persuaded to vote, may change the course of the election. To persuade people is a difficult task, however. They are impervious to propaganda and to attempts to tell them how they should behave. They are influenced more in election campaigns by situations which may be contrived. The election of June 1951, offers a vivid case study.

In the region around Peyrane, the Communist Party made the first strategic move. Toward the end of April 1951, the Ochre Workers

Union, an affiliate of the Communist dominated Confédération Générale du Travail, called a strike. This was a vulnerable point at which to attack, for the situation of the ochre workers was notoriously bad. They are the hardest-working and poorest-paid workers in the region. As a general rule no one works in the mines if he can avoid it. It is the sort of work that attracts Algerians who accept low wages and live in squalid conditions. The average ochre worker earns about twenty-three cents an hour, but since a good many days are lost because of rain and layoffs, the average take-home pay is about thirty dollars a month. In 1951, in spite of the rapidly increasing cost of living, there had been no increase in pay rates for several years. The demands formulated by the Union seemed reasonable. The principal demand was for an increase in wages of three cents an hour.

The management handled the affair poorly. When the Union sent a delegation of men to discuss the situation, it was kept waiting an hour in the office of the spokesman for the various ochre companies and was finally sent away without talking to anyone. Management declined every opportunity to make contact with the Union, and the strike went on for days. Finally, in the third week of a strike which in the beginning was expected to last half a day, public pressure forced the management to adopt a more reasonable attitude. Even conservative people in the community sided with the workers. The workers got their three cents an hour increase and went back to the mines.

Since the commune of Peyrane has only a few small ochre mines, most of them owned by patriarchal figures known personally by the workers, the conflict was not so bitter as it was in Gargas and Apt, where there are big mines owned by a large corporation. The miners of Peyrane did not blame their employers too severely, for it was obvious to them that the individual employers could not counter the policy of the Big Corporation any more than the workers could. In fact, the relations between the Peyrane owners and their workers had been so good that before the strike only one miner from Peyrane belonged to the Union. That was Pouget, the secretary of the Communist Party.

By the time the strike was in its second week, however, the situation had changed. Membership of the Peyrane workers in the Union was one hundred per cent. Thus the Confédération Générale du Travail increased its strength in this predominantly rural community, at least until after the election in June. Since the management of the ochre mines had behaved so stupidly in the affair, and since everyone knew that the Communist Party had really engineered the strike through the unions it dominated, the net effect was to weaken the position of the conservative candidates and to strengthen the position of the Communist candidates throughout the region.

Before the Communist Party had completed the ochre strike maneuver, Mayor Ginoux had quietly started a counterattack in the Peyrane area by replying with the New School Gambit. It will be recalled that the school in Peyrane is a shambles. In the neighboring town of Goult, no larger or more wealthy than Peyrane, there is a new school, a modern building with plenty of light and air, built by a Communist administration soon after the war.

Peyrane, too, had planned to build a new school. Several years ago the Mayor and the Town Council approved the building. The Ministry of Education approved. Architects came to the village and drew up plans. Just as it seemed certain that Peyrane would soon have a new school, difficulties began to arise. There was a squabble among the people of the village over where the school should be located. Finally this argument was settled in favor of building the school on the site of the old school. Then a new obstacle was encountered when the Administration of Primary Education and the Administration of Fine Arts, both sections of the Ministry of Education, could not agree. The plans of the former called for a modern school building, but the Administration of Fine Arts would not approve on the grounds that a modern building would destroy the picturesque harmony of Peyrane.

At this point everyone interested in the project began to despair. To secure the approval of one government agency for any purpose is difficult, but to get two governmental agencies to settle a difference and to agree on a course of action is an almost impossible task. Nothing more was done. In the spring of 1951, the new school of Peyrane still reposed in the files of the Ministry of Education. Goult, with a Communist administration, had an impressive new school. Peyrane, with a Socialist Radical administration, had a school that was a menace to the health and safety of the children.

One afternoon toward the end of April, I was in the Town Hall talking to Rivet when the Mayor arrived. After he had seen the people who were waiting for him, he began to go through the papers Rivet had prepared for him. As he signed letters and permits and certificates, thus making Rivet's work official, he brought up the subject that was on his mind.

"Marcel," he said, "What about the school?"

Rivet answered with a shrug of his shoulders. Monsieur Ginoux said nothing for a few minutes while he looked through his papers. He signed his name to still another document without looking up and then he tried again.

"Marcel. . . It's time we did something about the school."

Rivet hooted. "From the way you talk, Monsieur Ginoux, you'd think we hadn't done anything about the school!"

After a moment the Mayor said softly, "Goult has a new school. Peyrane hasn't. That's bad, especially now."

Rivet let this remark pass, but he no longer shrugged his shoulders. His position as Town Clerk depended on the success of Monsieur Ginoux's Socialist Radicals.

"Perhaps, Marcel, we should write a letter to Daladier."

Rivet could not resist a sarcastic remark: "All right, Monsieur Ginoux, I've written him so many times about the school that I know my letter by heart."

"I think, Marcel, that this time it will be different." Monsieur Ginoux still concentrated on the papers in the dossier. "The election will be close. . . If we could figure out a gimmick (*truc*) Daladier could use to stir up the Ministry of Education, he might use it this time."

Now Rivet became interested in papers on his desk; Ginoux and he sat absorbed in work. Then the conversation began again.

"Monsieur Ginoux. . . Perhaps it wouldn't be bad. . .

"Ah?"

". . . to organize a spontaneous revolt of the parents!"

Monsieur Ginoux put his papers on the desk and looked at Rivet. Then he stared out the window and shook his head.

"No, Marcel . . . it might complicate things. . . We want to stir things up in Paris, not in Peyrane."

"All right, Monsieur Ginoux, but you wanted a gimmick for Monsieur Daladier to use. This is it."

"No, I'm afraid it might mean trouble."

"But, Monsieur Ginoux, can we help it if there's a spontaneous revolt?"

"No, Marcel, I'll have nothing to do with it. . ." Monsieur Ginoux went back to his papers, but in a moment he added, "I hope you'll not implicate me when you talk to Madame Baume about it this evening."

Madame Baume is the retired schoolteacher of Peyrane and the President of the Conseil de Parents d'Élèves. I was not with Rivet when he talked to Madame Baume, but the result of their conversation became obvious two days later when Johany brought a note home from school. The children who could not yet write had been given notes written by the older children as part of the morning's work.

> There will be a meeting of the Conseil de Parents d'Élèves in the Meeting Room of the Town Hall next Sunday at four o'clock. Urgent business will be discussed.

Francis Favre, the postman, took copies of the note to parents whose children were absent from school that day.

On Sunday afternoon at four-thirty, eighteen of the eighty putative members of the Conseil des Parents d'Élèves were in the Meeting Room of the Town Hall. When Madame Baume was able to get the attention of the parents the meeting began.

"It has been suggested," Madame Baume said, "that we can do something about the new school. Maybe if we refused to send our children to school until They authorize the new building, They might do something about it."

Conversations broke out immediately all around the room. Madame Baume assured the parents that other villages had been successful in their strikes against the Government, that the Government had not retaliated, that there was no danger in the proposal. Reassured, the parents tacitly assumed that the proposal would be accepted. Any proposal directed against the government, involving no risk, perhaps achieving something everyone wanted, was a proposal that would be adopted as a matter of course. After a half-hour the meeting ended. No vote was taken. The meeting ended because no one cared to discuss the subject longer.

The next afternoon, Jacques Leporatti and Georges Vincent knocked at our door and asked us if we would be willing to sign a petition they were circulating among all the children's parents in the village:

> We, the undersigned, parents of the school children of Peyrane, have

united our voices to protest against the delay in the construction of our new school. Fearful that the collapse of the old building is imminent, we have determined no longer to risk the lives of our children. If the construction of the new school is not authorized by June 1, we shall after that date keep our children at home.

Jacques and Georges said that other older children were circulating the petitions in the *quartiers* outside the village and that the Postman was taking petition to *quartiers* where there were no older children. Within three days all the parents had signed the petitions. No one had refused. After all, the matter of the new school was not a political matter, it seemed; there was no reason for anyone to refuse to sign.

Madame Baume sent the petitions to the Minister of Education on May 25. On May 30 the Mayor received a telegram from the Minister announcing that the construction of the new school building had been authorized. The election was to be held on June 17. On June 7, the following item was published in the Vaucluse edition of the Radical Marseille *Méridional.*

Peyrane's New School

M. le Maire is happy to announce that the Ministry has just authorized construction of our new school. He is anxious to call to the attention of the people the fact that it was the collaboration of M. Edouard Daladier that helped assure the success of our project. M. Daladier intervened repeatedly in our behalf.

The construction of the school has been delayed because the Administration of Fine Arts objected to certain details in the school plans which might prevent the school from fitting in with the architectural style of our village. These details have been changed and authorization has been granted.

Now the delay may be forgotten since only the end result matters, and we trust that the prospect of seeing a new school soon rise on the site of the old one will bring joy to everyone. The Mayor wishes to express our gratitude to those who have contributed in making possible this necessary and useful addition to our village.

The Socialist newspaper, *Provençal,* had an item on Peyrane's new school, too, but it did not mention Daladier.

The Influence of Our Representatives

M. Geoffroy, Senator from the Vaucluse, has received from M. P.-O.

Lapie, Minister of National Education, the following letter, dated June 5:

My dear friend,

Thank you for calling to my attention the school construction project in the commune of Peyrane.

I am pleased to inform you that the Special Section in charge of the Buildings of France has studied the project. The objection raised by the Bureau of Sites concerning the location of the new school has been removed. Of course, the new building must be architecturally appropriate. It must have narrow openings, the appropriate color, and a roof of rounded tiles.

Very cordially,
Lapie

Lapie and Geoffroy are members of the Socialist Party. Daladier, a Socialist Radical, had obviously worked with Geoffroy on this project. Coöperation was appropriate in this election since the two parties were *apparentés* in the Vaucluse, so that a victory for one meant a victory for the other. However, each newspaper made sure to give credit to the representative of its own party.

The Communist *Marsiellaise* made no mention of the new school, of course. There was no point in their giving publicity to the success of the Mayor's New School Gambit. Instead, the *Marseillaise* played up the success of the ochre strikers.

Public election meetings were scheduled by all the parties except the RPF. The first meeting was announced on a big poster displayed in the window of the Voisin café. It invited the voters of Peyrane to gather in the *Salle des Fêtes* at six o'clock on June 1 to meet the leading candidate of a new political party, The Independent List of Republicans of Peasant, Economic and Social Action. This candidate bore the unbelievable name of Alcide Macabet, which has in French the same comic effect that its rough translation — Hercules Cadaver — might have in English. No one in the village knew anything about this party or about Macabet. The Communists suspected he was a tool of the Moderates trying to syphon off some of the Communist votes. The Moderates thought he was a tool of the Communists trying to divert conservative votes. No one was interested enough in the Macabet mystery to attend the meeting, however. The only people present were Monsieur Macabet and his wife, one of the old men of the village (who vent to all free meetings though he was too deaf to hear what was said), Assistant Mayor Aubenas, and Garde-Champêtre Franchet (both of them required by law to attend such a meeting), and myself.

Although the MRP, RGR, and SFIO announced public meetings, the meetings were not held. Couston, the leading MRP candidate, came to Peyrane and was met by his only party member in the village, Edouard Pascal. Pascal took Couston to Vincent's for lunch and then showed him the picturesque sights in the village. Edouard Pascal had arranged no meeting because, he said, the villagers were too stupid to appreciate Couston.

Daladier and Lussy, the perennial Socialist Député from Vaucluse, announced their intention of visiting Peyrane, but neither of them came. In their place came the RGR Senator, Pellenc, and the SFIO Senator, Geoffroy, who were not up for re-election but were campaigning for Daladier and Lussy. Pellenc had lunch at Vincent's restaurant with Monsieur Ginoux. Geoffroy had lunch at Vincent's with Aubenas. Election meetings were not held, Monsieur Ginoux said, because everyone was busy working in the fields to catch up after a rainy spring; no one could be expected to take time to listen to political speeches.

The Communist Party of Peyrane held its election meeting as it was announced, in the *Salle des Fêtes* at six o'clock on the evening of June 5. Sixty people came to hear René Arthaud, the Communist deputy who was up for re-election, speak for forty-five minutes on the sins of the Government, the iniquities of American capitalism, the invasion of the Vaucluse by Americans, the magnificent victory of the Ochre Workers Union. He ended by encouraging all present to work for the success of the list of candidates presented by the Communist Party, that is the *List of Republican, Resistant, and Anti-Fascist Union for National Independence, Bread, Liberty and Peace*. The applause which frequently interrupted the speaker was not enthusiastic, but it was adequate for the occasion.

In the days before the election, the conversation in the café turned more and more to politics, but it cannot be said that anyone was really excited. Underlying every conversation was the generally accepted assumption that all politicians are a "pile of bandits," that after all it didn't matter much who won. The heat of the discussion came from the participants' personal hostility toward each other rather than from their differing political opinions. This does not mean that no principles were involved in the discussion. The political campaign simply gave people an opportunity to express their hostility toward each other under the guise of anonymous ideals. But the hostility never got out of bounds. Arguments might flair up to a sudden peak, but if they were about to become violent they were stopped. There was never even a suggestion of a physical threat.

On election day most people went about their work as usual. Only the principal party workers and the town officers in charge of the election took the whole day off. The lower floor of the Town Hall was set up with tables and voting booths. The party workers used the Voisin café next door as headquarters. Voisin put tables in front of the café where people could sit and talk. There was no heavy drinking although a good many drinks were consumed, since Chanon and Ginoux were more eager than usual to offer free drinks.

In the Town Hall the voting moved slowly. Only three hundred and twenty-nine people voted during the day, and the polls were open for ten hours. Monsieur Ginoux, Franchet, the Garde-Champêtre, the electoral committee of the Municipal Council, and the watchers for each party sat quietly waiting. Every hour or so one of them would go to the café and return with a tray of glasses, pastis, and a pitcher of water. No exciting event enlivened their day. They sat and talked and joked, coming to attention only when someone came to vote.

This voting procedure was simple. As one entered the door of the Town Hall, he found Franchet sitting at a table on which there were six piles of ballots, a pile for each of the parties competing in the election: Independent, Communist, RPF, SFIO, RGR, MRP. Each ballot contained the name of the party, the names of the candidates and their principal qualifications. Thus Daladier was described as "Present Député, former Prime Minister." Less well-known figures offered a more elaborate or intimate description of themselves. Roger Adam described himself as "Businessman at Carpentras, escaped prisoner of war, member of the department directing committee, president of the Professional Union." Denise Jumontier was labelled, "Secretary, Mother of a Family, Widow of the 1939–45 war."

Three of the parties indicated further on the ballot that they were *apparentés* with each other — MRP, RGR, and SFIO. The *apparentement* was a system worked out by these parties and enacted into the electoral law to prevent the RPF and Communist parties from winning the election. According to this complicated system, any parties could proclaim themselves *apparentés* and count their votes together as though they were one party. If together they had a majority then each of the parties individually won the election. We shall see how the system worked in the Peyrane election.

When the voter came in the door he picked up an envelope and a ballot from each of the six piles. He went into a curtained voting booth in the middle of the hall where he chose the one of the six ballots he preferred, and he then threw away the other five. Or he might split his ticket, deleting certain names and inserting others on one of the six ballots. In either case he folded one of the ballots, put it in the envelope and went from the booth to the big table at which were seated the Electoral Committee and the party representatives, and in the middle of which stood the electoral urn. The voter announced himself, and after the officials had called off and checked his name he was asked to drop the envelope into the urn. There was little joking at this moment. One sensed that it was a solemn occasion in spite of the cynical attitude toward politics and elections.

There was even less joking than usual when Moïse came to vote. People always joked with Moïse but they did not joke this time, even though his appearance gave them an admirable opening. To show how seriously he took this democratic procedure, Moïse had shaved and put on his best suit, wrapped a brilliant red sash around his waist and donned his red tie on which was painted Picasso's dove of peace. When he entered the Town Hall he did not deign to pick up a ballot from each of the six piles. Everyone knew his convictions and he took advantage of the opportunity to flaunt them. He picked up only the Communist ballot, walked through the booth without stopping, came out putting the ballot in the envelope, and presented himself at the table. No joke was cracked until he left the building and was going down the steps. Monsieur Ginoux was just going in. I asked if they wanted their pictures taken together. Of course they did, and as they shook hands, everyone came to the door to banter them.

Most of the party workers were inactive except for the Communists. All day one of their men sat at the voting table with a list of the registered voters, checking off all those who voted. The other parties did not bother. Now and then a knot of Communist officials huddled at the bar or at one of the tables. Then Pouget or Léon Favre would leave in a car, returning sometime later with a voter. They even brought in the nameless old woman who sat all day huddled up in a field near Raoul Favre's, holding the leash of her goat. She had become so much a part of the landscape that seeing her out of her field gave one the feeling that an unnatural phenomenon was taking place.

At seven o'clock the polls were officially declared closed by Monsieur Ginoux, and the counting began. Now the Town Hall became crowded with people who massed around the electoral table as the votes were called off and tabulated. The Electoral Committee kept official score, but each party worker counted for himself, too. The counting lasted for forty-five minutes, and then news of the results circulated through the crowd. There was no expression of jubilation or of despair. One could not tell from the people's faces whether their candidates had won or lost. Finally I worked my way up to the table and got the results from Rivet.

Registered voters	467
Votes cast	329
Invalid	10
Valid votes cast	319
Arthaud (Communist)	141
Daladier (RGR)	77
Lussy (SFIO)	40
Couston (MRP)	37
Mazo (RPF)	21
Macabet (Independent)	6

The Communists had received the most votes, but since the RGR, SFIO, and MRP were *apparentés* they won the election, for together they received thirteen more votes than the Communist candidate. Thus were the moderate parties of Peyrane able to combine to win the election in 1951.

As we left the Town Hall and went back to the café, I found myself with Lucien Bourdin, who had voted SFIO. He shook his head and said, "You Americans must think we are awfully dishonest to fix (*truquer*) the election like that." However, Lucien Bourdin was the only non-Communist to speak in such terms. Most people felt that since politics are dishonest in the first place, one could scarcely *fix* a political event. Nevertheless, the Communists were outraged by the results of the election. They said it only proved the hypocrisy and decay of the so-called "political democracies."

To speak thus in terms of parties is in a sense misleading, since party labels are less important than personal relations in determining attitudes and actions. It may be true in general that "the Communists say this" or the "MRP voters do that," but the fact cannot be over-emphasized that the relationship of one individual to another is funda-mental. The existence of political labels permits easy generalizations, but if we speak only in terms of political labels the impression we give is false.

To illustrate this point, it might be useful to tell how Léon Favre sabotaged his own party meeting. Léon Favre is Peyrane's number two Communist, the most important after Chanon. The other men listen to him because they know he is *serious*. He holds no office in the party, but it is he who makes important decisions. His party connections did not prevent him from associating with me, and our families even spent evenings together. When Léon was in the hospital in Cavaillon after his motorcycle accident, I took his wife to see him, and when he was ready to return home, I went to get him. During his convalescence, since he had nothing better to do than sit and talk, he became one of my most coöperative informants.

Toward the end of April, as a part of the general "Peace Offensive" of the Communist Party, that is, as a partially disguised election ma-neuver, the Peyrane Communists were planning a big meeting to "at-tempt to bring the public together in a nonpartisan effort to secure peace, menaced by American capitalism." When Pouget asked me if I planned to come to the meeting I told him that I attended meetings of all kinds at which I was permitted to be present. He assured me that I would be welcome, and later he wrote me a formal invitation. I thought this was peculiar on his part, but thanked him for the invita-tion and again assured him that I intended to come.

One evening, a few days before the meeting, I was out walking and met Léon Favre. He said that he was on his way to our house, for he had something to tell me confidentially.

"You're coming to our meeting?" he asked.

"Of course. Pouget said I might."

"Do you know the main purpose of the meeting?"

"I thought Maury was going to speak." (Maury was a Communist candidate in the election and secretary of the *confiseurs'* union in Apt.)

"Yes, but the main thing is to collect signatures on the Peace Movement Petitions."

"That doesn't concern me. I can come and watch, can't I?"

"No, and that's the point. Either you sign or you don't. If you sign, we'll have it in the papers — *American signs anti-American petition!*"

"And if I don't? Because you know I won't."

"Then the Communists will all be mad. And if you do sign you'll have everyone else against you."

"In other words, I'm on the spot."

"Not necessarily. . . Didn't you say something about wanting to see Switzerland before you leave?"

"Yes."

"They say it's nicest in May, you know."

We were in Switzerland when the Peace Meeting took place.

The fact that the people of Peyrane are more interested in local situations and in each other as individuals than in political parties and national issues may be seen in a comparison of the participation of registered voters in the municipal and national elections in the village since the war.

National Elections		*Municipal Elections*	
May 1946	67%	April 1945	80%
June 1946	68%	October 1947	80%
November 1946	73%	April 1953	90%
June 1951	70%		

Everyone told me that municipal elections were much more bitterly fought than national elections, but unfortunately, there was no municipal election the year I was in Peyrane. It would have been illuminating to witness the municipal election of April 1953, for people in the village wrote me that it was particularly hot. It had looked for a time as if the Communist faction, or rather the Chanon-Favre faction, would not even be able to put up a slate. The group had been badly split. They had quarrelled over whether it was fair to hunt rabbits with ferrets. Pouget's zeal and lack of discretion had annoyed former friends of the party. Chanon had lost so much money when he was Mayor after the war that he insisted he would no longer accept the position if he were elected. In the last three elections the party had polled a smaller and smaller percentage of the votes — 51 per cent in 1946, 46 per cent in 1947, 45 per cent in 1951. The outlook did not seem hopeful for the Communists. Then three things happened that improved the situation. The rabbit epidemic killed off all the rabbits and settled the ferret question. Pouget moved away from Peyrane. Jouve called on Chanon.

Jouve is the thirty-three-year-old son of a prominent ultra-conservative, ultra-Catholic family of Avignon. He intended to study medicine, but the war interrupted his education and by the time he would have been able to go to medical school he had decided that what he really wanted to do was to return to the soil. As a good Catholic, he felt it was his duty to live as a peasant, to help bring religious faith back to other peasants and to raise a large family.

For several years Jouve was kept busy learning to be a farmer, but little by little he became bored and — according to Rivet's sharp tongue — decided that the people of Peyrane needed an intelligent, well-educated man like him to run their commune. He talked the matter over with Ginoux, hoping to be given a place on the Moderate ballot in the municipal election. He even brought pressure to bear on Daladier so that the latter suggested to Ginoux that Jouve should be accepted as a candidate for the municipal council on the Moderate ticket.

Ginoux would have nothing to do with Jouve. Jouve obviously had no political future in Peyrane and would only be a liability on the Radical Socialist-Socialist ticket. Jouve was an outsider. He was a city man. He went to mass every Sunday. He kept his four little girls at home to be educated by his wife instead of sending them to the village school. He had living with him as a farm worker the son of an Avignon collaborator executed after the war. He could not be too serious a farmer since he tried any new modern method he read about. He worked actively for the Coöp, which was threatening to ruin Ginoux's business. Ginoux resisted all attempts to foist Jouve onto the Moderate ticket.

Jouve then called on Chanon and proposed an alliance with the Communist faction. This action is not too surprising. Jouve was on good terms with his Communist neighbor, Raymond Laurens. Laurens was President of the local CGA (the Farmers Union), and Jouve was Secretary. In this part of France the CGA is Communist-dominated.

Jouve told me that he joined the CGA to bore from within, for he thought the Catholics could use this technique as effectively as the Communists. Jouve could justify his participation on the Chanon ticket on the grounds that he was boring from within.

Chanon and Léon Favre talked the matter over and decided that they were in no way frightened by Jouve's effort to bore from within and that his overture might give them the means to win. Their faction could normally count on about 45 per cent of the vote. Perhaps Jouve could swing for them the three dozen votes of the devout Catholics, and with these extra votes they would win the election. It was true that Jouve insisted on being Mayor if their slate won the election, but that did not worry them. Chanon had no desire to be Mayor. He would be Assistant Mayor, and he would easily be able to control Jouve, because of Jouve's political ambition and, they believed, because of his stupidity.

Chanon accepted Jouve's offer, and a coalition slate was formed with six active members of the Communist Party (Chanon, Laurens, Vidal, Maurice Favre, Avenas, and Seignon), three members of the ultra-Conservative Catholic faction (Jouve, Joly and Gleizer), and four *serious* friends to add weight to the ticket (Borel, Jaumard, Mitifiot, and Fortias). This slate seemed strong to Chanon, aged thirty-eight, and to Jouve, aged thirty-three, because of its youth. Only two of their candidates were over fifty, while only two candidates of the Moderate slate were under fifty. Léon Favre pointed out that youth was not necessarily an advantage in an election.

The Ginoux-Aubenas slate was made up of seven incumbent municipal councillors and six new candidates. The latter were Gaston Jouvaud, and Julien Vincent, two of the most *serious* and successful men of the village, Madame Baume, the retired teacher who was disliked by some people but respected by most as their former teacher, le père Imbert, the father of a large brood of adult voters and the father-in-law of the postman, Brousse, a farmer who was supposed to be *in* with the devout Catholics, and Antoine Charial, a farmer only thirty-three years old who might serve as proof that the Ginoux-Aubenas faction was not against young people as a matter of principle.

With these opposing slates, the electioneering began. The issues concerned the need for a sewage system, the erection of public baths (or rather moving the showers from the unused soccer field to a new structure near the public square), and the new school. Yes, the new school was still an issue. In spite of the promises made before the election of 1951 the school had not been built. The class that met in the upstairs room, the room which was immediately threatened by a cave-in, had been moved to Lataud's former café, but the other two classes still met in their rooms in the old building. But, of course, the most effective electioneering did not concern these issues at all; it concerned rather the *histoires personnelles* that I might have heard if I had been in Peyrane. Unfortunately, my correspondents seem loath to put *histoires personnelles* in writing. When I press for details, they answer, "Oh, you know, these *histoires personnelles* that no one believes, but that everyone talks about."

The results were close. The majority necessary for election was 204 votes; no candidate received more than 217, and no candidate received less than 172. The results are shown below.

List of Republican Union for the Defense of Communal Interests (Socialist Radical–Socialist)		*List of Peasant & Workers Union for the Defense of Local Interests* (Catholic–Communist)	
ELECTED			
Marnas, Louis	217		
Arnoux, Lucien	216		
		Chanon, Raoul	216
Jouvaud, Gaston	216		
Aubenas, Albert	213		
Sanape, Marcel	213		
		Mitifiot, Aimé	212
Vincent, Julien	210		
Ginoux, Laurent	210		
Baume, Geneviève	208		
		Fortias, Jean	206
		Jaumard, Roger	206
DEFEATED			
Laplace, Léo	203		
Brousse, Paul	203		
		Borel, Louis	202
Charial, Antoine	202		
		Laurens, Raymond	202
Massot, Georges	200		

Imbert, Marcel 199

Vidal, Guy	191
Gaston-Jouve, Henri	190
Seignon, Elie	180
Favre, Maurice	177
Joly, Paul	177
Gleizer, Joseph	175
Avenas, Maurice	172

It is obvious that party lines have little to do with local elections. This fact was even more apparent the following Sunday. Since only twelve of the candidates had received a majority of the votes, a run-off election had to be held to elect someone to the thirteenth seat of the Council. After consultation, the moderates Laplace and Charial withdrew in favor of their friend Brousse. The Communist-Catholic group decided to run Borel against him. If the Socialist Radical group had been able to enforce party discipline, Brousse would have won the election easily, but when the votes were counted, it was found that he had lost to Borel, 224 to 160!

A statistician knowing nothing of the personalities involved in this election might sum up the results thus: The Moderates won 8 seats, the Communists 5. The Moderates got fifty-two per cent of the popular vote, the Communists forty-eight per cent. This is three per cent more than the Communists received in 1951. Hence the Communists have gained strength in Peyrane in the last three years.

Obviously this is not the case. Even if we were to admit that Communism is an issue in this case, it would be necessary to point out that all the Communist Party members except Chanon were badly defeated. The only members of the Chanon-Jouve coalition who were elected were the *serious* men who were added to the slate to give it weight. Chanon himself was elected because he is a village hero. The regular Communist Party members like Avenas, Maurice Favre, Seignon, and Vidal were defeated along with the extreme conservatives Jouve, Joly, and Gleizer.

Rather than raise the issue of Communism in such an election, it would be wiser to seek other, more fundamental issues. We might say, for instance, that the election was a victory for the farmers. This would scarcely be surprising in a commune in which three-fifths of the voters are farmers and farmers' wives. Seven of the thirteen councillors elected are farmers. Yet, this is certainly not a basic factor. In view of the high proportion of farmers on the ballot, they did no better than chance.

A more important factor is that of the origin of the candidates. All four of the candidates born outside the Vaucluse were defeated. It does not seem to have mattered to the voters, however, what part of the Vaucluse the candidates were from. Of the ten candidates born in Peyrane, five were elected. Of the eleven candidates born elsewhere in the Vaucluse, seven were elected.

Candidates living in the village itself seem to have been preferred to those living in the country, even though a majority of the voters live in the country. Seven of the eleven village candidates were elected, while only six of the fifteen country candidates were successful.

Still more important is the question of age. The median age among the successful candidates is fifty-three; among the unsuccessful candidates it is forty-four. This is scarcely surprising in a community in which the proportion of elderly people is unusually high. Jouve was wrong, as Léon Favre warned him he might be, in assuming that it was an advantage to have a "young, energetic slate."

Yet, the factor of age is not the most decisive factor. The seventy-year-old Imbert and sixty-four-year-old Massot, both of them farmers born in the Vaucluse, were defeated, while the thirty-two-year-old Fortias and the thirty-eight-year-old Chanon were elected. There must be still another factor which is more basic.

The one factor which correlates almost perfectly with success and failure in the election is simply a personality trait. If we make a list of all the candidates — regardless of their party label — who have the reputation of being *sérieux*, who mind their own business and seem indifferent to the affairs of other people, our list coincides with the list of successful candidates. There is the possible exception of Chanon, but even Chanon, though not considered *sérieux*, minds his own business. The relations of these men with other people are sufficiently warm. But they are the kind of men who are never accused of prying into what does not concern them.

This explains the curious victory of Borel over Brousse in the run-off election. When it was obvious after the first election that the Ginoux-Aubenas slate had won a majority of seats in the Council, the supporters of that slate did not hesitate to drop Brousse. He has the reputation of being a black reactionary and the unpleasant habit of telling people what they ought to do and think, which is never what they want to do and think. Borel, on the other hand, maintains cordial relations with other people, but he always gives the impression that he is indifferent to them. He has built up a profitable business simply by working hard and staying to himself and his family. He goes to the café but does not hang around. He plays boules now and then, but he does not have a passion for the game. He has been friendly with Communists but only as he has been friendly with everyone else. He is slightly *bien* with everyone and *brouillé* only with people detested by everyone, like Monsieur Martron. He is the kind of man the voters could count on to pry as little as possible into their family affairs and to be as fair as it is possible for a man to be when he is given power. Of the two candidates, Borel was the one that was less easily identified with the *ils* of the village and with the *ils* that lurk beyond the borders of the commune. Regardless of their party labels, Borel was elected and Brousse was defeated.

Adult Recreation and Pleasures

Chapter 11

At The Café

The Cafetier and The Drinking Circles

In Peyrane each family, each home remains the center of existence for its members in recreation as in work. The one institution that most nearly fills the role of a public recreational center is the café. It is not only a recreational center, however. It has other functions that make it an important institution in the community. First, it is a store like other stores but specializing in the sale of beverages, alcoholic and nonalcoholic. People who do not make their own wine and who do not like the wine sold at the groceries buy their wine at the café just as they buy their meat at the butcher's. One of the chores of some of the children when they get home from school at noon is to take an empty bottle to the café to have it filled with wine for lunch. A man whose wife is sick may come to the café to buy her a bottle of Vichy water.

Since the café is also a *tabac*, a tobacco store, it is an official government agency. The ownership and the management are licensed by the government and cannot be changed without its authorization. The manager of the store must be bonded, and he is inspected periodically by government agents. The café sells other products on which the government has a monopoly besides tobacco. One may buy matches, lighters, postage stamps, and lottery tickets there. The café has the forms on which all those who make brandy must declare officially the amount they have made. Finally the café sells tax stamps which must be put on all legal documents.

In the life of the village one of the main functions of the café is to serve as a neutral meeting ground, the only neutral spot where villagers and outsiders may come and go freely. Tourists, strangers, salesmen, any of the people coming to the village who have no access to a home, may go to the café to rest and refresh themselves. Natives want-

ing to meet on neutral grounds to talk over a private affair can find
a back table where they will be undisturbed. A politician coming to the
village to talk over party affairs with his local agents will meet them
in the café.

When I began to give Rorschach tests, I either made arrangements
to meet my subjects at their home or I invited them to our house. I
soon found that both arrangements were unsatisfactory. In their home
I was a guest, and my call was necessarily considered a social call. As
a guest I was unable to keep other members of the family from taking
part in the test. In our house I found people felt ill at ease. Their dual
roles of guest and subject were confusing to them, and for some of the
more humble villagers the relative comfort of our house was disturbing. Soon I discovered the ideal location for the tests — a back table in
the café which came to be known as my office. There we were on neutral, familiar ground. Both the subject and I felt at ease, and the café
owner coöperated in keeping curious clients from disturbing us. Furthermore, people saw that something intriguing was going on and
wanted to participate. I soon found that I had more willing subjects
than I could handle.

Since so many different kinds of people go to the café for different
purposes and since few leave without chatting a bit with the café owner
or his wife, the establishment has naturally become the unofficial information bureau of the town. All the information and misinformation
gathered by the extensive network of gossip circles throughout the
community is eventually funneled into the café. The town clerk spends
two hours or so in the café every day. The doctor often drops in for
an apéritif when he comes to town. People from outlying sections of
the commune who come to the village only on official business at the
Town Hall drop into the café and leave news of their neighborhood.
Through the café owner the postman relays messages with which he
has been charged on his route. With these and many other sources of
information at his disposal the café owner usually knows better than
anyone else in the village the news of the community.

The café also serves as a home, a substitute *foyer*, for the Lonely
Ones, five or six of the poorest adult males of the community — bachelors, widowers, divorcés — who live alone. They make the café the
center of their existence. They are too poor to buy more than a couple
of *canons* a day. A *canon*, a small glass of red wine, costs only three

cents. So the café owner makes little profit from the Lonely Ones. Still, when they are not working or sleeping they are at the café. They read the café newspapers, use the café playing cards, unload their hearts to the café owner's wife, or just sit doing nothing. At mealtime they often bring their bread and cheese and sausage to the café and eat in the company of the café owner's family.

The Lonely Ones are the bane of the café owner's existence. Monsieur and Madame Chobaut had the café when we moved to Peyrane. They had been there only a few months. Before that they had lived in Nice where they said they had had a café so popular and prosperous that Madame Chobaut became *un peu fatiguée* from the strain. To give her a chance to recover her health they sold their place in Nice and bought the café in Peyrane. There they found that they had overestimated the quiet, restful atmosphere of rural life. Madame Chobaut got no rest. She had to be on her feet from early in the morning until late at night, if only to keep shop while the Lonely Ones made their forlorn conversation with her. She had been a governess in England, she said, and she was accustomed to the sophisticated conversation of her clientele in Nice. She felt sorry for Monsieur Maucorps and Pierre and Marino and *lou Frisé*, but she found that ten hours a day in their company were unbearable. Her health deteriorated, and after a few months her husband sold the café in Peyrane and bought a sheep farm in the southern Alps. There Madame Chobaut hoped to find the rest and peace she needed.

The Chobauts were replaced by the Voisins. Voisin, a forty-year-old adolescent who had never been able to become *sérieux*, had tried several trades but had not been satisfied with any of them. When we moved to Peyrane, he was a baker. The bread he made was not bad, but Voisin was unhappy. His work interfered with his one passion in life — playing *boules*. Being a baker in the winter when it is too cold to play boules was all right, but in the summer when he played boules until one or two o'clock in the morning and then had to start baking at three or four he couldn't get enough sleep. Three days a week he had to fill his car with bread and deliver it to farms around the commune. On the other days when he could have caught up with his sleep, he would no sooner get comfortably settled in bed than he would hear the clicking of boules in the *place* beside his house. He tried to ignore the noise, but eventually his passion won out over his need for sleep, and he spent the rest of the day playing boules. His wife and his father nagged him, but it did no good. He got so little sleep that by September he was *fatigué* and had to give up the bakery.

His wife and daughter and he went to live in Apt with his father, where he spent several months resting and vaguely looking for a job. Finally he heard that the Chobauts were leaving, and he thought he had found his calling at last. As soon as government authorization could be obtained, he replaced Chobaut as *cafetier*.

By that time the boule season had opened, and Voisin found that he was finally able to combine business with pleasure. While his wife stood behind the counter, he spent the day playing *boules*. Unfortunately, Voisin is not a good player. In spite of his enthusiasm and his constant practice his game does not improve so that whenever Voisin plays, he loses. The client gets his drink free instead of paying for it. Voisin also loses at cards, and he loses in his business since he doesn't have the courage to say no when anyone asks for credit. Madame Voisin tries to make up for this, but when she has to leave the bar in charge of her husband she says it's *la catastrophe*. She returns home from shopping and finds a whole page of the little black book filled with names of people who have charged their drinks while she was away. Rivet said to Voisin one day (he is the kind of unfortunate goat who seems to ask to be insulted), "The only reason you're going to keep this café without going bankrupt is that you lose every contest you enter. You lose at boules. You lose at belote. You're bound to lose to your wife who'll keep the café going in spite of you."

Of course, no one could make a living from the trade of the Lonely Ones. The sale of government monopoly items like tobacco is not lucrative, although it helps attract customers who may buy a drink. The café as an information center and as a neutral meeting ground brings in a few customers a day. The sale of table wine brings some income. For most of his income, however, the *cafetier* depends on his sale of drinks during the time when the café is serving as a recreation center — during the apéritif hours, at boules and belote contests, and when the café is turned into a movie house.

As a men's social club the café functions principally during the apéritif hours, from twelve to one o'clock before lunch and from six to seven o'clock before dinner. The two apéritif hours are quite different. The noon hour is the hour of the city men. Rivet the town clerk,

Avenas, the tailor, Porte, a retired naval radio operator who moved to the country to hunt — all three of them from Marseille — are always at the café at noon. Barbier, the Notaire, often comes. He was born in Peyrane, but he was educated in Aix and Paris. Doctor Magny usually drops in on Mondays and Fridays, and sometimes on Wednesdays if he is not too busy. Chobaut, the suave *cafetier* from Nice, held this group together and participated in it. Of course, the Lonely Ones are present too, but their presence is scarcely noticed and they do not join in the conversation. Now and then one of the men at the bar feeling mellow will say, "Well, Monsieur Maucorps looks thirsty. Serve him a drink, too," and the *cafetier* takes a *canon* of red wine to Monsieur Maucorps who murmurs his thanks.

The group at the bar does not drink red wine or pastis but more sophisticated and more expensive city drinks of the vermouth type. The number of drinks consumed by each member of the circle depends on the number present, for it is customary for each to pay for a *tournée*, a round. This is a fixed procedure, but it can be varied easily through a special excuse. If someone has to leave before he has offered his round of drinks, he says, "Tomorrow will be my round." If someone has to leave before profiting from a round due him, he says, "That will be for tomorrow." When "tomorrow" comes, everyone has forgotten the postponed drink.

The conversation of the noon apéritif circle usually centers about the lack of sophistication in this town where they are fated to live. They are amused by incidents and scandals which emphasize the village atmosphere, so different from the city they profess to prefer. It was from this group that I learned the details of such scandals as the Aubenas-Roche *brouille*.

When politics is mentioned, Avenas, for he is the only Communist in the group, tries to start an argument. No one takes him seriously, so political discussions are saved for those days when he is not there. When Avenas is there, he is inevitably the butt of all the joking. He is ribbed sometimes because of his incapacity as President of the Hunting Society, and sometimes because of his putative excessive sexual drive. When Avenas is away the Lonely Ones become the targets, but they profit from the situation since they are offered a free drink whenever anyone takes notice of them.

Talk about sex is reserved for the days when the Notaire is absent.

He is not puritanical in the least, but he is the Notaire and deserves respect. On days when he is there the conversation turns more to trips he has recently made to Italy or Spain or Paris, the hotels where he stayed, the good meals he had. Automobiles are another safe and rich source of conversational matter. The Notaire has the biggest, newest, finest car in the commune.

At one o'clock when most of the townspeople have finished their dinner and the children are going back to school, the noon apéritif group breaks up and goes home for a one o'clock lunch.

The evening apéritif circle is a larger and less intimate group. There are usually ten or fifteen ochre workers, artisans and farmers, in addition to the Lonely Ones. The preferred drink is neither red wine, the poor man's apéritif, nor vermouth, the bourgeois drink, but pastis, the anis-flavored, milkish-colored, sweet-tasting drink which is the most popular apéritif in any café in southern France. The drinking ritual is fundamentally the same as that of the noon circle, but it is less formal in the evening. The groups of men standing at the bar or sitting at the tables mingle, and the *tournée* groups, that is the set-up groups, become so confused that often it is not clear whose turn it is to pay. Only the café owner's wife can keep the intricate network of debts in mind. She knows exactly who has paid for whose drink, and above all who still owes her money. In the confusion, a man who does not have enough money to pay for a whole round of drinks can order a drink for only himself without being embarrassed.

The language used by the evening circle is primarily the local Provençal dialect, and the conversation principally concerns hunting, war experiences, gossip, and politics. When the men start to talk about politics, the atmosphere becomes more tense. If someone loses his temper, others save the situation by introducing a bantering note, and the argument calms down. The butt of the joking mutters to himself for a few moments, but soon he overcomes his resentment and joins the conversation again.

The men in the evening circle drink more than those in the noon circle. Most of them are obviously stimulated by the alcohol. Voices are raised, and the conversations become animated, but there is rarely any drunkenness. The only chronic alcoholic in the community drinks alone. Almost the only cases of drunkenness I saw were on the rare occasions when a Lonely One had had a job, had just been paid, and consequently had had more to drink than he was accustomed to. On these occasions the Lonely One comes to life. He aggressively takes part in the *tournée* groups. He insists on setting up the house. He takes too active a part in the conversation. He never gets rolling drunk, but his conduct is embarrassing to the other men. If, as he drinks, he becomes more gentle, the men remain friendly to him, but they joke with him as they would with a small child who has not developed rational control. If he becomes loudly or violently aggressive, they turn away from him. The *cafetier* refuses to sell him more drinks and tells him to go home to rest. Rebuffed, he goes out the door muttering to himself, and the atmosphere in the café returns to normal.

By seven o'clock most of the men have gone home. If one lingers, his wife sends a child to tell him that supper is ready. But the child is greeted so cordially that he often forgets the purpose of his errand. The men shake hands with him, joke with him, and the father gives him a sip of his pastis. Then the *cafetier* mixes a drink of grenadine or mint syrup and soda water and gives it to the child who remains the center of attention until he says, "Thank you, Monsieur."

Usually after a few minutes the father and child shake hands with everyone, thank the *cafetier* again, and go home to supper. If they do not go in a reasonable length of time, his wife will come to the café door, angry but smiling.

"Aimé, your supper is getting cold. Didn't the child tell you?"

"Yes, yes, yes. I'll be right there."

He doesn't go right away. He must remain a few minutes more to preserve his self-respect. But after a few moments he pays his bill and hurries off.

By seven-thirty all but the Lonely Ones have left, and the *cafetier* and his wife can sit down to their supper.

In the evening the café is quiet. Usually only four or five habitués drop in: little Avenas and his wife, two or three older unmarried men, and Raoul Pascal who seems eager to spend the evenings away from home. They play cards while the Lonely Ones sit and watch them. If an extra hand is needed, one of the Lonely Ones will be asked to play, too. The evening drags on, especially for the *cafetier* who sells scarcely enough drinks to pay for the light and heat. By ten or ten-thirty the card games are over, and the losers pay for the drinks. Conversation drags on for a while, and eventually the Avenases go home, followed by the other habitués. The Lonely Ones are gently but firmly urged to leave, and finally the *cafetier* is able to close up and go to bed.

Unfortunately for him, there are occasions when this habitual group gets lively. It may happen that Raoul Pascal, who has been losing steadily all evening, is the object of so much joking that he finally appears to be insulted. He insists on starting another game and raising the stakes from a drink to one or two packages of cigarettes. With these high stakes the excitement grows, and everyone may stay until one or two o'clock to see the outcome of the match. Unless the *cafetier* himself is involved in the challenge, the situation is scarcely bearable for him. Light and heat are consumed for three hours more; he gets three hours less sleep; the increase in his evening's profits is inconsequential.

The *cafetier's* lot is not a happy one, his wife and he are quick to assure you. They get up early and go to bed late. They are on their feet most of the time. They have no privacy at mealtime. They must listen to much dreary conversation, and the wife must be able to smile impassively when salty remarks are made. They dare not join in political disputes, yet they must subscribe to newspapers and magazines representing the shade of opinion held by a majority of their clients. They are plagued with the problem of credit — *la plaie du commerce*. The life they lead is not a normal one, and still the income from the long hours of work is not sufficient. In order to make ends meet they must organize special activities to bring them more business.

Boules

Painted on the weathered façade of the café is a sign:

BOULES TOURNAMENT
EVERY SATURDAY NIGHT
NINE O'CLOCK

By organizing this tournament and by making his café a center for men who like to play boules, the *cafetier* attracts a larger clientele and increases his income substantially.

After the gardens are planted in the spring and before the hunting season opens in the fall, there is usually someone playing boules on the *place* across from the cafe — even if it is only Voisin practicing by himself. Lights are strung across the *place* (the *cafetier* pays the electric bill) so that those who share Voisin's passion for boules can play at night as well as in the daytime. In the summer, a dozen or so men play boules until one or two or three o'clock every morning. They make so much noise that the property on the *place* has actually decreased in value. Three houses are vacant. No one wants to live in a spot that is so noisy. Most of the men who play so late are, unlike Voisin, serious workers. Raoul Pascal, who plays every evening, has one of the best-run farms in the commune.

"How can you work the next day when you stay up late every night? Aren't you sleepy?" I asked him.

He seemed surprised. "Sleepy? What does that matter? You just go ahead and work anyway."

Most of the men, however, do not come to play except in the tournament on Saturday night, or on a Sunday afternoon when there is also a tournament if enough men want one. A tournament may be organized or canceled on the spur of the moment. There are formalities, but no one feels that they are rigid.

Although the Saturday night tournament is advertised as beginning at nine o'clock, very few of the men arrive so early. They drift in slowly after their dinner, order a drink, and carry on conversation normally as though no activity were planned. Finally a couple of the men say, "Well, we have to begin to think about that boules tournament," and they informally assume the responsibility for organizing it. They collect a fee of twenty-five cents from each of the twenty or thirty men who are interested in playing. This money forms the pot out of which the first, second, and third prizes will be given to the winning teams. They write down the name of each participant and put a number beside his name. Then the *cafetier*, who is too busy serving drinks to help organize the affair, gives them a cigar box of old slips of cardboard which they dump into a béret to draw for teams. Each man finds his partner or partners, gets his boules from the old case in the back of the café, and goes out fondly clicking the boules together. By the time the tournament begins it is ten-thirty.

The balls with which the game of boules is played used to be made of wood studded with tacks, but in the twentieth century this old-fashioned boule was replaced by a cast bronze or steel ball called *intégrale*. Today the best boule is made of stainless steel, the "J. B. Boule." If a man takes his game of boules seriously he must acquire a set of three "J.B.'s" which cost about four dollars apiece — a considerable sum for a man from Peyrane.

The game of boules is relatively simple, but as formulated by the F.F.B.J.P.P. (La Fédération Française Bouliste du Jeu Provençal et Pétanque — the French Federation of Pétanque and Provençal Bowlers) the rules cover three pages of fine print. Every possible contingency is foreseen — what happens if a boule breaks, what happens if a spectator interferes with the game, what happens in case of rain or *force majeure*, etc. We need not worry about all the fine points of the game here. We shall not even make the distinction between the two games of *pétanque* (from the Provençal expression meaning "feet together") and *provençal* (also called the "long game" or "Marseille game"). It does seem essential, however, that we have a general understanding of this sport which is as important in southern France as softball, horseshoes, croquet, bowling, and shuffleboard combined would be in the United States.

A team is made up of one, two, three, or (rarely) four men, each man having two or three boules. A boule must be from two and one-half to three and one-third inches in diameter and must not weigh more than about two pounds. The game can be played on any terrain, but the best terrain is a hard, smooth surface. (When the impassioned players of Peyrane get bored with their usual terrain, they go play on the macadam highway!) There are no limits to the playing field, no lines restricting the play; the game can be played anywhere. The only equipment needed is the boules themselves and a little wooden ball about an inch in diameter, which is called *le but* (the target) or *le bouchon* (the cork).

A member of one team starts the game by tossing the cork from fifteen to seventy-five feet in any direction. He then throws one of his boules, trying to place it as close as he can to the cork. A member of the opposing team then throws a boule, trying to place it still closer to the cork. After that the other boules are thrown, each team trying to get as many as possible of its boules closer to the cork than the nearest boule of the opposing team. For each of its boules closer to the cork than the opponent's closest boule, a team scores one point. The game goes on until one team wins with a score of fifteen points. Then the losers buy a drink for the winners.

The real complications of the game arise from the different possibilities for getting a boule closer to the cork. One can "point," that is, simply try to roll the boule close to the cork. One can "fire," that is, throw a boule at an opponent's boule, knocking it out of its position close to the cork. One can "fire at the cork," that is, throw a boule directly at the cork, knocking it away from an opponent's boule or knocking it closer to one's own boule.

The real interest in the game lies in the decision a team has to make each time a boule is about to be thrown. Should a boule be "pointed?" If so, in what manner? Should it be rolled with a lot or a little backspin? What tiny slopes or pebbles are there in the course that might influence the roll of the boule? Is the terrain hard and fast or soft and slow? Such questions could be multiplied many times, and they are! The members of a team may argue for fifteen minutes about how a shot should be made. The wit, the humor, the sarcasm, the insults, the oaths, the logic, the experimental demonstration, and the ability to dramatize a situation give the game its essential interest. Spectators will ignore a game being played by men who are physically skilled but who are unable to dramatize their game, and they will crowd around a game played by men who do not play very well but who are witty, dramatic, shrewd in their ability to outwit their opponents. The most popular players are, of course, those who combine skill with wit.

One Sunday afternoon a large crowd of spectators gathered to watch a match between two of the best teams in the village. On one team were Rivet, Paul, and Pascal; on the other Prayal the tailor, Henri Favre, and Fraysse. It was the final game in a tournament. All these men play unusually well, and all of them have a sense of drama. A tense moment arrived. Rivet's team had 14 points, Prayal's team 11 points. Rivet's team had thrown all its boules and had one boule closer to the cork than any boule of Prayal's team. This might be the winning boule. However, Prayal still had one boule to throw, and his team had three boules closer to the cork than Rivet's second closest boule. The outcome of the game and of the tournament depended on the boule that Prayal was about to throw.

The question was how he should throw his remaining boule. He could "point" it. That is, he could simply try to roll it closer to the cork than Rivet's winning boule. If he succeeded his team would get one point; the score would be Rivet's team: 14; Prayal's team 12. The game would go on. If he failed to beat Rivet's winning boule, the game would be over.

There was the alternative of "firing" this last boule, that is, hurling it directly at Rivet's winning boule. This shot had attractive possibilities. If Prayal "fired" accurately, his boule would hit Rivet's winning boule squarely and send it flying, while his own "fired" boule would spin and settle down in the winning position now occupied by Rivet's boule, a perfect billiard shot. In this case Prayal's team would score not only one point, but four points, because with Rivet's ball removed Prayal's team would have four boules nearer the cork than the closest boule of Rivet's team. The score would be Prayal's team: 15; Rivet's team: 14. Prayal's team would win both the game and the tournament.

The cork, however, lay fifty feet from the spot from which Prayal had to throw. Prayal is an excellent "firer," but he stood no better than a fifty-fifty chance to make good on this shot, for it is extremely difficult to "fire" accurately at this distance. On the other hand, although it is normally much easier to "point," the terrain on which the game was being played was rocky and bumpy, and a tiny pebble or slope may deflect a boule disastrously when it is rolling. There was no safe way to play the boule. It was probably safer to "point" than to "fire," but the decision was difficult.

Prayal and his teammates, Favre and Fraysse, studied the situation silently for a while, walking around, surveying the angles, thumping the terrain, considering the distance. Finally Prayal broke the silence:

"I'm going to fire it. It's all or nothing."

Favre's expression showed amazement and contempt: "Are you mad? You're not in form today, or we'd already have won."

Prayal was indignant: "What do you mean, I'm not in form! I haven't missed a shot. If you'd played as well as I have, we'd already be in the café having a drink."

The argument developed. Prayal and Favre each called on their teammate, Fraysse, and on the spectators to testify in his behalf. The spectators remained silent, but Rivet — their opponent — hoping to add fuel to the fire and upset them still further, yelled:

"Come on and get it over with. It's our point any way you play it.

Everyone knows that Prayal can't "fire," and he's off on his "pointing" today, so he might as well throw and have it over with."

Prayal was insulted, and an argument developed between Rivet and Prayal concerning which one was responsible for losing the last time they were paired together in a tournament.

Meanwhile Fraysse had been examining the terrain, and had finally reached a conclusion:

"Look, Prayal. This is the way to play it. You've got to "point" it. Toss it all the way up to this spot to avoid the stones there in front of you. Land right here where it's solid. Not too much backspin. Then this little bump will make it roll right in between Rivet's boule and the cork. We win the point. It's simple. Look!" He pretended to throw a boule and then ran to imitate the trajectory which he predicted the boule would take.

Favre rejected this suggestion: "No, there are too many pebbles. The thing is to throw the boule high with plenty of backspin so that it will land right next to the cork — and there's our point. You can't let it roll. Look at those pebbles."

Fraysse said, "That's all right. We'll clean them away from the path." And he started to brush away the pebbles from his preferred course. This was against the rules. Rivet's team rushed in, furious, pushing the pebbles back where they had been, yelling.

A furious argument broke out. The men, who had been speaking Provençal, now burst into French, as they always do when there is an argument over rules. Fraysse feigned disgust for Rivet and his men, "little people who would argue over a few pebbles," but he knew the rules were against him.

Prayal called to Fraysse, "Don't bother about the stones, Fraysse. Don't upset the little men with them. I'm not going to 'point' anyway. I'm going to 'fire' and get it over with."

Favre objected to this reckless manner of making a decision. He tried to show Prayal that the only logical, sensible, safe way of playing the point was to "point" the boule as he, Favre, had suggested — to throw it high above the pebbles and with enough backspin so that it would not roll too far. This was certainly the reasonable shot to make, but Prayal was obstinate. He still insisted that he was going to "fire" the boule.

Although Rivet had openly disparaged Prayal's ability to "fire" he knew that in reality Prayal could "fire" better than anyone else in the village. He wanted to keep him from making a shot that might well win the game. So he said,

"If I were on your team, I'd tell Prayal to go ahead and 'fire' it. You know he's got to because he's afraid to 'point.'"

Prayal was taken in. He now wanted to "point" just to show that he could do it. He refused to admit that he had changed his mind, but eventually he let himself be persuaded by his teammates who wanted him to "point" it. Prayal then found himself in an enviable position. He was going to "point" instead of "firing." He was going to play the shot safely and reasonably. At the same time he was getting credit for wanting to make the more reckless, dramatic shot, "firing" it. Furthermore, he had evaded responsibility. If his shot went wrong he could say that it was the fault of his teammates who persuaded him to do it their way in spite of his better judgment.

"All right," he said finally, "I'll 'point' it, but that's not the shot called for here. It would be less complicated to 'fire' it and finish the game, but if this is what you want, here it is."

Favre saw Prayal's trick and did not intend to be taken in by it: "Oh, no, you don't. You can't blame us if you miss your shot. Have it your way and 'fire' it, if you want."

Prayal started to reply, but Fraysse interrupted. Fraysse had made a side bet of two packages of cigarettes on the game and couldn't afford to lose.

"Leave him alone, Favre," he said. "Prayal, you know what we think, but do as you like."

Prayal surveyed the terrain again. There was more discussion about brushing away the stones, but all the drama had been drawn from the situation. Prayal was finally ready to make the throw.

"This is what you wanted. Here it is," he said.

Prayal stood poised. Fraysse kneeled and remained frozen pointing to the spot where he thought the boule must land to win the point. Favre squatted and pointed to the place near the cork where the boule must roll. The moment had arrived, but Prayal stood mentally rehearsing the throw he was about to make. Finally, with deliberation but with a free movement, he tossed the boule. It was a perfectly executed shot. The boule landed at the spot where Fraysse was pointing, rolled almost to the spot where Favre was pointing, and came to rest near the cork. However, it did not roll quite far enough to win the point decisively. It looked as though it were exactly at the same distance from the cork as Rivet's boule. Was it a tie?

No word was spoken. Teams and spectators closed in, gathering round the boules lying near the cork. Rivet picked up a straw to measure the distances but found it was too short. With an impatient gesture he whipped off his belt and crouched down, using the belt to measure the distances. He measured them, and it was at once obvious that his boule had won the point, and that his team had won the game and tournament. Still nothing was said. He repeated the measurement two or three times. No one said a word, but the spectators started to walk away, and the players picked up their boules.

The climax of the drama had been long; the anticlimax was extreme. Prayal had failed by a half inch to win the point. The evidence was convincing, and no one felt a need to comment on it. Spectators and players, who a few moments before had been tense, now stood completely indifferent. You could not tell from the expression on the faces of the players which ones had won and which had lost.

As the men drifted back to the café, Prayal muttered in a voice just loud enough for Fraysse to hear it:

"I should have done what I wanted to and 'fired' it instead of listening to Fraysse."

Fraysse was furious. "That's right. That's Prayal for you. You blame me when anyone can see it's your fault. You put too much backspin on the boule. When you threw the boule, I knew we were going to lose because of that backspin. Besides, if you'd 'fired' you'd have missed for sure."

The two walked back to the spot where the point had been played, set the cork and the boules up in the position in which they thought they had been, and began their arguments again. Fraysse said he'd show Prayal how the shot should have been made, and he bet him a package of cigarettes that he could roll his boule right next to the cork. He tried — and failed badly. His boule struck a stone and rolled three yards off to the side. Prayal gloated, and bet another package of cigarettes that he could "fire" his boule precisely as he had bragged he could. His attempt was perfect. The opponent's boule went flying, and Prayal's boule snuggled next to the cork.

Prayal was exultant. He had exonerated himself. He had lost the game, but he felt he had proved that he should have followed his own judgment. He should have made the bold "firing" shot which would have won the game instead of the sensible, safe shot that Fraysse had insisted on.

Fraysse was miserable. He knew that he was right, but he had lost four packages of cigarettes as well as first prize, and he had allowed Prayal to maneuver him into the position of responsibility. He knew that Prayal's so-called "proof" proved nothing at all except that luck had been on Prayal's side in the demonstration. Everyone would secretly agree with Fraysse, but no one would admit it because he had allowed himself to become the scapegoat for the defeat.

Rivet called from the door of the café, "How about the drinks you owe us?" Prayal and Fraysse picked up the boules and walked back to the café. Sitting around the table drinking pastis, all the men seemed to have forgotten the situation. The conversation concerned other subjects besides boules. Only now and then did Rivet make a crack at Prayal, and Prayal turned the joke onto Fraysse. The dramatic situation had become a matter for joking. It assumed its former importance only two months later when Prayal and Fraysse were again thrown together on a team. In another tense moment Prayal made a point of reminding Fraysse and the spectators of how one time Fraysse had lost them a tournament by insisting on having his own way instead of listening to Prayal.

The indifference with which the spectators and all the players except Prayal and Fraysse appeared to witness the end of this crucial match is difficult for an American to accept. There are no handshakes, no applause, no congratulations, no condolences. The only emotion expressed is amusement at the discomfiture of someone who may have become the butt of a joke during the game.

When Léon Favre had his motorcycle accident and returned from the hospital in Cavaillon to Peyrane, his recovery was discouragingly slow. His facial paralysis did not disappear. He was unable to work for weeks. As the time dragged on, Léon seemed to lose confidence in himself and in the future. His friends and family were alarmed by his depression as much as by his physical difficulty.

It was at this time that the big boule tournament of the spring fête was held. Léon did not plan to play, but at the last minute one of the players dropped out, and Léon was asked to replace him. To everyone's surprise, Léon's team won game after game, and by the middle of the afternoon it was in the final match. Opposing it was a team of semiprofessional players from Apt, the best team in that part of France, the team that later was sent to Algeria to take part in the French national boule tournament.

The game was close. The Apt team was not playing as well as usual and Léon's team was outdoing itself. The outcome of the game was uncertain down to a final shot which Léon himself made, a difficult shot on which an expert player might easily have failed. Léon won the point, the match, and the tournament with this shot.

I was moved by the situation, for it seemed to me that this unexpected public triumph might help Léon recover his self-confidence. Perhaps other people were moved, but no one showed it. The game ended and the crowd walked away. There were no congratulations, no applause. No one seemed excited by the upset. Nothing was said by anyone except by two members of the losing team who got into an argument over the manner in which the final point should have been played. I caught up with Léon Favre who had picked up his boules and was walking alone. When I shook hands with him and congratulated him on playing so well, he seemed surprised that I should have spoken to him. He was not displeased, but because my congratulations were unexpected, he did not know how to accept them. From the expression on his face one would have thought that his victory was a matter of indifference to him.

Belote

After the biggest tournament of the year, the tournament held at the Saint Michael's Day Festival, interest in boules begins to wane. The most enthusiastic players still come to the *place* every night, but the Saturday-night tournaments are soon abandoned. Some of the men are preoccupied with the grape harvest and with making their wine. Other men like to play only in warm weather. As the weather gets cooler it is not comfortable to spend the afternoon or evening out on the open *place*. The mistral begins to blow. Voisin, Rivet, Fraysse, and Léon Favre do not give in easily, but eventually even they are forced to abandon the sport. The steel boules chill their hands so that it is no longer possible to control the backspin. By mid-November the boule season has ended. By that time, moreover, the hunting season has opened, and hunting takes the place of boules in the daytime. At night or on rainy days when they cannot hunt, some of the men spend their leisure time playing cards.

Several card games are played in Peyrane. *Manille* and *écarté* enjoy a certain popularity. A few people play bridge, but it is considered a city game. Only Bonerandi, Viquier, Aubenas, and Vincent play bridge with enthusiasm. In the winter they meet three nights a week at the inn to play.

By far the most popular game in winter is *belote*, which is said to resemble bezique and pinochle. Everyone in Peyrane knows how to play belote, and it is one of the few games in which both men and women participate. The schoolteachers and their husbands, who form an almost closed social circle, often play belote when they spend the evening together. When the Arènes have closed their store and finished their late supper they usually play a few hands before they go to bed. On cold, rainy Sunday afternoons some of the men sit in the cafe and play belote for four hours without stopping.

The *cafetier* takes advantage of this enthusiasm for belote by organizing a Saturday-night tournament to take the place of the boules tournament. He finds the belote tournament even more rewarding than the boules tournament. When men sit around playing cards they naturally buy more drinks than they do when they have to come in from the boules grounds outdoors to get a drink. Moreover, since belote tournaments are held during the hunting season the prize for the winners usually is game — hares or thrushes shot by the *cafetier* himself or by one of his debtors. The prize therefore costs the *cafetier* nothing, and he pockets the twenty-five-cent fee paid by each of the participants — "to cover the cost of heat, lighting, wear-and-tear on the cards and other equipment."

The tournament is vividly advertised by the *cafetier* for several days before the tournament. He pencils a large sign, "Belote Tournament Saturday Night," and puts it in his window. Below the sign he hangs the prizes, a couple of hares or four thrushes, to whet the appetite of the men who pass.

The turn-out is always good. There are rarely fewer than fifty or sixty men taking part in the tournament, and there is always one woman. Little Avenas doesn't play, but his amazon wife never fails to show up. Perhaps other women would like to play in the tournament, but no woman except Madame Avenas dares. The men joke with her about her presence, but her rejoinders may be so devastating that she is usually accepted as though she were one of the men. Behind her enormous back, however, some of the men continue to remark that if she were *their* wife *they* would know how to put her in her place, and they have contempt for Avenas.

There are more players than spectators at a belote tournament, because belote is not a very interesting game to watch. Partners are not allowed to argue with each other over how they will play a point. Crucial decisions regarding strategy cannot be made collectively and openly as they are in boules. Belote players make their decisions individually and silently. Belote games can be tense, but by their nature they cannot be as dramatic as a good game of boules.

Of course, men like Rivet and Prayal cannot avoid making the most of every dramatic opportunity. When they are dealt an ordinary hand they play it in silence, but when they are dealt an extraordinary hand, a triumphant hand which cannot possibly be beaten, the rule of silence goes by the board and they loudly proclaim every play they are about to make. As they start to play the hand the other people in the café draw around to watch the display.

At such a moment Prayal sits forward tensely, holding his cards close to his chest so the bystanders cannot see them. As his opponent leads a club, he holds a card high above his head and throws it exultantly on the table, yelling: "That's the way it is. You play a club. I *cut* it with a heart and the lead is mine." He holds up another card and slams it on the table: "And there's the jack of hearts to take away one of your trumps." The other three men follow suit docilely. Another card thumps on the table: "And there's the nine of hearts to take another of your trumps. You were a fool, Baume, to bid hearts when I had the two top cards." Baume looks downcast as he reluctantly follows suit. Another card thunders down: "And there's the ace of spades, and another trick is mine . . . And there's the ace of diamonds — for my last trick. You have a measly little trump left, Baume, so you can have the last trick. You're lucky you're not *capot*." As the spectators make their way back to their own tables, Baume flares up: "It's easy for a person to brag when he's lucky enough to have all the good cards." Prayal ignores this remark, which he and everyone else know is true. He stares into space showing no inclination to argue a completely irrelevant point. He claims no merit for playing the hand well. He is content to have played his role well. He and his spectators are satisfied.

The only time a serious argument arises over a belote game is when two men are accused of cheating by using prearranged signals. It is dangerous to make such accusations, however, because they are hard to prove and because there are few terms more insulting than that of "cheater." A man knows that if he accuses another man of cheating, whether he thinks the charge is justified or not, he will be *brouillé* with his opponent. Even when Biron and Ginez won the Saturday-night belote tournament for three weeks in succession no one openly accused them of cheating, but their winning streak aroused suspicion and was the subject for gossip. Some men went so far as to make broad hints or joking references in their presence. Biron and Ginez preferred to ignore these hints, and since no one was willing to accuse them directly, no violent dispute resulted. The two men understood the position they were in, however, for on the fourth Saturday night each of them sought another partner.

Although violent arguments are rare, less serious disputes occur frequently, especially between partners. At the end of a game, resentment that has built up during the enforced silence often boils over. A man accuses his partner of having played the game stupidly or carelessly. He has not counted the trumps accurately when they were played, or he has overbid when vulnerable, or he has not led back in accordance with conventional indications. The accused partner never takes criticism docilely. His partner and he have played so many games of belote with each other over the years that each remembers examples of his partner's stupidity. As they argue, their opponents pay no attention unless an insult is phrased with art. Then they join in the laughter. The butt of the joking sees that everyone is turning against him, and drops the argument. When he speaks again it is as though nothing had happened.

With fifty or sixty men and Madame Avenas participating in the tournament, it takes a long time to finish it. Like the boules tournament the belote tournament is scheduled to start at nine o'clock, but it never starts before ten or ten-thirty. Consequently it often lasts until two or three o'clock Sunday morning. Few of the men sleep late on Sunday morning. If they do not have work to do they get up even earlier than usual to go hunting. This loss of sleep does not appear to affect them.

Movies

Armand Foullet, a young man from the neighboring village of Goult, has developed a profitable business since the war. With his portable 32-millimeter projector and portable screen he brings movies to the people living in the villages near his. There are seven villages on his circuit, and he has made arrangements with the *cafetier* in each of them to turn the café into a movie house one night a week. The *cafetier* is repaid by the profits on the increased number of drinks he sells. Foullet furnishes the film and pockets the admission fees of fifteen cents.

Tuesday night is Peyrane's turn. When Foullet is a mile from the village he clamps his hand on the horn of his car and holds it down until he drives up in front of the café. This blast is the loudest noise heard in Peyrane all week. When he has parked his car and carried his equipment into the café the *cafetier* helps him shove back the tables and arrange the chairs, set up his projector, loud speaker and screen, take down the poster advertising the evening's showing and put up a poster announcing the movie for the following week. By eight-thirty when the movie is scheduled to begin, Foullet is ready, but since few customers have arrived he sits down with the *cafetier* for a drink and a few hands of belote.

Customers drift in slowly. The clientèle varies but little; the same people, thirty or forty of them, come to the movies week after week. Almost all the adolescents attend regularly. Three or four families, families like the Henri Favres and Bellets who never miss any opportunity for "distraction," come with all their children. The Lonely Ones who have fifteen cents for a ticket are always present. Lucien Bourdin, Elie Seignon, and the other thirty- and forty-year old bachelors attend without exception. However, very few "serious" people ever come to the movies. A few of the wives of the more proper families let their love of the cinema overcome their sense of propriety; Madame Vincent, Madame Bonerandi, Madame Borel, Mademoiselle Héraud, the postmistress. The one other group that makes up the regular clientèle is the cluster of Algerian ochre workers. Their appearance at the movies marks their only participation in any public occasion. Even then they do not mingle with other people. No one scorns them, not even Madame Vincent or Mademoiselle Héraud, but they remain segregated as though by mutual agreement.

By nine-fifteen or nine-thirty most of the spectators have arrived and taken their usual places in the rows of chairs. Foullet and the *cafetier* interrupt their belote to collect fifteen cents from everyone present except the children, who are charged no admission. The lights are turned off, and the movie begins.

The people have no voice in the selection of the movie they are to see, and the variety of productions they are shown is great. They may see the best Pagnol film or the most insipid Tarzan picture, a bedroom comedy or a fantastic murder mystery, a surrealistic Cocteau production, or a western with Hopalong Cassidy speaking French argot. Foullet has no voice in selecting the film he shows, either. He has a contract with a distributing company in Paris which sends him a film, a short, and a newsreel every week. He may make suggestions and express preference, but his point of view appears to have little effect on the distributing company. Since his customers in Peyrane understand his helpless situation they do not blame him when they pay to see a boring film. They do not like it, but they know that he does not like it either. In fact he often warns them before they pay their admission that they are in for a bad evening. They accept his apology and are reassured when he tells them that the film for the following week will be better.

The favorite films are French, but foreign films are popular, too. They like some American films although they condemn others because they are insultingly naïve or unrealistic. They laugh at Hopalong because they say he never has to stop to reload his pistols. They feel cheated when an American film has a happy ending when an unhappy ending would have been more logical and realistic. On the whole, however, the films are accepted for what they are, and neither praise nor criticism is expressed spontaneously.

While the movie is being shown, little reaction is heard. The children laugh at the slapstick scenes, but as the evening progresses and the children fall asleep the comic element is accepted passively. From the dim light of the screen one can see no expression on the faces of the spectators. There is no whistling, no hissing, no stamping of feet, no applause. Almost the only time during the year that the spectators reacted violently was during a French newsreel. The scene was a burning native hut in Korea. A maimed child was crying at the side of its dead and badly disfigured mother. When this scene was flashed on the screen, everyone in the audience gasped in horror. Some of the men whistled loudly to show their disapproval.

When the main film is half finished and Foullet has to change reels, the lights are turned on, and the audience is given an intermission of ten or fifteen minutes. The women usually stay in their seats. The men file out resolutely as though they were leaving for prearranged business. The first evening I attended the movie I followed the men to see what could be attracting them. They all unhesitantly walked across the street and took their places facing the wall across from the café. Several years of this collective, periodic urination have discolored the wall from a height of two feet down to the ground.

Back in the café the men have a drink — a beer, a fruit syrup with soda or a glass of wine. Usually there is little discussion of the movie beyond a word or two of approval or disapproval. The conversation centers about situations in other movies or experiences in the life of the men themselves that are recalled by what they have seen in the first part of the movie. War movies are naturally the most evocative of all, and they are judged on the basis of their resemblance to the wartime experiences of the men.

The intermission ends. The lights are turned off, and the rest of the film is shown. By eleven-thirty or twelve the show is over. The people get up and file out silently. There is no conversation. Fathers and mothers carry their sleeping infants and rouse the older children so that they may stumble home behind them. Madame Vincent and Mademoiselle Héraud, Madame Borel and Madame Bonerandi walk directly home in pairs. The Algerians wait until the others have left, and then they leave the café in their silent cluster. In a few moments the café is almost deserted. The Lonely Ones settle back in the corners which they inhabit, and some of the bachelors sit down for a few hands of belote before they go home.

This same scene was repeated every Tuesday night during the year I was in Peyrane. Only once did the movies excite more general attention in the village, and that was the night when the film *Marius* was shown.

Marius is a movie about a young man torn between his love for a girl and his longing to go to sea. Both families, the girl herself, and the neighborhood, whose life centers in his father's bar on the Marseille waterfront, try to persuade Marius to marry Fanny and settle down. In the end, Fanny realizes that Marius will never be happy at home, and above all that he will never be a dependable husband and father. She sends him away.

The principal actor in this movie is Raimu, who was one of the most popular and beloved actors in the history of the French movies. He plays the role of Marius' father, César, the big Marseille barkeep who protects his tender feelings by directing witty shafts at the people of whom he is most fond. Incarnate in César are the humor and pathos of the southern French stereotype.

Marius was filmed in 1932, but it is still one of the most popular movies in France, especially in the Midi. Two later films, *Fanny* and *César*, produced by Marcel Pagnol to round out this story of a Marseille family, lack whatever it is that attracts spectators to *Marius*. On the Tuesday evenings when they were given, there were no more spectators than usual and the atmosphere was calm.

The Tuesday evening when *Marius* was shown was very unusual. Instead of the few dozen movie fans, there were over a hundred people crowded into the hall. Everyone was in a good mood, smiling, chatting, and even happy to be together. Most of the people had seen this movie eight or ten times, but that made no difference. They only loved it more. There was a feeling of unity in this gathering, almost a feeling of corporative worship that was notably lacking at all other public events, even at funerals or at Midnight Mass.

When I asked people why they were so fond of *Marius*, they first mentioned Raimu. They said they always loved to see him on the screen. However, when the other two movies of the trilogy were shown, only the old movie habitués came to see them, and when Raimu appeared in still other movies during the year he did not draw an unusual attendance.

I pointed this fact out to people, and everyone's reaction was the same. "Oui, mais *Marius*, c'est tellement ça!"

"Ça . . .?"

"Oui, c'est tellement ça, la vie."

So people thought that *Marius* was "so much like *life*." It was realistic for them. That's why they said they liked it, and beyond that they could not explain their feelings. Yet, viewed literally and objectively, this movie is *not* realistic. What is there in this mixture of farce and melodrama that gives the people of Peyrane the illusion of life? What is there that gives them at the same time an almost religious experience?

It would be hard to imagine a people more realistic than the people of Peyrane. "C'est comme ça" is the phrase that is most frequently on their lips. They complain about the problems of life, but they face them. From childhood they have learned to face them — the physical discomforts, the domination of tender but severe parents, the plagues of nature and governments, the necessity of trying to live up to family and community rules, all the family worries that beset everyone, the difficulty of getting along with *les autres*.

To live successfully in Peyrane one must learn to endure all this and to endure it alone. No consolation can be expected from *les autres*, and there is no solace for most people in formal religion. Each person must find solace in the depth of his own personality. This inner loneliness is hidden by a sort of gay, sarcastic banter that gives the illusion of lightheartedness. People see themselves in Raimu's César, the suffering parent.

But how many people, consciously or subconsciously, also feel with Marius an urge that they will always suppress but which he obeys — to go off, away, far? "Partir . . . N'importe où, mais très loin. Partir," Marius says. Expressed in simple terms, disguised with a strong element of farce, this movie answers a need felt by people who are weighed down by social restraints. Beneath the farce and the melodrama it describes a psychological situation which for them is realistic. If they were more sophisticated they might have a taste for the poetry of Baudelaire, Rimbaud, Mallarmé. Marius, and the people who go to the movie to share in his conflict, would understand a contemporary poet who also went to sea:

> Emportez-moi dans une caravelle,
> Dans une vieille et douce caravelle,
> Dans l'étrave, où si l'on veut, dans l'écume,
> Et perdez-moi, au loin, au loin.
> — *Henri Michaux*

At Home

Work and Talk Circles

Tuesday night, the movie night, is the only time during the week when the café as a recreation center is open to women. They may go to the café to buy wine or stamps or tobacco, or they may go to pay a social call on Madame Voisin, the *cafetier's* wife, but as a rule women never go to the café to play cards and drink. The only women who fail to observe this rule are the city wives of the men in the noon apéritif circle. Occasionally Barbier or Doctor Magny may bring his wife to have an apéritif with him and his friends just as he would invite her to go with him to the café in Marseille or Paris, but even these bourgeois wives never go to the café alone. The only woman who goes to the café and anywhere else she wishes is Madame Avenas. Her behavior might be normal for a woman in certain circles in Marseille. In Peyrane it is not. No woman born and bred in Peyrane goes to the café except on business or to the movies.

There is no institution in the village that draws a large group of women together as the apéritif or boules or belote draws the men together. It is difficult to imagine women abandoning their productive activity to devote themselves to amusement. Men are freer to do what they wish. They may play games, or stand and drink with each other, or simply sit and do nothing. Women must work. A woman's day of necessity is so full that she must contrive to combine her recreation with her work. She could finish her daily shopping in a fraction of the time it usually takes her, if she did not use her marketing tour as an opportunity for recreation. She stops to talk to friends she meets in the street. While she is waiting her turn at Reynard's grocery she chats with the other women who come in. After Reynard has waited on her, she may stay to talk to him for ten minutes. At Canazzi's bakery and at Biron's butcher shop the scene will be repeated. When she eventually returns to her house, the housewife of Peyrane has caught up on all the village news and has had a rest from her household tasks and worries.

The women living on farms outside the village lack this opportunity for they shop only once or twice a week, and on the days when they do not go shopping their life is lonely. When the older children were asked to write a theme on their parents' activities during a typical day, Colette Magnan told in detail of her mother's day on the farm.

Maman gets up at five o'clock; she lights the fire and heats a cup of coffee for papa and then she gets breakfast, comes and wakes us up and pours out our breakfast. Then she feeds the rabbits and goats, lets the chickens out and feeds them. She breaks an egg to feed the little chicks. Then comes breakfast with papa. Then she takes the goats out, sweeps the house, washes the dishes, dusts ("raises the dust"), cleans the bedrooms, wet-mops the tile floor of the kitchen, bedrooms, and hall. Then she gets dinner ready, washes my sisters' smocks. Then she sets the table and we have dinner. Then she sweeps around the table and does the dishes again. She ties the asparagus into bunches, washes them and carries them down to the road. Then she goes into the vineyard to help papa with the work he has been doing all morning. Then she comes back and fixes *goûter* for papa and continues her work. Then she goes out to get grass for the rabbits. When she comes back it is dark and she feeds them and the chickens, closes them up in their coop and gathers the eggs. She feeds the goats and chicks and closes the chicks up in their box. Then she goes to milk the goats. Before she went out for grass she prepared supper, sorted the vegetables, and lit the fire. When she gets back after dark, she sets the table and we have supper. Then we go to bed. Maman mends our clothes. Papa listens to the radio or reads the newspaper. Then they go to bed because the next day they have to go out early to cut asparagus.

On such a day Madame Magnan has little opportunity to see anyone outside the family. Her neighbors live only a few hundred yards away, but they are as busy as she. She would not be a "serious" adult if she spent much time calling on them. On such a day as the one described, Madame Magnan's best chance to meet other women is when she takes the asparagus down to the road. There she may find women who are waiting for Monsieur Borel's big truck to collect the neighborhood's asparagus production for the day. It is not surprising that the farmer's wife looks forward to the Saturday morning trip to the market at Apt. Her isolation makes her life very different from that of the women living in the village.

The village women are alone when they are doing their household tasks, but much of their work they can do in the company of other women. Marie Fratani, Madeleine Pian, Madame Biron, and their children go foraging in the country several afternoons a week. In the fall they take baskets and gather mushrooms. In the winter they push a two-wheeled cart to the woods on top of the neighboring hill and gather sticks and light branches. In the spring they carry large sacks for grass and mulberry leaves. These expeditions are profitable from an economic point of view, they are also a pleasant form of recreation.

When the women stay at home and have only sewing or knitting to keep them busy, they often invite a friend or two in to have a cup of coffee with them. The friends bring their sewing or knitting and, after sipping their coffee, they get to their handiwork. If the weather is warm and sunny they carry their chairs out in front of the house to work and talk in the open.

There they may be joined by one or two other women, and many of the people passing by stop to chat a moment, but these work-and-talk circles are essentially small and they are essentially stable. It is usually the same three or four women who get together day after day. A mother-daughter combination is frequently the nucleus of a group. Marie Fratani spends her time with her daughter Madeleine Pian and with Madame Biron who shares her house. Madame Pleindoux sits and works with her daughter Nicole Favre and Madame Voisin, the wife of the *cafetier*, who lives across the square. Madame Borel sits with her daughter, Françoise Bonerandi, and her son's fiancée, Nicole Magnan. Other groups are based on friendship rather than kinship. Giselle Favre spends all her time with Marie Mazon; the two have been close friends since childhood. Marcelle Jouvaud works and chats with her elderly neighbor, Madame Grandgeon. Berthe Fraysse and Renée Fortias do not live near one another but they both have a city background.

These work-and-talk groups are self-sufficient. They rarely coalesce, and women from different groups are seldom seen together unless they happen to meet on the street or in the grocery. Some women in this village never see each other socially from one year to the next. Most of the men of the village are brought together now and then, if only as spectators at a boules game. The contacts of the women with each other are much more limited.

15. *Monsieur Maucorps at the café*

16. *Monsieur Marnas serves as election observer*

17. *Monsieur Anselme casts his ballot*

18. Moïse Jannel reading election results

19. The Borels' "new" car

20. *The Volunteer Firemen of Peyrane*

Because the conversation in these groups so often centers on village events and especially on village personalities, and because the conversation is usually critical, the men complain about the evil effects of the gossip groups. More characters are assassinated, they say, and more reputations are ruined by these circles than in any other way. This complaint is justifiable, although the men also indulge in character assassination. No woman ruins reputations so effectively as the sharptongued Edouard Pascal. But on the whole, the men are more interested in sports and political argument than in local gossip, while for the women the gossip circles are the most important form of recreation.

The woman's group that I was able to observe most naturally was the one that met in front of Madame Pleindoux's house. On sunny days this group sits in a corner of the Town Hall Square across from the café. This is a strategic spot because anyone who goes anywhere in the village is almost forced to pass this way — whether he is on his way to the bakery, to the grocery, to the butcher shop, to the Town Hall, to the café, to the public laundry, or to the public toilets. Since the *cafetier's* wife is a member of the group, the women of the group also have access to most of the information passed over the bar during the apéritif hours. Few women of the village are better informed concerning village affairs!

One morning as I sat with this group, life was dull. The women were knitting and had little to talk about. Two-year-old Dédou Favre was playing about the square, throwing a rubber ball and occasionally stopping to suck on the pacifier hanging from a string about his neck. Since there was little to interest the women Dédou received more attention than usual. Whenever he got into a pile of dirt, his mother yelled threats at him. This led her to complain about all her children — Dédou and his three older sisters — who were always getting dirty and tearing their clothes, thereby increasing her load of work. She held up a pile of mending at her side for proof. Madame Pleindoux, her mother, contradicted her, defending her grandchildren and pointing out that they were much better behaved than other village children. She cited the children of Marcelle Jouvaud as children who were really dirty and ill-behaved.

This conversation was interrupted by the arrival of Madame Peyroux who had just been to Reynard's store to buy yarn. She announced that the price of a ball of yarn had been raised another ten francs. This brought forth from all the women protests against those mysterious forces which seemed intent on destroying them. "So, *they've* done it again. *They* raise the price first on wool, then on coffee, then on sugar, and now *they're* starting all over again."

Madame Pleindoux, who always took a more optimistic view than her daughter, pointed out that at least yarn was cheaper, more available and of better quality than during the war. The other women admitted this, and the thought of what they had gone through from 1940 to 1945 changed the course of the conversation. It turned to hardships they had endured and difficulties they had had in providing for their families during those years. In spite of everything, life was better now. Then someone mentioned the fact that life was still better in the days before the war, and this brought the group back to the subject of the present rise in the cost of living.

This topic would have been pursued the rest of the morning, as it often was, if Madame Fraysse had not dropped by with news of the latest escapade of Paul Jouvaud. Paul, the adolescent moronic son of Simon Jouvaud, was feared by everyone in the village, especially by the women. He was strong as an ox and was reputed to have an abnormally large sexual organ. Everyone was afraid that his strength and his "animal-like" mind and his growing sexual craving would sooner or later bring about a catastrophe in the village. Only a few days before he had slipped up behind old Madame Pleindoux, stroked her white hair and had whispered, "How beautiful you are! How beautiful you are!"

Madame Fraysse reported that a few minutes before, her husband had been passing an abandoned house up on the top of the hill. He heard shouts and when he went to investigate, he found that Paul had made twelve-year-old Suzanne Canazzi go in the house with him and wouldn't let her leave. Fraysse slapped Paul, hoping it might teach him a lesson.

Everyone in the group was outraged. The expected catastrophe had almost taken place. Everyone had been telling Simon and Marcelle Jouvaud that they should send Paul away to a "school," but Marcelle always cried when the suggestion was made. Simon said that only Marcelle and he understood Paul. If they sent him away, he would die of loneliness. And if Paul died, he, Simon, would kill himself.

The women expressed pity for the Jouvauds, but, they said, "What can you expect from such people?" Simon and Marcelle were first cousins. They had always been in love with each other, but their parents would not let them marry. Simon married another woman but he continued to see Marcelle, and Paul was born of this relationship. After Simon's parents died, he divorced his wife and married Marcelle. He and Marcelle then had four more children, all of whom were normal.

So although the women in Madame Pleindoux's circle all felt sorry for the Jouvauds, they felt self-righteous in saying that the Jouvauds had brought their troubles on themselves. Furthermore, the Jouvauds were dirty, they had too many children, they did not pay their debts, and Simon drank too much. To the proper inhabitants of Peyrane, the Jouvauds symbolized all that was not proper.

Confronted by the menace of Paul Jouvaud, the women agreed that if no satisfaction could be obtained from the Jouvaud family, the authorities of the town should take the matter in hand. This led to criticism of the Mayor and the Town Clerk. The Mayor didn't even live in the commune, and didn't care what happened to it. The only reason he wanted to be Mayor was to further his business. As for the Town Clerk, he had tried to run the inn before Vincent took it over and he had failed. How could he be expected to help run the town? Back in the days when "poor Monsieur Prullière" was Mayor, things were different. He wouldn't have tolerated a scandalous situation like the present one with Paul Jouvaud loose in the village.

The Jouvaud affair nourished the conversations of the gossip groups for several days, but on the morning in question the conversation came to an end when the town clock struck twelve. The women gathered up their sewing and knitting, exclaiming that they had forgotten about the time. Madame Favre hurried home, and Madame Pleindoux followed her slowly, holding Dédou by the hand. Madame Voisin took her time, for the Voisins could not have lunch until after the noon apéritif hour. She walked back to the café, and the sunny corner in the square was left empty until the middle of the afternoon when the women would meet again.

The women went back to their homes refreshed. They had had a chance to talk about their problems. They had relieved themselves by attacking the Jouvauds, the Mayor, the Town Clerk, and the vague

forces lying beyond the horizon of the village. They had found consolation in talking about former days that were harder and former
days that were easier. The Paul Jouvaud affair had brought drama into
their lives.

La Veillée

Since the café and work-and-talk circles are public institutions
easily observed by an outsider, they appear at first to be the center of
all village recreation. As a matter of fact many people do not take part
in either the café or circle activities. Their usual recreation is harder
to observe because it is private. As one walks through the streets in
the evening most people are not in evidence. Except for the homes of
the Pougets and Malitournes who seem lacking in *pudeur,* all the
houses have their shutters closed. There is no way of knowing whether
the other people are at home, and if they are at home, what they are
doing. This darkness creates an atmosphere of mystery, but there is
really nothing dramatic about what is going on in the houses. Most
people are simply spending the evening quietly at home.

The evenings are short. In the winter supper is not finished until
at least eight o'clock, and in summer it is often nine o'clock or later
when the table is cleared. During the school year the children have
homework to do. They sit at the table in the *salle* working on problems and reciting their lessons. The older children help the younger
ones, and the parents are consulted when necessary. The father reads
the paper and listens to the news on the radio. Occasionally he leaves
the radio on after the news to listen to another program. His wife is
sewing or knitting or ironing. A friend may drop in, but unannounced
calls are short and purposeful. The family is ready for bed by ten
o'clock.

Once or twice a week the family is invited to spend the evening with
another family, or they may invite friends to spend the evening with
them. *Faire la veillée chez des amis,* is the favorite recreation in Peyrane. Because it is an informal occasion it takes time for an outsider
to recognize the pattern followed by most families during the *veillée.*
It is easier to learn to play a game of boules in which the rules are
explicitly stated. To learn to pay or receive a call according to local
custom is a subtle problem.

The *veillée* is a simple occasion; men feel compelled to shave, but·

neither hosts nor guests wear their best clothes. Best everyday clothes are more appropriate. Guests are usually invited to come between eight or nine o'clock, but the precise time is not important. They are expected whenever they have had time to clean up after supper.

The whole family is invited and the children are expected to come. We tried to follow our custom of putting our children to bed by seven o'clock regardless of where we intended to spend the evening. It seemed that it should not be difficult to get a baby sitter since the adolescents needed money and had time to spare, but the institution of baby sitting was not really understood in Peyrane. The ambiguity of the roles of guest and employee, the confusion of friendly favor and paid service, the strangeness of giving an outsider responsibility within the family circle seemed queer to people. They did not feel comfortable sitting alone in our house at night. We were considered odd for complicating life by putting our children to bed instead of including them in the evening's entertainment.

Whenever we arrived at the home of friends — let us say the Favres, who were typical of our hosts — they expressed regret that we had not brought the children, although our stand on this question was known. The next exchange of remarks inevitably dealt with another of our quirks — our notorious habit of keeping our *salle* well heated. As we were taking off our coats, Monsieur Favre always said, "I don't know what's the matter with that fire. It's much too cold in here." In spite of our protest he poured some briquettes into the stove in honor of his guests. When the fire had been stirred up, Madame Favre put the pot of coffee on to warm. At the Favre's, as in most homes, the fireplace had been abandoned in favor of a kitchen stove, and it seemed more natural for us all to sit around the table in the *salle*.

Madame Favre served the coffee presently, and a bowl of lump sugar was passed around. Like the other guests we took only one cube of sugar, but Madame Favre immediately insisted, "Oh, help yourself. Take two." We all protested, but in the end we each took a second lump. As we drank our coffee Monsieur Favre went to a cupboard and brought back a bottle of his *marc*, a home-distilled raw brandy. Madame Favre got out glasses for everyone but ritual did not require that everyone accept a drink of *marc*. It is a very strong drink, and it is recognized that some people have stomachs and livers too delicate to cope with it. The men who accept *marc* drink it straight, sipping a few drops now and then during the evening. The few women who accept it take only a few drops in a glass. They are also given another sugar lump, and they consume the *marc* by dipping the sugar lump into it and sucking on the sugar.

We were told that some people spend the *veillée* together playing cards, but at our *veillées* with the Favres and other friends the conversation was so lively that there was no need for any organized entertainment. The traditional way to spend the evening is *faire la castagnade* (to roast chestnuts), but the custom is dying out. Chestnuts must be bought at the grocer's, and as the chestnut blight creeps across France they are becoming more and more expensive. Besides, while chestnuts may be roasted over a stove, much of the pleasure of a *castagnade* is in its association with the open fireplace. Among the friends with whom we spent the *veillée* only the elder Pians had not replaced their fireplace with a stove. It was only at their house that we took part in a *castagnade*.

Madame Pian brought out a special long-handled frying pan so old that the bottom had worn through in spots. Since it could no longer be used in the kitchen, more holes had been punched in it, making it the family chestnut pan. Then she brought out a bag of chestnuts and a paring knife with which she slashed each chestnut before putting it in the pan. She pointed out that she had to be careful in doing this because if a chestnut slips into the pan without being slashed it may explode and hurt someone. When she had the bottom of the pan covered with chestnuts, she roasted them over the coals until they browned and popped open. Then she poured them into a woolen cloth and wrapped them up tightly, for chestnuts must be "smothered" for a few minutes before they are good to eat. Meanwhile Monsieur Pian had opened a bottle of his best white wine. Chestnuts and white wine, like cheese and red wine, are best appreciated together. They "marry" well. There was usually at least one person at the Pians who could not share the pleasure of the *castagnade* because the chestnuts were too heavy for her stomach and the white wine was too enervating. The Pian grandchildren also were warned not to eat too much because children's stomachs are too "delicate" to stand the "weight" of the chestnuts.

In most homes the refreshments were not so picturesque. At eleven o'clock the hostess went to the cupboard and got out glasses. With a special embroidered dish towel she polished each one carefully. As she set them around the table, the host opened a bottle of his homemade dessert wine, a heavy, sweet wine sometimes flavored with herbs. On special occasions he produced a bottle of his own sparkling wine. If a family does not have its vineyard, a bottle of dessert wine must be purchased at Reynard's store. It is expensive, but it is so sweet that no one drinks more than a small glass, and one bottle will last for several *veillées*. For special occasions the hostess baked a custard pudding or a tart or a cake, but usually she served sweet wafers bought from Reynard.

Conversation continued during the refreshments, but when they had been eaten, the evening was over. Friends who had brought their children roused them and put them through the torture of having their coats put on and their long scarves wrapped around their necks. The torture was increased by the laughter of the adults who found the children especially *mignons* when they were sleepy. After the hosts had been thanked and everyone had shaken hands with everyone else, the guests departed.

Chapter 13

Community Celebrations

The Fate of the Feast Days

The work-and-talk circles, the *veillés*, and the activities centered about the café are the routine forms of recreation for the adults of Peyrane. Older people say that in the days before the first World War the daily routine was frequently broken by special occasions, so that there was always something to look forward to.

On New Year's Day no one worked. People spent the day calling on friends to wish them a good year and good health. Children were given presents by their relatives and godparents, and in groups they went from house to house collecting sous and candy in return for New Year's wishes.

On Epiphany evening friends gathered to eat a special cake made in the form of a crown. In the cake a bean or some little favor was baked, and the person who found it was supposed to furnish a cake for the same group the following Sunday. The traditional joke was to give the piece of cake with the bean in it to the stingiest person there. The others in the group were in on the secret that he had the special piece, and they watched him closely so that he would not swallow the bean in order to avoid having to provide another cake.

On Candlemas everyone went to church to have a candle blessed. A candle blessed at Candlemas and lighted during bad storms was supposed to protect the family from lightning. Candlemas was also the day when the bear was supposed to come out of his hole. If the weather was bad he went back in, and forty days of bad weather ensued.

Saint Joseph's Day was a special day for the children. They went to Mass with their parents and were given holy medals and cakes that the priest had blessed. At home a special meal was prepared for them, a meal with all their favorite dishes.

Then came Carnaval, Lent, Mid-Lent, Holy Week. Palm Sunday

was another children's day. Olive branches, rather than palm leaves, were blessed at Mass, and when they were taken home they were decorated with candied fruit. When the fruit was eaten the branches were saved. Like the Candlemas candles, the olive branches were burned during bad storms to protect the family from lightning. On Maundy Thursday the children kept a close watch on the church belfry and the sky around it, for on that day the bells were supposed to fly through the air on their way to Rome to be blessed. They would not return until Easter Sunday. Since there were no bells to announce Tenebrae, groups of children walked around the village three times making a racket with pans and rattles to call the people to Mass.

Then came Whitsuntide, the time for trips and long *promenades.* For Rogations, the priest and many of the people made a procession throughout the countryside and held brief services at the tiny chapels and crosses scattered along the roads and in the fields. For Corpus Christi there was a procession in the village itself. The women hung their best sheets along the front wall of their houses and made a little altar before the doors. The procession passed through the streets, the children walking first scattering flowers, followed by the priest and his acolytes and then, say the old people, by "le bon Dieu" himself, carried on a platform by several men. As the procession passed, the priest blessed the family altars.

On Saint-John's night everyone lit a bonfire. If you climbed to the top of the hill you could see that the whole countryside was dotted with spots of light. Even up on the mountains there were fires burning; each lonely shepherd burning his fire on Saint-John's night felt close to the people down in the valley. The evening's sport was to jump over a bonfire, for the saying was that if you jumped over a Saint-John's fire you wouldn't be bothered by fleas the rest of the year.

On August 15, the Day of the Assumption of the Blessed Virgin, the priest, followed by the villagers made a pilgrimage to the little Chapel of Saint Michael, a half-mile down the hill below the town, for the special Mass that was celebrated there once a year.

The feast of the patron saint of Peyrane, Saint Michael, brought a whole week of ceremonies and celebration toward the end of September. This joyful occasion was followed a month later by the most serious day of the year, All Souls' Day. The bell ringer tolled the church bells all night on Halloween to prepare the villagers for the All Saints'

Day ceremonies the next day. The following day, the solemn All Souls'
Day, was spent at Mass and at the cemetery. In the evening families
stayed at home. This was not a time for calling on friends. Each family
spent the *veillée* alone.

Christmas was not the outstanding feast of the year it is in some other
countries, but it was an important occasion. Today there are only two
bakeries in Peyrane, but in the old days there were seven of them, and
they were all kept busy at the Christmas season baking the traditional
nougats, made of nothing but honey and almonds, and flat cakes called
gibaciers. This was the season when the farmers customarily showed
their appreciation to the bakers by bringing them presents of eggs and
meat.

At Midnight Mass the church was crowded, and afterwards each
family ate one of the biggest feasts of the year. This *réveillon* might
last from the time the family got home from Midnight Mass until it
was time to go to the first Mass on Christmas morning. When the yule
log was put on the fire, the head of the family took a stalk of celery,
dipped it in wine and sprinkled the log with the wine as he said a
blessing. Then everyone solemnly drank a bit of the wine in which the
celery had been dipped. After that the celebration began.

There were many other days that called for special ceremonies. January 2, Saint Clair's Day, was a servants' holiday. Seamstresses did
not work for it was said that if they sewed on that day they would
go blind. On the night of Saint Vincent's Day the women of the town
would parade through the town with torches and call on the men
named Vincent, and all the Vincents were supposed to offer the women
a drink. The tradesmen and artisans had their special feast days: the
carpenters on Saint Joseph's, the blacksmiths on Saint Eligius', the
cobblers on Saint Thomas'. Assumption was the feast day for the
masons. On that day they were expected not only to refrain from work
but to get drunk. Why the masons were supposed to be less moderate
than the other artisans and tradesmen is not clear.

Today the masons do not drink more or less than any other group
in Peyrane. Assumption is no more a special occasion for them than
it is for anyone else. The men named Vincent receive no more attention on Saint Vincent's Day than on any other day. The seamstresses
sew on Saint-Clair's Day. Few people have more than a snack when
they come home from Mass on Christmas eve. The church bell is silent

on Halloween. There is no procession to Saint Michael's chapel on Assumption; the little chapel has been boarded up for years. The priest does not lead a procession through the streets of the village on Corpus Christi to bless the family altars.

When the teachers discovered that the children knew practically nothing about the celebration of Carnaval, they organized a class project. Each child was to question his parents and grandparents about the Carnaval celebrations they remembered. All the information was brought to class, and together the children wrote the following report.

Our Investigation Concerning Carnaval in Our Village

Today the Carnaval celebration has almost completely disappeared. All we do is make pancakes on Candlemas (February 2). It used to be that in order to be rich all year, people made pancakes holding the handle of the pan in the right hand and holding a gold piece in the left hand. Those who respect this tradition today hold any kind of coin in the left hand. We also make fritters and oreillette cakes which we share with our friends. When we're together eating them we play a joke on someone whom we secretly designate in advance. We make him a pancake or oreillette in which the cook has put thread or pepper or salt. If it's thread he pulls it out when he eats. If it's pepper he coughs, makes a funny face and asks for something to drink. Everyone laughs at him and makes him wait before giving him his white wine.

It used to be that there were many masked balls on Carnaval. The biggest one was held on Mardi Gras. After midnight some good old man announced the arrival of his Majesty *Caramentran* and his wife *Carême* (that is, Beginning-of-Lent and his wife Lent). These were dressed up figures of straw. The *cafetier* made a pitcher of hot wine which was drunk in their honor. They were placed on the platform beside the musicians and the dance began. People who did not know how to dance guarded His Majesty. At four o'clock everyone went to supper, and Caramentran presided at the meal, with his guards at his side. Then the young people painted their faces and went out into the country where they made the rounds of the farms asking for eggs, sausage, poultry, wine, etc. If they got more eggs than they wanted, they would try to trip one of the people carrying baskets of eggs.

On Wednesday evening or the following Sunday they made pancakes which they gave to everyone who came to the dance. If there were old people at the dance they were given a bowl of *café au lait*. After the dance which lasted a long time the food collectors had a big feast with the food they had collected. In the afternoon they had a mock trial of Caramentran and he was condemned to death. Then they shot him and carried him to the cemetery as they all sang, "Goodbye, poor Caramentran." In the cemetery they burned him. The young men who had collected the food put on women's nightgowns and nightcaps and danced a devilish farandole around the fire. That was the celebration of the "Camisards" ("Shirted Men") which they danced to the sound of trumpets and drums.

The Carnaval we spent in Peyrane some of the people spoke of having pancakes for dessert. Reynard had some masks for sale in his store, but our sons were the only ones who bought them. Jeanne Reynard's father gave her a mask. We bought a mask for Colette Favre, who wanted one but was told by her mother that she had "no money for such foolishness." Jeanne, Colette, and our boys were greeted sympathetically as they paraded through the streets. Only two of the adolescents dressed in costumes and masks that night. A few of the neighbors came in to admire their old Provençal costumes, but the boy and girl did not walk through the village. When they were ready they got in the family car and drove off to a dance in Cavaillon. These activities were all that remain of the celebration of Carnaval in Peyrane.

The only traditional celebrations that are still widely observed are All Souls' Day, Midnight Mass at Christmas, the festival of the village's patron saint, and the festival of the patron of the volunteer firemen.

All Souls' Day

All Saints' Day, when the saints in heaven are honored, and All Souls' Day, when prayers are said for the souls suffering in purgatory, have become somewhat confused in the tradition of Peyrane. The name of the first has survived, but its function has no hold on the minds of the people. It is popularly applied, rather, to the second of the two days which is solemnly observed even by those who rarely go near the church.

In the last days of October, the path to the cemetery, usually deserted by all except tourists, becomes a thoroughfare for the villagers. Everyone spends his spare time giving the family plots and tombs a cleaning. Fathers and mothers, leading their children and carrying garden tools, climb up the cemetery hill. Out-of-town cars are parked where the path meets the road, for families who have moved away from Peyrane make a special trip back to the village to put their family plot in order. Everyone is busy pulling weeds, spreading and raking fresh gravel on the walks, sweeping the tombs.

Our children carried on the American celebration of Halloween and made paper jack-o'-lanterns and cut out witches and ghosts. We confined these activities to a back room, however, for to let the people of Peyrane know that we were confusing Holy Evening with Carnaval would not have been tactful. Most of the people of Peyrane are not devout but "after all one owes respect to the dead."

The church bell did not ring all night as it used to on Halloween, but it rang frequently on the morning of All Souls' Day, for three masses were sung. Though few people went to Mass, the ringing of the church bell created the feeling that there was something special about the day. The town was also busier than usual because of the cars arriving and departing.

The Prayals went off to Goult for the day. The Louis Pians went to Gordes, and the Vernets went to Pernes. Madame Girard made a long bus trip to a village in the next département. The Martrons, who moved to Apt a few years ago, returned to Peyrane for the day. The Carles drove over from Saint-Saturnin. There were many people in the village whom I did not know. Houses that were closed the rest of the year were opened by their owners for the day. Every family that could was returning to the village where most of the family was buried. On the streets, people who had not seen each other for a year stopped and embraced cordially but not joyfully. The black suits and dresses everyone was wearing were reminders that the occasion was solemn.

All during the day the cemetery was full of people arranging flowers on the tombs they had cleaned a few days before. Though Madame Jouvaud, the mason's wife, is the only person in Peyrane who raises flowers simply for their beauty, some families raise a few flowers in order to decorate the family graves on All Souls' Day. It is less expensive than buying the chrysanthemums which old Monsieur Grandgeon raises to sell to people for this occasion.

Vespers was the best attended service of the day. After the service the priest led the faithful out of the church in a procession to the cemetery. As the procession wound through the streets down the hill many people joined it who never go to Mass but felt a need to participate in the ceremonies at the cemetery. By the time the procession started up the cemetery path, it had grown from a score of people to almost a hundred.

Within a half-hour the ceremony was over, and old Monsieur

Autrand, the priest, came walking into the village as fast as he could. He was worn out by the ceremony and eager to get back to the presbytery to remove his heavy cope. Georges Vincent was his only acolyte. People who were in Peyrane only for the day said goodbye to their friends and drove away. The villagers did not stop to visit with each other but went directly to their homes. At the apéritif hour the café was deserted except for the Lonely Ones.

Midnight Mass

All Souls' Day is observed in an atmosphere of solemn religious respect, but not many people attend the Mass. At Christmas almost everyone goes, but not many people are moved by the religious significance of the occasion. They go to Midnight Mass as they go to the Prize Day exercises at the school. The few devout people are lost in the crowd of others making their annual appearance in church.

Since Christmas Eve is the only time during the year when the church is filled, it is the only opportunity l'abbé Autrand has to make an impression on the majority of the villagers. He begins to prepare the program weeks before Christmas, and does his best to make Midnight Mass an impressive ceremony.

First, l'abbé Autrand concentrates on organizing and training a choir. Since there are not enough young people in the homes of the devout families to make up a choir, he is obliged to recruit in the homes of people who are indifferent toward the church. It is humiliating for l'abbé to admit every year to the weakness of the faith in the village, although he never has trouble recruiting his choir. No matter how indifferent people are to the church or what their political affiliation is, they are always proud to see their children perform in public.

In training his choir, l'abbé Autrand is hampered because music does not play an important role in the life of Peyrane. The children are taught songs at school. One of the schoolchildren is taking trumpet lessons in Apt and hopes to become a musician. Now and then one hears a woman singing as she works. Otherwise the only music that is heard in the village comes over the radio. No one has a piano or even an accordeon. There is no village band. Dance orchestras have to be brought in from other towns.

There is an old harmonium in the church, although some of the more cynical villagers question whether it is really a musical instrument. At any rate, it serves as one and is played by Mademoiselle Héraud, the postmistress. She is one of the few faithful attenders at church and before Christmas she spends all her spare time in its damp, chilly interior preparing her special numbers.

L'abbé Autrand is also fortunate in having Monsieur Gérard to help him with the music for the Midnight Mass. Years ago when Gérard, a Parisian, still hoped for a successful career as a singer, he met a girl from Peyrane and married her. For a year or two he sang in music halls, but he became *fatigué*, and had to move to southern France for his health. It was natural that he should go to Peyrane to live. Madame Gérard had gone to Paris to get away from home, however, and she could not resign herself to living in the village again. She left her husband and went back to Paris, but Gérard stayed on for a few years. He now lives in Apt and always comes to Peyrane to sing "Minuit Chrétien," at the Midnight Mass. L'abbé Autrand can always be sure that this one number will be appreciated by everyone.

At the Christmas Mass that I attended all the benches were filled, and a score or more people were standing in the back of the church. Léon Favre and his family and relatives were present to hear Louise sing in the choir. Chanon, the chairman of the local Communist organization, and Pouget, the secretary of the party, were there with their families, although their children were too young to take part. Roche, the anticlerical Assistant Mayor, was there. Rivet, the agnostic Town Clerk, was there with his wife. It seemed as though the whole village were present, although some must have been absent, for the building would not be big enough to hold everyone. In spite of the crowd, the church was icy. The chill from the stone floor penetrated one's whole body, although no one seemed bothered by it.

The music held the interest of the people. There were a few smiles when Mademoiselle Héraud played her special numbers on the harmonium, but the old Provençal carols sung by the choir of girls were received with serious appreciation. When the girls were not sure of themselves, l'abbé Autrand raised his voice to carry them on. He had a bad cold, but his coughing spells did not disturb him.

For most people the ceremony reached its climax when Monsieur Gérard sang "Minuit Chrétien." After he had sung people began to leave. L'abbé Autrand had turned to the altar and was continuing the Mass. Edouard Pascal, Monsieur Charpier, Madame Reynard, and the other faithful who were sitting toward the front of the church remained in their seats.

Some of the people who left went straight home; others stopped in the café to warm themselves at the stove and with a glass of rum. They had a mixed attitude toward the Christmas celebration, but they appreciated the efforts of Monsieur Autrand. "He certainly does the best he can," they said. "He had the girls singing beautifully. And Monsieur Gérard was wonderful as usual. But Mademoiselle Héraud and the harmonium . . . You couldn't tell whether it was Autrand or the harmonium that was coughing sometimes!"

After the Mass some people went to the home of friends for wine, pâté, and cake, but there were no big dinners. Since the war no one celebrates *réveillon*, the Christmas feast that traditionally followed Midnight Mass. Monsieur Vincent had no parties coming to his restaurant; his door was closed, and his windows were dark. Although Marcel Rivet had told me that this tradition had died out because everyone felt too poor to indulge in such a luxury, it was obvious that the real reason for the lack of celebration was not so much poverty as indifference. Most people had had their dinner as usual; they had not fasted before going to Mass. Few people had any thought of going to the early morning Mass on Christmas. Christmas had little meaning for most people.

A few days after Christmas an article on Midnight Mass in Peyrane appeared in the Marseille newspaper. It had been written by Edouard Pascal, the only devout young man in the village, who is the head of the tourist bureau. His article was inspired both by his religious devotion and by his desire to spread the fame of Peyrane at the expense of a nearby village, Les Baux, where Midnight Mass attracts a crowd of several thousand. The celebration described in Pascal's article was so different from the actual event that even the devout were amused.

In the Old Church in Peyrane in the Vaucluse Mountains the Old Carols of the Fifteenth and Seventeenth Centuries Lived Again

Peyrane is one of the golden cities for tourists in this region. It is an eagle's nest in the Vaucluse Mounts. It is a haven of peace in the midst of the tortured mountain which bleeds floods of gold and blood in an atmosphere lifted from an illustration of the Apocalypse.

Christmas Eve was clothed in unaccustomed splendor here, but not with a noisy splendor deriving from a crowd of tourists more interested in the feast to follow than in the spirit of faith which should characterize this holy ceremony. It was a splendor inspired by the simple piety of the whole village, all of whose inhabitants, regardless of their differences in opinion, were eager to assemble at midnight before the illuminated altar.

Here there was no exuberant manifestation of folklore. It was in the pure tradition, and only a few visitors, invited by the outstanding people of the village representing this tradition which has endured for centuries, shared this magnificent spectacle which was offered to all the people of the village.

Thanks to the zeal of the priest of Peyrane, l'abbé Autrand, a choir of girls had been organized. Thus we were privileged to hear for the first time, not "standardized carols," but beautiful and rare scores of the fifteenth, sixteenth, and seventeenth centuries, and especially those airs which on Christmas Eve were sung at the court of the Sun King.

The only concession made to modern usage, with a pious deference, was that of "Minuit Chrétien," interpreted by an excellent singer of the Gaîté-Lyrique Theater of Paris, M. Gérard, accompanied on the harmonium by Mlle Héraud.

"Ite missa est." After the ceremony the crowd dispersed into the streets where wander the shades of William of Cabestang and his brothers the troubadours, while the moonlight flowed over the slopes of the roofs, pouring its serenity over the valley whose wild aspect seemed to be miraculously softened.

Peyrane is one of the rare villages in the Vaucluse and in the region where tradition still lives.

Fête de Saint Michel

The most important occasion of the year in Peyrane is unquestionably the votive fête in honor of Saint Michael, the patron of the village. In one of his letters Marcel Rivet wrote, "It's too bad you missed the Fête this year. I say *the* Fête, because for every person born and raised in Peyrane that's the only fête that really counts."

Early in September, the Municipal Committee on Celebrations draws its plans and has large posters printed and posted throughout the region.

COMMUNE OF PEYRANE
VOTIVE FÊTE OF SAINT MICHAEL

Program of Events

Saturday, September 28, Café Voisin

8 p.m. PETANQUE BOULES TOURNAMENT

Teams of Two Players, Three Boules Each

Prizes of 5000 francs in addition to the pool

9 p.m.   Extraordinary Movie Program

Sunday, September 29

10 a.m.   Café Voisin

TOURNAMENT OF BOULES A LA LONGUE
Teams of Three Players Drawn by Lot
Prizes of 5000 francs in addition to the pool

2 p.m.   Café–Hôtel Vincent

GAMES AND RACES FOR ALL
Children, Women, Grandfathers
Sack races, 100 Meters Races, etc.

4. p.m.   Post Office Square

SYMPHONY CONCERT
Under the Direction of the Maestro
PIERRE MONTI
and his nine piece orchestra

5 p.m.   Festival Hall

OPENING OF THE BALL
with the celebrated
PIERRE MONTI
and his formidable singer
YVES RICHARD

Entry Free

You are invited to be the guests of the town

8 p.m.   Illumination of the Public Buildings and Monuments
Parade through the City by the
BUGLE CORPS OF THE CITY OF APT

9 p.m.   Superb Fireworks Displayed on the Peak of the Hill
overlooking
THE BEAUTIFUL CLIFFS OF PEYRANE

10 p.m.   Festival Hall

GRAND BALL
with the famous
PIERRE MONTI
And His Orchestra

Entry Free

Monday, September 30

10 a.m.   Café Voisin

GRAND REGIONAL TOURNAMENT OF BOULES A LA LONGUE
Over Thirty Teams of Champions
PRIZES OF 20,000 FRANCS

5 p.m. Festival Hall

Afternoon Dance
with the Music of Pierre Monti

10 p.m. Festival Hall

GRAND BALL
with the Music of the Great
PIERRE MONTI
and His Nine-Piece Orchestra

Free space available for side shows and booths
The fête will be sonorized
Special Buses will bring the crowds from surrounding cities
Get information at your bus station

The Committee takes no responsibility
for accidents occurring at the celebration

The people in the surrounding region respond in large numbers to this invitation, for the fête of Saint Michael in Peyrane has the reputation of being one of the best in the département. In 1951 the town officials counted one hundred and eighty cars from out of town parked in or near the village. Five buses were chartered to bring people from cities and other villages. Bicycles and motorcycles were parked everywhere. The streets and cafés were crowded. The large play yard in front of the school was transformed into an amusement park. There were rifle ranges, swings for children and adults, a merry-go-round, roulette booths, candy stands. The noise was terrific. Each booth kept a victrola playing continuously, and the music was broadcast at full volume over loud-speakers. In the evening, the music from the dance orchestra was broadcast over six loud-speakers strategically placed throughout the village. This was what the announcement on the poster meant: the fête was "sonorized."

Peyrane swarmed with people who had come to see the parade and the fireworks. The dances were crowded. The boules players paid little attention to the rest of the celebration. The unusually high stakes increased the element of drama in the game. The only event that was not carried out according to the announcement was the program of games and races for children, women, and grandfathers which was supposed to be held in front of the hotel on Sunday afternoon. I was there with my camera well before two o'clock, but no children or women or grandfathers or members of the Committee appeared. When I asked Madame Vincent about it, she was puzzled. I showed her the announcement on the poster and she laughed. "Oh, there won't be any of that, The Municipal Committee on Festivals thought it would be a good idea to advertise our restaurant on the poster in some way, and that seemed to be the way to include us."

For many people in Peyrane, the importance of the Saint Michael's fête is that it brings former residents back to the village. Some of them come back for All Souls' Day, but that is a solemn occasion. At the Saint Michael's fête families and old friends are brought together for a joyful celebration. As they walk down the street people stop every few feet to embrace and joke with old friends they have not seen for weeks or perhaps years. There are big family dinners. Monsieur Biron, the butcher, sells more meat during the last week in September than at any other time.

This is the happy moment of the year for the people of Peyrane. The children are excited by the booths and sideshows put up in front of the school. If most of the children have only enough money to ride a couple of times on the swings and to buy a little candy, they still have the excitement of watching other people enjoy themselves. The adolescents get to go to four dances in two days. The "boulomaniacs" have three days of boule tournaments. The women and old men enlarge the gossip circles to include old friends. The tradesmen have almost more business than they can handle. Voisin's café is full of customers from morning until late at night, customers who buy drinks and don't just sit and enjoy the free heat and electricity. Everyone looks forward to the Saint Michael's dinner — the biggest feast the family has all year.

The fête of Saint Michael was traditionally the most popular religious celebration of the year. A procession of all the villagers made a pilgrimage to the chapel of Saint Michael bearing a huge statue of the saint. The Abbé not only led the procession; it was he who planned the fête itself. Now there is a special mass, but only the few faithful attend. The fête has become completely secularized. It is planned and directed by a committee appointed by the Town Council.

Yet, l'abbé Autrand does not appear forlorn. In coming to Peyrane he had no illusions, for he was born and raised in the Vaucluse and knew the indifference of the people in villages like Peyrane. Although in his devotion to religion he is unlike these people, he is like them in other respects. He shares their ability to accept unpleasant realities for what they are. He knows that some of the younger priests cannot accept this reality and organize soccer teams and scout troops to win the young people to the church. He suspects that these efforts are futile, that the indifference of the people lies deep in their character.

Chapter 14

Organizations

The Firemen's Banquet

Each craft guild in Peyrane used to celebrate the fête of its patron saint just as the village as a whole celebrated the fête of Saint Michael. Now there are no carpenters, no cabinet makers, no barrel makers, no harness makers, no shoemakers, no sabot makers, no millers as there used to be. The only group of artisans active enough to carry out a celebration are the eleven mason-builders in town, but among them there is no professional bond. Gaston Jouvaud and Arcangelo Caselli, who own the town's two construction enterprises, are *brouillés* and do not speak to each other. Caselli's helper shares the *brouille* and does not speak to the men employed by Jouvaud.

Officially Jouvaud employs only two men, his brother and Elie Seignon. Actually he has six other masons working for him regularly, but by calling them temporary day laborers he avoids making a contribution to their social-security fund. They are bitter, but they do not protest because if they lost their jobs they would have to go to work in the ochre mines at much smaller wages. Among these men there is a certain *esprit de corps*. Most of them are bachelors still interested in having a good time. Most spent five years as prisoners in Germany and belong to the same political party. Most of them play belote together at Lataud's café every evening.

After the war Elie Seignon was appointed by the Government to reorganize the firemen of Peyrane. He was named Lieutenant and sent to Paris with all expenses paid for a month's training. On his return it was natural that he should organize his corps around the group of men with whom he had much in common. Five of the firemen are masons working with Seignon for Gaston Jouvaud. The others are close friends of theirs, Francis Favre, the postman-electrician-plumber, Raoul Favre, the owner of the sawmill, Maurice Favre, an ochre worker,

Sansom Aubenas, a tractor driver, André Saut, a farmer, and Charles Prayal, a road mender.

These men accept Seignon as their leader because of his prestige and because in France firemen have a military tradition. If as president of the Boules Club or Hunting Club he tried to give orders the members would resist. The same men, as Volunteer Firemen, submit to a little discipline, and the organization functions effectively. Most of the men come out for maneuvers one Sunday morning every month. They take turns buying a bottle of pastis to drink after the maneuvers are over. They coöperate in organizing a Spring Festival. It is not surprising that this group should be the only organization in Peyrane to carry on a traditional guild fête, the Feast of Saint Barbara. Needless to say, Saint Barbara, the patroness of artillery men, miners, firemen, and all those who need protection from explosions and fire, has little real meaning for the firemen of Peyrane. They call their celebration the *Fête de la Sainte-Barbe*, but it has no religious significance. It simply offers an excuse for the most elaborate gastronomic ceremony performed in Peyrane during the entire year.

The firemen began to plan their December banquet early in the fall. As they sat in the café after the September maneuvers, they discussed plans in general. A month later at the October maneuvers, a committee was delegated to go over the matter with Monsieur Vincent. After the November maneuvers, the suggested menu was discussed. Although the proposed dinner would cost each man two days' wages, it was agreed that it was not elaborate enough, that if this was to be a real *gueuleton* (blowout) another course should be added. The men were willing to make the sacrifice of a third day's wages in order to *faire les choses bien*. "We want to do things up right," they said. It was also agreed that the Mayor should be invited as guest of honor and that other people might be invited if they were willing to pay. Since I had a typewriter, they decided to buy fancy menu cards and I was asked to type a menu for each guest.

There was also some discussion about the day on which the banquet should be held. Saint Barbara's Fête fell on a Monday that year. Should they keep to the tradition and miss a day's work, or should they change the date? It did not take long to agree that they could not afford to pay three days' wages for the banquet and, just for the sake of Saint Barbara, lose the wages of a fourth day. The dinner would be on Sunday, December 3, at one o'clock.

At twelve-thirty on the day of the banquet most of the men were already at the café. They wore their black suits and were drinking their pastis in an atmosphere of unusual dignity. There were three or four men present who were not firemen but were obviously dressed for the dinner. I assumed that they had accepted the general invitation to anyone who was willing to pay for his own dinner, but Seignon told me that no one in the village had accepted the invitation except me. These men were there because it had been decided at the last minute to have a double celebration. The Association of Former Prisoners of War usually have a dinner every year. Since most of the Firemen are members of the Association of Former Prisoners of War, the men decided it would be sensible to combine the two dinners. The non-Firemen who were standing at the bar were members of the Association of Former Prisoners of War.

At one-fifteen the Mayor arrived and in his best election-day manner had an apéritif with the Firemen and Former Prisoners, all of whom had arrived by this time. When he had finished his glass, we filed ceremoniously out of the café and into the Town Hall next door where he was to offer the Firemen an official toast on behalf of the town of Peyrane. In the room that was usually reserved for marriage ceremonies there was a bottle of pastis, a pitcher of water and a tray of glasses which Laure Voisin had brought up. We stood silently and rather awkwardly in a circle around the green, felt-covered table while the Mayor prepared the drink and passed out the glasses. When everyone was served, he raised his glass and made an eloquent speech praising the Volunteer Firemen of the Town of Peyrane, who every day stood ready to risk their lives to protect the property and the lives of the other people of the village. Peyrane was fortunate, he said. The only fire that had occurred during the year had been a chimney fire immediately extinguished by one of the firemen who, with great presence of mind, had dropped a tile down the chimney. A disaster had been averted. The Mayor proposed a toast to the Volunteer Firemen who were alert to the dangers that threatened Peyrane. After we had drunk the *apéritif d'honneur*, we filed out of the Marriage Hall as ceremoniously as we had entered.

In the street the men relaxed, and the group straggled down the hill toward the hotel. On the way Seignon told me they were worried because the café owner, Lataud, would resent their having had an apéritif at Voisin's café instead of his. He would be hurt that his best friends had gone to the other café at a time of celebration. As they may or may not have anticipated, I invited the group for an apéritif *chez* Lataud. After the drinks were served, I realized that the men were waiting for me to make a toast. I tried to rise to the occasion by offering a toast to Franco-American amity and to the men of France who had suffered for humanity by spending five years of their life as prisoners in Germany.

We then went on down the hill to Vincent's hotel where Monsieur Vincent, in an unusual display of generosity, stood ready to toast the Firemen of Peyrane with another round of pastis before they sat down to the dinner. By the time we had finished this last *apéritif d'honneur* it was two-thirty, but even Monsieur Vincent was not disturbed. As he said, "Dinner is not a military attack in which the H Hour is sacred."

Madame Vincent had decorated the dining room as attractively as when the Prefect of the Département came to dinner. The tables, arranged in a square in the center of the dining room, were covered with her best linen and decorated with flowers. At each guest's place there was one of the menus I had typed:

MENU DE LA SAINTE-BARBE
Choice Hors d'oeuvre
Lobster à l'Américaine
Civet of Hare du Ventoux
Hearts of Artichoke Peyrannais
Alpine Thrushes canapé
Homemade Pastries

———

Local Red Wine
Rosé Wine Reserve
Sparkling Wine
Coffee — Liqueurs

There was an atmosphere of leisure. All the men concentrated on enjoying the best dinner they could have by paying the equivalent of three days' wages. The occasion was important, for one has all in all few such gastronomic and social experiences in a lifetime. Whenever wine was poured, there were more toasts, not formal toasts to all those present but toasts from individual to individual with a simple "to your health." This was gradually shortened to "to yours," or "health," and finally became merely a nod of the head and a glance of recognition. After the first hour of the dinner, conversation had become so general and so gay that it would have been difficult for anyone to make himself heard by the whole group. Everyone was involved with his food, his drink, and with conversation with those nearest him. Several times the Mayor tried to get everyone's attention, but even he had to content himself with the limited audience of the men on either side of him. Although the men were enjoying themselves and their conversation was cruder than the pious ears of Mademoiselle Héraud could have endured, there was no rowdiness.

At four o'clock, as the artichokes were being served, Maurice Favre rose, excused himself and went into the lobby of the hotel where he lay down on a bench. The men watched him go with sympathy and concern. André Saut, next to whom I was sitting, explained to me that before the war Favre had been able to eat and drink as well as any other men. While he was a prisoner, he almost starved to death and this had shrunk his stomach. Favre lay on the bench and rested for a half hour or so. When he came back into the dining room, he was greeted with applause. He settled back into the situation with the same grace with which he had left it.

At five o'clock, when the coffee was being served, I realized that my training had not prepared me for such a "gueuleton." I went home.

When I went to the café later in the evening, I found a few of the firemen there, dressed in their everyday clothing, standing at the bar or playing belote, looking as though no special event had taken place. However, they were discussing in detail the whole affair, evaluating each course of the dinner and each of the wines, comparing the dinner with others they had had and still others they had heard about, criticizing Monsieur Vincent on some scores but praising him on others. When I asked what had happened after I had left, I let myself in for some joking, but then there was a serious discussion about the training necessary for such occasions. The men agreed that the main thing is to enjoy such a dinner occasionally so that the stomach will be used to it. Americans cannot be used to it, they said, for it is obvious in American movies that Americans do not spend much time eating.

And Americans do not drink wine; they drink whiskey. Some of the men admitted that during the war they had drunk whiskey with American soldiers with catastrophic results. They had drunk too much before they realized it and had disgraced themselves. When I asked if the Americans did not get drunk, too, they replied, "Yes, but the Americans seemed to want to get drunk."

The Coöperatives

By far the healthiest organizations of Peyrane are the coöperatives to which many of the farmers belong. There are wine coöperatives in the neighboring communes of Bonnieux, Lumière, and Apt; the farmers of Peyrane belong to the one of these that is located nearest their property. There is a coöperative distillery at Costellans, about ten miles from Peyrane. In Apt there is a granary coöperative combined with a farm supply coöperative to which many of the Peyrane farmers belong. Finally there is the tractor and ploughing coöperative which has its headquarters and garage in Roussillon and serves the farmers of all the surrounding communes.

The simplest indication of the success of these organizations is the worry they cause the Mayor of Peyrane, for he complains that they are destroying his livelihood. He used to sell most of the fertilizer and sprays used in the commune, but now that the farmers have joined the supply coöperative he has had to reduce his prices to keep his few remaining customers. His main earnings now come during the harvest season when he buys up the farmers' produce and trucks it to the Cavaillon market, but recently there has even been talk among the farmers of organizing a marketing coöperative. Monsieur Ginoux asked me what was done in the United States to protect the business-man from "insidious organizations like coöperatives." He said that he was working within his political party for legislation to tax them so that competition would be less unfair.

The officials of the coöperatives are less disturbed by the Mayor's campaign to tax the coöps than they are by the problem of personalities which plagues all organizations in Peyrane. Now and then there is an outburst like the one that occurred just before the election when Louis Aubenas was hired as one of the tractor drivers. A group of members threatened to withdraw from the coöperative because they said the officials were playing politics in hiring him. They said he was given the job because his father was assistant mayor and in spite of the fact that he was inexperienced, did not need the money, was not a responsible worker, and was too young for such heavy work. The executive committee ignored the threat, and after the election the dissident members cooled off. They could not afford to withdraw from the coöperative because it ploughed their land for half the price it cost them to have it ploughed by the private concern in Cavaillon that used to do the work.

Economic necessity keeps the coöperatives alive as business undertakings, but the educational and recreational aspects of the coöperative movement remain insignificant. Every Saturday morning during the winter months when the farmers are not too busy, a lecture is given at the office of the supply coöp in Apt by an agricultural expert from a government agency or school. The lecture is followed by a practical demonstration at one of the farms near the city. Of the hundreds of members of the coöp only a dozen attend these meetings.

Jouve took me to a lecture on pruning one Saturday morning. The lecturer, a professor from the departmental Direction des Services Agricoles, was at first embarrassed by my presence because his subject was the difference between American and French methods of pruning, but he assured me that there were no political implications in what he had to say. With the aid of excellent charts and blackboard drawings he showed how the American method of pruning sacrifices the longevity of the plants and the quality of the fruit for the sake of quantity. The French system does not produce so much, but it prolongs the life of the plant and produces fruit of better quality. After the lecture we rode out to the farm of one of the men where everyone was given a chance to prune a grape vine under the guidance of the expert.

The twelve men who attended the lecture were not typical of farmers of the region. The only man from Peyrane was Jouve. Three of the attenders were middle class Belgians who had come to southern France during the war and had decided they would rather farm than return to the cities of the north. The educational and recreational program of the coöperative does not appeal to the average farmer. Even Bourdin and Joly, the two most intellectual farmers of Peyrane, pay no attention to it. When I asked Bourdin why he never went to the meetings, he said, "I'm too busy working to go to meetings." But regardless of work he never missed a business meeting of the coöperative.

The Hunting Club

Hunting is the great passion of most of the men of Peyrane. From the opening to the close of the hunting season the men spend as little time as they can at home and in the fields. The boules lie unused in the rack at the back of the café. Belote is played only at night. At apéritif hours the conversation is devoted to hunting and cooking and eating game. The town dogs, which the rest of the year are left to fend for themselves in the garbage at the bottom of the cliff, suddenly look sleek. During the hunting season they are cared for like children.

The best place to go hunting is, of course, off in the mountains a few miles from the village. There one may still find big game, even wild boars, but the hunting land in the mountains has become more and more restricted as private clubs from the cities have bought up tracts for game preserves. Besides one does not always have the time to go off into the mountains, and it is difficult to find transportation. Most of the men of Peyrane have to hunt within the narrow limits of the commune itself, so game in Peyrane's few square miles has become very scarce. Usually when the men return after spending a morning hunting, they have only a rabbit and one or two birds in their game bag. Often they return with the bag empty.

By birds, I do not mean quail or pheasant or woodcock. Such birds are highly prized by the hunters of Peyrane but they have become so scarce that no hunter expects to see one. When the men talk about hunting for birds, they mean almost any kind of bird except crows and magpies and sparrows. Thrushes are esteemed, but even more prized as game birds are the *petits oiseaux*, "little birds" of all kinds — nuthatches, titmice, kinglets, warblers, European robins, etc. Although a man may get only one or two of these little birds on a single hunting expedition, they keep well, so that they may be accumulated until there are enough of them for a feast. Some of the men boasted that they had eaten as many as fifty or sixty at a single dinner, but they admitted that a normal serving of "little birds" would be only a half-dozen.

Little birds are not cleaned before they are cooked. They are merely plucked, larded, put on a spit and roasted in front of the fire. Pieces of bread are placed to catch the drippings. To eat the birds one takes a piece of the bread, toasted and permeated with the drippings, and smears as much of a bird on it as possible. This is the most tasty part of the dish, although one also eats the rest of the bird, including the bones and head, which have little more consistency than sardine bones.

The hunters complain that there are fewer little birds than there used to be. (The farmers also complain that insect pests are now more destructive.) In order to attract the birds, blinds are built in the woods, and live decoys are placed in front of the blinds. Some of the men raise their own decoys, but Aldo Leporatti makes a business of raising them. He has dozens of tiny cages for the birds which he tends carefully all year in order to sell them or rent them during the hunting season.

If game were plentiful, there would be no need for a Hunting Club, but since it is so scarce the men are obliged to band together to preserve what game remains and even to try to increase it. So the Hunting Club manages to weather the storms of individualism and live through one crisis after the other. It employs two hunting guards for a few dollars a year and entrusts them with the task of protecting the game of Peyrane from poachers and from predatory animals. If they discover poachers, they notify the *garde-champêtre*, the town constable, who has the authority to arrest the miscreants. If a den of foxes is discovered, the guards don their gas masks, gas the foxes out, and shoot them. The Hunting Club may be affiliated with other clubs of the region and with the general hunting club of the département. This affiliation gives the members certain courtesy privileges in other communes.

Once a year, toward the end of the hunting season, the club holds a meeting to decide on its affiliation with other hunting clubs and on what kind of seed-game will be released during the year. Although most of the men of the Commune belong to the Hunting Club, only about thirty showed up at the meeting which was held at the Town Hall at four o'clock, January 28, 1951. The executive committee of the club sat at a table at one end of the room. Moïse Jannel, one of the guards serving as sergeant at arms, had a bell to keep order. As the members came in they sat on benches arranged in rows in the rest of the little meeting room.

When it seemed that all the members who were going to come had arrived, Monsieur Avenas, the president, called the meeting to order. Avenas is the little tailor with the big wife. During the hunting season,

Avenas temporarily recovers the masculine role in his family. He goes hunting, and his wife stays at home. As Avenas called for order, Moïse began to shout and ring the bell. Because of the din the men had to talk even louder in order to continue their conversations. Finally Avenas got the attention of four or five of the men, and the meeting was opened. Avenas announced the two questions on the agenda: Were they to affiliate with the Roussillon Hunting Club? What seed-game should be released this year?

At once everyone began to talk. Finally Raoul Figeard rose and succeeded in getting the attention of most of the men so that he could make himself heard. He said that he was not a hunter and not a member of the Hunting Club, but he had come because he had something to tell the members of the club. The year before a pair of seed-hares had been released near his house, and in the early spring they had destroyed his newly planted asparagus. He had come to the village to see the guards, but they had just laughed at him so he went home and shot the hares himself. He had come to the meeting to complain that the guards had not done their duty.

At once both of the guards, Moïse Jannel and Charles Pian were on their feet shouting explanations, and everyone began to talk again. Avenas called for order. Moïse grabbed the bell and pounded the table with it as he tried to press his point of view. The din quieted, and Avenas succeeded in saying that the purpose of the meeting was to discuss the matters on the agenda, not to give nonmembers a chance to complain about the guards. In a fury Figeard shook his head and left the room. Avenas then called on Buisson, a member of the executive committee, to report on the questions up for consideration. Buisson was unable to get the attention of the members. Nevertheless, he read his report calmly to the accompaniment of the bell which Moïse continued to ring.

After Buisson finished his report, Avenas called for general discussion of the questions. Christian Laplace rose and by shouting he got the attention of the members. The bell was silent for a moment. However, instead of speaking to the question before the organization, Laplace continued where Figeard had left off. Figeard's criticism of the guards was perfectly justified, he said. Laplace had discovered a den of foxes which were destroying his chickens. He came to the village and told the guards about it, but they had simply replied, "We'll do it when we get around to it. You can't tell us what to do." It took them a month to get around to destroying the foxes, and by that time most of his chickens had been killed.

It was difficult to know what the members thought of this accusation because all of them were on their feet talking at once. Moïse gave up ringing the bell and shouted to make himself understood. Finally he flung the bell on the table in front of Avenas, took his guard's badge out of his pocket and shouted, "I don't get paid enough to ·take such criticism!" He threw the badge on the table and walked out of the room.

Everyone was startled, and Avenas took advantage of the quiet to remark that the meeting still had to decide whether it would affiliate with Gordes and Goult. At that moment Robert Peretti came into the room and said he wanted to tell the club something: "You all know that I dropped out of the club a year ago because I wanted to hunt with ferrets. Well, now I want to come back into the club."

Charles Pian, the second guard, jumped up and shouted, "Sure, now that you've killed off all the game with ferrets, you're ready to stop."

He moved over to Peretti and they stood nose to nose, shouting at each other. They were now speaking Provençal so furiously that they were hard to follow, but their insults soon had nothing to do with hunting. They were reviving an old feud and were talking about something that had happened during the German occupation when they were both in the *maquis*. Their friends took sides with them and shouted as loud as Peretti and Pian. Avenas had the bell that Moïse had abandoned, and he rang it desperately, but no one paid any attention to him.

Finally Avenas shouted, "Is it agreed then that we should affiliate with Roussillon and that we should buy three pairs of hares to release as seed-game?" Most of the men did not know that he had spoken, but the members of the executive committee and a few members in the front row heard him. One of them shouted back, "Of course, that will be all right." The executive committee shouted its assent. Avenas banged the bell on the table and yelled, "The meeting is adjourned!"

He and the members sitting at the front of the room started to leave. The other members realized that the meeting was over, and the argument died down as they, too, drifted out. Soon all were back in the café drinking a pastis. Everyone seemed jovial, cordial, in a good mood.

21. *Grandfather and Granddaughter*

22. *The controversial housetrailer*

23. *The funeral*

24. Mayor Ginoux

25. The clock tower of Peyrane

A few days later the following item appeared in the Vaucluse section of the Marseille newspaper.

Peyrane
The Hunting Club Met Sunday

Sunday, January 28, there were many hunters who listened respectfully to the speech of our dignified president, Avenas, while he explained the development of the club since he was elected to office.

When he had commented on several possible projects, the president asked the members to express their opinion concerning the agenda. Several hunters made comments, and then the motions embodying the projects were unanimously adopted.

One important event must be noted. Monsieur Moïse Jannel, one of the two guards, resigned from his office. For personal reasons he turned in his badge and expressed his regret at being no longer able to serve the organization.

All in all, it was a good meeting, successful in every respect.

We must congratulate the Executive Committee and above all its president, Avenas, who succeeded in directing the deliberations in an atmosphere of complete calm and courtesy.

This article which had been sent in by Rivet, the paper's correspondent in Peyrane, was the big joke at the apéritif hour for several days. Rivet told me that everyone knew Moïse himself had poached and closed his eyes when he found any of his friends poaching, but if any of his enemies were caught breaking the rules, he informed the constable immediately. Moïse was about to be asked to turn in his badge. He took advantage of the situation to resign dramatically.

Chapter 15

Ideal Recreation

The Steam-Roller Incident

Rivet was pleased with the success of his practical joke, but at the same time he was embarrassed. As a city man grafted on to village life he was a bit ashamed because he thought it was a kind of small-town trick. "What can you expect here in Peyrane?" he said. "There's not much going on in a village this size, so we have to find ways to amuse ourselves."

It is true that from the point of view of city people there is little entertainment of the professional sort to which they are accustomed. Except for the weekly movie and the occasional visit of a one-horse circus, a small-time magician, a troupe of comedians, or a family of clowns and strong men who travel the village circuit, there is no professional entertainment in Peyrane.

The performers in these shows say that Peyrane is not a bad show town. The people are more hospitable than in many villages, and the audiences are average. A circus draws about fifty people, and the smaller shows can count on an audience of a dozen or two. Generally speaking, one sees the same people at these performances as at the weekly movie — only a small proportion of the population of the village. When I asked other people why they did not go to the shows, the answer was always the same: Since the war no one can afford such things.

Yet most people are not interested in professional entertainment even when it is free. One Sunday afternoon a big truck rolled into town bringing an exhibit sponsored by an Alsatian fertilizer company. The men in charge of the exhibit rented the café hall to show three films to which the public was invited. One film advertised fertilizer, but the other two, a travelogue and a comedy, were to attract the public which was invited to the show by loud-speaker and public crier. The only people who came were the Lonely Ones, the village children, the

Algerians, the three or four families who attended every sort of entertainment, and one farmer — Jouve. All the other people ignored the free show. They preferred to sit and chat in the sun or to take a walk around the village.

In contrast with this fiasco, an incident took place a few evenings later that attracted the entire village. As we were eating dinner, there was a crash, and our house trembled. We ran to the door but found it blocked. We ran upstairs and looked down from the window to the street below. Wedged between our house and Arène's store was a tremendous house trailer, pulled by a steam roller. The driver had tried to get the engine and house down the narrow street, but he had misjudged the pitch of the road. The top-heavy homemade trailer had careened, crashing its top into our house and its bottom into Arène's.

By the time we had reached our window fifteen villagers had already arrived at the scene of the accident. Within five minutes there were twenty more, and within ten minutes all the children, all the men and some of the women were there. The driver was on the roof of the trailer studying the situation. He tried to ignore his wife who stood screaming at him that he had broken every dish in the trailer. Their child clung to her skirt, crying with fear. The audience stood in little groups discussing the scene and the events that led up to it.

The steam roller was the vanguard of a road repairing crew which was coming to repave one of the village streets. As the driver had come into town he had seen at once that the logical place to park the steam roller and set up housekeeping was in the schoolyard. He had just gotten his trailer parked when Edouard Pascal, bursting with the importance of his position as President of the Peyrane Tourist Bureau, arrived. Pascal said that a cavalcade of tourists was expected the following Sunday, and the town could not be disgraced by having this unsightly steam roller and house trailer where everyone would see them. The driver would have to move on around back of the town. The driver, overcome by Pascal's importance, had moved on. As he started down the rue de Gordes, however, someone stopped him and warned him that it was not safe for so heavy a load. There were old ochre mines running under the street, and the street might cave in under a steam roller.

There were only two other possibilities open to the poor man. One was the rue Centrale, leading up to the Place de la Mairie, but it was

obviously much too narrow for a steam roller. Our street, the rue de
la Fontaine, looked just wide enough, so he had tried it, with tragic
results. His trailer was jammed. It looked as though its roof were
sprung. The buildings were damaged. His wife was furious with him.
She stood screaming, "It's a catastrophe! A catastrophe!" His child was
crying. The whole village stood discussing him. He climbed down
from the trailer and surveyed all angles of the situation. The comments
the men made to him were not intended to be helpful: "You should
have seen that the street was too narrow." "You should have measured
it." "You should have stayed in the schoolyard and told Edouard Pascal
to go to the devil." "You should have gone down the rue de Gordes.
Steam rollers have been over it before." "You're stuck there for good."

Of course, with all the man power present, the trailer could probably
have been lifted out of its position, but the men were not there to help.
They had come to see the spectacle and comment on it. Finally someone
arrived whose job it was to help. Alain Peyroux, the road mender, was
a state employee and was to work with the road-mending team. Peyroux
and the driver discussed the situation and finally decided on a strategy.
The driver would uncouple the steam roller, go on down the hill and
all the way around the town, come up the rue de Gordes to the head
of the rue de la Fontaine where the trailer was stuck, hitch on to the
back of the trailer and pull it out of its position.

Since the steam roller had almost a mile to go before it backed up
to the trailer the maneuver was going to take time. Meanwhile the rest
of the village women had arrived. They had not come sooner because
they were busy getting dinner. Since the steam roller was just starting
off down the hill it was easy for the women to persuade their husbands
and children that dinner would be over and they could all return before
the steam roller had time to make the circuit of the town.

Forty-five minutes later everyone was on hand. The steam roller
backed up to the trailer, the two were hitched, and with a frightful
splintering sound the trailer was pulled free. After it had been dragged
the eight or ten yards to the top of the slope, another problem arose.
The trailer had brakes when it traveled forward; it had no brakes when
it was pulled backwards. Now it had to be pulled backwards down the
slope to a place wide enough for it to be turned around. The roadmen's
solution to this problem was hair-raising. When the trailer started to
roll backwards downhill — but before it had gained enough momentum

to crash into the steam roller — the roadmen would jump in front of it and throw four-by-fours under the wheels. As the wheels bumped against these beams the trailer and the steam roller shuddered to a stop.

Yard by yard they lurched the thirty yards down to the little square in front of the post office where the trailer could be turned around and hitched up to the steam roller as it was meant to be. They then went off to the schoolyard to settle down for the night in spite of Edouard Pascal. The roadmenders and their wives were invited by the driver's wife to have a glass of wine. (The glasses were not *all* broken!) The rest of the crowd drifted toward home.

During the year we were in Peyrane, the village would scarcely recover from the excitement of one event before there was another that aroused everyone's interest. There was the bad collision between Henri Favre, riding a motorcycle, and Francis Favre, riding a bicycle. There was the Christmas brawl of the Bellets and the subsequent suicide attempt of Madame Bellet. There was the theft of the bathrobe from the public clothesline, and the investigation by the police. There was always the threatened drama in which the moronic Paul Jouvaud would have a leading part. There was the theft of the tomato plants by Louis Gayol which led to the most startling *brouille* of the year.

The most successful comedy involved a Parisian woman who was spending Easter vacation in a house without a toilet. One morning, just when all the women were out shopping, the Parisian went to the public toilet, slipped, and fell into the pit. She had a dreadful time getting out, and when she finally managed, she had to walk home in front of all the women.

Such incidents satisfy the need for entertainment more fully than a movie or any organized diversion because they are an integral part of the life of the village itself. People feel involved as both participants and spectators. Artfully they utilize each incident to create for themselves the drama that nourishes imagination and conversation.

Growing Old in Peyrane

Chapter 16

Old Age

A stranger walking through the streets of Peyrane gets the impression that it is a town of old people. Although the impression may be exaggerated when the children are at school and their parents are at work, it is fundamentally accurate. In the United States about twelve per cent of the population is over sixty years old. In France, and in the commune of Peyrane as a whole, the proportion is about seventeen per cent. But in the village of Peyrane itself twenty-five per cent of the people are more than sixty years old.

The most obvious reason for this situation is that in most country towns the percentage of old people is higher than in the surrounding country because people frequently move from farm to town when they retire. In Peyrane the situation is magnified because so many young people have moved to the city. The decrease in the population to half of what it was a hundred years ago has been at the expense of its younger element.

The fact that one quarter of the village is over sixty years old does not mean, of course, that one quarter of the population is senile and unproductive. Although the people of Peyrane consider that old age begins at sixty, people do not become inactive when they reach that age. On the contrary, some of the most productive people in the commune are over sixty. The three men with the reputation of being the hardest-working farmers in the neighborhood are Roussel, sixty-four years old, Anselme, sixty-seven years old, and Pierre Pian, seventy-one years old. The two blacksmiths in the commune, Prayal and Jouvaud, are sixty-eight and seventy years old, and Prayal puts in as hard a day as any younger man. Old Mazon, "lou Frisé," still puts in a full day in the ochre mines, and he is seventy years old.

Not all the older people are as active as these men, of course, but most of them continue to work as long as they can. When they are forced to give up their normal adult activity they work at whatever tasks they are capable. "Ils font de la bricole," they say; that is, they putter about and do odd jobs. Monsieur Grandgeon repairs bicycles and grows flowers to sell on All Souls' Day. Madame Grandgeon takes in sewing. Mademoiselle Pamard gives sewing lessons to two adolescent girls. Monsieur Favarel raises a few chickens and sells eggs. Old Anglade is the street-sweeper. Madame Charrin peddles the milk from her cow. Madame Pernet delivers the newspapers in the village; she does not get paid for this work, but she gets her own newspaper free.

When there are no odd jobs to do, there are always the chores that the older people share with the children. They gather wood and mushrooms and herbs and grass. They watch the smaller children. They work in the garden. They watch over the sheep and goats.

There comes a day when age and sickness curtail activity to the point that a person cannot even putter around at odd jobs and share the chores with the children. Then one sits patiently and demands as little attention as possible so that others will not be distracted from their work. Madame Donnadieu is blind and sits all day in the chair at the kitchen table. She used to listen to the radio, but now she is too deaf to hear it. Monsieur Isnard, the father of Madame Baume, lies in bed, helpless from a stroke.

Old Jaumard can walk around the village, watch the boule games and even take part in the Saturday night belote tournaments, but he is becoming childish and demands an increasing amount of care from his daughter, Madame Paul. She complains to her friends of this responsibility, but it would never occur to her to try to avoid it. Every pressure has been placed on her since she was a child to prepare her to accept it. Her reputation would be ruined if she neglected her father. Furthermore, French civil law requires children to support their needy parents. For these reasons Madame Paul would never neglect her father, however much she might complain of the trouble he gives her.

According to the moral code of the village one must not only support one's parents materially, one must also love, respect, fear, and obey them throughout their lives. Fear, respect, and obedience are often incompatible in the relationship between aged parents and adult children, however. Madame Paul can hardly fear, respect, and obey old Jaumard, for his mind and behavior are those of a child. Instead she must treat him as a child, and he must respect, fear, and obey her, his daughter.

As older people become more like Jaumard, losing their physical, mental, and economic power, the roles are reversed. The more they act like children, the more they are treated like children. They are expected to do children's chores. They are disciplined like children. They become witnesses rather than principal actors in the family and village dramas. Their opinion is no longer sought, and if it is offered it is not heeded. They are subjected to the same sort of kindly joking to which children must submit.

The only old people who complain seriously of their lot in life are those few individuals who live alone because their children have moved to the city. Bellet's only child, a daughter, moved to Marseille to work years ago. She and her husband seldom visit Peyrane. They send the Bellets money now and then — not much money, for they do not have much, but enough to ease their conscience. Bellet is bitter against his daughter and against children in general. Why work and worry yourself almost to death raising children, he says, when they grow up, move away, and don't appreciate anything that you've done for them?

Madame Pernet has more self-respect than Bellet so she does not complain openly about her children, but she is bitter. They live in Apt, and yet they come to Peyrane only on important feast days. They do not meet their obligation to support her. They send her very little money. She would be willing to live with them, but they have never asked her. She says nothing to the authorities for she does not want to get her children in trouble.

Although few old people are prosperous, many of them have incomes from one source or another. Some receive income from their farms. Madame Pleindoux is the widow of a farmer. When her husband died she moved to Peyrane to live near her daughter, Nicole Favre, and rented her farm to Figeard's son who had just gotten out of the army. She lives modestly but comfortably on the rent he pays her. Madame Isnard also receives an income from her farm, which she has entrusted to a *métayer*. She complains that he is dishonest, and he complains that she does not contribute sufficiently to the upkeep of equipment, but they both manage to live from the income from the farm.

The rental or sale of small properties in the village is also a frequent source of income. When Lataud bought old Charrin's café, Charrin did not want a lump sum; he wanted 2,000 francs (six dollars) a month for the rest of his life. Lataud went broke and left town after two years, but Charrin was fortunate in persuading the municipality to buy the building as a post office and to accept the responsibility of continuing the life annuity contract. This type of contract is very popular with older people, especially people like Charrin who have no children and are concerned only with having an income for the rest of their lives.

Another source of income for the aged is the old-age insurance issued by the government Social Security Agency. Both wage earners and the self-employed (independent artisans, merchants, professional men, farmers) are eligible for a pension. Since this system of old age insurance was not fully developed until after the Second World War, few older people have contributed to the fund over a long enough period to draw more than a nominal pension. Until the fund builds up, temporary allowances are made to assist "old workers" and "economically weak" people. Any person sixty-five years old or older who can prove that he lacks resources is eligible for a pension of one hundred to three hundred dollars a year, depending on his status and dependents. In order to secure this pension almost every elderly person in the village keeps his financial resources a close secret so that he may be classified as destitute. A careful examination is made of each case, however, and it is hard to deceive the cantonal commission which has the responsibility of investigating the financial status of everyone who applies for an old age pension.

One day the Avenases appeared at the noon apéritif hour sputtering with more than their usual fury. That morning they had been notified that Madame Gontier, the mother of Madame Avenas, had failed to convince the cantonal commission that she was destitute. The commission had turned down her application on the grounds that although she had no income and no resources of her own she had three wage-earning children. The Avenases ranted over their apéritif. They saw at once, however, that even their friends in the café did not take them seriously, for it was obvious to everyone that Avenas made money as a tailor, and Madame Avenas made money as a hairdresser, that they had no children and lived in one of the nicer houses in the village. When they saw that they were receiving no sympathy they presented another argument which did appeal. Other people with more money had been granted old age allowances. Everyone agreed it was too bad that Madame Gontier had failed where others had succeeded in "pulling their carrot out of the government."

A person who is honestly destitute and forced to live on old age allowances can scarcely manage on the one to three hundred dollars he receives. As a last resort, a person can count on the charity of the townspeople, who know exactly who really needs help and who does not. They can never be fooled like the cantonal commission. They know, for instance, that old Maucorps has only the house he lives in, the rags on his back, his truffle dog, and his garden plot at the foot of the hill. Besides the bread which Bonerandi and the town council give him, Maucorps can always get a free lunch at the school cantine. Now and then he finds a few truffles or sells a few vegetables to pay for wine and tobacco. The men at the café often buy him drinks and offer him cigarettes. So Maucorps, the poorest person in Peyrane, manages in poverty but not in misery. As he says, "One day bumps the next one along."

Old Maucorps is seventy-five years old, and he cannot expect one day to go on bumping the next indefinitely. Life must end, and according to the Provençal proverb which he likes to quote:

> "Entre setanto e quatre-vint
> Pau de gènt reston sus lou camin."
>
> (Between seventy and eighty
> Few are left on the road.)

A hundred years ago, when the population was twice what it is today, there were ninety people in their sixties (5.5 per cent of the population), sixty in their seventies (3.5 per cent), six in their eighties (0.3 per cent) and none in their nineties. According to the census of 1946, there are seventy-one people in their sixties (9 per cent), fifty-one in their seventies (6.5 per cent), eight in their eighties (0.1 per cent) and two in their nineties. The normal span of life has increased in the last hundred years, but the proverb still expresses the true situation. Few people survive the seventies. We could narrow down the crucial period still more to show that the big break occurs in the group seventy-five to eighty.

The attitude of the older people toward their approaching death is one of acceptance and resignation. On the conscience level, at least, they want to be *raisonnable* about death as about life. There is still considerable variation among individuals, depending on their health, religious faith, material comfort, and their feeling of being wanted.

Old Maucorps certainly has a minimum of material comfort. His health is neither good nor bad. He is usually a little "fatigué" though he feels better when he has had a glass or so of wine. He has no close relatives, no one to love or who might love him except his dog. He is liked by the villagers and must feel wanted by them, although they tease him. His relations with the church are tenuous; he has not been inside one since his mother died fifty years ago. You might think that Maucorps would have little to live for — or for that matter little to die for. Yet he has a zest for life that many younger, healthier, wealthier people do not have.

An even more lively person is ninety-seven-year-old Madame Pamard, le Mélanie, the oldest person in the commune. She is blind in one eye and deaf in one ear. She lives with her unmarried, crippled daughter. She is not so poor as Maucorps, but she is far from wealthy. Her house might be a forlorn spot, but it is not. La Mélanie and her daughter are two of the gayest people in the village. When I gave la Mélanie the Rorschach test she would smack her lips loudly when she came to a card with color' on it and say, "*That* is a pretty card. It pleases me!" She is in no hurry to die. Like Maucorps, she says, "When the day comes you may carry me out, but *ça ne presse pas.* There's no hurry."

Monsieur Marnas has a different attitude toward death. He complains constantly that the good Lord does not see fit to take him away. He is ready to go. He has settled his affairs. He is leaving everything, and everything in his case means one of the biggest estates in the commune, to his adopted daughter. He is one of the few men to go to Mass faithfully. He has made peace with God. He has no interest in farm or village, though he has always been a model farmer and citizen. His health is good, but he has little zest for working or for enjoying himself. He says that since his wife died several years ago he has lost all interest in living, but other villagers told me he had always had a long face. People respected him, but he was never a gay companion.

In the cases of Maucorps and Marnas, such factors as health and material comfort are obviously less important in determining their attitude toward life and death than deeper personality traits. These men seem to represent two extreme types in the village. Maucorps has a zest for life, Marnas does not. More typical of a majority of the older people is Pierre Pian. He still lives as actively as he can, but he has had to slow down his pace. He now talks of selling his farm and retiring. This prospect seems to make him neither happy nor sad. When I said goodbye to him on our departure from the village I told him I hoped we would see each other again in seven years. "Don't count on it," he replied in a matter of fact way. "I'm seventy-one, and you know that between seventy and eighty few people are left on the road." He did not anticipate death eagerly as Marnas did, but on the other hand he did not dread it excessively.

Monsieur Roche, the first assistant mayor, was eighty years old, and for a person his age he seemed to have more than his share of zest for life. At least when I first knew him there was some gossip about his amorous activities. During the months that we lived in Peyrane, however, his health declined noticeably. Soon he became "bien fatigué," and Doctor Magny was called. After a few days Doctor Magny finally overcame the family's objections to send Roche to the hospital in Apt for observation and treatment.

A week later I met Roche's son on the street and inquired about his father.

"Didn't you hear?" he asked sadly. "We brought him home from the hospital last night."

I started to say that I was happy Roche was well enough to be brought home from the hospital, but the expression on the son's face made me cautious. I simply answered that I had not heard the news.

"Yes," he said, "they called up from the hospital yesterday and told us to come get the old man. He was about to die, so we brought him home. I'm on my way now to get l'abbé Autrand." Just as the people of Peyrane believe that babies should be born at home, they believe that people should die at home, surrounded by their family, the only people who really care for them.

There is also a practical reason for bringing a dying person home. According to law, a permit must be secured to move a body from the commune in which death occurs. In bringing old Roche home to die, his son not only accomplished his filial duty of making sure that his father expired in the bosom of the family; he was also avoiding unnecessary complications. There is already enough to worry about when someone dies.

Usually a close friend or a relative less affected by the death than members of the immediate family is entrusted with the task of observing formalities and making arrangements for the funeral.

If the doctor has not been present at the time of the death, he must be called to pronounce the death officially. He makes out a special form, stating the time and the cause of death, and puts it in an envelope which he closes with his official seal. This certificate must be taken within twenty-four hours to the town hall where it is presented with the *livret de famille* or the birth certificate proving the identity of the dead person. The town clerk then makes out a death certificate and issues a burial permit. The burial cannot take place for twenty-four hours after death, except under special circumstances. It usually takes place on the morning following this twenty-four hour waiting period.

On leaving the town hall the person in charge of arrangements must go up the hill to the church to talk to the priest. Theoretically one may choose between a *missa cantata*, for which the usual offering is 1200 francs, and a low mass, for which the usual offering is 800 francs, but only a family wanting to display its wealth would ever have more than a low mass. L'abbé Autrand has never sung a high requiem mass in the years he has been at Peyrane. Sometimes when a family cannot be brought together immediately, only a simple benediction is given on the day of the interment, and the regular requiem mass is postponed for a week.

When the representative of the family receives the burial permit from the town clerk, he also obtains permission to use the municipal hearse, which is stored in a cellar dug in the cliff. But he must find a farmer who is willing to bring his horse and drive the hearse in the ceremony. The rate of this service is normally 2000 francs. He must also buy a coffin. This is not easy for there is no carpenter in Peyrane. In the past, Raoul Favre has sometimes been persuaded to put together a rough coffin at his sawmill, but he rarely has the appropriate wood and he finds the chore distasteful, so the coffin is usually bought in Apt or ordered from a carpenter in the neighboring towns of Saint-Saturnin or Goult. The price of a coffin is 4000 francs.

Usually a family already has a plot or a small mausoleum in the town cemetery, but it is necessary to check to make sure that all is in order and that the rent is paid. The town charges 630 francs a square meter for perpetual concessions, 270 francs for thirty-year concessions and 120 francs for fifteen-year concessions. It is important that these arrangements be clear, for it is expensive to have to make changes later. Anglade, the gravedigger, charges 1800 francs to dig a grave and just as much to reinter a body. If several bodies in a plot are to be moved at the same time, however, his rate is less. To reinter the second body costs only 1400 francs, the third 1000 francs, the fourth 700 francs and any others 500 francs each.

Relatives and close friends are told immediately of the death, but one of the elderly women of the town, usually Madame Pernet, is asked to notify the other townspeople officially. She goes from door to door throughout the whole village bringing news of the death and announcing plans for the funeral. The postman is asked to notify people living in the country.

When a child or a young person is buried the hearse is not used. The coffin is carried by pallbearers chosen among the young friends of the deceased. At the funeral of an adult there are pallbearers, too, but they do not carry the coffin through the streets.

At the home of the deceased the death room is cleaned. The windows are closed, and the mirrors are covered with a cloth. (The vases are not covered as they traditionally are in some parts of France.) Members of the family, often aided by a close friend, lay out the body on the bed. Every effort is made to give the deceased the best possible appearance. He is buried in his best clothing.

Members of the family look to their own clothing, too, for they must go into mourning, although mourning is not formally declared until the *messe de mise en deuil* takes place a week after the funeral. For men to wear mourning simply means wearing their best clothing, since their best suit and best hat are always black. Yet a man cannot wear his best suit every day. He wears it only at the funeral and afterwards wears a black band on his hat or merely a black rosette in his lapel. Some men wear a black band on one of their sleeves, but this custom is disappearing. Women wear black shoes, stockings, dress, hat, and if they can afford it, a heavy black veil for the funeral.

Officially the period of mourning lasts until the *messe de sortie de deuil* one year later, but observance varies with individuals and families. The older women often wear black the rest of their life. Younger people wear mourning only six months. During the period of mourning everyone refrains from having too good a time in public, although this practice varies, too, from family to family. Generally speaking, the younger people of the community feel that too much stress has been placed on mourning and that it involves unreasonable expenditures of money.

Every adult member of the community is expected to go to a funeral. Even at the height of the harvest season men will take time off from work. Family feuds are temporarily forgotten. If it is impossible for a whole family to attend, at least one member of the family will be there. Anyone who for personal reasons detracts from the respect which the community is paying the dead will arouse universal indignation. Even if the deceased has in fact been disliked by everyone, he is respected from the time of his death until he is decently laid away.

People gather at the home of the deceased a few minutes before the time of the funeral. They stand in the street talking quietly in small groups. Now and then an individual or group moves toward the door and goes in the house to view the body which lies in state until about ten minutes before the ceremony is to begin. Then it is placed in the coffin, and the top is nailed down.

When the priest arrives the coffin is placed in the hearse, and flowers and beaded decorations are arranged around it. The procession departs for the church. First come Georges Vincent, the acolyte, and the priest, dressed in his funeral cope. They are followed by the hearse behind which walk the family, the friends, and then the general population. Halfway up the hill where the new city meets the old and where the procession must go through the clock tower of the old wall, the procession stops as the driver of the hearse negotiates a very difficult turn and persuades the horse to continue up the narrow street in the old town.

At the church, the big central doors, which are usually closed, are opened and the pallbearers carry the coffin into the church to place it on a platform set up in the aisle. The doors are closed, and mass is begun.

Most of the women have gone into the church, but very few men have entered, other than those who are members of the family or close friends of the deceased. The rest of the men stand out in front of the church, quietly talking in little groups. A few of them drift down to the café for a drink and a game of belote while mass is going on.

After the mass is ended the procession forms again and moves down the hill. As it goes by the café the men who have been playing cards fall into line — rather furtively. The driver of the hearse works to secure the brake as he goes down the steep rue Centrale. It would be a catastrophe if he lost control at that dangerous spot. Once he has turned the corner at the foot of the street the going is safe for a few minutes. The procession goes on by the post office, the inn, the smithy, the school, then turns up a rocky path that climbs Piquebaure Hill. The road goes so near the edge of the red cliffs, that a man must be sure of his horse to accept the job of driving the hearse.

The pallbearers carry the coffin to the edge of the grave, and the people of Peyrane gather around. Even the indifferent ones stand piously as the priest gives the benediction and the coffin is lowered into the grave. The lamentation reaches its peak, but even at this moment the emotion is restrained. There has been constant but not excessive weeping all during the ceremony. A member of the family who could not control her grief at the funeral would not have come. She would have stayed at home with someone to care for her.

The ceremony is over. The priest and the altar boy leave first, walking rapidly back to the church. The family of the deceased moves slowly out of the cemetery. As the mourners leave, each one walks past the open grave, picks up a clod of earth and drops it on the coffin below. Soon everyone has left except old Anglade, who has been standing apart leaning on his spade.

The people and the church of Peyrane have taken leave of a Peyranais. At the town hall, Rivet has noted the death on the *livret de famille* and on the birth certificate of the deceased. If the deceased was born in another commune, Rivet has notified that commune of the death. He has also notified the office of the Department of Health in Avignon. Finally he sends a death notice to the regional office of the National Institute of Statistics at Marseille. The Peyranais has now officially ceased to exist.

Epilogue

Chapter 17

Peyrane Today

Letters from Peyrane are like letters from any little town. The news is of the same order: marriages, births, deaths. People have moved away and others have moved in. A public sewage system has been installed. The old shower bath down at the soccer field has been moved into a new public bathhouse next to the public laundry. An artist from Paris is living in one of the windmills. The Charrins' cow died, and they closed up their house and moved away. Madame Pamard is now one hundred and two years old. She survived both the public celebration of her hundredth birthday and the catastrophic cold wave of January 1956. L'abbé Autrand died, and the church of Peyrane has been closed. Since the flock in Peyrane was not fervent enough to support a full-time priest, a priest is sent up from Apt to say Mass on Sundays and on special occasions.

These events seem in the order of things. They could not have been predicted, but there is nothing surprising about them, and above all there is nothing about them that would lead us to change our conception of Peyrane. When one lives in Peyrane, of course, such events take on important proportions. City events lose their impact because they fade into the surrounding activity. Even a small event in a village looms up, especially if it can qualify as drama.

Undoubtedly the most dramatic event in Peyrane in the last five years was the invasion by the Gaumont Moving Picture Company. With almost no warning a crew of actors, actresses, directors, and technicians arrived to make a movie entitled "Le Paradis retrouvé," and for several weeks the red cliffs of Peyrane became the backdrop of a romantic tale. All I have been able to learn about the tale is that it concerns Adam and Eve, who are not dead, after all. They rediscover themselves and Paradise in Peyrane. However, they bump into the Wandering Jew and this encounter touches off a series of events which make up the plot of the movie.

One can imagine what the filming of this movie did to Peyrane. Rivet wrote: "The village is upside down and has been for a month. I was named Impresario and Official Liaison Officer between Directors and Villagers. Many scenes were shot in the village and around the cliffs. I even had a rôle — I was the Postman, and I'm in several scenes in my son's uniform. Others were given rôles, too, and still others had technical jobs. The famous Moïse and young Philippe Aubenas worked with the technicians. The inside scenes were filmed in my house. Most of the actors and actresses found places to stay in the village, but some had to be lodged in Apt. The stir made by this event has changed the village completely."

The spectacular changes were temporary, but there were other changes that had lasting effects. For instance, the filming of the movie made the Voisin café go bankrupt. It had been expected that Voisin's passion for boules would ruin him, but it was his prosperity, not boules, that finally did it.

When the Gaumont company moved into Peyrane it brought actors and technicians who had time and money to spend in the café. It also brought tourists who came to the café to see the actors and actresses. Voisin was so awed by the actresses and by the flowering of his business that he was paralyzed. Madame Voisin took over. She hired Jacques Leporatti to help her and sent her husband away to play boules so that he would not be behind the bar to give credit and drinks on the house. For a while the Voisins thought Peyrane was really "Paradise Regained."

Madame Avenas, the owner of the beauty shop next door, was prospering, too. Her appointment book and her extra rooms were filled with people from the movie company. Still she was jealous of the Voisins. It seemed to her that they were making easy money. Her tenants gave her the idea of actually cutting in on the café trade. Dissatisfied with the high price they paid for meals in Vincent's Guide Michelin restaurant, they persuaded Madame Avenas to give them board as well as room. Next they asked for apéritifs before their meals, and then for drinks at the other times of the day, and soon Madame Avenas found herself in the café business. She paid her patent, hired Charles Pouget as waiter, and became a *cafetière* in earnest. Needless to say, the relations between Madame Voisin and Madame Avenas deteriorated.

An unexpected complication made the competition ever more intense.

The owner of a café in Marseille, Jean Mauron, heard of the little town where a movie company was attracting many tourists. His wife was *fatiguée* and needed a change of air, so he closed the Marseille business and moved his city fixtures and equipment into the empty shop next door to Madame Voisin's.

For a few weeks there were three cafés lined up in Peyrane's little Place de la Mairie. They all lasted through the stay of the Gaumont Company, but when the glamorous actors departed, *c'était la catastrophe*. Normal business was scarcely enough to keep one café alive. Each of the three settled down to wait for the other two to die. The first to give up were the Voisins. They had the advantage of their tobacco business, but they lacked capital to hold them over. As soon as they could make arrangements to settle the exchange of the government tobacco patent they moved away from Peyrane. That left Madame Avenas and Mauron sparring for an advantage.

This incident would hardly be worth telling if it were not for its political ramifications. Madame Avenas is the number three communist in the commune. Chanon is the leader. Léon Favre is the brains. Madame Avenas is the dynamo. Pouget, the waiter she hired for her new café, is number four, the worker and local Secretary of the Party. However, it turned out that Mauron was also an active Communist, and he brought with him the prestige, the self-assurance, and the influential relations of a big operator from Marseille. He started at once to take over the direction of the Party in Peyrane.

From reports it appears that the reaction was violent. When Madame Avenas shouts and beats her breast it seems as though something awful were about to happen. Mauron, who is a caricature of the popular conception of a Marseillais, was a match for her. The Place de la Mairie became an unpleasant place. Even the boule players were disrupted. Rather than choose between the two cafés, and consequently take part in the internecine struggle, they moved their game to another part of the village. Meetings of the Communist cell became impossible because Madame Avenas and Mauron equated party loyalty with café loyalty. The party had not been in so bad shape since the dispute over the use of guns and ferrets in rabbit hunting.

It was at that moment that Prime Minister Faure called an election. The followers of Mendés-France could have been no more outraged than members of the Communist Party of Peyrane. They were caught in an awkward moment in history. It took all the patience and common sense of Léon Favre to patch up the ranks. Perhaps, of course, it was good for the Party that it came so suddenly. The surprise shocked members into a semblance of discipline.

The campaign was short, and it was more furious than any election since just after the war. The fury was stirred up by a new political force that muscled its way into the center of the traditional political situation — Poujade's middle class antitax movement. It had been said that the best way to undermine the Communist Party in Peyrane was to invent a party that would represent an even more violent protest. But since all the parties in Peyrane are protest parties, Poujadism endangered them all. Poujade was even more dangerous in the Vaucluse than elsewhere because in that département he multiplied himself. That is, there was not one Poujade candidate, there were three — one for the tradesmen, one for the peasants, and one for the consumers. The three candidates were, of course, affiliated, so that according to the electoral law of 1951 each one was credited with the combined success of all three.

The heat of the campaign can be measured most precisely by the fact that more people turned out to vote in this election than in any other national election since the war. It may be recalled that usually about 70 per cent of the registered voters of Peyrane vote in a national election. In the election of January 1956, 79 per cent of the voters came to the polls.

The results of the election bring further confirmation of our concept of politics in Peyrane. Their meaning is clear when they are compared with the election returns of 1951 (see page 231).

	1951	*1956*	*Difference*
Registered Voters	467	457	−1
Votes Cast	329	361	+32
Invalid Votes	10	14	+4
Valid Votes Cast	319	347	+28
Communist (PC)	141	130	−11
Socialist Radical (RGR)	77	44	−33
Socialist (SFIO)	40	42	+2
Popular Republican (MRP)	37	27	−10
de Gaulle (RPF)	21	–	−21
Independent	6	–	−6
Poujade	–	104	+104

Almost a third of the Peyrane voters supported Poujade's candidates! Who were these voters? We cannot answer definitely, but the preceding tabulation is suggestive. If we add the 81 votes of those who apparently deserted the traditional parties to the 32 votes of those who voted in the election of 1956 but not in the election of 1951, the total is close to the 104 votes received by the Poujade candidates.

There were three principal sources of support for Poujade. First, there was the vote of people like Figeard who have always had such contempt of politics that they did not bother to come to the polls. The destructive oversimplifications of Poujade's statements appealed to them more than any party statements had before, so they voted instead of staying at home. Then there was the support of the score or more people who always vote to the right, who had voted in 1951 for the conservative candidates on the Gaullist and Independent tickets.

The strongest support, however, seems to have come from the Socialist Radicals who deserted Daladier. Their switch is not surprising, for on the whole they are people of substantial means who bear the heaviest tax burden in the commune. Poujade's denunciation of the system of taxation appealed to them directly. He also gave them an opportunity to express their traditional feeling of extreme protest against impinging forces without at the same time associating themselves with the other extreme protesters, their Communist neighbors. So their vote for Poujade was a vote against taxation; it was an extremist vote against government; it was also a means of differentiating themselves still more radically from their neighbors.

For a person who is fond of Peyrane it is painful to acknowledge that it gave Poujade stronger support than did most of the other communes in the Vaucluse. Unfortunately, this is not the first time that Peyrane has distinguished itself by offering support to less admirable candidates. François Goguel, in an unpublished analysis of the electoral history of Peyrane, points out that in several elections at the turn of the century Peyrane gave proportionally more votes than did other Vaucluse villages to the ex-socialist, ex-Boulangist, nationalistic, and alcoholic adventurer Georges Laguerre. Professor Goguel warns us, however, that it is dangerous to read too much meaning into any one such fact. It might seem that Peyrane has a penchant for demagogues if we were not aware of another fact that implies a quite different motivation in the Laguerre vote. It was Laguerre who worked with the Mayor to secure for Peyrane one of the first munioipal water systems in the region. Election statistics may be revealing, but they may also be misleading, especially if they are studied without regard for other factors and if the numbers involved are as small as they are in the commune of Peyrane.

The election results of 1956 are in a sense just as misleading. It is a fact that in this election, roughly one-quarter of the voters did not vote, one-quarter voted Poujadist, one-quarter voted Communist, and one-quarter voted for moderate candidates. Logically, one might conclude that revolution seethes in Peyrane since only one-fourth of the adults support the Fourth Republic, while three-fourths of them are either indifferent to it or favor its destruction.

We know that the opposite is true. Peyrane is profoundly conservative. The vote does not mean that they want to change the order of things. It means quite the contrary, that they want to be left alone so they will not have to change. Not that the state of things is good as it is. It is neither good nor bad; it is tolerable. Or rather it would be tolerable if it were not for the malevolence of human beings organized into groups. For organization means power, and power means the oppression of the individual.

Even at the local level where individuals know each other personally we have seen that the only successful organizations are coöperatives whose benefits have been concretely demonstrated to outweigh their oppressive nature. Other groups lead a precarious life, and usually they disintegrate entirely. People say they do not want to belong to an organization because they do not want to put themselves in a position where other people will spy on them, boss them, criticize them, burden them with responsibilities, make them the butt of gossip and ridicule, commit them to action against their will.

They can ignore or disrupt local organizations, but whether they like it or not they are under the control of the French Government and the hidden forces which they believe run the Government. They react characteristically. The person who does not vote pretends to ignore the Government as he pretends to ignore a person with whom he is *brouillé*. He symbolically assassinates it. The person who votes adopts an even more popular form of defense. Just as he insults and gossips about his enemy, inflicting harm on him orally, he uses the ballot as an insult to organized power. A few literal-minded voters cannot content themselves with expressing a destructive vote. They write insulting words on the ballot, even though they know the writing will cause their votes to be thrown out.

Seen in this light the political behavior of Peyrane loses its paradoxical appearance. In context it becomes understandable — if not right — that a conservative people should thus assert its will to protect the individual from collective human power.

This explanation raises three basic questions. Why should the people of Peyrane feel that collective human power is essentially baleful? Why do they not act collectively and creatively to control the power instead of simply cursing it? Why do they not make positive use of the one real weapon at their disposal — the vote?

The answers to these questions must be implicit in the facts of life in Peyrane as they have been described, but cultural, psychological, and historical information is still too fragmentary for me to think in terms of causal relationships. The best I can do is to suggest certain parallels which may have some bearing on the questions.

When I think of the individual of Peyrane faced with collective human power, an image immediately occurs to me. I see Alphonse Peretti stoically walking from school up to the church with his messy school theme pinned to his back so that people along the way will make fun of him. Or I see a little girl walking in a circle in the school yard, alone, with her hands on her head, with the sign "thief" pinned to her back, while the other children point at her and mock her. These are extreme and unusual cases, but they point forcefully to the essential disciplinary tools — shame and ridicule — which adults use with children both at home and at school. Children need not fear violence, mutilation, loss of love, separation from parents, threats of damnation or any of the other weapons which people in the world use to secure obedience from children. They are constantly faced, however, with shaming fingers and mocking laughter. To avoid the pain of public shame and ridicule children must learn to conform — on the surface at least. The revenge that is sometimes tolerated is for them to stand at a safe distance and shout insults.

How can a child avoid feeling as he grows up that people are ready to assail him collectively with the force of public scorn whenever he deviates from the behavior that is expected of him? And since no one can live without deviating from an ideal social code — both in action and in thought — almost everyone feels that society has cause to attack him. He is even further convinced that humans collectively are hostile because he assumes that they feel as hostile toward him as he feels toward them.

As the child grows up these personal feelings about collective human power are reinforced by conventional attitudes that have undoubtedly been current in Peyrane since the first individuals settled on the red hill. For there has never been a time since the beginning of Peyrane's history, when contact with organized humanity has meant anything but the exploitation and manipulation of the individual. The wandering hordes, the Romans, the feudal lords — including the neighboring papal rulers, the agents of Provençal counts and French kings, the nineteenth-century régimes set up by Paris, the twentieth-century bureaucracy centralized in Paris — all these form an unbroken past in the vague memory of the village. They all mean domination by a human power beyond the control of the individual. At best the domination has brought unsought modifications in living habits. At worst it has brought disaster. And so it has become conventional to think of human power as a plague to be classed with the plagues of nature: the odious government, the leveling mistral, the flooding Durance.

Later when adults come into actual contact with government these inner feelings and conventional attitudes toward human power, and especially toward government, seem to be confirmed. The most intimate contact a young man can have with a government agency comes through his military service. Whatever else one may say of an army, it is not designed to change the mind of a young man from Peyrane about his relationship with collective human power. He returns home changed in some respects but not in that one. And as he establishes his own family and assumes adult responsibilities, he personally suffers from the direct and secondary effects of all the ills he has always heard attributed to government — war, taxation, inflation, legal restraints, administrative callousness.

But he also enjoys the benefits of government. How can he ignore the good that government accomplishes for him as an individual and for his family? Some of the benefits, like public health protection, eliminate suffering, and it is hard to feel and to appreciate an absence of suffering. Social security benefits are concrete and important, but they are obscured by inflation, red tape and charges of favoritism. Other benefits, like mail service, have become so natural a part of life that one accepts them unthinkingly. Others, like French honor in the French Union, are too abstract, too remote, and too tainted with private interests to evoke more than an indifferent or cynical reaction. The benefits of government as a whole lack the provoking immediacy of its oppressive effects. Confronted by this oppression, people want to seal themselves off so that outside authority can exert none of its malevolent control within the invisible frontier that separates the *foyer* from the rest of the world. Unable to do this, they stand back and shout insults —if only symbolically through the ballot.

To stand back and shout insults is not a constructive approach to the solution of a problem. Why do they not act instead of shouting?

The feeling of frustration does not paralyze all their activities. We have seen that when immediate family concerns are at stake there is no such despair. Members of the family participate positively in every aspect of family life. A child learns very young that he must share the problems. One after another, responsibilities are thrust on him, so that he acquires a growing sense of responsibility for the family's welfare. In this sphere he is impelled to act constructively.

But in other spheres of life, corporate responsibility and constructive participation by the individual are not stressed. We have seen that the school experience tends toward passivity and immobility. Children are not made to feel that the initiative is theirs as it is in the family. Spontaneity is not officially recognized in the educational system as it operates in Peyrane. A child who acts spontaneously risks being punished, and the punishment consists of forced immobilization of the body combined with shame. In formal learning emphasis is placed on deduction: children are not encouraged to "discover" a principle by themselves; it is presented to them as something to accept passively. Even in art class there is no place for free expression; children are asked to reproduce as realistically as possible a flower or a vase that is put before them. Recess play on the playground is unplanned, but children must behave with civilized caution. School experience does not, on the whole, develop an urge to act, to act adventurously to dominate one's own situation, to act coöperatively to improve the situation of the whole group. So far as the average student is concerned responsibility is something to be avoided. It may be recalled why Jacques Leporatti worked hard in school: "So they'll leave me alone!"

The school experience is paralleled in other spheres of life, especially in the relationship the child comes to have with his government. No government in the history of the village has tried seriously to give the individual a feeling of active, responsible participation. In the last hundred years he has been able to vote, but the centralization of the government is such that the individual still feels much more acted upon than acting. We have seen a good example of this in the episode of the new school building: the welfare of the village is frustrated by a remote centralized agency of government. Such incidents have more effect in the formation of attitudes than the "beautiful sentences" in the civics books. These sentences slide over the surface of the child's personality as smoothly as the injunction to be kind to little birds. He grows into adulthood and finds that outside the limits of the family he is treated on the whole more like a manipulated thing than a participating personality.

Of course, other peoples in the world may share this predicament and still believe individually that fate is in their individual hands. The people of Peyrane could reply only that this feeling of omnipotence is an illusion which they cannot share. They reject easy illusions and prefer to look unpleasant truths in the face. Once recognized for what they are, unpleasant truths may be accepted. One cannot act against them. Resignation is the remedy. The most common expression in Peyrane is, we have seen, "C'est comme ça."

But still there is the vote. Why do so many people throw away this one opportunity? Every vote cast has in intention the same negative meaning. Why should it not be used positively?

The attitude toward the vote may be given perspective by another aspect of the classroom situation. The immobilizing effect of the school experience is in a sense relieved by the existence of a sort of jungle area in which the formal system of punishments and rewards does not function. This, we have seen in the chapter on the school, is the area called "favors." The granting of favors is governed by unpredictable and rather mysterious feelings of one person toward another. Both parents and children expect the teacher to have pets because human likes and dislikes cannot be dictated. Spontaneity is not constrained here any more than it is in the *bien* and *brouillé* relations of the children and their parents among themselves. There is no resentment in the granting of favors so long as the official system of school laws is not infringed upon. A favor has nothing to do with laws because it has nothing to do with right and wrong. The fact that it is recognized as an exception guarantees the sanctity of the system itself.

As a child grows up he learns that this duality characterizes life. There is on the one hand the paralyzing network of official laws and regulations. Beneath this is the area of human relationships where with resourcefulness one may move freely to accomplish what may be legally unattainable. The existence of these two worlds may be amply documented with incidents that occur in Peyrane, but the most dramatic illustration is the case of Paul Rivet's hearing aid.

Through an improbable chain of efforts and coincidences Paul was sent a hearing aid by Big Joe Rosenfeld, the director of an American radio program called "Happiness Exchange." The customs officials at the Marignane airport notified Paul's father that the package could not be sent on until Rivet produced an import licence and ninety-six dollars customs duty. Since Rivet had not purchased the hearing aid he had no import licence, and he certainly could not produce the customs fee which was three times his monthly salary. He went to Marignane to explain the situation to officials. No reasoning could prod the hearing aid loose. Local officials could not or would not find a loophole in the rules and regulations so that a humanitarian purpose might be served. ("The law is the law, and we have no authority to change it. You'll have to see my superior. . .") After weeks of frustration on different levels of official channels Rivet found a solution. He telephoned a childhood friend of his in Marseille who, he said, owns a bar and a string of racehorses. I do not know how the friend maneuvered to accomplish what he did, but I do know that he soon appeared in Peyrane with the hearing aid for Paul.

Frustrated in the area of rules and regulations, Rivet had retreated to the jungle area of human relations where he could move freely and effectively. He had utilized the "Système D" — the art of wangling, which is an essential lubricant in the stiffly functioning French legal machine. It is through this system that individual human rights may triumph over official restrictions when the two are in conflict. If one develops sufficient skill and good connections one can nullify the restricting force of rules and regulations. So a person's power depends less on his official position in society than on his skill in manipulating human relationships. Who would have thought that a little town clerk could successfully challenge the collective will incarnate in the Marignane customs clerks?

Generally speaking the people of Peyrane believe that effective action is accomplished not officially through legal channels but unofficially through personal contacts. Most people do not have contacts as powerful as Rivet's outside the commune. Without the "belles relations" necessary to maneuver in the area of favors and obligations they feel paralyzed in the area of laws and regulations. What is their power compared with the power of Rivet's friend? What is his power compared with the truly great powers in Paris? Against such forces the individual's vote is no more than an empty legal gesture. One would be naïve to take it for more than that. Offered to the individual as a gesture, the vote is used as a gesture — a gesture of defiance.

The exasperation of the citizen of Peyrane is intensified by his contradictory position. He would like to divorce himself from the rest of the world — and yet he does not want to. Monsieur Marnas cuts, cleans, and bunches his asparagus and takes it down to the edge of the road. Monsieur Borel comes along in his truck and takes it to Cavaillon where it is shipped to London. The amount of money that goes into Monsieur Marnas' wallet depends on the many factors that separate him from a London housewife who takes money out of her purse. These factors interest Monsieur Marnas. This is a bond with the outside world that he has no inclination to cut. It is a bond that is concrete and immediate, but beneficent rather than maleficent. If only for its sake, Monsieur Marnas and the people of Peyrane should be helped to think in more constructive terms of their relationship with the rest of the world.

They might be helped if there were in Peyrane a strong force to counter the traditional attitudes. Perhaps it would help if there were an agent of articulation, an Articulator who could interpret Peyrane and the outside world to each other. For this task one would need patience, sympathy, intelligence, imagination. Especially imagination, for this is probably the quality that the people of Peyrane lack most seriously — the imagination to grasp abstract goals beyond their concrete experience. They need a Complicator who could show them that oversimplified solutions do more harm than good.

But who could serve as Articulator, as Complicator? It is a tragedy that every year the two or three children who show qualities of creative leadership are encouraged to move away to the city. Their potential influence is lost to the commune. Of course, almost every village suffers the same loss, but most villages have a teacher or priest or mayor to exercise leadership. Peyrane has been unfortunate in this respect. Teachers stay only until they can secure transfer to the city where they can find intellectual companionship and supplementary sources of income. The priests who have been sent to live out their purgatory in Peyrane have been old, tired, and resigned, and now there is no resident priest at all. No mayor has served as a real leader since Monsieur Prullière. Rivet is intelligent and imaginative, but he lacks patience and confidence.

The only possible leaders in Peyrane are Chanon and Edouard Pascal. Chanon is friendly and has the confidence of people, who trust him despite his party affiliation, because "he's not so bad underneath." But Chanon lacks the intelligence and imagination to exert positive influence, and although he showed real courage in the *maquis* he curls into a ball whenever Pascal deigns to snarl at him. Pascal has imagination and intelligence, but his sour disposition, his nasty tongue, and his contempt for the villagers make him the most powerful destructive force in the community. His influence only reinforces the psychological barriers that frustrate human coöperation. Politics always leads to personalities in Peyrane, and our attempt to elucidate the political behavior of the people has led us to the gloomy personality of Edouard Pascal.

To many an American the political behavior of the people of Peyrane is the most puzzling aspect of their culture. We have dwelt on it because it needs interpretation. However, by emphasizing this one factor we risk leaving a distorted impression. After all politics is only a small part — and the least attractive part — of the general pattern of life in Peyrane. If we look at the pattern as a whole, each element falls into its proper perspective, and the little corner of political behavior assumes its proper proportion. Seen as a whole, what is life in Peyrane?

Peyrane is a place where a person can live with himself. He sees himself in the perspective of time and nature. He thinks it is important to "see things as they are," and he readily acknowledges the unpleasant along with the pleasant aspects of existence. He knows that his knowledge and experience are limited, but he respects the pursuit of knowl-

edge both for its own sake and for the practical benefits he may derive
from it. He has a clear conception of his roles in life, and he makes
an effort to fulfil them without violating his inner needs. He enjoys
being with himself. He can sit alone with no other entertainment than
the contemplation of what goes on within him and around him. He
listens to the radio occasionally and goes to the movies and to church
now and then, but organized entertainment, comics, and pulp magazines do not interest him.

He also enjoys and is even stimulated by the company of other
individuals. His relations with other people and his observation of
their personal dramas bring warmth and excitement into his life. The
somewhat tolerant regulation of sexual expression keeps a certain balance between his needs and those of society. He accepts his emotions
but moderates them because he fears their extreme expression. He feels
anger readily, but anger rarely results in physical violence. A tongue
lashing usually brings sufficient release to calm him down, although
he may feel compelled to "cut the other person dead" for years. Peyrane is a community where crime is almost unknown, a community
with almost no homicide, suicide, theft, juvenile delinquency, or crim-
inal assault. Consumption of alcohol is general, but there is almost
no drunkenness.

Life in Peyrane is centered about the family, and the family is a
strong, healthy organism. Children are wanted. They are treated with
love, and they are carefully trained. There is little divorce. Old people
are cared for. The most solemn occasion of the year is the celebration of
All Souls' Day which unites the family about the family tomb. Formal
religion is given formal recognition, but the deepest religious feelings
relate directly to the family.

Peyrane is a hard-working, productive community. Though only
one-third of the land is profitably arable, though it is inefficiently distributed, and though there are few other important natural resources
in the commune, the people produce more than they consume. The
wealth of the community is rather evenly divided: no one is extremely
rich, and there is no misery. The health of the community is good.
Housing is poor, but everyone is sheltered. Clothes may be patched,
but everyone is clothed. Food is expensive, but everyone is fed.

If Adam and Eve were to return to life as they did in the Gaumont
movie, they might well choose Peyrane as their Paradise Regained.

Compared to most communities in the world today, Peyrane is well off. Its pattern of life seems balanced and sane. There is a bit of madness in the relationship of the Peyranais with the rest of the world. But when we look at life there and life elsewhere, it is not always clear on which side the madness lies.

Chapter 18

Peyrane Ten Years Later

As we drove into Peyrane for a return visit in the summer of 1959 we were surprised to find the way barred at the entry to the village. A sign directed all cars to a parking lot which turned out to be the old school yard now covered with macadam. We left our car there and walked up toward our old house. In the center of the streets of the village there were deep trenches where Algerians and Spaniards, yellow with ochre dust, were shoveling earth into mounds. Trenches branched off into the houses on either side of the streets. A zigzag of planks made a bridge for the workmen's wheelbarrows — and for the children who were playing follow-the-leader. In front of Madame Favre's a group of ochre-yellow workmen clustered, joking with the Favres who had come to the door to watch the activity.

Through the open doors of the houses one could see the reason for the upheaval. New porcelain sinks, water closets, and an occasional bathtub had recently been delivered and were being installed in each house by the masons of Peyrane. For years the Town Council had talked about having a sewage system in Peyrane, and at last it had come to pass. The village had not been torn up like this since 1912, when water was piped in from springs in the Luberon Mountain. Peyrane had been one of the first communities in the area to install running water; now in 1959 it was one of the first to put in a modern sewage system. The improvement of 1912 had been facilitated by the development of a new industry in the village, ochre mining. What economic justification could there be in 1959 for the installation of the sewers?

Certainly in 1951 it would have seemed unsound to think of this kind of improvement for the village of Peyrane. With technological progress the center of the commune seemed moribund. Even though the farms around it were moderately prosperous the village itself scarcely benefited from this prosperity because it had lost its function as economic center. Modern transportation enabled the farmers to sell their produce and do their marketing more efficiently in the commercial city and rail center, Cavaillon. Synthetic dyes had replaced ochre in the world market; the mines were closed and most of the workers had moved away. The village of Peyrane remained only the administrative center of its little commune. Farmers came there to vote and to fill out harvest declarations and applications for tractor fuel. Babies were brought for baptism to the church, and couples were married there. A few — very few — women came to the village for Mass on Sunday. Most of the children attended the village school. The little stores and café, however, served primarily the handful of civil servants and elderly people — remnants of the prosperous nineteenth-century village — who continued to inhabit the *bourg*. In many ways Peyrane had appeared to be a dying village. Why should a new sewage system be installed now?

By 1959 the village of Peyrane had found a new function which, curiously, developed from the depression it suffered, especially the depression of real estate prices. In 1950 the value of property in Peyrane was extremely low. Who would buy property in a village without a future? Americans? At that time the Notaire had suggested that I might be interested in acquiring an abandoned windmill and the whole hill on which it stood for $90. When the Charrins moved away from Peyrane in 1953 they wrote us asking if we did not want to own a bit of property in the community of which I was so fond. They offered to sell me their house and land for $450. When their next-door neighbors, the Leporattis, died, their house remained empty for months until it was finally sold for $500.

Most of the property in neighboring villages had suffered the same fate several years earlier, for they had not even had the ochre industry that kept the village of Roussillon alive until after the war. Gradually city people began to discover this cheap property. They found that for a few thousand francs they could buy an old house where they might spend vacations, in the southern sun far from the cold rain and exhaust-choked streets of Paris. For a few thousand francs more — though several times the sale price of the property — the house could be transformed into a quaint and convenient hideaway where Parisians could satisfy the traditional French urge to play at being peasants.

Villages that were almost completely dead and where property was cheapest were the first to be invaded by city people. By 1950 Oppède and Gordes had been "discovered." For $60 a sociologist from the Sorbonne bought a ruin in Gordes. He thought it was a two-story house, but on cleaning it out he found that it actually had five stories built into the side of the hill — the accumulation of centuries. For $2000 he transformed the ruin into a picturesque vacation spot. Proud at having this distinguished new citizen, the Town Council of Gordes bought the ruined property next door and gave it to the professor for a garden. Among his interesting neighbors was the painter Chagall. Of course, these intellectuals and artists were followed by other city people, and soon the property bargains in Gordes became rare.

As the prices rose and as artists fled from the non-artists, other villages in the region became refuges. Eventually it was the turn of the beautiful ochre-colored town of Peyrane — and the invasion by city people began. Real estate prices rocketed. Today the $90 windmill is not for sale; the Notaire told me that the present owner had just turned down an offer of $3000! The $450 Charrin house belongs to a well-known American violinist who would undoubtedly not sell it for ten times that amount. The $500 Leporatti house was sold for $3000. The tumble-down house of Mme. Favre, closed and deteriorating since her death twenty years ago, located in the least sunny corner of the town, would bring $2000 if the heirs could end their *brouille* and agree to sell it. The Notaire told me that vacant lots which could not be sold ten years ago for $150 are now worth $2000 an acre. In the midst of this real estate boom the installation of a sewage system is a sensible investment.

As Peyrane has developed its new function as a resort town the last vestiges of the former agricultural center have almost disappeared. Old Monsieur Jouvaud closed his smithy in 1951 and died a few months later. No one replaced him. Monsieur Prayal retired as blacksmith at the age of seventy, two years later. His son Roger, who had worked with him and was to succeed him, moved to Apt to work as a clerk in a hardware store. Since the farmers were selling their horses and buying tractors there was little to keep him in Peyrane. The Prayal smithy is boarded up.

Since all of the Prayals' nine children have left Peyrane to live elsewhere, the Prayals are understandably lonely, increasingly lonely since their old friends are fast disappearing. When we returned to Peyrane in 1961 we found the old couple sitting with their friend Madame Lanval on a bench in the shade outside the closed smithy. They found distraction in watching the tourists and summer people drive in and out of the village, but they must also have peopled the streets with memories of lost friends. In 1950 when we first went to Peyrane it seemed a town of older people. A quarter of the population was over sixty years old. Now many of these people have died. The joyous dean of the commune, Madame Pamard, la Mélanie, as she was called by everyone, died at the age of 102. Old Maucorps fell ill and was taken to the hospital in Apt. He lingered for a time, but without his truffle dog, his place in the café, and his frequently-filled glass of wine he soon lost the will to live. Most of his friends, the Lonely Ones, who used to inhabit the café, have also died. So have the more respected and prosperous farmers of the commune — M. Marnas, M. Pian, M. Anselme. So have most of the elderly widows whose black clothing was so characteristic a feature of the village. At the top of the hill in the old town there remains only Madame Lestapis, who seems unchanged and ready to take the place of la Mélanie as dean of the commune. With the disappearance of the older women Peyrane takes on a gayer air, for the younger women, even the widows, do not wear mourning as they used to. The young women dress more like city women, so there is little incongruity between the villagers and the tourists and summer people who gather beneath the gay umbrellas in front of the three cafés on the Place de la Mairie.

These umbrellas — along with the stainless steel *café espresso* machines — are the symbols of the new function as a resort town, for as a result of the changed economy the café business is booming. In 1950 there were two cafés, but one of them had so little business that it closed within a few months. Now, at least during the resort season, three cafés prosper, and there are a restaurant and an inn as well. In 1950 Julien Vincent had just moved to Peyrane to take over the old restaurant-hotel and was trying hard to make ends meet. Fortunately it was not long after his arrival that the transformation of Peyrane began. Indeed, he helped bring about the transformation, for within a few months his *civet de lièvre du Ventoux* and the view from the terrace of his restaurant were famous, and he eventually gained a starred reference in the *Guide Michelin*. His success was such that his only child, Georges Vincent, a star pupil in my English class in 1950, gave up the study of engineering and has returned home to learn his father's trade. By 1961 Georges was doing most of the cooking so that Julien was free to wander from table to table on a busy Sunday afternoon, receiving the compliments of the guests. By 1963 Georges had married, and his wife was learning from Mme. Vincent the complex métier of *patronne* — how to keep accounts, to manage servants, to soothe the kitchen, to treat each category of customer with the appropriate nuance of respect.

Madame Avenas, the beauty shop owner who opened a café when the Gaumont movie company came to Peyrane, has completely given up her original profession and has made a success in the hotel business. Under her adopted *nom de guerre,* "Maman Jeanne," she mothers the inhabitants of her *pension de famille.* Every room of this simple inn on the Place de la Mairie is full during vacation periods. In the winter the dining room is a gathering place for neighbors who have no television sets of their own.

Next to Maman Jeanne's, its umbrellaed tables continuing hers on the terrace, is the oldest café, the one which was run by Jean Voisin in 1951. When he gave up the business in 1953 he was succeeded by a Marseillais who ran a seafood stand in Paris during the winter but liked to return to his wife's home, Peyrane, so he might play boules during the summer. He eventually tired of the café business and moved away as soon as his tobacco license could be transferred to his successor, Robert Peretti. This was Robert's first venture into business; until then he had worked as a mason for Gaston Jouvaud. Now he is married to Jacqueline Favre, one of the little girls in my English class years ago, so that this café is the only one run by native Peyranais. It will undoubtedly serve even more effectively as the nerve center of the gossip system of the community.

There is still another café on the little Place de la Mairie, the Café du Castrum, owned by another Marseillais, who left the city for reasons of health. He also has a terrace with umbrellaed tables. On a hot summer day, when the tables of the three cafés are filled with summer people watching the boules games across the street, the atmosphere of Peyrane seems as gay as a scene from a musical comedy — gay, but just as artificial, for underneath there is a current of tension. The Marseillais proprietors especially keep a close eye on the customers of their competitors and maintain an efficient system of mental bookkeeping, so that they know just which customer takes a drink at which café, when and with whom. If you go to the Café du Castrum three times in a row without stopping for a drink at Maman Jeanne's or the Café des Sports you realize that the owners seem to avoid speaking to you as a punishment for favoring their competitor. Sometimes they even avoid speaking to each other, which makes for a complicated situation since they do live cheek by jowl — or at least umbrella by umbrella.

Furthermore, all three owners were ardent workers of the Communist Party. Since it is through political opposition that personal and business conflicts may most effectively be expressed in Peyrane, the ideological accord of these three ménages could not endure. It was reported that the problem was solved during the Poujade period by the action of the Avenases in embracing the cause of the Great Pierrot. This eased the conflict since their café stood between the other two and cushioned their relationship. City people, grafted onto village life, seem far to outdo the villagers in the intensity and complexity of their *brouilles*. Country life is not the Arcadia they expected to find when they moved from the city, and they take out their bitterness on each other.

The owners of the cafés and restaurants think their competition has been intensified within the last two years by the establishment of another inn. The finest house in the commune, the old Cavalier house, built by a prosperous notaire in the eighteenth century but neglected by the owners in recent years, has been taken over by an English architect who has turned it into an exquisite country inn with modern comforts as well as a beautiful view. Each of the few rooms has a bath and telephone, and the cuisine is good. As a matter of fact, the new inn — called *La Rose d'Or* — offers less competition than the other restaurant and café owners believe it does, for there is a division among the clientele coming to Peyrane. Maman Jeanne attracts the lower-middle-class people to her boarding house. The Café du Castrum really serves only snacks. Monsieur Vincent brings the tourists who follow the *Guide Michelin* and the *promeneurs* from all over the Vaucluse who drive to Peyrane for a special meal on Sunday or on holidays. The Rose d'Or fills a quite different role, for it attracts the well-to-do tourist who is enchanted by the picturesque village but nonetheless insistent on comfort.

The leaders of the Syndicat d'Initiative of Peyrane hope that the Rose d'Or may raise the aesthetic standards of the village. Most of the villages in the area which have become resort centers — Oppède, Gordes, Lourmarin, Murs — have not lost their characteristic architectural charm, but Peyrane seems somehow to have attracted too many whose taste led them to destroy the traditional simple architecture. In its place they have built the gingerbread houses so characteristic of the Riviera and of so much of French suburbia. This development is ironical, since Peyrane is *classé*, so that by law the plans of every change in the architecture of the village should have the approval of the Ministry of Fine Arts. When the village authorities have written to the Ministry to protest the construction of gingerbread houses painted salmon or apricot, however, they have received no answer. The local masons continue to build the houses according to the taste of the resorters, and the Town Council is strengthened in its belief that it never does any good to appeal to Paris for anything.

The most important effect the Ministry of Fine Arts has had on Peyrane was the seemingly interminable delay in the construction of the new school. The Ministry insisted that the building be in harmony with the traditional style and coloring of Peyrane, but the Ministry of Education refused to accept plans for any but a modern, well-lighted, well-ventilated school. Only after fifteen years was this conflict resolved, and finally in 1961 I had an opportunity to visit the new school, an excellent compromise between the two extremes at first envisaged. Built at the edge of town, not far from the Rose d'Or, the school with its simple lines and traditional ochre color blends with the tastefully reconstructed Cavalier house. Still the school has modern conveniences and sanitation. Big windows on the south flood the schoolrooms with the sun of the Midi.

The building was shown to us by the new principal, Madame Manuel, justly proud of her school. At last Peyrane has a teacher who is not only good at her job but has an active interest in the welfare of the whole community. Her husband, the nephew of a senator from a nearby community, has the movie business in the surrounding towns, and the people of Peyrane have shown their respect for him by electing him to the Town Council. The Manuels live with their four little girls in the new apartment built into the school, and it looks as though Peyrane may have acquired new, and badly needed, potential community leaders.

Of course, since someone always criticizes everything in Peyrane, there are criticisms of the new school. It looks more like a garage than a school building, it is said. This judgment must be taken with some skepticism, however, since a contractor from Avignon rather than a local mason was given the contract for constructing the school. But the masons of Peyrane need not complain, for they already have more work than they can do. In 1950 there were only two contractors in Peyrane; today there are three and a crew of helpers. They were even too busy to help remodel the Rose d'Or, so outside workers were brought in. Not only is there the continuing task of remodeling the old village houses for the summer people — and even for the people of Apt, who find it pleasant to live on the red hill and commute to work in the city — but there is a great deal of building going on in the farms around the village. Peyrane, like most of France, has undergone an architectural transformation in the last few years.

Naturally the building boom has brought prosperity to the masons of

Peyrane. Jouvaud, the most popular mason, has sold his neat house in the village and built himself another one, larger, more modern, more ornate, a kilometer from the village. Emile Pian, Jouvaud's first assistant, has gone into business for himself and has been so successful that he would like at least to remodel his house, but he cannot find time to work on the project because of the two activities that now absorb his extra time — television and traveling.

Television came to Peyrane in the late fifties, when a transmitter was erected on the Luberon Mountain in order to bring the Marseille programs to the communities of the valley around Apt. Emile bought a set at once, or rather he brought it home and paid for it on the installment plan over a period of twelve months. This sort of transaction was new to him and contrary to his family training and tradition, according to which one should never buy on credit. Now, however, he is convinced that he has been foolish all these years to stay out of debt. "The way prices keep going up," he said, "it's stupid not to get what you want when you want it — within reason, of course." Since every year he has more business and there seems to be no end of it, the future appears less insecure. His attitude is that of the younger people of Peyrane, an attitude new to Peyrane since 1950 when the blacksmith Prayal had said to me: "No one here will ask for credit if he can avoid it. No one wants to be obligated to anyone."* Most of the television sets operating in Peyrane were bought on the installment plan. How many are there? In 1961 the postman, Francis Favre, did me the favor of counting them as he made his rounds. He reported twenty-three sets in the village and seventeen on the farms.

The effect of television on community life is noteworthy. The farmer Paulin never used to miss a boules tournament. Yet I met him on Sunday afternoon in the summer of 1959 walking toward home instead of to the café where a tournament was being organized. "I don't play much any more," he said when I asked him about this change in his habits. "Sometimes I watch, but not much because it's mostly just the resort people playing boules. I'd rather stay at home and watch a good program on the *télé.*"

When I met Paulin I had just come from Emile Pian's, where we had had a big Sunday dinner. The dinner had been delicious, complicated, and so prolonged that Emile had barely been able to contain himself while the coffee was served. He wanted to turn on the television set. An international

* See above, p. 183.

swimming meet in Paris took the place of the conversation we used to
have over coffee.

In the evening I dropped into the Café des Sports, hoping especially to see
Pascal and the Avenases, who used to meet there every evening for a few
games of belote. Neither was there.

"They both have the *télé*," Gavaret said, "so they don't come around in
the evening very often."

Television seems to have atomized still further the social contacts of the
people of Peyrane, which were already badly fragmented in 1950. However,
the Peyranais who watch television instead of playing boules with their
neighbors and gossiping about village affairs no doubt feel as though they
have more in common with Frenchmen in general who are also watching
the swimming meet in Paris. This is only one example of many influences
which act upon the people of Peyrane to increase their sense of integration
with the rest of France today.

Now that Emile Pian has a different attitude toward buying on credit
and being in debt he has satisfied another long-standing desire: he travels.
In 1959 his wife and he thought nothing of driving to a remote corner
of the department on their new scooter to visit friends and relations, and
by 1961 he had acquired a Citroën 2CV truck so that his son and parents-in-
law could go along, too. (Of course, the truck serves him in his business
on weekdays.) In 1950 we had taken the Pians to call on Emile's mother
and sister, who live on a farm in the next commune; they had not seen
each other for months. Now they see each other at least once a week. The
Pians also make frequent trips to another neighboring village where they
never used to go, Saint-Saturnin, to swim in the municipal swimming pool,
the new pool built by the government. (According to the Peyranais, Saint-
Saturnin has a government pool because the senator lives there!) The day
of the boules tournament Emile was not playing because Madeleine and
he had gone off with their family to the top of Mount Ventoux, the big
mountain that dominates the Vaucluse landscape. Before he got his scooter
he had climbed Mont Ventoux once. Last year they made the trip twice,
and now they have pushed their horizons back into other departments of
the Midi.

The new cars in Peyrane have destroyed the picturesque automobile
array we saw in 1951. Pascal still has his 1923 Citroën, and its motor
purrs as beautifully as ever, but most of the other old cars have disappeared.
The development of transportation has also destroyed another picturesque
vestige of the past: the Volunteer Fire Company of Peyrane is now

obsolete! The Town Council decided it was more efficient to pay for the services of the better-trained and equipped firemen in the city of Apt, five miles away, than to maintain its independent corps and equipment. The Apt firemen can, it is claimed, reach Peyrane almost as fast as the Peyrane volunteers can assemble. So the volunteers were disbanded. There are no more Sunday maneuvers on the Place de l'Ecole, no more *gueuletons* at Vincent's restaurant on Saint Barbara's Day, no firemen's spring festival. The firemen rather bitterly protest that the change was politically inspired: most of them were Communist and the Town Council had a Radical majority. But they are easily consoled, for most of them are married now and preoccupied with family responsibilities. Their successors, the young bachelors of today, do not complain because they are less dependent on local activities to fill up their leisure time. They prefer to get on their "motos" and go dancing in Cavaillon.

The modernization of transportation has had an important effect on another institution. It keeps the church from being closed. The Curé Autrand died in 1953, and the diocesan authorities decided that a priest could no longer be supported in Peyrane. The rectory was closed, and arrangements were made for a missionary priest at a nearby mission training school to carry on the rudiments of religious life in Peyrane as well as in neighboring villages whose religious practice and financial contributions are minimal. The faithful of Peyrane were made responsible for driving the Father up from Notre-Dame-de-la-Lumière to Peyrane on Sunday morning, however.

The question arose who might transport the Father. A score or two of people attend Mass, but since normally women do not drive and since only two men go to Mass the choice of drivers was limited. Edouard Pascal had no car, so Lucien Bourdin inevitably had the finger of responsibility pointed at him. He accepted the task of driving to Notre-Dame-de-la-Lumière every Sunday morning and bringing Father Bertin to Peyrane; afterward he delivered him to Goult for Mass there.

Bourdin had no real objections. He is a bachelor and without family responsibilities. He rather enjoyed his conversations with Father Bertin. However, as the weeks passed he felt more and more ashamed of being a *poire* (sucker). At Mass he could see all the women whose husbands had cars and who should be taking turns with him — Bonerandi, Jouvaud, Favre, Vincent — and the idea possessed him that all four had newer cars than he and could more easily afford to buy gas.

Finally he went to see Vincent and explained his point of view frankly.

Vincent is no anticlerical, so he took the suggestion well. However, he pointed out to Bourdin that the restaurant and church businesses were irreconcilable. The chef's biggest day is Sunday, so from four o'clock Sunday morning until four o'clock Sunday afternoon the chef must be in his kitchen. He cannot even go to Mass, not to speak of driving to Notre-Dame-de-la-Lumière to fetch Father Bertin.

Bourdin found this reasonable, so he went to see Léon Favre. Favre is foreman at the ochre mine in Apt and is free on Sunday. Besides, although he is one of the leading Communists in Peyrane, he has never been actively anticlerical. There are only two Communist families in Peyrane who refuse on principle to send their children to catechism, and Favre has little sympathy with these ardent city Communists who have moved to the village and try to run things. His wife and daughter go to Mass, and his son is a choir boy. He took Bourdin's proposal gently, but two days later told him he had thought it over and decided he could not coöperate. It was one thing not to object to religious activity of members of his family: that was tolerance. But actively to further the work of the Church, a formidable anti-Communist institution, was more than could be asked of him. That would be really inconsistent with his principles.

Bourdin also found this point of view reasonable, so he went to see Jouvaud. Jouvaud's wife, daughter, and mother-in-law go to Mass. He is not a Communist, so he ought not have scruples about lending a hand. However, Bourdin did not have a chance to explain his point of view fully, for the shrewd Jouvaud understood from his first words what was about to be asked:

"Listen, Bourdin," he said, "we masons have more work than we can do in a six-day week. I work on Sunday, and I go to work in my truck. If the priest needs a car for his work he should get his own instead of sponging off of us."

Bourdin tried a last time. Bonerandi's women go to Mass. He has always been anti-Communist. He does not work on Sunday. Bourdin did not go to see him first because he is considered one of the least obliging persons in the community, but Bourdin hoped he might be sympathetic this once. This was a foolish notion, as Bourdin told me later:

"Bonerandi just laughed at me and said I could be a sucker if I wanted, but he wasn't going to join me. If his women wanted a priest, they could use a wheelbarrow to fetch him."

With this insult flung at him Bourdin gave up, and he even gave up

going for Father Bertin. He was not going to be considered the village
poire. He was through, and he told the Father this the next Sunday. A
week later Father Bertin appeared in a "new" secondhand 2CV Citroën.
Of course, this led to the inevitable rumor that the missionaries were making so much money in Peyrane and the neighboring villages that they were
buying cars and living high. Bourdin does not know how the car was
acquired, but he is relieved not to have this problem on his conscience
any more.

From this episode it is obvious that one aspect of Peyrane life persists
amid all the economic, technological and architectural change: human
relations in the village seem about the same. Perhaps the coming of the
city people has made the general atmosphere even tenser, for they seem
to get along together even less well than the people who were born and
raised in the commune.

However, I know now that there are fewer old-time Peyranais living in
Peyrane than I thought when I wrote the book. Then I was aware that
only one-quarter of the population was born in the commune, but I have
since learned that there is even more demographic change than I suspected.
In the summer of 1959 I went over the census of 1954 with Marcel Rivet,
who took the time to tell me what had happened to every individual who
had left the commune in those five years. We had already equivalent statistics for 1946–1951, so this gave me two comparable five-year periods.
Various patterns of migration appeared. Then, by making a card for every
person present in the village at these four points in time, I discovered
several interesting and quite unpredictable facts. The first was the large
number of people who had lived in Peyrane between 1946 and 1959. Although there were never more than 779 at any one moment there were
1150 cards in my files, representing 1150 Peyranais living in the commune
at one, at least, of my points of time, 1946, 1951, 1954, 1959. But I knew
that many people had moved into Peyrane and moved away without being
counted at any of the four points in time. Actually, then, there were far
more than 1150 people who during the thirteen-year period had lived in
Peyrane long enough to call it their home. It would take extensive research
in the town archives to determine just how many, but there may well have
been as many as 3000! So when we make the assumption that the population of the commune simply dwindled from 779 to 680 between 1946 and
1959 we wrongly imagine that a few people left but most of the others
stayed. We assume there must be a sort of permanent population core of

about 700 people. Nothing could be farther from the truth. The population is constantly transformed by migration to and from the commune.

But of all the individuals living in Peyrane during the thirteen-year period from 1946 to 1959, how many lived there for all thirteen years? Only 275! And of these, 137 were not born in Peyrane! At this point I begin to wonder what I mean when I refer to "the people of Peyrane." It seems now that this expression refers primarily to the small number of people who apparently remain in the community and transmit its culture to the many individuals who move in, remain for a few months or years, and then move away.

It may be imagined that Peyrane is less stable than most rural communities, and this idea is reinforced by the periodic changes in its economy emphasized in this book. To gain a point of comparison a parallel study has been started in a very conservative community in western France, but there also we are amazed to learn that there is far more demographic turmoil than expected and almost as much as in Peyrane. It begins to look as though our traditional image of the stable rural community is an inaccurate one, developed principally by middle-class city people nostalgic for a stability they lack but which they wrongly ascribe to rural communities.

It is not hard to see how this illusion is created. When I return to Peyrane and see old Madame Favre — la Léoncie — sitting in the same chair in the town square surrounded by the other women of her gossip circle, I have the impression that nothing has changed. When I go into the café and find Henri Favre standing at the bar where I said goodbye to him ten years ago, I have a feeling of continuity. This is true even though the members of Madame Favre's gossip group have changed, even though the owner of the café and the men standing at the bar beside Henri Favre are not the same ones who used to be there. On seeing old friends we have a sense of stability. The truth is, however, that except for this small core of villagers who do not move away there are few people who have spent their whole life in Peyrane.

It is surprisingly difficult to generalize even about this core population. In many ways they seem like all the other, but more transient, Peyranais. Some of them own property; some do not. Some are powerful in the community; some are among the most humble citizens. It is interesting to point out, however, that most members of the Town Council are members of the core population. In the municipal election of 1959 nineteen of the twenty-six candidates were members of the core, a far larger percentage of the population than one would expect by chance. Ten of the thirteen winning candidates were from the core group. Two of the three others were understandable exceptions: one was Julien Pecquet, a Parisian man of letters and functionary, who had become interested in Peyrane; the other was Jean Manuel, the husband of the new schoolteacher and nephew of a senator from the Vaucluse. With these exceptions the representatives of the core population dominated the election.

Since the election of 1959 offers a good opportunity to illustrate both change and stability in Peyrane's human relations I should like to describe it here in some detail. It was a particularly bitter election in spite of the determination of several leaders of the community to avoid the usual battle. Because of the tension in personal relationships in Peyrane, the Notaire and Edouard Pascal, President of the *Syndicat d'Initiative,* decided it would be unfortunate for the reputation of the community and harmful to the resort business to allow a bitter election battle. But how could there be an election without a battle? Whether they actually thought in terms of providing a local de Gaulle for Peyrane, no one told me, but it is clear that Pascal must have had the national political situation in mind when he sought a means to avoid a squabble. The Notaire and he developed a plan so that an outsider, someone "above it all," a non-partisan or rather suprapartisan leader could be elected mayor. To achieve this goal it was necessary to persuade all political factions to agree on a common slate of candidates. Then there would be no bitter battle.

Pascal went first to call on Mayor Ginoux, who offered no resistance to the plan. He had been mayor since the war and had had his fill of criticism, and besides, his health was poor. He was not, he said, planning to run for re-election under any circumstances. Of course, this is what any mayor would have said in his place, and it would still not have prevented him from accepting the nomination if the voters had insisted. No one insisted this time. One of the mayor's strongest points had been that he was the friend of the departmental deputies, Lussy and Daladier, but they had been defeated by Gaullist candidates a few months before. The mayor's reputation for having pull in the right places suffered accordingly. There was no popular move to draft him for the election.

With the mayor out of the picture Pascal could go directly to the heads of the political groups of the commune, those who were identified with national parties more out of convenience and because of vague ideological association than because of real affiliation or loyalty. The MRP's, the smallest group in the commune, were no problem, since Pascal himself was the most influential spokesman. The largest and most important group to win over were the Communists, against whom all other groups usually must combine forces in order to win. Chanon, the leader of the Communists, was the most serious obstacle to the formation of a single slate, but it turned out that he accepted it easily. It seemed to Chanon that the plan gave his group real power in the community without giving him the onerous task of serving as mayor. He had had enough of that after the war.

Pascal's plan gave Chanon and his followers a strong influence on the community. The new mayor, Peyrane's de Gaulle, whoever that might be, could not be expected to live in Peyrane and concern himself with day-to-day business in the Town Hall. But he was not really needed for this function. Rivet already ran the practical affairs of the commune by himself. If he needed advice and confirmation he could turn to the two assistant mayors. And who would they be? The heads of the two largest political groups, of course. Chanon would be the first assistant mayor, and the second would be Madame Baume, the retired schoolteacher who represented the tradition of the Socialist Party in the neighborhood. In effect, therefore, Rivet would run the commune under the direction of Chanon and Mme. Baume. The new mayor, the Outsider, would offer them an *umbrella* by accepting responsibility for their decisions, and he would actually intervene only to settle a dispute.

Madame Baume was as enthusiastic over Pascal's plan as Chanon was. (Indeed, some believed that it was originally her own idea.) It corresponded to the formula that had made the French civil service work so efficiently for centuries: give the power to a local functionary, but cover him by attributing the responsibility to an official living in Paris!

But who could be Peyrane's de Gaulle? As President of the Syndicat d'Initiative Pascal had over the years developed a wide acquaintance with intellectuals, some of whom he had already attracted to Peyrane. Among the property owners in the commune were a German painter, a Dutch photographer, an American violinist, a French novelist who worked in the Unesco office, a Canadian journalist and member of the Académie Franco-Canadienne, an architect from Moulins, a sub-préfect from Paris. They had even started a literary review — *Soleils* — with Peyrane as its editorial headquarters. In this group was Jean Pecquet, a government employee, formerly high in a ministry in Paris, who owned property in the nearby town of Cabrière d'Avignon. He was responsible, well-liked but uncommitted to any group. Pascal persuaded him to accept nomination to the Town Council with the understanding that the Council would elect him mayor after the election. His name would appear on the ballot of the single party, set up under the name "Consolidated Slate for the Commonweal of Peyrane," along with other nominees chosen among the most "serious" citizens of Peyrane regardless of party identification.

There remained a stumbling block, however, for still another political group remained to be consulted — the small group of conservatives, of whom the most influential was Julien Vincent. These people were regarded as the old Gaullists, that is, those who had continued to support his ideas from 1946 to 1958, although some of them had momentarily been attracted to Poujade. Since their principal idea was that France needed a strong hand to rid it of political differences, it might have been assumed that they would accept a de Gaulle-like solution to the problems of Peyrane.

Nevertheless when Pascal talked to Vincent he met with a determined refusal. What took place during the interview is a matter of conjecture. It depends on whether you accept Pascal's or Vincent's version — or one of numerous other versions circulating in Peyrane. At any rate, Vincent's reasons for refusing to coöperate were clear. As a matter of principle he opposed any alliance between Catholics and Communists: it was unnatural and immoral. Furthermore, it would have been logical for Vincent himself to become mayor, or at least first assistant mayor instead of Chanon. In the previous election he had been elected to the Town Council by a strong majority. In the past nine years he had put Peyrane on the map by giving it a first-class restaurant, and he had literally put it on the prestigious maps of the *Guide Michelin*. In many ways he had taken the lead in the transformation of Peyrane. He had even revived the village soccer team, paid for clearing the old field and repairing the shower house, supported the team which, captained by his son, won the regional championship. It was only logical that he should assume more official responsibility in the affairs of the community, so his friends and he had decided to present their own list of candidates in the election.

Pascal argued with Vincent but could not make him change his stand. Chanon went to see him. Madame Baume went to see him. Rivet and the Notaire went to see him. It was even suggested that Vincent become second assistant mayor in the new administration. But Vincent would accept no compromise. He would have no part in bringing in an outsider from Paris as mayor. Above all, he would not join hands with the Communists. Let Edouard Pascal, a practicing Catholic who went to Mass every Sunday, accept such an alliance. He, Vincent, had a conscience with a longer memory.

We now see the ideological positions defined and the battle lines drawn up, but if we remain at this political level we shall not really understand the situation. Since political disputes serve primarily to express hidden and inexpressible antagonisms, we cannot understand the situation without knowing what Vincent's relations were with each of the people who had come to labor with him. We must also know about the economic and social evolution of the farmers around the village, and this was not even mentioned during the election, even though it was a primary factor.

So far as personal relations are concerned, we already know of the antipathy between Rivet and Vincent. It had been inevitable from the time Rivet had given up running the restaurant in 1950 and had become Town Clerk. Their relationship had been proper but cool. Aware that there were deep reasons for mutual antagonism, they made sure that there was "nothing between them."

Pascal, on the other hand, had for years been an ally of Vincent's, and it was partly through the Syndicat d'Initiative that the fame of Vincent's restaurant was spread. But as Peyrane grew in fame and attracted more and more artists and intellectuals and sub-prefects, it became obvious to members of the Syndicat d'Initiative that Vincent's restaurant needed a face-lifting. It was dingy, and the belief was that Vincent was not interested in beautifying the restaurant to turn it into a first-rate establishment. Disagreement on this issue grew into estrangement, so that when Pascal organized a banquet of the editors and collaborators of *Soleils,* Peyrane's literary review, he made arrangements not *chez* Vincent, but — of all places — in the little dining room of Maman Jeanne's *pension de famille!* This obviously brought to an end the collaboration between Vincent and Pascal.

As for remodeling the restaurant, Vincent carefully explained, whenever· anyone suggested the possibility, that he would like nothing better than to invest his savings in an operation that might put his restaurant into a higher Michelin category. Unfortunately, the property belonged not to him but to Madame Baume, the sister-in-law of the retired schoolteacher who was now trying to run the politics of the town. The Baumes had refused to listen to any idea for improving the property and thereby contributing to the progress of Peyrane. Madame Baume not only refused to sell him the property; she would not give him a long enough lease to let him transform it and still get his money out of it. Pascal and the boosters of Peyrane might do better to try to overcome the backwardness of Madame Baume instead of going off to have their literary banquets in a boarding house run by a Marseillaise hairdresser turned cook.

An even more bitter blow had come from the Notaire, who had been instrumental in getting the old Cavalier house turned into the Rose d'Or. Everyone agreed that Vincent's cuisine was better than that of the Rose d'Or, but competition was serious because the Rose d'Or attracted a prosperous foreign clientèle to whom the delightful modern inn particularly appealed.

Between Chanon and Vincent there was also a personal hostility that lay beneath the ideological disagreement. As a farmer and as a Communist, Chanon represented the interests of both the rural population of the commune and the poorer people of the village. Among both these groups Vincent had acquired the reputation of haughtiness. It was said that when the more humble people came to Vincent's to arrange for baptism and wedding banquets he discouraged them by raising his prices. Consequently they stopped coming, and more and more people began to celebrate their baptisms and marriages at home. To this development Vincent was rumored to have replied: "The peasants would rather celebrate their daughters' marriages in a stable than in a proper place." Whether he actually said this or not, it poisoned the relationship between Chanon and Vincent.

Under these circumstances it is scarcely surprising that Vincent should have reacted as he did when Rivet, Pascal, Madame Baume, the Notaire and Chanon came one by one to persuade him to support their single election ticket and a Parisian as mayor. Far from accepting the proposal he fought it.

Vincent had an ally in Louis Borel, a self-made man and one of the most prosperous entrepreneurs in the region, as we have seen.* Every time we returned to Peyrane we found that his business and his establishment had grown. His filling station became a garage. He built more and more vats to store the cherries which he buys from local farmers at the peak of the season and later sells to canners in Apt when prices are highest. He acquired more trucks to transport the asparagus, melons and beans which he buys from the farmers and sells at the regional market in Cavaillon. He now trucks fertilizers and insecticides into Peyrane and sells

* See above, p. 176.

them to the farmers. In the 1953 election he was elected for the first time
to the Town Council. At that time Vincent and he were on different
slates—Vincent on the conservative list and Borel on the Communist. Since
then, however, Borel had given up his Communist connections, first supporting Poujade and then de Gaulle.

The alliance between Borel and Vincent seemed natural, since both of
them had done so much for the economy of Peyrane. Why should the
voters of the commune not support two of the most "serious" citizens?
They had in their favor two issues that could not fail to harm their
opponents: the interference of Parisians in the affairs of the village and the
unholy alliance of Catholic conservatives and Communists on the opposing
ticket. Furthermore, Borel and Vincent had been active in supporting de
Gaulle in the fall of 1958; they could profit from the momentum of this
movement. Accordingly, they decided to oppose the move toward political
unity in Peyrane and to form a list of their own. They recruited Bonerandi
(Poujadist-Gaullist baker and father of Borel's son-in-law), Aubenas
(former Socialist-Radical assistant mayor) and seven farmers who were
on good terms with Borel.

When it became known that Vincent and Borel had formed a separate
slate it was assumed that the original plan for unity would not work,
because Pecquet had assured Pascal he would run for the Council and
accept the office of mayor only if he were elected as head of a single,
unopposed slate. He did not want to get involved in politics. He was
persuaded nevertheless to let his name remain on the ballot. He need not
become involved. Indeed, he could and should remain "above it all" so
that when he was elected he could carry on in a detached de Gaulle-like
manner.

In Pascal's opinion there was no doubt as to the outcome of the election.
On the unity ticket there were in addition to Pecquet the three leading
Communists, two conservative Catholics and seven of the most "serious"
men of the commune, vaguely Socialist-Radical in tendency, representing
both village and farm. They had with them Jouvaud, the most popular
contractor and builder in the commune. More important, Pascal realized
that Vincent and Borel had committed the most serious social crime of
Peyrane. Not only were they successful, but they had — rightly or
wrongly — acquired the reputation of being *fier* (proud). Furthermore,
Borel had alienated the Communists by detaching himself from their
group. He also suffered the fate of all middlemen; even though people

need the services of a middleman they resent the fact that he makes a living from buying and selling what they produce. Borel's vats and trucks and garage were tangible reminders of his commercial success and his political weakness.

With this background we can readily understand why the campaign was one of the most murderous in years. It is unnecessary to recount the events of the campaign itself and especially the "petites histoires" that were used as evidence in this slanderous contest. As a matter of fact, it would undoubtedly be libelous to record them here.

The surprising thing is that down to the moment the votes were counted, each side thought that it was winning the election. Any inkling of the outcome was obscured by the heat of the campaign. It turned out that the whole struggle was extremely one-sided, for Vincent and Borel were pitilessly crushed. The Parisian, Pecquet, received 292 votes, Chanon 297, while Vincent received only 119 and Borel 116. The weakest candidate on the coalition slate got 248, and the strongest of the Vincent-Borel slate 133. For Vincent and Borel *c'était la catastrophe!* And the worst part of the defeat was that they had to stay to watch the votes counted even though it was obvious from the beginning what the outcome would be. Partisans of the coalition told me — somewhat too gleefully — that even they began to feel sorry for the two men who sat in a daze at the counting table with everyone around snickering at what had happened.

When I saw the Borels and Vincents a few months after the election it was obvious that the experience had been racking. The Borels preferred not to talk about it. The Vincents were bitter: "To think that people would act like that! . . . We don't go out much any more (Nous ne fréquentons presque plus) and just stick to our business. Oh, Monsieur, it's lucky we know how to take it (heureusement qu'on est philosophe)!"

When one hears an analysis of the election from the main participants, it would seem that it had been an ideological quarrel motivated by personal interests, but as I went out into the country and talked to the farmers I realized the importance of the changed economic situation and state of mind of the farm people in the commune. They have a new awareness of their professional status and dignity, which is reflected in the growth of their professional organizations and in their sense of solidarity with farmers elsewhere. They are no longer peasants, awed and overwhelmed by villagers and city people; they feel superior to the local squabbles of village and regional politics. Although some of the farmers had been persuaded to run for office, and although once the campaign began almost no one could keep from becoming emotionally involved, this very involvement intensified the farmers' conviction that the old game of politics was no longer for them.

When I went to talk with Marc Peyre, the manager of the Tractor Coöperative, he was so eager to show me the new garage built by the coöp at the fork in the road leading into town that it was difficult to get him interested in telling me about the election. It was not until later that I realized the connection between the prosperity of the coöp and his indifference to politics.

Marc has been with the coöperative since it was begun in 1945. When we lived in Peyrane in 1950 it had one tractor and two plows for its forty-eight members from Peyrane and the surrounding communes. When we returned to Peyrane in 1959 it had three tractors and three full-time employees. By 1961 it owned the big new garage that Peyre was showing me with such pride, and there were 225 members. The organization owned a whole assortment of plows for different kinds of soils and crops. Peyre wrote out the following list of additional equipment that had been acquired with the aid of government loans:

1 diesel bulldozer
1 diesel caterpillar tractor for plowing
1 diesel caterpillar tractor for vineyards
3 diesel wheel tractors of different horsepowers
1 gasoline tractor for towing
2 asparagus earthing machines
1 gyropulverizer
3 rotavators
1 forage press
1 grain harvester
1 rotor for subsoiling the earth

(All this equipment was in addition, of course, to the tractors owned by individual farmers in Peyrane — fifty-seven, of which thirty-three were modern diesels. And in 1950 there had been scarcely a tractor in the commune!)

As Peyre kept talking about the coöperative I kept trying to get him to tell me about the Town Council elections. Finally he grew a bit exasperated and said:

"Look! That election took place two years ago, and even then I tried not to get involved in it. There was quite a squabble up in the village, but

1. Why a new sewage system?

2. Old houses become 'new' summer homes.

3. The retired blacksmith and his wife sit with Madame Lanval and watch the tourists.

4. *Place de la Mairie is a gay resort center.*

5. Vincent's restaurant has a star in the Guide Michelin.

6. Madame Jeanne's pension de famille is full all summer long.

7. Peyre blocks the road with his tractor.

8. The most stable element in Peyrane is the way in which the children are brought up.

the people up there have time to squabble. In the country we're more serious."

"But surely it mattered to you who was going to run the commune," I replied.

"The people in the village think they're running things just as they always did, but they aren't! If I want something done, do I go see the mayor? No, I go to Avignon and talk with Monsieur Mauron, the head of the Services Agricoles of the département. For money do we go to the notaire? We don't even go to the banks in Apt any more. We go see Maître Rouvière. He's president of the Crédit Agricole."

"But just the same, how did the farmers vote?"

"How could a farmer have voted for Vincent? And how could a member of the coöperative have voted for Borel? It's not the old political game; times have changed. You know how we get things done!" And he pointed to a placard standing in the corner of his office. It read:

C. U. M. A.

de P E Y R A N E

Je représente

250 petites

exploitations

familiales

manacées de

disparaître

par M. DEBRÉ

OUVRIERS PAYSANS

U N I S S E Z - V O U S !*

---

* C.U.M.A. (Coöperative d'utilisation du matériel en commun, i.e., tool-sharing coöperative) of Peyrane: I represent 250 little farms threatened with extinction by M. Debré. Peasant workers, UNITE!

I knew exactly what Peyre meant because two weeks earlier I had seen similar placards in western France. Exasperated by the governmental agricultural policies, and blaming them on de Gaulle's prime minister Michel Debré, the farmers of France had organized a mass demonstration. They blocked the roads with their tractors. They paraded in the streets of the département capitals. Then sent delegations to call on government officials. I took part in the demonstration in Angers with the farmers from the village of Chanzeaux. Although a few of the more rowdy demonstrators (not from Chanzeaux) tried to throw potatoes through the windows of the préfecture as a reminder that potato growers were not getting a fair price, generally these mass demonstrations were dignified and effective. My Chanzeaux friends had carried placards reading:

DEBRÉyons Chanzeaux!*

PARITÉ

des PRIX AGRICOLES

et

des PRIX INDUSTRIELS**

TOUS UNIS contre la POLITIQUE
GOUVERNEMENTALE†

It was impressive that the farmers of France had united in this demonstration. In Angers, the conservative, Catholic farmers of Chanzeaux marched figuratively shoulder to shoulder with the Communist farmers of Vaucluse in Avignon. Furthermore, it was obvious that French farmers were in agreement that if they wanted action there was nothing to be gained by talking to elected officials. Instead they paraded in front of the departmental préfecture and entrusted their various union officers with the responsibility of seeking appropriate administrative action to change the agricultural policies. At last they had come to feel that their most effective political representatives were not the traditionally elected officers —

---

* A pun implying: Let's rid Chanzeaux of Debré!
** "Parity for agricultural and industrial prices."
† All united against the government policy.

deputies and senators — but farmers themselves who had been elected to office in professional organizations. This is what Peyre meant when he pointed to the placard and said, "You know how we get things done."

In talking with Peyre it became obvious that one of the principal reasons for the defeat of Vincent and Borel in the municipal elections was that they represented the old style of political behavior. The farmers of Peyrane had voted against them not only because they had the reputation of being *"fier,"* or because Borel was a successful middleman between the local producer and the market, but because the farmers had lost faith in the old political game. They voted for the ticket that seemed to promise a successful, though non-political-solution to their problems.

The same trend characterized the national elections of November 1962. I was in Chanzeaux for the campaign and was struck primarily by the fact that all six candidates for député disassociated themselves from the traditional parties in order to court the voters. What was generally called a personal victory for de Gaulle was in fact due less to enthusiasm for him than to distaste for his political opponents. In Paris after the election I had lunch with Mayor Pecquet of Peyrane who brought news of the campaign in the Vaucluse. Superficially the election in Peyrane had been the opposite of that in Chanzeaux, for in Chanzeaux the Gaullist candidate had won while in the Peyrane the Gaullist incumbent (our old druggist from the city of Apt, M. Santoni) was defeated by a Communist-Socialist-Radical coalition. However, as Mayor Pecquet and I discussed the campaign, I realized that beneath the party labels the elections in the two communities had much the same significance. In Peyrane the winning coalition was the same which had rejected the traditional political game in the municipal elections of 1959. In 1961 they still remained united, even though it was against a Gaullist candidate who normally might have been considered the non-political candidate. In Peyrane the staunchest Gaullists were Vincent and Borel and Bonerandi. In Chanzeaux the voters had supported the Gaullist candidate who was opposed by candidates of more traditional politics. In both communities the principal implication of the election was that the voters had had enough of traditional politics and political representatives.

The economic and professional development of Peyrane's farmers, the purchase of matériel by organizations and by individuals, the prosperity of both the coöperative and the middleman Borel, all imply an important change in the point of view of the farmers. In 1950 they still raised wheat

and refused to plant fruit trees, even though agricultural experts insisted
that trees were better suited to the soil and climate than grain. Lucien
Bourdin had explained their resistance to change: "Plant orchards so that
the Americans and Russians can use them for a battlefield? Thanks. Not
so dumb!"* The farmers had not felt secure enough about the future to
plant something that would take several years to produce income. They
might not even be there in several years — the trees, the farmers, or the
farmers' children.

But in 1961 as I stood at the top of the hill overlooking the countryside
of the commune, I could see fruit orchards in every direction. Not only
had the farmers planted apricot and apple trees, but they had even
replanted many of the old olive groves that had been killed in the great
cold spell of 1956. The new olive trees would not bear for twenty years.
It is true that the government granted subsidies for replanting the olive
groves, but the farmers would not have used valuable land for a crop with
so long deferred income if they had not had more confidence in the future
than they had in 1950.

However, I have come to realize that in 1950 in Peyrane, as in all of
France, the morale had probably never been lower. The dream that had
kept the French going from 1940 to 1945 was that after the war France
would return to the mythical age of happiness symbolized by the expression
"before the first war." By 1950 it was obvious that this was impossible.
Political squabbles, technological change, changes in family structure, housing problems, the dissolution of the French union, the growing strife in
Algeria — everything seemed to have got worse rather than better. Even
the value of gold, the last refuge of the distrustful, dipped to a new low in
1950. Still the old dream of a return to an imagined golden age paralyzed
creative initiative.

The characteristic Peyranais attitude had been a shrug of the shoulders
and the expression: "C'est comme ça!" At length, however, despair became
so great that even the dream of returning to a golden age died. Once
there was no more hope of turning back, once the inevitability of change
was accepted, it at last became possible for people to devote their energy
to seeking new solutions for their problems. People acquired a greater
sense of freedom to act for their own welfare. The rejection of the old
political system, the modernization of the farms, the tractor demonstrations,
the development of farmers' organizations are to a certain extent, mani-

* See above, p. 33.

festations of this changed spirit. Paradoxically, the confidence of 1963 had grown from the despair of 1950.

This is not only a change in the attitude of the Peyranais. It must not be forgotten that there had actually been a change in the population itself. Obviously many of those who clung most tenaciously to the old dream were the older generations who dominated the community in 1950. Today, most of these people have either died or retired. Their places have been taken by younger people with less nostalgia for the past and more compulsion to act in the present to prepare for the future. These younger men are not so content just to vote against the government; their inclination is rather to drive their tractors into the cities to demonstrate in favor of a different agricultural policy. They are less concerned with ideological issues and more concerned with economic problems.

These problems are serious. Some of them have grown out of progress itself. The modernization of the farms has increased the productivity of each farmer at the same time it has increased his indebtedness. In order to pay for new material the modern farmer must sell more of his produce at higher prices. But the markets have not expanded at the same rates as production, and the system of distribution has not been sufficiently reformed to meet the requirements of modern agriculture. In attempting to solve these problems, France has resorted to ever increasing state planning. Although the traditional policy of the French government had been to protect the farmer, even to favor him over the industrial worker, in the new planning the situation seemed to be reversed. Today the French farmer receives a far lower percentage of the national income than he did a hundred years ago or even twenty-five years ago. He feels that the paternalistic government favors his younger brothers, the industrial worker, the white collar worker, and the *fonctionnaire,* and he is therefore demanding that his status be raised at least to a level of equality with them. The French farmer seeks advantages favoring him rather than the city capitalist who invests in land; he demands higher fixed prices, a reform of the market system, expansion of foreign markets, tax relief and improved technical education for his children.

These are the problems one reads about in the newspapers, but the farmers of Peyrane talk more about others which seem to confront them more directly. One is the lack of water. In 1950 although there was no great abundance of water and in the dry seasons there was some drought, the water supply seemed sufficient. However, the modernization of village

and farm, while solving old problems has created new ones. The worst
of these was a water famine which was first apparent in the village itself.
The water supply, coming from springs in the Luberon Mountains for
fifty years had been sufficient until the day the new sewage system was put
to use. As soon as there were flushing toilets and bathtubs in the houses,
there was a water shortage. As soon as electric pumps and irrigation
ditches were installed on the farms, many of the old wells and springs were
inadequate. It has been necessary to tap the Durance River miles to the
east of Peyrane to bring water by canal to all the communes in the area
to help solve the problem.

The introduction of modern farming methods has intensified another
old problem — the division of each farmer's property into small fields
interspersed among the holdings of other farmers and scattered over a
wide area. This problem has already been mentioned,* but it had become
far more serious than it was in 1950 because of the introduction of tractors.
Modern farm machinery cannot be used efficiently in small plots of land,
as many farmers who bought equipment on credit have found. Their
operations are to their dismay so inefficient that they cannot pay for the
machinery which was expected to pay for itself.

It is difficult to believe how cut up a farmer's property is in Peyrane until
one is shown a specific case. A visit to Carette's farm in the summer of
1961 was for me the ideal object lesson. I had seen Carette in the village
when he came up for tobacco at the café. It was only by chance that we
met, for he said at once that he rarely came to the village anymore. He
usually bought his tobacco in Apt or Cavaillon on Saturday morning. He
invited me to his house, so we got into his 1929 Peugeot. He showed me
how to adjust the spark for him as he cranked the car.

"Yes, it's the same old crate. There are not many old ones left, but I only
need it to go to market, and it does the job. Why get a new one? But just
wait 'til you see my tractor!"

On the way down the hill he told me about his children. His son had
just finished his military service in Algeria and was coming home.

"I wanted him to go on to school," Carette said, "but he says he wants
to get back to the farm and to the animals — a good change from people.
Maybe he'll change his mind when he starts driving the tractor around all
day, listening to its putt-putt and smelling the fumes of the exhaust."

"Why did you buy the tractor, then?" I asked.

* See above, p. 22.

"I had to. I couldn't get any help, so I have to do most of the work myself. This way I can get the work done, at least."

Back at Carette's house we sat in the shade and — in deference to our livers — drank a glass of raspberry-flavored water. His house is located in what was a hamlet of three houses built near a common well. The middle one, which he inherited from an uncle, is empty and has been for years, but Carette keeps it in repair.

"It's handy," he said. "I store crops in it, and the kids bring their friends and have parties. In the summer I go there to take my siesta. Since it's all closed up it's cool, and no one is there to bother me."

The third house belongs to Alexandre Ruffat, whose various pieces of property are so interlocked with Carette's that I thought the two men must have problems.

"Oh, no. There is no trouble between us because we don't pay any attention to each other," said Carette. "When we have to we lend each other a hand, but most of the time we go our own ways."

As we walked out across the fields to a place where Carette wanted to show me a beautiful view, I was all the more impressed with his ability to get along with his neighbors. In finding out exactly which field belonged to whom, I discovered that the properties of all the farmers in the neighborhood were tightly interlaced. We had to go through Ruffat's chicken yard to reach the place where some of Carette's best vines were located. These fields were cut up by other fields belonging not only to Ruffat, but to Figeard (who lives on the other side of the road), and to Ricard (who lives on a hill a half-mile away). Carette, on the other hand, owns fields near Figeard's and Ricard's houses as well as elsewhere in the commune.

When I was amazed by the hodgepodge, he said, "If you think this is a mess, look at Ricard's house on the hill over there. The house belongs to him, but the barn to the left belongs to Figeard and me. That is, I own the middle part of the barn — with the rounded tile roof — and Figeard owns the two ends with new, flat tiles. Look on the other side of the house. That shed belongs to Ricard's brother, who lives in Cavaillon, but the lean-to at the end belongs to me."

When I asked why Carette didn't take advantage of the *remembrement* program,* he said, "Sometimes it works, but usually it doesn't. And do you think I'd ever give up this field?"

---

* A program sponsored by the government to help farmers trade so that they may round out individual holdings and diminish the parceling up of property.

We had reached the place we had originally started out to see, an extraordinary spot where one could look out over the whole Apt valley and its surrounding highlands — the Luberon Mountain, the village of Saignon perched high, the city of Apt hiding in its gully, the Perréal hill where the Romans once warded off an invasion by the Cimbri. It was a scene peopled with characters from Giono's novels. No? Who would trade this field for another, however productive the exchange might be?

"I used to be able to look at this view while I cultivated the vines," said Carette. "My horse knew the way. Now I drive a tractor and have to keep my eyes glued on the row all the time. That's progress!"

It was late. The sun was setting, and I was expected back in the village, but Carette insisted that we poke around the field and find some bits of Roman tile to take back to the children. The field was full of them, he said. So, a Roman had built his house on this spot two thousand years ago! He, too, had enjoyed seeing the reflection of the setting sun on the Luberon Mountain.

It is sad to realize that Carette's economic situation will inevitably get worse. Besides wasting too much time and energy going from field to field with his equipment, he wastes the potentiality of the equipment because his fields are too small for it to be used most advantageously. Carette's total holdings are not more than fifty acres, and most of them are not favorable for the specialized crops that can make a small farm profitable. It is difficult to see how he can meet the growing competition of the Common Market and eventually of the world market. Having a diversity of crops is an advantage if a family is trying to be self-sufficient, but now it only hinders Carette in his need to compete with the great vineyards of Languedoc and the wheatfields of the Beauce, not to mention the ranches of Argentina, the wheatfields of Russia, and the corn fields of Iowa.

Land reform, further development of coöperatives, experimentation with other forms of collaboration in production, financing, and marketing — through these means or others, the farms of Peyrane will eventually be changed. Before a new and stable pattern evolves, however, there will be even more heartbreak and social unrest than there already has been, for the Carettes of France will not give up without a struggle. Through their professional organizations and by such shows of direct force as the tractor demonstrations of 1961, the farmers may be able to force the government to ease the process of transition, but the change is inevitable.

Carette is in exactly the same position as the few surviving shopkeepers in the village of Peyrane who try to scrape a living from their small independent operations. When we lived in Peyrane there were five grocers. Since then two of them, Arène and Saindol, have given up, and their shops are closed. A third grocery has changed hands three times, as each new grocer vainly thinks he can make a go of it. A fourth grocer manages to survive, but only because he also runs a bakery and spends a great deal of time and labor in trucking groceries and bread directly to the farmers throughout the countryside. The fifth grocer seems to be making a living, but in the summer of 1961 he told me he was looking for someone to buy his store. His wife and he were tired of working an eighty-hour week to make a simple living.

It is these little farmers and little shopkeepers who represent the gloomier aspect of French economic life today, since in a modern economy their operations seem too inefficient to survive. It was they who out of desperation supported Poujade in the '50's. They have now rejected his rhetoric and look to other sources for hope. Instead of relying on political solutions, the farmers turn to their professional associations — farmers' unions and coöperatives. The shopkeepers have no effective equivalent organizations. Some turn to de Gaulle, who reassures them, or to the Communists, who protest so vigorously. Some find hope in the Independents because, perhaps, the name reflects their own yearning. Finally, some withdraw more and more to nurse their bitterness in back rooms of their little shops. Unless these people find a way to reconcile their dream of independence with economic reality, other Poujades will undoubtedly profit from the paradoxical plight in which these people find themselves.

So in Peyrane we have two aspects of France today — the glamorous side of change and prosperity, and the darker side of what it means for many of the human beings caught in this change. In the country, the brighter side is seen in the adoption of modern farming methods, in the growth of the coöperatives and especially in a new sense of participation in the commonweal that did not exist in 1950. In the village we find that Peyrane has a new function, symbolized by the remodeled houses, the modern sewage system, the gay umbrellas in front of the cafés. Peyrane is today a young community teeming with children who have a constantly improving opportunity to study in a modern, well-lighted, well-equipped communal school or to go to the city for more advanced and more technical education.

The darker side is symbolized by the *cadastre*, the huge tomes in the Town Hall where the records of property ownership are kept. There one sees the intricate patterns of land tenure, mirroring the perpetually complicating factors of marriage, birth, death, and the consequent sharing of the family heritage. Before the problem of regrouping the madly dispersed plots of land is solved — or drifts toward a solution, since it seems unlikely that a rational and acceptable solution may be found — many of the people of Peyrane will have lost their independence. It is not clear what will happen to the children and grandchildren of Carette, Chanon, Marchal, Seignon, and most of the other farmers who have been the subject of this book.

Of course, when we speak of the threat to the independent farmers and shopkeepers, when we describe the modernization of France, it is often assumed that France as we knew it has disappeared. Modernization has always been equated with "Americanization," "mass culture," the "death of individuality" — the loss of those very ideals and values that seem to have characterized French culture and that have appeared to depend on the economic independence of the little men.

There are other forces, however, that hold back economic change or pattern it so that the traditional values are still expressed in new forms. Carette's son may have to give up farming and work for Shell Oil in Berre, but he cannot divest himself of the basic values he learned at home and at school in Peyrane. It is precisely in the area of child training and education that life in Peyrane has changed least since 1950. The relationships of members of a family, the way children are brought up and learn to perceive the world about them, the way in which they learn to think and to feel about nature, about people, about themselves — all these things have changed relatively little. The school building is new. The textbooks are far more attractively designed. There is less print on a page; illustrations and photographs abound. Still, the same basic method of learning is followed: the child is taught a principle which is simply presented to him and he then learns systematically to apply the principle to his own experience. The function of the teacher and his relationship with the children remain the same. The system of rewards and punishments remains the same. More children now go to the city to continue their education, but even there the methods and the spirit are the same. These are forces which act to preserve the Peyrane we knew. At the same time, other important forces transform it. Probably the element of life in Peyrane that will change last is the most basic element in French civilization — the sense of the dignity of the individual that impels a man to humanize the world about him and that permits him to participate in a sophisticated culture but still maintain a ferociously independent personality.

Chapter 19

Twenty-Five Years Later

On the number of visits I made to Peyrane and Chanzeaux since 1970 I became increasingly aware that Peyranais and Chanzeans alike no longer feel themselves defined, in any sense of the word, by the limits of their community. At first, on these returns to Peyrane, which I felt I knew so well, I planned to arrive just before noon so that I could greet my friends at the apéritif hour. I could not count on finding most of the 1950 habitués. Still, it was likely that even though individuals would have died, moved away or simply might be staying away from the bar because of their livers, others would have taken their places. In the past the Town Secretary, the doctor, the postman, the *notaire,* the husband of the schoolteacher, the café owner had, as a group, been the town's vital nerve center. By spending an hour with these men I had always been sure that no important event, past or present, would escape me.

I found to my disappointment that there was no longer a regular group at the bar. On my first return visit in 1973 I met Rivet, but he told me at once that since retiring three years before as Town Secretary, he no longer "comes up" to the village regularly. His successor, Madame Girard, a professionally trained administrator brought in from the outside, does not frequent the café. She is smart, says Rivet: she knows how to stand apart and not get herself involved in squabbles as he did. Rivet had never looked happier now that he could devote himself to playing in the regional boules contests. As he left after a few moments for Cavaillon, he reminded me I might see him on TV in a few hours if, as often happened, he reached the finals in that afternoon's tournament.

I now realize why the noon apéritif group has disappeared: Peyrane has ceased to be a tight little community in which such a group plays an essential role. The Peyranais no longer feel themselves to be — in fact no longer are — a unit functioning as autonomously as possible in defense against the Outside World; they have become an integral part of the world they once staunchly resisted.

The same change has taken place in Chanzeaux, that Angevin village where I have also spent so much time. There the weekly gatherings at the cafés and at the coöperative drinking society after mass on Sunday were equivalent to Peyrane's daily apéritif group. In the past I was sure to catch up on important news by sitting around a table with the Mayor, the Town Secretary, the president of the regional farmers' union, the "responsable" of the *Mouvement familial rural,* and the chairman of the parochial school committee. Now it is not certain that these people will even be in town then, for nowadays Sunday is the day for family excursions. Chanzeans often go to mass on Saturday evening in order to have Sunday free, or they go to church with the friends they are visiting in a distant town. It is rumored that some may not even go to mass — once they escape the social pressure of their neighbors.

This evolution cannot be surprising, for in studying the histories of the two communities I have been impressed more by their constant transformation than by their stability. City people like to think of rural communities as unchanging, but we have seen that in Peyrane, as in Chanzeaux, shifts in the population and changes in the life-style generally have been more steady and more rapid than is commonly assumed. The illusion of permanence is nourished by a small core of families remaining in a community from generation to generation. In Peyrane the Jouvaud and Favre families play this role, though as a matter of fact many more members of these clans have left Peyrane than have stayed.

When some readers suggested that the mobility of the population of Peyrane was unusual for a rural French community, my students and I decided to compare its population movement with that of Chanzeaux, a considerably more conservative commune and well outside the tourist circuit. We discovered that although the state of the national economy affects the rate of change, the trend during the last 150 years has been toward a constant annual turnover of five per cent of the population. A majority of the people born there now live elsewhere in France; most of the people living there were born elsewhere.*

The flux of the population has, of course, been related to the transformations in the general character of these particular rural communities. In 1790, Peyrane and Chanzeaux lived in relative isolation, producing principally what was necessary for them to be self-sufficient. By mid-nineteenth

* See *Chanzeaux, A Village in Anjou* (Cambridge, Mass., Harvard University Press, 1966), p. 156 ff.

century, improvements in transportation permitted them to specialize in production for a much wider market: in Chanzeaux, meat and wine; in Peyrane, silk and madder, the plant from which red dye was made for British military uniforms. By 1860 the populations of the two communities, stimulated by this economy, reached their peak, almost double today's total. By 1900 Chanzeaux had changed little, but Peyrane had evolved into a quite different place: it had become a mining village with a large number of foreign workers brought in to help produce ochre from the red hills. During the Second World War the villages both returned to an economy of near self-sufficiency. By the fifties, when I first began to study them, their nature was less clear. They were groping to see how they could live in a modern world. Their sense of loss of control over their destiny was summed up in a phrase of resignation, *c'est comme ça*. Ten years later this atmosphere of grim acceptance had been lightened. The population was rejuvenated. City people were reviving the village. Farm people had the hope that by modernizing their operations they, too, might share in the benefits of a soaring French economy. The spirit of resignation implicit in "c'est comme ça" was reserved for poor health, bad weather, and disappointing offspring.

By the mid-seventies, however, it became obvious that the new prosperity was not to benefit all Peyranais and Chanzeans equally. Those who for one reason or another could not adjust to the new life were more despairing than ever. Rivet had suggested that I call on Lucien Bourdin, an old friend who was "fatigué," in fact seriously depressed. In 1950 there had been a dozen Peyrane farmers living in the *bourg*. With the blacksmiths and other artisans catering to the farmers, they gave a rural atmosphere to life there. Today there are no rural artisans, and Bourdin is the only farmer left. He lives with his mother, who answered my knock. I found the 58-year-old bachelor sitting, unshaven and uncombed, in a corner of the dark little *salle*. He tried to greet me cheerfully and told his mother to give me a glass of her liqueur, made of his brandy, green almonds, and herbs. He immediately began to talk about the problem he had fixed on as the cause of his depression. Bourdin finds the government and the whole economic system against him, and he has given up trying to fight them. With their savings and a little garden, his mother and he can manage — though barely — so he has stopped going to his fields. His asparagus had not been harvested. His cherries would not be picked. His melons could rot on the vine.

Bourdin needs a psychiatrist, as his mother and the local doctor keep telling him, but he had fixed on a rationalization that no one could dispute. Most of the farmers of Peyrane and Chanzeaux, though without Bourdin's neurosis, feel the same way about the system. For generations the small land-owning peasant was the symbol of social stability; he was protected by all governments of every political persuasion. But France is now primarily industrial — in agriculture as well as in manufacturing — and the small agricultural unit is no longer viable. The very protection given the small farmers for decades proved their undoing; there was no need for them to evolve in order to compete in the world market. After the war they were encouraged and helped to modernize their operations, and many of them went into debt to buy new equipment, but modern farm machinery is efficient only for extensive farms like those in Beauce and Picardy. In Peyrane and Chanzeaux, as in many parts of France, most of the farms have fewer than 50 acres, and the fields are scattered over a wide area. Faced with the competition of the Common Market, the Bourdins of France cannot survive. The Government is not oblivious to the problem of the little farmer, but the official assumption is that he is doomed. The Concorde has replaced the Peasant as the national symbol the Government chooses to subsidize.

Periodic outbursts of violence in regions where farms are characteristically small, and most dramatically in Brittany and in southwestern France, are symptomatic reactions to changes in government policy. Recently when a tax collector was accused of hounding a recalcitrant farmer in Chanzeaux, the farmer's friends tried to keep the official from examining the records in the Town Hall. Among the group was one of the most sedate and respected farmers in Chanzeaux. He is now under indictment for having jostled the collector. Cardin's new machines, his wife's modern kitchen and the luxury items in the house point up the dilemma which moved Cardin to action against the Government. Were Cardin satisfied with his grandfather's low standard of living, he could still make a living from his farm, but he and his wife both reject the traditional lot of the peasant. They insist that their hard work entitles them to share the general French lifestyle held before them as a model on television and in the women's magazines. When they adopt this style and cannot make ends meet from the earnings of their farm, the result is frustration and anger.

The immediate solution for the small farmer seems to lie in specialization, in growing crops which require the sort of intensive care that cannot be given on industrially managed farms. In this regard the vintners are well off. With the fantastic growth in the world market for French wines, and as the well-known wines price themselves out of the ordinary market, there is a demand for "little" wines that makes them a shrewd choice. Since Beaujolais is too expensive for the ordinary consumer, neglected possibilities are discovered in a Bourgueil, a Gigondas, even in an Auvergne. In Chanzeaux, the few farmers who produce Anjou *rosé* on the slopes of the Layon River are doing well. In Peyrane, the vintners can market all their wine profitably through the nearby coöperative of Goult.

Farmers whose lands make growing grapes impractical or who are not technically or psychologically tooled up for viticulture turn to other labor-intensive crops. In Chanzeaux, where families are traditionally large, the labor of women, children, and retired relatives makes it possible to produce tobacco, camomile, mint leaves, pansy seeds. In Peyrane, the sun and soil make truck farming and orchards profitable. Although labor is scarce and the farmers cannot bring in foreign workers through government contract because their operations are too small, they have shown ingenuity in solving the problem of procuring sufficient help. When I went to see Paul Carette in his asparagus field, I found him working with two soldiers from the atomic defense installations near Apt. They were earning a little extra on their day off.

Another solution open to the farmers of Chanzeaux and Peyrane would be for them to band together in coöperatives, as many vintners have. They say that vegetables, fruit and meat present more difficulties in coöperative marketing than wine, but I suspect that a major obstacle is psychological. Traditionally French farmers are jealous of their independence; they coöperate only to defend themselves against the government. A few years ago when an equipment coöperative was begun by a group of Chanzeaux farmers who had grown up together in the Catholic rural youth movement, I thought that necessity, strengthened by a unifying ideology, might bring a change in the traditional resistance to coöperation. But after five years the coöperative was abandoned. Aversion to joint planning and use of equipment was too great. In Peyrane, the Tractor and Ploughing Coöperative has been phenomenally successful under the leadership of an ardent Communist, Marc Peyre. I had thought the group's success was related to the strength of the Communist party among the farmers in the region, but departmental agricultural officials assured me that it is the charisma and organizational ability of Peyre, not his politics, that account for the success of the coöperative.

Logically, the solution to the problem of property structure would be to reorganize it completely, a procedure which, in theory at least, appeals to the French Cartesian mind. For years the government has actually sponsored a program of *remembrement*: at the request of a commune, government specialists will analyze the local property structure and then arrange the practical and legal procedure for reshaping and exchanging fields and rights of way so that every farmer can have a more compact holding of large, adjoining fields. But few communities — certainly neither Chanzeaux nor Peyrane — have the will to undergo this major, corrective surgery. Among the excuses people have found for avoiding it is their contention that in the long run it would be futile because the constant division and dispersion of fields through death and inheritance would soon recreate the old structures. Furthermore, farms are rarely limited to the confines of a commune; a solution would have to involve a joint effort by several communes. And communes have as great a problem in coöperating as farmers.

Change in the property struction is slowly taking place through attrition, however. As farmers can no longer compete, they are forced to abandon their land; the remaining farmers can then expand their operations. During the last 50 years the number of farms in Chanzeaux has gradually diminished from 150 to less than 100. Still, it is generally agreed, there is room for no more than 10 viable farms in the commune. The farmers' predicament is further complicated by the growing competition of city people in the purchase of rural property. The question has become: *which* farmers will survive?

The former head of the Farmers' Union of Chanzeaux is one of the few who openly recognized his predicament and acted before necessity made action painful. Eugène Bourdelle retired early and moved to the *bourg*; his farm has been rented to a young neighbor; his son was dissuaded from becoming a farmer and was trained as a Government agronomist. Given human nature, Bourdelle says, no farmer will admit that he will be among those forced off his land. Each one sees himself as winning out and eventually acquiring enough land from the surrounding farms to raise beef for an insatiable market.

The *bourgs* remain the administrative and educational center of the *communes,* but they are no longer the functional center for the farm economy. The farmers relate more to the city market than to the nearby village. In 1950 it was not clear what the future of these obsolete villages would be, but I see now that they were already evolving new functions. The *bourgs* of Peyrane and Chanzeaux today are adjuncts of the city. Their function is to furnish living quarters, second residences and retirement homes for people from the city.

Workers used to move to the city to be near their jobs. Now they prefer to live at home and commute. Workers already living in the city try to move from the huge, urban housing developments to small, single houses in not-to-distant villages. Peyrane is only five miles from Apt, which used to be a sleepy little town but is now thriving because of the nearby launching sites for France's atomic missiles. The mayor of Chanzeaux, Jean-Pierre Gardais, a self-educated farm hand who has become head of a departmental social-service agency, drives to work in Angers in his Citröen 2CV every day. He has a large family, and housing is cheaper and life more pleasant in Chanzeaux than in Angers. For most people the bottlenecks at the bridges over the Loire keep Chanzeaux and Angers from being accessible to one another, but factory jobs in the booming city of Cholet, a few miles to the south, are not too far from Chanzeaux.

Undoubtedly the popularity of the *bourgs* as *villages-dortoirs* (bedroom communities) would be greater were it not for another phenomenon which has forced the value of village property higher than many workers can afford. It used to be that only the well-to-do had a *résidence secondaire*, a country house, as well as a city dwelling. Now most middle-class people have a house in the country, and the upper classes seek a third and even a fourth residence, one for the sun in the Midi, one in the mountains for the snow, one in Brittany for the ocean. Now that the French working class has been largely replaced at the bottom of the social scale by foreign workers, the aspiration for a *résidence secondaire* is beginning to reach these French, too. The Communist party newspaper, *L'Humanité*, carries advertisements of property supposedly within their means: "*Aulnay-sous-Bois: Spécial weekend, anciennes dépendances de château, bord de rivière, océan de verdure.*" "*Sup. pav! pl-pied gd liv 3 chbres/cuis bns ch cent jard park pêche chasse.*"

Each village acquires a new personality according to the type of city people it attracts. Chanzeaux, less beautiful, less known than Peyrane, less expensive, is attractive to shopkeepers, petty functionaries, skilled laborers. Peyrane, with its spectacular ochre cliffs and the sun of the Midi, has attracted sophisticated city people. The house we rented the year we lived there was bought and modernized several years ago by an Italian sculptor. At the back of our courtyard, near the edge of the cliff, the shed where our landlord's wine-making equipment was stored was torn down and replaced by a swimming pool overlooking the valley. Recently the house was bought by one of the best-known journalists in Paris. There are no more bargains in real estate!

Many of the *résidences secondaires* are acquired with retirement in mind. One-half of the house we lived in at Chanzeaux has been sold to a Paris truck driver and his wife who rented it for a summer and then decided to retire there. A retired construction worker from the shipyards of Nantes has bought the other half. Peyrane has once more become a town of older people. When we lived there, a quarter of the population was over 60. Then the increased birth rate following the war created a community dominated by the young. Now, with the increasing number of retired people, the atmosphere is not unlike that of a Florida retirement community. The Mayor is a retired engineer; the Assistant Mayor is a retired army officer. The game of boules is played all day now because so many people are not working. Boules in Peyrane reminds one of shuffleboard in St. Petersburg.

The possibility of a family exploration in the ochre cliffs followed by an extraordinarily good meal in the village fills Peyrane with excursionists every Sunday. The little restaurant Monsieur Vincent took over the year before we arrived now has a wide reputation. The rustic tables at the edge of the cliff where in fair weather tourists used to eat truffled omelette and roasted thrush, have been replaced by a substantial building that can be used all the year around. Vincent has retired, and the restaurant is run by his son, Georges, who gave up his plans to be a civil engineer and became a chef. Georges is friendly, outgoing, and especially popular in Peyrane because he organized a soccer team and starred as its center forward. As he grew older his popularity drew him into politics, and he was soon elected town councillor, then assistant mayor. It looked as though he might furnish the leadership Peyrane had so long needed, but after a few years the restaurant had grown so much that Georges felt he must devote all his energies to it. To help run the kitchen he brought back Jacques Leporatti, a classmate in the English class I taught years ago, who had finished his chef's training in a tour of Riviera hotels. Now that the Vincent restaurant has become a regional institution and Peyrane's sense of community is diminished, Georges is naturally less tempted by the idea of a local political role. This natural leader came on the political scene a generation too late to meet the needs of Peyrane.

The Rose d'Or, Peyrane's luxury inn, has also prospered, but it has always remained aloof from the community. In order to avoid embroilment in local quarrels the manager brings help in from outside instead of hiring Peyranais. The inn's location emphasizes its isolation, for it is both in and out of the village. Built on a spur of ochre cliff, it remains separated from village life: its guests, lunching comfortably on the terrace, look across the narrow valley at the village as observers rather than as participants. Visitors who want involvement in the life of the town — visiting Peyranais relatives, artists and sociologists — most usually stay at the *pension de famille* started by Maman Jeanne. Maman Jeanne has retired, however, and the *pension* has been taken over by Georgette Jannel, who has returned to her native Peyrane with her Italian husband and their children. Reports are that one eats well chez Georgette as one takes part in — or just observes — the new bustle on the Place de la Mairie.

Maman Jeanne, no longer interested in either business or politics, now devotes herself to one of Peyrane's favorite past-times. The lurid beauty of the cliffs has always been an attraction for a certain kind of artist, and this enthusiasm has been communicated to some of the natives. Rivet was a prolific painter before he became so involved in competitive boules. Maman Jeanne finds painting a source of income as well as pleasure, for her canvasses sell for 1,000 francs. "Je suis un primitif," she says. In the summer Peyrane even has an art gallery in what used to be the shed for Monsieur Prayal's buzz saw. At the top of the hill, where Madame Lestapis was for so long the lone survivor of another age, a young silversmith and his wife have a shop where they sell his work as well as that of other serious regional artisans. With the death of Madame Lestapis all the houses on the top of the hill are now occupied by "city people."

The economy of the village is geared to the needs of its new population. When we lived in Peyrane, there were five groceries; now there is one. The old groceries had the only refrigerators in the village. We shopped from meal to meal at Arène's, four yards from our front door. His grocery was our larder and our pantry. Now every house in the village has a refrigerator, and for most of their shopping people drive to a city supermarket. The remaining grocery, combined with a bakery, is viable only because it is mobile: Monsieur Bonerandi trucks his wares through the countryside, while his wife and mother take care of the little store.

In the fifties we were surrounded by artisans. Across the street in Chanzeaux was the wooden-shoe maker. Our landlord was a harnessmaker. Chanzeaux and Peyrane both had two overworked blacksmiths. Now there

is scarcely a horse in either community; the smiths and the harnessmaker
have retired. Wooden shoes and tin pails have been replaced by plastic ones
bought in the city. The widow of the tinsmith tries to supplement her
social-security payments by selling kitchenware.

Supplying energy to modern homes brings prosperity to some merchants.
When we were in Peyrane, Monsieur Borel used to bring truckloads of
oak logs and *petits bois* to our courtyard; our fireplace and the wood stove
in the kitchen provided the only heat in the house all winter. Now Borel's
sons carry on a prosperous business in bottled gas for the cooking and
heating facilities of the whole village. Bottled gas has also helped transform
farm life in Chanzeaux. Farmers no longer spend long winter hours harvesting branches from the trees in the hedges that separated the fields.

In Peyrane, what little trash there was in the past was customarily
dumped over the cliff into the surrounding valley. In 1950 every old bottle,
every piece of paper, every piece of cast-off clothing was put to use. When
we bought olives at Monsieur Reynard's grocery, he wrapped them in a
neat square of newspaper taken from a pile he used only when necessary.
We saved the oily paper because we learned it was helpful in starting a
fire. Now newspapers seldom have a second use. Wood fires are not used
for cooking and heating; for wrapping, everyone has a supply of plastic
bags saved from trips to the supermarket; the coming of toilet paper elimi-
nated another use for newspapers. The dump at the foot of the cliff is a
growing pile of paper and plastic flapping in the mistral.

In the fifties, there was a water shortage in both villages. "Chanzeaux
sans eau," complained the critics of the Town Council. Then Chanzeaux had
water piped in from the Loire, 20 miles away. Peyrane's new supply comes
from the Durance River. But water was plentiful only for a brief time.
The supply was soon outrun by new demands — for irrigation, toilets,
bathtubs, clothes- and dishwashers, even swimming pools.

When the French standard of living began its phenomenal rise during
the nineteen-fifties, many French saw in it the corruption of French culture
by "Americanization." They denounced the *civilisation du gadget* and the
Coca-colonisation of France. These terms are not heard now. Everyone knows
that the increase in the standard of living was simply the result of the
modernization of a country that had so long remained economically backward. Today the French proudly repeat the prediction, made by the Hudson
Institute in the U.S., that by the 1980's their country will be the first industrial power of Europe. They take it for granted that all French (though

perhaps not the foreign immigrant laborers) should enjoy the comforts of a highly industrialized society.

In the light of the changes described so far, it is surprising to find stability and continuity in those aspects of life most directly related to ideology. In the legislative elections of 1972, Chanzeaux voted decisively in favor of the Gaullist candidate. Peyrane, temporarily united by agreement at national levels between Socialist and Communists, voted decisively against the Gaullist mayor of Apt. The political characteristics, defined in terms of national parties, persist. Though the terms "left" and "right" have been applied in quite different situations in each generation, Peyrane maintains a position to the left and Chanzeaux to the right.

Religious behavior also remains constant, at least when measured in statistical terms. In Peyrane the number of faithful attending mass is still about 5 per cent. When the Abbé Autrand retired, he was not replaced; a missionary now comes every Sunday and for any emergency. In the huge church at Chanzeaux, most people attend mass as they always have. But these statistics are a measure of custom rather than of religious fervor. Long ago the priest of Chanzeaux pointed out to me that most people, in most communities, are religiously indifferent: the 5 per cent figure for Peyrane probably corresponded to the 5 per cent of the Chanzeans whom he considered truly devout. Most of the people of Chanzeaux go to mass because in that part of Anjou one goes to mass; in the Vaucluse, the custom is not to go to mass. These distinctive customs, like the political behavior, have prevailed for centuries.

The devout of 1950 were different from those of 1970, however. From the beginning of the century, after the law of 1905 separating church and state, the gentry supported and dominated the church and parochial schools. Today the devout 5 per cent comes from a young elite who were trained in the Catholic rural youth movement in the forties and fifties. These leaders support social change generally, as well as change in the church, and are dismissed by the conservative gentry as "Communists disguised as clergymen."

At first sight, a startling transformation seems to have taken place in education. Peyrane has a new school, large, sunny, well-ventilated. In Chanzeaux, where there are only parochial schools, the buildings and equipment have been completely modernized since public funds became available to the parochial system. The audiovisual aids are impressive. Textbooks have been redesigned and are profusely illustrated. Beneath these visible signs of change, however, education appears to be essentially what it has been for decades. It involves the same basic conceptions, usually labeled Cartesian, of what cónstitutes knowledge and how it ought be acquired and used. The textbooks, despite their changed appearance, preserve the traditional structure and subject matter. The ultimate function of examinations is still to assign individuals a proper niche in the social hierarchy.

One aspect of school life is markedly different from what I observed in the fifties, however. Because the change is also seen in family life, I find the development particularly significant. In both teacher-child and parent-child relations, the traditional figures of authority are less sure in their exercise of power and have communicated their lack of conviction to the children.

Twenty years ago the five-year-old Dédou Favre might occasionally have talked back to his mother; he might even have been impudent to another adult, if he were verbally clever — and stayed out of reach of a punishing hand. Fundamentally, Dédou expected to obey his elders, however. In the single classroom for two dozen 4- to 6-year-olds, the discipline was stern but was such effective training that in the upper classroom one scarcely heard a whisper. This year I saw Dédou's nephew, another Dédou Favre, having a tantrum in the street in front of his house; his mother seemed completely indifferent to what in the past would have been a neighborhood scandal. In school, children now speak more freely, just as at home they take part in adult conversations without being regularly silenced with the traditional "Mange et tais-toi!"

The loss of control is even more obvious with older children, especially with adolescents who in increasing numbers go to the city every day, some to work, some to continue their education. A few parents try desperately — and unhappily — to enforce traditional patterns of authority and hierarchy, but in most families there is acceptance, though tinged perhaps with nostalgia, of the young people's new independence. Village parents may be shocked by their children's involvement with city schoolmates in the lycée revolts of recent years, but at the same time they rather wonderingly admire the daring of the young in confronting authority.

The French are puzzled by this evolution and often not sure how it ought be handled. When the old and new attitudes coexist and action is required, conflicts develop. Observers wonder why French officials — from school principals and police officers to Cabinet members — have been unable to cope with recent student uprisings. Why should the most powerfully centralized state in the Western world be baffled by a few thousand young people? The explanation may lie in the fact that many of the officials, like the parents and teachers of Peyrane and Chanzeaux, feel a growing ambivalence toward the exercise of authority and find their public and private roles conflicting. Publicly there persists a belief in hierarchical law and order, but private experience in many families has undermined this conviction. At home people have learned to tolerate — even to enjoy — a less authoritarian social atmosphere.

Despite the evolution in human relations, the families I know in both the provinces and Paris seem more unified than before. The belief in hierarchy has given way to a concern for each individual's will, a mutual respect, a tolerance of differences that I would never have thought possible. The independence of the individual has grown, while the unity of the family is less tense and even more solid. I conclude with more conviction than I did in 1960 that the most basic and enduring element in French civilization is the individual's acceptance of his responsibilities in the family with his concomitant refusal to compromise his right to independence.

Index